PREFACE.

THE plan of narrative adopted in the ensuing page the sanction and the example of very learned antiquity; since, without referring to the numerous classical volumes, which have been written upon the same principle, two of the most ancient and esteemed works on English Jurisprudence have honoured it with their selection. Of the accuracy of the historical events here recorded, the authorities so explicitly cited are the most ample proofs; and, that they might be the more generally interesting, whatever may have been their original language, the whole are now given in English: so that an argument should lose none of its effect from its too erudite obscurity, nor an illustration any of its amusement by requiring to be translated.

The collection and arrangement of these materials have been a labour so unexpectedly toilsome and extended, as, it is hoped, fully to excuse every delay in the work's appearance; and, but for the valuable aid of those numerous friends who have so kindly assisted its progress, it must have still been incomplete. Of these, the first and the most fervent has been JOHN GARRATT, ESQ., who, by a singularly happy coincidence, was at once the founder of the New London Bridge, as Lord Mayor, and a native, and Alderman, of the Ward containing the Old one. Of other benefactors to these sheets, the names of HENRY SMEDLEY, ESQ.; H. P. STANDLEY, ESQ.; HENRY WOODTHORPE, ESQ., Town Clerk; MR. JOSEPH YORK HATTON; MR. JOHN THOMAS SMITH, of the British Museum; MR. WILLIAM UPCOTT, of the London Institution; and MR. WILLIAM KNIGHT, of the New Bridge Works; will sufficiently evince the importance of their communications; to whom, as well as to the many other friends, whose kindnesses I am forbidden to enumerate, I thus offer my sincerest acknowledgments. The Historians of the Metropolis have hitherto passed over the subject of this work far too slightingly: it will be my most ample praise to have endeavoured to supply that deficiency, by these

CHRONICLES OF LONDON BRIDGE.

June 15th, 1827.

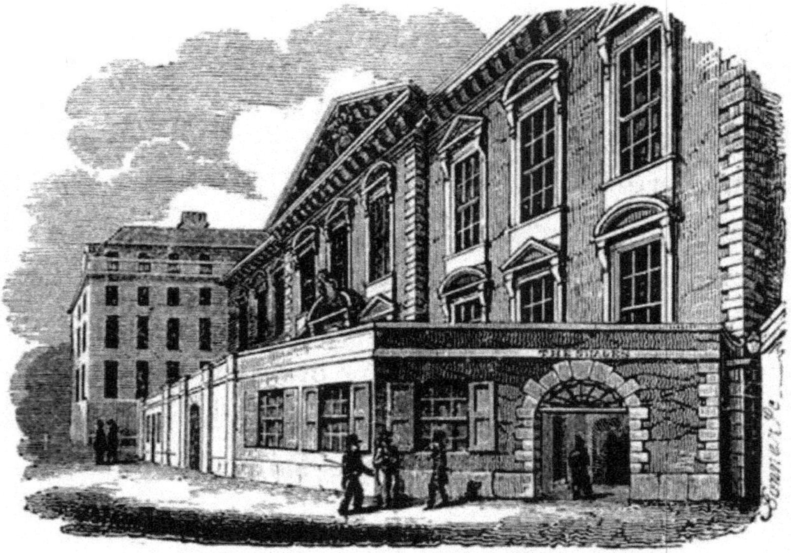

Chronicles of London Bridge

Richard Thompson

Alpha Editions

This edition published in 2024

ISBN : 9789367249123

Design and Setting By
Alpha Editions
www.alphaedis.com
Email - info@alphaedis.com

As per information held with us this book is in Public Domain.
This book is a reproduction of an important historical work. Alpha Editions uses the best technology to reproduce historical work in the same manner it was first published to preserve its original nature. Any marks or number seen are left intentionally to preserve its true form.

Contents

PREFACE. ....- 1 -
CHRONICLES OF LONDON BRIDGE.................................- 3 -

CHRONICLES OF LONDON BRIDGE.

So numerous are the alterations and modernisms in almost every street of this huge metropolis, that I verily believe, the conservators of our goodly city are trying the strength of a London Antiquary's heart; and, by their continual spoliations, endeavouring to ascertain whether it be really made "of penetrable stuff." For my own part, if they continue thus improving, I must even give up the ghost; since, in a little time, there will not be a spot left, where any feature of age will carry back my remembrance to its ancient original. What with pullings-down, and buildings-up; the turning of land into canals, and covering over old water-ways with new paved streets; erecting pert plaister fronts to some venerable old edifices, and utterly abolishing others from off the face of the earth; London but too truly resembles the celebrated keepsake-knife of the sailor, which, for its better preservation, had been twice re-bladed, and was once treated with a new handle. One year carried with it that grand fragment of our city's wall, which so long girdled-in Moorfields; while another bedevilled the ancient gate of St. John's Priory with Heraldry, which Belzebub himself could not blazon, and left but one of the original hinges to its antique pier. Nay, there are reports, too, that even Derby House, the fair old College of Heralds,—where my youth was taught "the blasynge of Cote Armures," under two of the wisest officers that ever wore a tabard,—that even *that* unassuming quadrangle is to be forthwith levelled with the dust, and thus for ever blotted from the map of London! Alas for the day! Moorgate is not, and Aldgate is not! Aldersgate is but the shadow of a name, and Newgate lives only as the title of a prison-house! In the absence, then, of many an antique building which I yet remember, I have little else to supply the vacuum in my heart, but to wander around the ruins of those few which still exist:—to gaze on the rich transomed bay-windows that even yet light the apartments of Sir Paul Pindar's now degraded dwelling; to look with regret upon the prostituted Halls of Crosby House; or to roam over to the Bankside, and contemplate the fast-perishing fragments of Winchester's once proud Episcopal Palace.

It was but recently, in my return from visiting the spot last mentioned, that I betook me to a Tavern where I was erst wont to indulge in another old-fashioned luxury,—which has also been taken away from me,—that of quaffing genuine wine, drawn reaming from the butt in splendid silver jugs, in the merry old SHADES by LONDON BRIDGE. I loved this custom, because it was one of the very few fragments of an ancient Citizen's conviviality, which have descended to us: a worthy old friend and relative, many a long year since, first introduced me to the goodly practice, and though I originally liked it merely for *his* sake, yet I very soon learned to admire it for its own. It was a most lovely moonlight night, and I placed myself in one of the window boxes, whence I could see the fastly-ebbing tide glittering with silvery flashes; whilst the broad radiance of the planet, cast upon the pale stone colour of the Bridge, strikingly contrasted with the gas star-like sparks which shone from the lamps above it. "Alas!" murmured I, "pass but another twenty years, and even thou, stately old London Bridge!—even *thou* shalt live only in memory, and the draughts which are now made of thine image. In modern eyes, indeed, these may seem of little value, but unto Antiquaries, even the rudest resemblance of that which is not, is worth the gold of Ind; and Oh! that we possessed some fair limning of thine early forms; or Oh! for some faithful old Chronicler, who knew thee in all thine ancient pride and splendour, to tell us the interesting story of thy foundation, thine adventures, and thy fate!"

It was at this part of my reverie, that the Waiter at the Shades touched my elbow to inform me, that a stout old gentleman, who called himself MR. BARNABY POSTERN, had sent his compliments, and desired the pleasure of my society in the drinking of a hot sack-posset. "My services and thanks," said I, "wait upon the ancient, I shall be proud of his company: but for sack-posset, where, in the name of Dame Woolley, that all-accomplished cook, hath he learned how to——? but he comes."

My visitor, as he entered, did not appear any thing very remarkable; he looked simply a shrewd, hale, short old gentleman, of stiff formal manners, wrapped in a dark-coloured cloak, and bearing in his hand a covered tankard, which he set upon the table betwixt us; after which, making a very low bow, he took his seat opposite to me, and at once opened the conversation.

"Your fame," said he, "MR. GEOFFREY BARBICAN, as a London Antiquary, is not unknown to me; and I have sometimes pleased myself with the thought, that you must be even a distant relation of my own, since tradition says, that the *Barbicans* and the *Posterns* originally received their names from having been gate-keepers in various parts of this fair city: but of that I will not positively speak. Howbeit, I am right glad of this fellowship, because I have some communications and reflections which I would fain make to you, touching the earlier days of that Bridge, under which the tide is now so rapidly running."

"My dear Mr. Postern," said I, in rapture, "nothing could delight me more than an Antiquary's stories of that famous edifice; but moralising I abominate, since I can do that for myself, even to admiration; so, my good friend Mr. Barnaby, as much description, and as many rich old sketches, as you please, but no reflections, my kinsman, no reflections."

"Well," returned my visitor, "I will do my best to entertain you; but you very well know, that we old fellows, who have seen generations rise and decay, are apt to make prosing remarks:—However, we'll start fairly, and taste of my tankard before we set out: trust me, it's filled with that same beverage, which Sir John Falstaff used to drink o'nights in East Cheap; for the recipé for brewing it was found, written in a very ancient hand upon a piece of vellum, when the Boar's Head was pulled down many a long year ago. Drink, then, worthy Mr. Barbican; drink, good Sir;—you'll find it excellent beverage, and I'll pledge you in kind."

Upon this invitation, I drank of my visitor's tankard; and believe me, reader, I never yet tasted any thing half so delicious; for it fully equalled the eulogium which Shakspeare's jovial knight pronounces upon it in the Second part of "*King Henry the Fourth*," Act iv. sc. iii.; where the merry Cavalier of Eastcheap tells us, that "a good Sherris sack hath a two-fold operation in it: it ascends me into the brain, dries me there all the foolish, and dull, and crudy vapours which environ it: makes it apprehensive, quick, forgetive, full of nimble, fiery, and delectable shapes; which, delivered o'er to the voice, (the tongue,) which is the birth, becomes excellent wit. The second property of your excellent Sherris is,—the warming of the blood; which, before cold and settled, left the liver white and pale, which is the badge of pusillanimity and cowardice: but the Sherris warms it, and makes it course from the inwards to the parts extreme. It illumineth the face; which, as a beacon, gives warning to all the rest of this little kingdom, man, to arm; and then, the vital commoners, and inland petty spirits, muster me all to their Captain, the heart; who, great, and puffed up with this retinue, doth any deed of courage; and this valour comes of Sherris: so that skill in the weapon is nothing, without Sack: for that sets it a-work: and learning, a mere hoard of gold kept by a devil, till Sack commences it, and sets it in act and use.—If I had a thousand sons, the first human principle I would teach them, should be,—to forswear thin potations, and addict themselves to Sack!"

Truly, indeed, I felt all those effects in myself; whilst my visitor appeared to be so inspired by it, that, as if all the valuable lore relating to London Bridge had been locked up until this moment, he opened to me such a treasure of information concerning it, that, I verily believe, he left nothing connected with the subject untouched. He quoted books and authors with a facility, to which I have known no parallel; and, what is quite as extraordinary, the same magical philtre enabled me as faithfully to retain them. Indeed, the posset and his discourse seemed to enliven all my faculties in such a manner, that the very scenes of which my companion spake, appeared to rise before my eyes as he described them. When Mr. Postern had pledged me, therefore, by drinking my health, in a very formal manner, he thus commenced his discourse.

"You very well know, my good Mr. Barbican, that Gulielmus Stephanides, or, as the vulgar call him, William Fitz-Stephen, who was the friend and secretary of Thomas à Becket, a native of London, and who died about 1191, in his invaluable tract '*Descriptio Nobilissimæ Civitatis Londoniæ,*' folio 26, tells us that to the North of London, there existed, in his days, the large remains of that immense forest which once covered the very banks of this brave river. '*Proxime patet ingens foresta,*' &c. begins the passage; and pray observe that I quote from the best edition with a commentary by that excellent Antiquary Dr. Samuel Pegge, published in London, in the year 1772, in quarto. Ever, Mr. Barbican, while you live, ever quote from the *editio optima* of every author whom you cite; for, next to a knowledge of books themselves, is an acquaintance with the best editions. But to return, Sir; in those woody groves of yew, which the old citizens wisely encouraged for the making of their bows, were then hunted the stag, the buck, and the doe; and the great Northern road, which now echoes the tuneful Kent bugle of mail-coach-guards, was then an extensive wilderness, resounding with the shrill horns of the Saxon Chiefs, as they waked up the deer from his lair of vert and brushwood. The very paths, too, that now behold the herds of oxen and swine driven town-ward to support London's hungry thousands, then echoed with the bellowing of savage bulls, and the harsh grunting of many a stout wild boar. But, as you have observed, *I* am to describe scenes, and *you* are to moralise upon their changes, so we'll hasten down again to the water-side, only observing, that the site of the ancient British London is yet certainly marked out to you, by the old rhyming stone in Pannier Alley, by St. Paul's, which saith:—

'WHEN Y^V HAVE SOVGHT THE CITY ROVND, YET STILL THIS IS THE HIGHEST GROVND.'

"Now, Julius Cæsar tells you in his Commentaries '*De Bello Gallico,*' *lib.* v. *cap.* xxi. that 'a British town was nothing more than a thick wood, fortified with a ditch and rampart, to serve as a place of retreat against the incursions of their enemies.' Here, then, stood our good old city, upon the best 'vantage ground of the Forest of Middlesex; the small hive-shaped dwellings of the Britons, formed of bark, or boughs, or reeds from the rushy sides of these broad waters, being interspersed between the trees; whilst their little mountain metropolis, the '*locum reperit egregiè naturâ, atque opere munitum,*' a place which appeared extremely strong, both by art and nature,—as the same matchless classic called those primitive defences,—was guarded on the North by a dark wood, that might have daunted even the Roman Cohorts; and to the South, where there was no wilderness, morasses, covered with fat weeds, and divided by such streams as the Wall-brook, the Shareburn, the Fleta, and others of less note, stretched downward to the Thames. As Cæsar and his Legions marched straight from the coast, worthy old Bagford was certainly in the right, when, in a letter to his brother-antiquary Hearne, he said, that the Roman invader came along the rich marshy ground now supporting Kent Street,—in truth very unlike the road of a splendid conqueror,—and, entering the Thames as the tide was just turning, his army made a wide angle, and was driven on shore by the current close to yonder Cement Wharf, at Dowgate Dock. This you find prefixed to Tom Hearne's edition of Leland's *'Collectanea de Rebus Britannicis,'* London, 1774, 8vo., volume i. pp. lviii. lix.: and many an honest man, since 'the hook-nosed fellow of Rome,' before a bridge carried him over the waters dry-shod, has tried the same route, in preference to going up to the Mill-ford, in the Strand, or York-ford which lay still higher. In good time, however, the Romans, to commemorate their own successful landing there, built a *Trajectus*, or Ferry, to convey passengers to their famous military road which led to Dover. But history is not wholly without the mention of a Bridge over the Thames near London, even still earlier than this period; for, when Dion Cassius is recording the invasion of Britain by the Emperor Claudius I., A. D. 44, he says,—'The Britons having betaken themselves to the River Thames, where it discharges itself into the Sea, easily passed over it, being perfectly acquainted with its depths and shallows: while the Romans, pursuing them, were thereby brought into great danger. The Gauls, however, again setting sail, and *some of them having passed over by the Bridge, higher up the River*, they set upon the Britons on all sides with great slaughter; until, rashly pursuing those that escaped, many of them perished in the bogs and marshes.' This passage, which it must be owned, however, is not very satisfactory, is to be found in the best edition of the *'Historiæ Romanæ,'* by Fabricius and Reimar, Hamburgh, 1750-52, folio, volume ii. page 958; in the 60th Book and 20th Section. The Greek text begins, 'Ἀναχωρησάντων δ' ἐντεῦθεν τῶν Βρεττανῶν ἐπὶ τὸν Ταμέσαν ποταμὸν,' &c.; and the Latin—*'Inde se Britanni ad fluvium Tamesin.'* I have only to remind you that Dion Cassius flourished about A. D. 230. Before we finally quit Roman London, however, I must make one more historical remark. The inscription on the monument which I quoted from Pannier Alley, is dated August the 27th, 1688; and if even at *that period*,—through all the mutations of the soil, and more than sixteen centuries after the Roman Invasion,—the ground still retained its original altitude, it yet further proves on how admirable a site our ancient London was originally erected:—well worthy, indeed, to be the metropolis of the world. This also is remarked by honest Bagford, in his work already cited, where, at page lxxii., he says,—'For many of our ancient kings and nobility took delight in the situation of the old Roman buildings, which were always very fine and pleasant, the Romans being very circumspect in regard to their settlements, having always an eye to some river, spring, wood, &c. for the convenience of life, particularly an wholesome air. And this no doubt occasioned the old Monks, Knights Templars, and, after them, the Knights of St. John of Jerusalem, as also the Friars, to settle in most of the Roman buildings, as well private as public, which thing, if duly considered, will be found to be a main reason why we have so few remains of them.'

"As I have always considered that the Romans had no more to do with Britain, than Joe the waiter here would have in a Conclave of Cardinals, I will not trouble you with any sketch of the dress or manners of the ferryman and his customers, during their government. Indeed, as a native of London, I always lament over it as the time of our captivity; and so I shall hasten on to the tenth century, when our Runic Ancestors from Gothland were settled in Britain;—when courage was the chiefest virtue, and the rudest hospitality——"

"Have pity upon me, my excellent Mr. Postern," interrupted I, "for I am naturally impatient at reflections; if you love me, then, give me scenery without meditations, and history without a moral."

"Truly, Sir," said he, "I was oblivious, for I'd got upon a favourite topic of mine, the worth of our Saxon fore-fathers; but we'll cut them off short by another draught of the sack-posset, and take up again with the establishment of a ferry by one Master Audery, in the year nine hundred and ninety—— Ah! see now, my memory has left me for the precise year, but nevertheless, Mr. Geoffrey Barbican, my service to you." When he had passed me the tankard, after what I considered a very reasonable draught, Mr. Postern thus continued.

"I hold it right, my friend, to mix these convivialia with our antiquarian discussions, because I know that they are not only ancient, but in a manner peculiar to this part of the water-side; for we find Stephanides, *Stephanus ab Stephano*, as I may jocularly call him, whom I before quoted, saying at folio 32, '*Præterea est in Londonia super ripam fluminis*,' &c. but we'll give the quotation in plain English. 'And moreover, on the banks of the river, besides the wine sold in ships'—that is to say, foreign wines of Anjou, Auxere, and Gascoigne, though even then we had some Saxon and Rhenish wines well worth the drinking,—'besides the wines sold in ships and vaults, there is a public eating-house, or cook's shop. Here, according to the season, you may find victuals of all kinds, roasted, baked, fried, or boiled. Fish, large and small, with coarse viands for the poorer sort, and more delicate ones for the rich, such as venison, fowls, and small birds. In case a friend should arrive at a Citizen's house, much wearied with his journey, and chuses not to wait, an-hungered as he is, for the buying and cooking of meat,

The water's served, the bread's in baskets brought,

Virg. Æn. i. 705.

and recourse is immediately had to the bank above-mentioned, where every thing desirable is instantly procured. No number so great, of knights or strangers, can either enter the city at any hour of day or night, or leave it, but all may be supplied with provisions, so that those have no occasion to fast too long, nor these to depart the city without their dinner. To this place, if they be so disposed, they resort, and there they regale themselves, every man according to his abilities. Those who have a mind to indulge, need not to hanker after sturgeon, nor a guinea-fowl, nor a gelinote de bois,'—which some call red-game, and others a godwit—'for there are delicacies enough to gratify their palates. It is a public eating-house, and is both highly convenient and useful to the city, and is a clear proof of its civilization.'

"Thus speaks Fitz-Stephen of the time of Henry II. between the years 1170 and 1182; and if you look but two centuries later, you shall find that John Holland, Duke of Exeter, held his Inn here at Cold Harbour, and gave to his half-brother, King Richard the Second, a sumptuous dinner, in 1397. Then too, when this spot became the property of the merry Henry Plantagenet, Prince of Wales, by the gift of Henry the Fourth, the same King filled his cellars with 'twenty casks and one pipe of red wine of Gascoigne, free of duty.' This you have on the authority of John Stow, on the one part, in his '*Survey of London*,' the best edition by John Strype, &c. London, 1754, folio, volume i. page 523; and of Master Thomas Pennant, on the other, in his '*Account of London*,' 2nd edition, London, 1791, 4to, page 330."

"Aye, Master Postern," said I, "and that same Cold Harbour is not the less dear to me, forasmuch as Stow noteth, in the very place which you have just now cited, that Richard the Third gave the Messuage, and all its appurtenances, to John Wrythe, Garter Principal King of Arms, and the rest of the Royal Heralds and Pursuivants, in 1485."—"True, Mr. Geoffrey, true," answered my visitor; "and you may remember that here also, in these very Shades, did King Charles the merry, regale incognito; and here, too, came Addison and his galaxy of wits to finish a social evening. Then, but a little above to the North, was the famous market of East Cheap; of which our own Stow speaks in his book before cited, page 503, quoting the very rare ballad of '*London Lickpenny*,' composed by Dan John Lydgate, of which a copy in the old chronicler's own hand writing, is yet extant in the Harleian Manuscripts, No. 542, article 17, folio 102, of which stanza 12 says,—

'Then I hied me into Estchepe;
One cried ribes of befe, and many a pie,
Pewtar potts they clatteryd on a heape,
Ther was harpe, pipe, and sawtry,
Ye by cokke, nay by cokke, some began to cry,
Some sange of Jenken and Julian, to get themselves mede;
Full fayne I wold hade of that mynstralsie
But for lacke of money I cowld not spede!'

"Lydgate, you know, died in the year 1440, at the age of sixty. In the present day, indeed, we have only the indications of this festivity in the names of the ways leading down to, or not far from, the river; as, Pudding Lane, Fish Street Hill, the Vine-tree, or Vintry, Bread-street,——"

"Hold! hold! my dear Mr. Barnaby," interrupted I, "what on earth has all this long muster-roll of gluttony to do with London Bridge? You are, as it were, endeavouring to prove, that yonder is the moon lighting the waters; for certes, it is a self-evident truth, that the citizens of London have from time immemorial been mighty trencher-men; nay, if I remember me rightly, your own favourite Stephanides says, 'The only plagues of London are, immoderate drinking of idle fellows, and often fires:' so *that* we'll take for granted, and get on to the Bridge."

"You are in the right," answered Mr. Postern; "the passage begins '*Solæ pestes Londoniæ*,' &c. at folio 42, and truly I wished but to shew you how proper a place these Shades are to be convivial in; but now we will but just touch upon the Saxon Ferry and Wooden Bridge, and then come at once to the first stone one, founded by the excellent Peter of Colechurch, in the year 1176. I would you could but have seen the curious boat in which, for many years, Audery the Ship-wight, as the Saxons called him, rowed his fare over those restless waters. It was in form very much like a crescent laid upon its back, only the sharp horns turned over into a kind of scroll; and when it was launched, if the passengers did not trim the barque truly, there was some little danger of its tilting over, for it was only the very centre of the keel that touched the water. But our shipman had also another wherry, for extra passengers, and that had the appearance of a blanket gathered up at each end, whilst those within looked as if they were about to be tossed in it. His oars were in the shape of shovels, or an ace of spades stuck on the end of a yard measure; though one of them rather seemed as if he were rowing with an arrow, having the barb broken off, and the flight held downwards. It is nearly certain, that at this period there was no barrier across the Thames; for you may remember how the '*Saxon Chronicle*,' sub anno 993, tells you that the Dane Olaf, Anlaf, or Unlaf, '*mid thrym et hundnigentigon scipum to Stane*,'—which is to say, that 'he sailed with three hundred and ninety ships to Staines, which he plundered without, and thence went to Sandwich.'

"Before I leave speaking of this King Olaf, however, I wish you to observe the paction which he made with the English King Ethelred, for we shall find him hereafter closely connected with the history of London Bridge. The same authority, and under the same year and page, tells you that, after gaining the battle of Maldon, and the death of Alderman Britnoth, peace was made with Anlaf, 'and the King received him at Episcopal hands, by the advice of Siric, Bishop of Canterbury, and Elfeah of Winchester.' On page 171, in the year 994, you also find this peace more solemnly confirmed in the following passage. 'Then sent the King after King Anlaf, Bishop Elfeah, and Alderman Ethelwerd, and hostages being left with the ships, they led Anlaf with great pomp to the King, at Andover. And King Ethelred received him at Episcopal hands, and honoured him with royal presents. In return Anlaf promised, as he also performed, that he never again would come in a hostile manner to England.' I quote, as usual, from the best edition of this invaluable record by Professor Ingram, London, 1823, 4to. It is generally believed, however, that the year following Anlaf's invasion, namely 994, there was built a low Wooden Bridge, which crossed the Thames at St. Botolph's Wharf yonder, where the French passage vessels are now lying; and a rude thing enough it was, I'll warrant; built of thick rough-hewn timber planks, placed upon piles, with moveable platforms to allow the Saxon vessels to pass through it Westward. A Bridge of any kind is not so small a concern but what one might suppose you could avoid running against it, and yet William of Malmesbury, the Benedictine Monk, who lived in the reign of King Stephen, and died in 1142, says, that, in 994, King Sweyn of Denmark, the Invader, ran foul of it with his Fleet. This you find mentioned in his book, '*De Gestis Regum Anglorum*,' the best edition, London, 1596, folio:—though, by the way, the preferable one is called the Frankfurt reprint of 1601, as it contains all the errata of the London text, and adds a good many more of its own; for I am much of the mind of Bishop Nicolson, and Sir Henry Spelman, who observe that the Germans committed abundance of faults with the English words. In this record, which is contained in Sir Henry Savile's '*Rerum Anglicarum Scriptores Post Bedam*,' of the foregoing date and size, at folio 38[b], is the passage beginning '*Mox ad Australes regiones*,' *&c.* of which this is the purport.

"'Some time after, the Southern parts, with the inhabitants of Oxford and Winchester, were brought to honour his'—that is to say King Sweyn's—'laws: the Citizens of London alone, with their lawful King'—Ethelred the Second—'betook themselves within the walls, having securely closed the gates. Against their ferocious assailants, the Danes, they were supported by their virtue, and the hope of glory. The Citizens rushed forward even to death for their liberty; for none could think himself secure of the future if the King were deserted, in whose life he committed his own: so that although the conflict was valiant on both sides, yet the Citizens had the victory from the justness of their cause; every one endeavouring to shew, throughout this great work, how sweet he estimated those pains which he bore for him. The enemy was partly overthrown; and part was destroyed in the River Thames, over which, in their precipitation and fury, they never looked for the Bridge.'

"I know very well that the truth of this circumstance is much questioned by Master Maitland, at page 43 of his '*History of London*,' continued by the Rev. John Entick, London, 1772, folio, volume i.; wherein he denies that any historian mentions a Bridge at London, in the incursion of Anlaf or Sweyn;

and asserts that the loss of the army of the latter was occasioned 'by his attempting to pass the River, without enquiring after Ford, or Bridge.' He affirms too, that Stow mistakes the account given by William of Malmesbury; and that the Monk himself distorts his original authority in saying that the invaders had not a regard to the Bridge. Now, if, as the margin of Maitland's History states, the Saxon Chronicle were *that* authority, the Library-keeper of Malmesbury had no greater right to speak as Maitland does, than he had for using those words which I have already translated,—'part were destroyed in the River Thames, over which, in their precipitation and fury, they never looked for the Bridge:' for the words of the Saxon Chronicle, at page 170, are, in reality,—'And they closely besieged the City and would fain have set it on fire, but they sustained more harm and evil than they ever supposed that the Citizens could inflict on them. The Holy Mother of God'—for the Invasion took place on her Nativity, September the 8th,—'on that day considered the Citizens, and ridded them of their enemies.' Here then is no word of a Bridge, nor, indeed, does any Historian record the event as William of Malmesbury does. *Lambarde*—whom I shall quote anon,—when he relates it, cites the '*Chronicle of Peterborough*,' and the '*Annals of Margan*,' but neither of them have the word Bridge upon their pages. He, most probably, took this circumstance from Marianus Scotus, a Monk of Mentz, in Germany, who wrote an extensive History of England and Europe ending in 1083, but, of this, only the German part has been printed, although it was amazingly popular in manuscript.

"We have, however, an earlier description of London Bridge in a state of warlike splendour, than is commonly imagined, or at least referred to, by most Antiquaries; and that too from a source of no inconsiderable authority: for the learned old Icelander Snorro Sturlesonius, who wrote in the 13th century, and who was assassinated in 1241, on page 90 of that rather rare work by the Rev. James Johnstone, entitled '*Antiquitates Celto-Scandicæ*,' Copenhagen, 1786, quarto, gives the following very interesting particulars of the Battle of Southwark, which took place in the year 1008, in the unhappy reign of Ethelred II., surnamed the Unready.

"'They'—that is the Danish forces—'first came to shore at London, where their ships were to remain, and the City was taken by the Danes. Upon the other side of the River, is situate a great market called Southwark,'— Sudurvirke in the original—'which the Danes fortified with many defences; framing, for instance, a high and broad ditch, having a pile or rampart within it, formed of wood, stone, and turf, with a large garrison placed there to strengthen it. This, the King Ethelred,'—his name, you know, is Adalradr in the original,—'attacked and forcibly fought against; but by the resistance of the Danes it proved but a vain endeavour. There was, at that time, a Bridge erected over the River between the City and Southwark, so wide, that if two carriages met they could pass each other. At the sides of the Bridge, at those parts which looked upon the River, were erected Ramparts and Castles that were defended on the top by penthouse-bulwarks and sheltered turrets, covering to the breast those who were fighting in them: the Bridge itself was also sustained by piles which were fixed in the bed of the River. An attack therefore being made, the forces occupying the Bridge fully defended it. King Ethelred being thereby enraged, yet anxiously desirous of finding out some means by which he might gain the Bridge, at once assembled the Chiefs of the army to a conference on the best method of destroying it. Upon this, King Olaf engaged,'—for you will remember he was an ally of Ethelred,— 'that if the Chiefs of the army would support him with their forces, he would make an attack upon it with his ships. It being ordained then in council, that the army should be marched against the Bridge, each one made himself ready for a simultaneous movement both of the ships and of the land forces.'

"I must here entreat your patience, Mr. Geoffrey Barbican, to follow the old Norwegian through the consequent battle; for although he gives us no more scenery of London Bridge, yet he furnishes us with a minute account of its destruction, and of a conflict upon it, concerning which all our own historians are, in general, remarkably silent. I say too, with Falstaff, 'play out the play;' for I have yet much to say on the behalf of that King Olaf, who, we shall find, is the patron protector of yonder Church at the South-East corner of London Bridge, since he died a Saint and a Martyr. Snorro Sturleson then, having cleared the way for the forcing of London Bridge on the behalf of King Ethelred, thus begins his account of the action, entitling it, in the Scandinavian tongue, Orrosta, or the fight. 'King Olaf, having determined on the construction of an immense scaffold, to be formed of wooden poles and osier twigs, set about pulling down the old houses in the neighbourhood for the use of the materials. With these *Vinea*, therefore,'— as such defences were anciently termed—'he so enveloped his ships, that the scaffolds extended beyond their sides; and they were so well supported, as to afford not only a sufficient space for engaging sword in hand, but also a base firm enough for the play of his engines, in case they should be pressed upon from above. The Fleet, as well as the forces, being now ready, they rowed towards the Bridge, the tide being adverse; but no sooner had they reached it, than they were violently assailed from above with a shower of missiles and stones, of such immensity that their helmets and shields were shattered, and the ships themselves very seriously injured. Many of them, therefore, retired. But Olaf the King and his Norsemen having rowed their ships close up to the Bridge, made them fast to the piles with ropes and cables, with which they strained them, and the tide seconding their united efforts, the piles gradually gave way, and were withdrawn from under the Bridge. At this time, there was an immense pressure of stones and other weapons, so that the piles being removed, the whole Bridge brake down, and involved in it's fall the ruin of many. Numbers, however, were left to seek refuge by flight: some into the City, others into Southwark. And now it was determined to attack Southwark: but the Citizens seeing their River Thames occupied by the enemy's navies, so as to cut off all intercourse that way with their interior provinces, were seized with fear, and having surrendered the City, received Ethelred as King. In remembrance of this expedition thus sang Ottar Suarti.'

"And now, Sir, as this is, without any doubt, the first song which was ever made about London Bridge, I shall give you the Norse Bard's verses in Macpherson's Ossianic measure, as that into which they most readily translate themselves; premising that the ensuing are of immeasurably greater authenticity.

> 'And thou hast overthrown their Bridges, Oh thou Storm of the Sons of Odin! skilful and foremost in the Battle! For thee was it happily reserved to possess the land of London's winding City. Many were the shields which were grasped sword in hand to the mighty increase of the conflict; but by thee were the iron-banded coats of mail broken and destroyed.'

And 'besides this,' continues Snorro, 'he also sang:'

> 'Thou, thou hast come, Defender of the Earth, and hast restored into his Kingdom the exiled Ethelred. By thine aid is he advantaged, and made strong by thy valour and prowess: Bitterest was that Battle in which thou didst engage. Now, in the presence of thy kindred the adjacent lands are at rest, where Edmund, the relation of the country and the people, formerly governed.'

'Besides this, these things are thus remembered by Sigvatus.'

> 'That was truly the sixth fight which the mighty King fought with the men of England: wherein King Olaf,—the Chief himself a Son of Odin, valiantly attacked the Bridge at London. Bravely did the swords of the Völscs defend it, but through the trench which the Sea-Kings, the men of Vikesland, guarded, they were enabled to come, and the plain of Southwark was full of his tents.'

"Such were the martial feats of King Olafus, upon the water; and now let us turn to his more pious and peaceful actions upon the land, that caused the men of Southwark to found to his honour yonder fane, which still bears his name and consecrates his memory. And in so doing, I pray you to observe that I am not wandering from the subject before us; for that Church is one of the Southern boundaries of London Bridge, and, as such, possesses some interest in its history. The other, on the same side, is the Monastery of St. Mary Overies, of the which I shall hereafter discourse; whilst the two Northern ones are St. Magnus' Church, and that abode of festivity which rises above us, Fishmongers' Hall, of which the story will be best noticed when we shall have arrived at the time of the Great Fire. There are within the City walls and Diocese of London, three Churches dedicated to the Norwegian King and Martyr, St. Olaf; and in consequence, Richard Newcourt, in his '*Repertorium Ecclesiasticum Parochiale Londinense*,' which I shall hereafter notice, volume i. page 509, takes occasion to speak somewhat of his history; collected, most probably, from Adam of Bremen's '*Historia Ecclesiarum Hamburgensis et Bremensis.*' He was the Son of Herald Grenscius, Prince of Westfold, in Norway, and was celebrated for having expelled the Swedes from that country, and recovering Gothland. It was after these exploits that he came to England, and remained here as an ally of King Ethelred for three years, expelling the Danes from the Cities, Towns, and Fortresses, and ultimately returning home with great spoil. He was recalled to England by Emma of Normandy, the surviving Queen of his friend, to assist her against Knute; but as he found a paction concluded between that King and the English, he soon withdrew, and was then created King of Norway by the voice of the nation. To strengthen his throne, he married the daughter of the King of Swedeland; but now his strict adherence to the Christian faith, and his active zeal for the spread of it, caused him to be molested by domestic wars, as well as by the Danes abroad: though these he regarded not, since he piously and valiantly professed, that he had rather lose his life and Kingdom than his faith in Christ. Upon this, the men of Norway complained to Knute, King of Denmark, and afterwards of England, charging Olaf with altering their laws and customs, and entreating his assistance; but the Norwegian hero was supported by a young soldier named Amandus, King of Swethland, who had been bred up under Olaf, and taught to fight by him. He, at first, overthrew the Dane in an engagement; but Knute, having bribed the adverse fleet, procured three hundred of his ships to revolt, and then attacking Olaf, forced him to retreat into his own country, where his subjects received him as an enemy. He fled from the disloyal Pagans to Jerislaus, King of Russia, who was his brother-in-law, and remained with him till the better part of his subjects, in the commotions of the Kingdom, calling him to resume his crown, he went at the head of an army; when, whilst one party hailed his return with joy, the other, urged by Knute, opposed him by force, and in a disloyal battle at Stichstadt, to the North of Drontheim, says Newcourt, page 510, with considerable pathos, they 'murthered this holy friend of Christ, this most innocent King, in Anno 1028,' but he should have said 1030. His feast is commemorated on the fourth of the Kalends of August, that is to say on the 29th of July; for Grimkele, Bishop of Drontheim, his capital City, a pious priest whom he had brought from England to assist him in establishing Christianity in Norway, commanded that he should be honoured as a Saint, with the title of Martyr. His body was buried in Drontheim, and was not only found undecayed in 1098, but even in 1541, when the Lutherans plundered his shrine of its gold and jewels; for it was esteemed the greatest treasure in the North. Such was St. Olave, to whose memory no less than four Churches in London are dedicated; for, says Newcourt, he 'had well deserved, and was well beloved of our English Nation, as well for his friendship for assisting them against the Danes, as for his holy and Christian life, by the erection of many Churches which to his honourable memory they built and dedicated to him.' I notice only one of these, because it is contiguous to London Bridge, which is called St. Olave, Southwark. It stands, as you very well know, on the Northern side of Tooley Street; and although many people would think St. Tooley to be somewhat of a questionable patron for a Church, yet I would remind you that it was only the more usual ancient English name of King Olave, as we are told on good authority, by the Rev. Alban Butler in his *'Lives of the Fathers, Martyrs, and other principal Saints,'* London, 1812, 8vo. volume vii. where also, on pages 378-380, you have many further particulars of the life of this heroic Prince. You may also meet with him under a variety of other names, as Anlaf, Unlaf, Olaf Haraldson, Olaus, and Olaf Helge, or Olave the Holy. Of his Church in Southwark I will tell you nothing as to its foundation, but remark only that its antiquity is proved by William Thorn's *'Chronicle of the Acts of the Abbots of St. Austin's Canterbury;'* which is printed in Roger Twysden's *'Historiæ Anglicanæ Scriptores Decem;'* London, 1652, folio. Thorn, you may remember, was a Monk of St. Augustine's, in 1380; and on column 1932 of the volume now referred to, he gives the copy of a grant from John, Earl of Warren, to Nicholas, the Abbot of St. Augustine's, giving to his Monastery all the estate which it held in 'Southwark standing upon the River Thames, between the Breggehouse and the Church of Saint Olave.' By this we know it to be ancient, for that grant was made in the year 1281. And now I will say no more of St. Olave, but that a very full and interesting memoir of him, and his miracles, is to be found in that gigantic work entitled the *'Acta Sanctorum,'* Antwerp, 1643-1786, 50 volumes, folio, and yet incomplete, for the year descends to October only:—see the seventh volume of July, pages 87-120.

"And now let me chaunt you his Requiem, by giving you, from the same authority, a free translation of the concluding stanza of that Latin Hymn to his memory, which Johannes Bosch tells us was inserted in the Swedish Missal, and sung on his festival; it is in the same measure as the original.

'Martyr'd King! in triumph shining,
Guardian Saint, whom bliss is 'shrining;
To thy spirit's sons inclining
From a sinful world's confining
By thy might, Oh set them free!
Carnal bonds are round them 'twining,
Fiendish arts are undermining,
All with deadly plagues are pining,
But thy power and prayers combining,
Safely shall we rise to thee!—AMEN.'

"One of the last notices of London Bridge which occurs in the days of King Ethelred, and I place it here because it is without date, is in his Laws, as they are given in the *'Chronicon'* of John Brompton, Abbot of Jorvaulx, in the City of York, who lived about the year 1328. His work was printed in Twysden's Scriptores, which I last quoted; and at column 897, in the xxiii. Chapter of the Statutes there given, is the following passage.

"'*Concerning the Tolls given at Bylyngesgate.*

'If a small ship come up to Bilynggesgate, it shall give one halfpenny of toll: if a greater one which hath sails, one penny: if a small ship, or the hulk of a ship come thereto, and shall lie there, it shall give four pence for the toll. For ships which are filled with wood, one log of wood shall be given as toll. In a week of bread'—perhaps a festival time, 'toll shall be paid for three days; the Lord's day, Tuesday, and Thursday. Whoever shall come to the Bridge, in a boat in which there are fish, he himself being a dealer, shall pay one halfpenny for toll; and if it be a larger vessel, one penny.'

"Concerning Brompton's translation of these laws, Bishop Nicolson, in his *'English, Scotch, and Irish Historical Libraries,'* London, 1736, folio, page 65, says that they are pretty honestly done, and given at large: but they may be seen with several variations and additions very fairly written in the collections of Sir Simonds D'Ewes, preserved with the Harleian Manuscripts in the British Museum, No. 596. John Brompton, however, at column 891 of his Chronicle, tells us one circumstance more concerning London Bridge before the Invasion of Knute; for he says, under the year 1013, 'After this, many people were overthrown in the Thames, at London, not caring to go by the Bridge;' that is to say, because it had been broken in the two recent battles as I have already told you, and there were also erected several fortifications about the City.'

"Perhaps it was the error of Sweyn in getting his Fleet foul of London Bridge, which made Knute the Dane, his Son, go so laboriously to work with the Thames, upon his Invasion in 1016; and I shall give you this very wonderful story in the words of the Saxon Chronicle, page 197. 'Then came the ships to Greenwich, and, within a short interval, to London; where they sank a deep ditch on the South side, and dragged their ships to the West side of the Bridge. Afterwards they trenched the City without, so that no man could go in or out, and often fought against it; but the Citizens bravely withstood them.' There are some who doubt this story, but honest William Maitland, who loved to get to the bottom of every thing, as he went sounding about the river for Cæsar's Ford, also set himself to discover proofs of Knute's Trench: and you may remember that he tells us, in his work which I have already cited, volume i. page 35, that this artificial water-course began at the great wet-dock below Rotherhithe, and passing through the Kent Road, continued in a crescent form to Vauxhall, and fell again into the Thames at the lower end of Chelsea Reach. The proofs of this hypothesis were great quantities of fascines of hazels, willows, and brushwood, pointing northward, and fastened down by rows of stakes, which were found at the digging of Rotherhithe Dock in 1694; as well as numbers of large oaken planks and piles, also found in other parts.

"Florence of Worcester, who, you will recollect, wrote in 1101, and died in 1119, in his '*Chronicon ex Chronicis*,' best edition, London, 1592, small 4to. page 413; and the famous old Saxon Chronicle, page 237; also both mention the easy passage of the rapacious Earl Godwin, as he passed Southwark in the year 1052. The tale is much the same in each, but perhaps the latter is the best authority, and it runs thus. 'And Godwin stationed himself continually before London, with his Fleet, until he came to Southwark; where he abode some time, until the flood came up. When he had arranged his whole expedition, then came the flood, and they soon weighed anchor and steered through the Bridge by the South side.' This relation is also supported by Roger Hoveden, in his Annals, Part I. in '*Rerum Anglicarum Scriptores post Bedam*,' by Sir H. Savile, folio 253[b], line 41.

"And now, worthy Mr. Barbican, before we enter upon the conjectures and disputes relating to the real age and founders of the first Wooden Bridge over the Thames at London, let me give you a toast, closely connected with it, in this last living relique of old Sir John Falstaff. You must know, my good Sir, that when the Church-Wardens and vestry of St. Mary Overies, on the Bankside yonder, meet for conviviality, one of their earliest potations is to the memory of their Church's Saint and the patroness who feeds them, under the familiar name of '*Old Moll!*' and therefore, as we are now about to speak of them and their pious foundation most particularly, you will, I doubt not, pledge me heartily to the Immortal Memory of Old Moll!"

"I very much question," returned I, "if either the good foundress of the Church, or she to whom it was dedicated,—if Mary the Saint, or Mary the Sinner,—were ever addressed by so unceremonious an epithet in their lives; but, however, as it's a parochial custom, and your wish, here's Prosperity to St. Saviour's Church, and the Immortal Memory of Old Moll!" Mr. Postern having made a low bow of acknowledgment for my compliance, thus continued.

"I have made it evident then, and, indeed, it is agreed to on all sides, that there *was* a Wooden Bridge over the Thames, at London, at least as early as the year 1052; and Maitland, at page 44 of his History, is inclined to believe that it was erected between the years 993 and 1016, at the public cost, to prevent the Danish incursions up the River. John Stow, however, in volume i., page 57, of his '*Survey*,' attributes the building of the first Wooden Bridge over the Thames, at London, to the pious Brothers of St. Mary's Monastery, on the Bankside. He gives you this account on the authority of Master Bartholomew Fowle, *alias* Fowler, *alias* Linsted, the last Prior of St. Mary Overies; who, surrendering his Convent on the 14th of October, 1540,—in the 30th year of Henry VIII.,—had a pension assigned him of £100 per Annum, which it is well known, that he enjoyed until 1553. This honest gentleman you find spoken of in John Stevens's '*Supplement to Sir William Dugdale's Monasticon Anglicanum*,' London, 1723, folio, volume ii., page 98; and from him old Stow states, that, 'a Ferry being kept in the place where now the Bridge is built, the Ferryman and his wife deceasing, left the said Ferry to their only daughter, a maiden named Mary; which, with the goods left her by her parents, as also with the profits rising of the said Ferry, built a house of Sisters in the place where now standeth the East part of St. Mary Overies Church, above the choir, where she was buried. Unto the which house she gave the oversight and profits of the Ferry. But afterwards, the said house of Sisters being converted into a College of Priests, the Priests built the Bridge of Timber, as all the other great Bridges of this land were, and, from time to time, kept the same in good reparations. Till at length, considering the great charges of repairing the same, there was, by aid of the Citizens of London, and others, a Bridge built with arches of stone, as shall be shewed.'

"The first who attacks this story is William Lambarde, the Perambulator of Kent, in his '*Dictionarium Angliæ Topographicum et Historicum*,' London, 1730, quarto, page 176; wherein he scruples not to call Prior Fowler 'an obscure man,' whom he charges with telling this narrative, 'without date of time, or warrant of writing,' and then sums up his remarks in these words. 'As for the first buildinge, I leave it to eche man's libertye what to beleve of it; but as for the name Auderie, I think Mr. Fowler mistoke it, for I finde bothe in the Recordes of the Queene's Courtes and otherwise, it signifieth over the water, as Southrey, on the South side of the water: the ignorance whereof, might easily dryve Fowler—a man belyke unlearned in the Saxon tongue,—to some other invention.'

"Maitland and Entick, at page 44 of their History, are not much more believing than Lambarde, the Lawyer; for they assert that the Convent of Bermondsey, founded by Alwin Child, a Citizen of London, in the year 1082, was the first religious house on the South side of the River, within the Bills of Mortality. The second, say they, speaking after Sir William Dugdale in his *'Monasticon Anglicanum,'* London, 1661, folio, pages 84, 940, was the Priory of St. Mary Overies, founded by William Giffard, Bishop of Winchester, in the reign of King Henry I. Now Bishop Tanner, in his *'Notitia Monastica,'* best edition by James Nasmith, Cambridge, 1787, folio, XX. Surrey,—for you know the book is unpaged and arranged alphabetically under Counties, of which Pennant heavily complains,—is inclined to think that Stow was in the right, although he had not discovered any thing either in print or manuscript to support his narrative. He is also willing to believe, that Bishop Giffard did not do more for St. Mary Overies, than rebuild the body of the Church: and, certainly, that he did not, in 1106, place Regular Canons there, since he refers to Matthew of Westminster to prove that they were then but newly come into England, and placed in that Church; whilst Bishop Giffard was himself in exile until the year 1107. The *'Domesday Book,'* also, the most veritable and invaluable record of our land, thus hints at a Religious House in Southwark; which, as that Survey was made about the year 1083, was, of course, long anterior to the times of which I spake last. You will find the passage in Nichols' edition of the register, London, 1783, folio, volume i. *Sudrie*, folio 32 a, column 1; and the words are as follow. 'The same Bishop,'—that is to say, Odo, Bishop of Baieux,—'has in Southwark one Monastery, and one Harbour. King Edward held it on the day he died.'—January the 5th, 1066—'Whoever had the Church, held it of the King. From the profits of the Harbour, where ships were moored, the King had two parts.' 'Now,' concludes the worthy Dr. Tanner, 'if *Monasterium* here denote any thing more than an ordinary Church, it may be thought to mean this Religious House, there being no pretence for any other in this Borough to claim to be as old as the Confessor's time, or, indeed, as the making of the Domesday Book, A. D. 1083.' *Vide* Sign. U u 2; *Notes* r, and s.

"Maitland, however, cannot be brought to believe in the foundation of a Wooden Bridge by the Brethren of St. Mary; and on page 44 of his work, already cited, he thus gives the reasons for his non-conformity. 'As the Ferry,' he commences, 'is said to have been the chief support of the Priory, 'twould have been ridiculous in the Prior and Canons, to have sacrificed their principal dependence, to enrich themselves by a wild chimera of increasing their revenues in the execution of a project, which, probably, would have cost six times the sum of the intrinsic value of their whole estate; and, when effected, would, in all likelihood, not have brought in so great an annual sum as the profits arising by the Ferry, seeing it may be presumed that foot-passengers would have been exempt from Pontage.' He next proceeds to quote a deed of King Henry I., which I shall produce in its proper order of time, exempting certain Abbey lands from being charged with the work of London Bridge: which he considers as a sufficient proof that the Priests of St. Mary did not preserve the erection in repair, and therefore, says he, 'as the latter part of this traditionary account is a manifest falsehood, the former *is very likely* to be of the same stamp.' He then sums up all by these bold words. 'As it appears that some religious foundations only were exempt from the work of this Bridge, and they, too, by charter, *I think 'tis not to be doubted*, but all civil bodies and incorporations were liable to contribute to the repairs thereof. And, consequently, that Linsted and his followers exceed the truth, by ascribing all the praise of so public a benefaction to a small House of Religious; who, with greater probability, only consented to the building of this Bridge, upon sufficient considerations and allowances, to be made to them for the loss of their Ferry, by which they had been always supported.' Such are the objections against the attributing the building of the First Wooden Bridge to the Monks of Southwark; but we may remark, by the way, that Stow was a laborious and inquisitive Antiquary, who saw and inquired, as well as read for himself, and, in all probability, had both seen and conversed with Prior Fowle; whilst Maitland and Entick were often contented to write in their libraries from the works of others, and speak of places with which they were but very slightly acquainted. We may add too, that, as the Priests of St. Mary were Regular Canons of St. Austin, by their rule they were not permitted to be wealthy, but were to sell the whole of their property, give to the poor, have all things in common, and never be unemployed. I know very well, that in opposition to Stow's account of Mary Audery's foundation, you may bring forward that assertion made in Stevens's '*Supplement to Dugdale,*' which I have already cited, volume ii. page 97; wherein she is called 'a noble woman,' and, consequently, could not be the Ferryman's daughter. But of this let me observe, that the authority of Stow's '*Survey,*' given in the margin, is mis-quoted; for although it is certain that the action itself was sufficiently noble, yet the old Citizen never calls her other than 'a Maiden named Mary.' You may see the place to which Stevens refers, in Strype's edition of the '*Survey,*' volume ii. page 10; and let me remark now, before I quit the history of St. Mary Overies, as connected with that of London Bridge, that there is yet extant there, a monumental effigy conveying the strongest lesson of man's mortality; it being the resemblance of a body in that state, when corruption is beginning its great triumph. Prating Vergers and Sextons commonly tell you, that the persons whom these figures represent, endeavoured to fast the whole of Lent, in imitation of the great

Christian pattern, and that dying in the act, they were reduced to such a cadaverous appearance at their decease. There has, however, been a new legend invented for this sculpture, as it is commonly reported to be that of AUDERY, THE FERRYMAN,

father of the foundress of St. Mary Overies. It was formerly placed on the ground, under the North window of the Bishop's Court, which, before the present repairs, stood at the North East corner of the Chapel of the Virgin Mary. Where it will be removed to hereafter, time only can unfold, for, as yet, even the Churchwardens themselves know not.

"In speaking of this person's tomb, I must not, however, omit to notice, that there is a singularly curious, although, probably, fabulous tract of 30 pages, of his life, the title of which I shall give you at length. '*The True History of the Life and sudden Death of old John Overs, the rich Ferry-Man of London, shewing, how he lost his life, by his own covetousness. And of his daughter Mary, who caused the Church of St. Mary Overs in Southwark to be built; and of the building of London Bridge.*' There are two editions of this book, the first of which was published in 12mo., in 1637, and a reprint of it in 8vo., which, though it be shorn of the wood-cuts that decorated the *Editio Princeps*, is, perhaps, the most interesting to us, inasmuch as it bears this curious imprint.—'*London: Printed for T. Harris at the Looking-Glass, on London Bridge: and sold by C. Corbet at Addison's Head, in Fleet-street, 1744. Price six pence.*' You may see this work in Sir W. Musgrave's Biographical Tracts in the British Museum; its first nine pages are occupied with a definition and exhortation against covetousness, in the best Puritanic style of the seventeenth century; and then, on page 10, the history opens thus:—'Before there was any Bridge at all built over the Thames, there was only a Ferry, to which divers boats belonged, to transport all passengers betwixt Southwark and Churchyard Alley, that being the high-road way betwixt Middlesex, and Sussex, and London. This Ferry was rented of the City, by one John Overs, which he enjoyed for many years together, to his great profit; for it is to be imagined, that no small benefit could arise from the ferrying over footmen, horsemen, all manner of cattle, all market folks that came with provisions to the City, strangers and others.'

"Overs, however, though he kept several servants, and apprentices, was of so covetous a soul, that notwithstanding he possessed an estate equal to that of the best Alderman in London, acquired by unceasing labour, frugality, and usury, yet his habit and dwelling were both strongly expressive of the most miserable poverty. He had, as we have already seen, an only daughter, 'of a beautiful aspect,' says the tract, 'and a pious disposition; whom he had care to see well and liberally educated, though at the cheapest rate; and yet so, that when she grew ripe and mature for marriage, he would suffer no man of what condition or quality soever, by his good will, to have any sight of her, much less access unto her.' A young gallant, however, who seems to have thought more of being the Waterman's heir than his son-in-law, took the opportunity, whilst he was engaged at the Ferry, to be admitted into her company; 'the first interview,' says the story, 'pleased well; the second better; but the third concluded the match between them.—In all this interim, the poor silly rich old Ferryman, not dreaming of any such passages, but thinking all things to be as secure by land as he knew they were by water,' continued his former wretched and penurious course of life. From the disgusting instances which are given of this caitiff's avarice, he would seem to have been the very prototype and model of Elwes and Dancer; and, as the title-page of the book sets forth, even his death was the effect of his covetousness. To save the expense of one day's food in his family, he formed a scheme to feign himself dead for twenty-four hours; in the vain expectation that his servants would, out of propriety, fast until after his funeral. Having procured his daughter to consent to this plan, even against her better nature, he was put into a sheet, and stretched out in his chamber, having one taper burning at his head, and another at his feet, according to the custom of the time. When, however, his servants were informed of his decease, instead of lamenting, they were overjoyed; and, having danced round the body, they brake open his larder, and fell to banqueting. The Ferryman bore all this as long, and as much like a dead man, as he was able; 'but, when he could endure it no longer,' says the tract, 'stirring and struggling in his sheet, like a ghost, with a candle in each hand, he purposed to rise up, and rate 'em for their sauciness and boldness; when one of them thinking that the Devil was about to rise in his likeness, being in a great amaze, catched hold of the butt-end of a broken oar, which was in the chamber, and, being a sturdy knave, thinking to kill the Devil at the first blow, actually struck out his brains.' It is added, that the servant was acquitted, and the Ferryman made accessary and cause of his own death. The estate of Overs then fell to his daughter, and her lover hearing of it, hastened up from the country; but, in riding post, his horse stumbled, and he brake his neck on the highway. The young heiress was almost distracted at these events, and was recalled to her faculties only by having to provide for her father's interment; for he was not permitted to have Christian burial, being considered as an excommunicated man, on account of his extortions, usury, and truly miserable life. The Friars of Bermondsey Abbey were, however, prevailed upon, by money, their Abbot being then away, to give a little earth to the remains of the wretched Ferryman. But upon the Abbot's return, observing a grave which had been but recently covered in, and learning who lay there, he was not only angry with his Monks for having done such an injury to the Church, for the sake of gain, but he also had the body taken up again, laid on the back of his own Ass, and, turning the animal out at the Abbey gates, desired of God that he might carry him to some place where he best deserved to be buried. The Ass proceeded with a gentle and solemn pace through Kent Street, and along the highway, to the small pond once called St. Thomas a Waterings, then the common place of execution, and shook off the Ferryman's body directly under the gibbet, where it was put into the ground, without any kind of ceremony. Mary Overs, extremely distressed by such a succession of sorrows, and desirous to be free from the importunity of the numerous suitors for her hand and fortune, resolved to retire into a cloister; which she shortly afterwards did, having first provided for the foundation of that Church which still commemorates her name.

"Such is the story related by this tract; and, if it were possible, one might suppose, that the pious maiden, out of her filial love, had placed that effigy in her fane, which I before mentioned to be sculptured in memory of her father; since it would, by no means, improperly represent the cadaverous features of the old Waterman. The figure, itself, is of the third form of the classes of Sepulchral Monuments, invented by Maurice Johnson, Esq.,—namely, tables with effigies or sculptures,—and the last of the arrangement adopted by Smart Lethullier, Esq., that is to say,—the representation of a skeleton in a shroud, lying either under, or on, a table tomb. Richard Gough, you know, in his *'Sepulchral Monuments,'* London, 1786-96, folio, volume i., part 1, Introduction, page cxi. where you will find all these particulars, attributes most of these figures to the fifteenth century, and Audery certainly died very long before the time of William I. However this may be, as I am laying before you all the illustrations of Bridge history, both authentic and traditional, which are now to be found, I must not omit to add, that the supposed effigy of Audery is six feet eight inches in length; and represents his decayed body lying in its winding-sheet. His hair is turned up in a roll above his head, though in the *'History of Southwark,'* by M. Concannen, Junior, and A. Morgan, Deptford, 1795, octavo, page 101, *Note*, he is erroneously stated to have 'a shorn crown,' and is, therefore, supposed to represent Linsted, the last Prior of St. Mary's.

"Captain Francis Grose has inserted this figure, not very respectably engraven, in his *'Antiquities of England and Wales,'* London, 1773-87, royal quarto, six volumes, in the Addenda attached to volume iv., plate iii.; and he observes, on page 36, that 'it is a skeleton-like figure, of which the usual story is told, that the person thereby represented attempted to fast forty days, in imitation of Christ,' as he remarks on the preceding page, but died in the attempt, having first reduced himself to that appearance. The best engraving of this effigy was published in *'Mr. J. T. Smith's Antiquities of London, and its Environs,'* London, 1791, quarto.

"Be this figure, however, who it may, the Waterman or the Priest, his tomb has outlived both his name and his dust. Whether he only carried passengers over the River Thames, or was occupied in teaching them how to cross that last fatal River,—which John Bunyan quaintly tells you hath *no* Bridge,— 'after life's fitful fever he sleeps well,'—

"Aye, and so shall I soon," cried I, stretching myself, and interrupting Mr. Postern; "let him rest in peace, my good Sir, and come out of Church now; for, truly, it's high time to close your Sermon, and let us hear somewhat about a River which *hath* a Bridge, that was once the wonder of the world."

"I thank you," replied my narrator, "I thank you, Mr. Geoffrey Barbican, for recalling me to the subject of our conversation; for this is the very point at which I would proceed with my history. You know, Sir," continued he, in a much brisker tone, "I have already observed to you, that the First Wooden Bridge was erected much farther to the East than yonder stone bulwark; for when King William I. granted a Charter to the foundation of St. Peter's Abbey, at West-Minster, in the second year of his reign, A. D. 1067, he confirmed to the Monks serving God in that place, a Gate in London, then called Butolph's Gate, with a Wharf which stood at the head of London

Bridge. This has ever been received as a well-established fact; for Stow relates it in his '*Survey,*' volume i., pages 22 and 58; and Mr. John Dart, in his '*History and Antiquities of the Abbey Church of St. Peter, Westminster,*' London, 1723, folio, volume i., page 20, supports it, in his List of Benefactors to the Abbey, in the time of King Edward the Confessor.

"The record is also given at length, by Stow, in English; but you may see it in the original Latin, in a curious Manuscript in the Cotton Library, marked *Faustina*, A. iii., which is entitled, '*A Registry of the Regal and Pontifical Charters, Privileges, Agreements, and Covenants, of the Bishops and Abbots of the Church of the blessed Peter of Westminster; many whereof are Saxon ones, written in the Norman-Saxon characters.*' This volume is a little stout quarto, written in a small fair Church text, on parchment; adorned with many vermillion initial letters, and rubrics, or heads of chapters. The Charter to which I have now referred you, chapter xliv., is the last but one in the reign of King William I., folio 63, b, of the modern pagination; and, put into English, is as follows:—

"'Concerning the lands of Almodus, of St. Butolph's Gate, and of the Wharf at the head of London Bridge.

"'William, King of England, to the Sheriffs and all Ministers, as, also, to his faithful subjects of London, French and English, greeting: Know ye, that I have granted unto God and to St. Peter of Westminster, and to the Abbot Vitalis, the House which Almodus, of the Gate of St. Botolph, gave to them when he was made a Monk; that is to say, his Lord's Court, with his Houses, and one Wharf which is at the head of London Bridge, and others of his lands in the same City, like as King Edward more fully and beneficially granted them: and I will and command that they shall enjoy the same well, and quietly, and honourably, with sake and soke, and shall hold all the customs and laws of the aforesaid. And I defend them that none shall do them any injury. Witness, Walkeline, Bishop of Winchester, and William, Bishop of Durham, and R., Earl of Mell., and Hugh, Earl of Warwick.'

"And now let me remark that, by this we are informed that the City end of the Bridge was not anciently the foot of it, which is asserted by the evidence of Richard Newcourt, in his '*Ecclesiastical History of the Diocess of London,*' London, 1708-10, folio, volume i., page 396, where he says, that 'St. Magnus' Church is sometimes called, in Latin, the Church of St. Magnus the Martyr, in the City of London, near the foot, or at the foot, of London Bridge.'

"This First Wooden Bridge, however, was not fated to stand long; for, on the sixteenth of November, the feast of St. Edmund the Archbishop, in the year 1091, 'at the hour of six, a dreadful whirlwind from the South-East, coming from Africa, blew upon the City, and overthrew upwards of six hundred houses, several Churches, greatly damaged the Tower, and tore away the roof and part of the wall of the Church of St. Mary le Bow, in

Cheapside. The roof was carried to a considerable distance, and fell with such force, that several of the rafters, being about twenty-eight feet in length, pierced upwards of twenty feet into the ground, and remained in the same position as when they stood in the Chapel.'

"The best accounts of this terrible event are to be found in the *'Chronicle'* of Florence of Worcester, page 457, which was literally copied into the *'Annales'* of Roger de Hoveden, Chaplain to King Henry II., printed in the *'Scriptores post Bedam,'* already cited, page 462;—in William of Malmesbury, page 125;—and in the *'Chronicle'* of John of Brompton, which I have also before quoted, page 987.

"During the same storm, too, the water in the Thames rushed along with such rapidity, and increased so violently, that *London Bridge was entirely swept away*; whilst the lands on each side were overflowed for a considerable distance. I cannot help observing how slightly, and erroneously, the *'Annals of Waverley'* notice this most dreadful devastation; for at page 137, of the best edition by Dr. Thomas Gale, volume ii. of his *'Historiæ Anglicanæ Scriptores* xv.' Oxford, 1691, folio, they merely state that 'a vehement wind struck down London the 6th of the kalends of November,'—that is to say, on the 27th of October,—'at the hour of six!' I doubt not but the truth was, that the good Monks of Waverley Abbey in Surrey felt nothing of this *ventus vehemens* themselves, and therefore gave a much more trivial record of it, than if it had shaken but a single bell in the turrets of their own *Cenobium*. The *'Annals of Waverley,'* you know, were, down to about 1120, almost a translation from the *'Saxon Chronicle,'* executed in the twelfth century. The following year, 1092, the sixth of the reign of William Rufus, was marked by a season fatal to bridges in general; although there is no mention that our's at London participated in the destruction. This fact is related by William of Malmesbury, page 125, and by Roger de Hoveden, page 464, in these words:—'Also, in his sixth year, there was such an excessive rain, and such high floods, the rivers overflowing the low grounds that lay near them, as the like was remembered by none. And afterward, in the winter, ensued a sudden frost; whereby the great streams were congealed in such a manner that they could draw two hundred horsemen and carriages over them; whilst at their thawing, many bridges, both of wood and stone, were borne down, and divers water mills were broken up and carried away!'

"Frequent destructions by fire seem, also, to have been a very general fate of all our ancient buildings; for, in 1093, the wooden houses and straw roofs of the London Citizens were again in flames, and a great part of the City was thus destroyed.

"Too soon after this calamity, at a most inauspicious time for commencing, or executing, expensive public works, in 1097, King William Rufus imposed a heavy tax upon his subjects for the re-building of London Bridge,—though *that* might very well be defended,—the erecting of the palace of West-Minster Hall, and the construction of a wall round the Tower. The *'Saxon Chronicle'* speaks of these ill-advised undertakings in the blended tones of sorrow and of anger. 'This was, in all things,' says that faithful old history, at pages 316, 317, 'a very heavy-timed year, and beyond measure laborious from the badness of the weather, both when men attempted to till the land, and, afterwards, to gather the fruits of their tilth; and from unjust contributions they never rested. Many counties also, that were confined to London by work, were grievously oppressed, on account of the wall that was building about the Tower, and *the Bridge that was nearly all afloat*, and the King's Hall that they were building at West-Minster; and many men perished thereby.'

"Our brave old River of Thames itself, however, is of the same changeful nature as Luna, the mistress of his tides; for, if at one time, he overflows his banks, blows up his Bridge, or drowns an invading army, by the fury of his waves; at another season he contracts his waters into their narrowest channel, or draws them back into his urn, without leaving enough to float a wherry over his bed. Of this I shall give you several instances, as we get lower down the stream of time; and now only remark, in chronological order, that on the 6th of the Ides of October, *videlicet* the 10th, in the 15th Year of the reign of Henry I. 1114, the River was so dried up, and there was such want of water, that between the Tower of London and the Bridge, and even under it, 'a great number of men, women, and children,'—says Stow, in his *'Survey,'* volume i. page 58,—'did wade over both on horse and foot,' the water coming up to their knees.

"The original account of this is to be found in the *'Annales'* of Roger de Hoveden, page 473; from whom we derive the additional information, that this defect of water commenced in the middle of the night preceding, and lasted until the darkest part of the next. The same historian, also, records, on the same page, that in the year 1115, the winter was so severe, that all throughout England the Bridges were broken by the ice.

"But although London Bridge was an edifice to which there was a continual and heavy cost attached, yet its possessions were, even anciently, very extensive; for you find that so early as in the 23d year of Henry I., A. D. 1122, Thomas de Ardern, and Thomas his son, gave to the Monks of Bermondsey, and the Church of St. George in Southwark, the tenth of his Lord's corn lands in Horndon, and the immense sum of Five Shillings per annum rent, out of the Lands pertaining to London Bridge. Calculate this, my good Sir, at twenty times its present value; for we know that in the Great Charter of King John, Chapter II. a knight paid but five pounds to the King as a Relief when he came to his estate; and *that*, Lord Coke tells you in his *Second Institute*, even several years later, was the fourth part of his annual income. Remember too, that sixpence by the week was then a living stipend to an ordinary labourer; that the Black Book of the Exchequer—which was written about the reign of Henry I.—ordains that a tenant shall pay one shilling to the King, instead of providing bread for one hundred soldiers for one meal; that the provender of twenty horses for one night, also to be paid by a tenant, was commuted for four pence; that in 1185, the tenants of Shireburn paid by custom two pence, or four hens, which they would; and, lastly, recollect, that in 1125,—called by Robert de Monte, the dearest year ever known,—a horseload of wheat was sold but for six shillings: in ordinary times, as in 1043, it was sixpence the quarter. Of all this you may see most abundant and curious proof, in Bishop Fleetwood's '*Chronicon Preciosum,*' London, 1745, 8vo. pages 55, 56; and therefore the gift of Thomas de Ardern was munificent.

"I should observe that Stow obtained the knowledge of this donation from the manuscript '*Annals of Bermondsey Priory,*' which are now preserved in the Harleian Library in the British Museum, No. 231, very fairly written in a good legible black text upon vellum; having vermillion rubrics of the King's Reign, and the date of the year. It is a rather small quarto volume, of 71 written leaves, delicately paged by some later hand; and the passage occurs on the reverse of folio 11. The Harleian Catalogue calls it, in Latin, 'the Annals of the Abbey of St. Saviour's of Bermondesie, from the year of our Lord 1042, down to the year of our Lord 1433; in which, beside the public affairs of each reign,'—told in the words of other Chronicles—'many things are narrated which belong to the history of the same Abbey.'

"You have already seen that London Bridge was a public work, to which all England furnished some labourers; but, as I mentioned some time back, Maitland, in his '*History of London,*' volume i. page 44, notices a deed cited by Stow, exempting the lands of Battle Abbey, in Sussex. This was granted by King Henry I. but is perhaps now lost, for it remains wholly unnoticed by the learned Editors of the new edition of Dugdale's '*Monasticon;*' and I must therefore give it you in the very words of the old Antiquary himself, who says, page 58, that in his time it remained with the seal very fair, in the custody of Joseph Holland, Esq.;—it is as follows:—

"'Henry, King of England, to Ralph, Bishop of Chichester, and all the Officers of Sussex, sendeth greeting. Know ye, &c. I command by my kingly authority, that the manor called Alceston, which my father gave with other lands to the Abbey of Battle, be free and quiet from shires and hundreds, and all other customs of earthly servitude, as my father held the same, most freely and quietly; and namely, *from the work of London Bridge,* and the work of the Castle at Pevensey: and this I command upon my forfeiture. Witness, William Pont de l'Arche, at Berry.'

"The second year of the succeeding King, however, namely Stephen, saw London Bridge in a state to require the exertions of all England to raise it: for, in 1136, a fire broke out in the dwelling of one Aileward, near London Stone, that consumed Eastward as far as Aldgate; and to the Shrine of St. Erkenwald, in St. Paul's Cathedral, to the West. On the Southern side of London the Wooden Bridge over the Thames was destroyed, but was soon after repaired, since Stephanides, whose description of London was written between 1170 and 1182, speaks of it as affording a convenient standing place to the spectators of the Citizens' Water Tournaments. I shall give you the whole passage, because it describes a very curious sport of the twelfth century, which was celebrated in the immediate vicinity of this very spot; and the account is at page 76, beginning '*In feriis Paschalibus*;' we'll content ourselves, however, with Dr. Pegge's translation of it, which runs thus.

"'At Easter, the diversion is prosecuted on the water; a target is strongly fastened to a trunk or mast, fixed in the middle of the River, and a youngster standing upright in the stern of a boat, made to move as fast as the oars and current can carry it, is to strike the target with his lance; and if in hitting it he break his lance, and keep his place in the boat, he gains his point, and triumphs; but if it happen that the lance be not shivered by the force of the blow, he is of course tumbled into the water, and away goes his vessel without him. However, a couple of boats full of young men is placed, one on each side of the target, so as to be ready to take up the unsuccessful adventurer, the moment he emerges from the stream, and comes fairly to the surface. The Bridge, and the balconies on the banks, are filled with spectators, whose business it is to laugh.'

"Of this singular sport, Joseph Strutt copied in his '*Sports and Pastimes of the People of England,*' London, 1801, 4to. page 92, plate x. a very curious illumination, contained in a volume of the Royal Manuscripts in the British Museum,—2 B. vii.—which consists of a history of the Old Testament, the Psalter, the Hymns of the Church, and a Calendar; all richly painted in water-colours, and beautified with gold,—'yellow, glittering, precious gold,'—so highly embossed, as to be 'sensible to feeling as to sight.'

"That volume brings back old days to my recollection, whenever I behold it; for, in the year 1553, it belonged to Queen Mary of England, and is bound in a truly regal style for her; being in thick boards covered with crimson velvet, richly embroidered with large flowers in coloured silks and gold twist; besides being garnished with gilt brass bosses and clasps, on the latter of which are engraven the Royal devices and supporters. Another, and more pleasing proof of its having been her's,—inasmuch as it records a good action of a London Citizen concerned with the affairs of this brave river,—is to be found in a Latin note written in a beautiful black text hand, on the reverse of the last leaf of the volume. 'This Book,' it states, 'formerly a gift, was afterwards carried away by a sailor; but that excellent and honest person, Baldwin Smith, Receiver of the Customs of the Port of London, hath restored and given it unto the most illustrious Mary, Queen of England, France, and Ireland, in the month of October, in the year of our Lord, 1553, in the first year of her reign.' The text of this volume is said to have been written, and the illuminations executed, in the fourteenth century, though, from their style, I cannot help thinking that the period is nearly an hundred years too late; for beneath the pages of the Psalter is a series of most interesting and excellent drawings, in pen-and-ink outlines, very slightly and delicately tinted with colours, which was certainly a far more ancient custom. However that may be, this series consists '*de omnibus rebus, et quibusdam aliis*,' for there are the representations of animals and birds, field-sports, games, legends, martyrdoms, battles, and fables, of an almost infinite variety; and in the course of them occur the figures of a water-quintain, both as it is described by Fitzstephen, and also of a more warlike character. The first of these was engraved by Strutt in the work which I have before referred to, and gives a very perfect idea of the RIVER TILTING OF THE TWELFTH CENTURY,

which the illuminator had, no doubt, personally witnessed in his own time. The other, which has also been engraven in the same work, page 113, plate xv. shews two armed knights getting 'grysly together,' as the '*Morte d'Arthur*' calls it, in boats;

and you will find it under the 60th Psalm, '*Dominus repulisti nos*,' &c.

"Stow, in his '*Survey,*' volume i. page 301, mentions a very rude imitation of this kind of jousting on the water at London; when he says, 'I have seen also in the summer season, upon the River of Thames, some rowed in wherries, with staves in their hands, flat at the fore-end, running one against another, and, for the most part, one or both of them were overthrown and well ducked.' In Queen Mary's Manuscript, under the psalm of '*Misericordiam et judicium cantabo,*' is also a representation of two fiends hurling a Monk from a rude stone Bridge; but as I rather think that did not occur at London, I mention it no farther.

"But now, to return to our subject:—Stow relates the particulars of the great fire of 1135-36, at page 58 of his '*Survey,*' citing in the margin the '*Annals of Bermondsey,*' and the '*Book of Trinity Priory,*' as his authorities. The latter of these is, perhaps, now no more; but in the former you may find the conflagration mentioned at page 13 b, where it is said to have happened in the year 1135, and to have extended to the Church of St. Clement Danes. It was probably in the Register of Trinity Priory, that Stow found a notice that London Bridge was not only repaired, but a new one erected of elm timber, in 1163, by the most excellent Peter of Colechurch, Priest and Chaplain; since I find it in none of the historians with whom I am acquainted. It is, however, much better authenticated that the same pious architect began his labours upon the first stone one in 1176; for, in the '*Annals of Waverley,*' at page 161, you find the following entry.—'1176. In this year, the Stone Bridge at London is begun by Peter, the Chaplain of Colechurch.' Here, therefore, ends the history of the infancy of London Bridge: and a very chargeful infancy it was, for, as old Stow says, 'it was maintained partly by the proper lands thereof, partly by the liberality of divers persons, and partly by taxations in divers shires, as I have proved, for the space of 215 years,'—And now, Mr. Geoffrey Barbican, your very good health."

"Sir, my hearty thanks to you," replied I, rubbing my eyes, "for this Bridge Story is as dull as proving a Peerage, where there's no reliance, and much doubting:—but how's this, Master Postern!" continued I, looking into the tankard, "you have drank, and I have drank, and yet the jug is as full as ever, and as hot as it was as first?"

"You're pleased to be facetious, good Sir," answered my visitor, "for truly I'm no Saint Richard to work such miracles; but, if you please, we'll now return to the Bridge again.

"We are here entering upon the golden age of London Bridge, for the new stone building, by Peter of Colechurch, was such an ornament as the Thames had never before witnessed; indeed, in my poor judgment, it very far surpassed that erection, of which I shall hereafter have occasion to speak; and perhaps, for its time, even that which now stretches itself across the flood. The person to whom was entrusted the building of the first stone Bridge at London, was, as I have already told you, named Peter, a Priest and Chaplain of St. Mary Colechurch; an edifice, which, until the Great Fire of London, stood on the North side of the Poultry, at the South end of a turning denominated Conyhoop Lane, from a Poulterer's shop having the sign of three Conies hanging over it. This Chapel, of which the skilful Peter was Curate, was dedicated to the Blessed Virgin, and was famous as the place where St. Edmund and St. Thomas à Beckett were presented at the baptismal Font; still it must have been something very like having a church on a first floor, for you may remember Stow says, in his '*Survey*,' volume i. page 552, that it was 'built upon a vault above ground, so that men are forced to ascend into it by certain steps.' Of the architectural knowledge of the Curate thereof, I have already shewed you that the Citizens of London had experienced some proofs, since he is said to have rebuilt their last wooden Bridge: and John Leland the Antiquary—whom I shall anon quote more particularly,— observes, in the notes to his famous '*Song of the Swan*,'—a book of which I will also speak hereafter,—that Radulphus de Diceto, Dean of London, who wrote about 1210, states from his own knowledge, that he was a native of this City. The same venerable Antiquary also tells us in his '*Itinerary*,' edited by Thomas Hearne, Oxford, 1768-69, octavo, volume vii. part I. marginal folio 22, page 12,—that 'a Mason beinge Master of the Bridge Howse, buildyd *à fundamentis* the Chapell on London Bridge, *à fundamentis propriis impensis*;' or, as we should now say, from bottom to top, at his own costs and charges. The property of Peter of Colechurch, however, would not stand Bridge-building by itself; and therefore the present will be the most fitting place, to give you some account of the other contributors to this great national work.

"Master Leland, in the same place which I last quoted, observes that 'a Cardinale, and Archepisshope of Cantorbyri, gave 1000 Markes or *li*. to the erectynge of London Bridge.' Now, the Cardinal who is here alluded to, was Hugo, Hugocio, or Huguzen di Petraleone, a Roman, Cardinal Deacon of St. Angelo, whom Pope Alexander III. sent, in 1176, to France, Scotland, and England, as his Legate; which you may find stated in Alphonso Ciaconio's noble book entitled '*Vitæ et Res Gestæ Pontificum Romanorum, et Sanctæ Romanæ Ecclesiæ Cardinalium*,' Rome, printed with the Vatican types, in 1630, folio, page 578, a work of about 3000 pages in extent; of an enormous size, fairly bound in embossed vellum, and adorned with a prodigious number of copper-plates and wood-cut Armorial Ensigns; by the latter of which we are shewn, that this foreign contributor to the building of London Bridge bore for his arms, Quarterly, Argent and Gules, and over all, in the centre point, a sieve of the first. Whilst the Cardinal resided in England, he took some notice of the dispute which was then going on concerning the Primacy, between the Archbishops of Canterbury and York: when at a meeting held at Westminster, Roger de Ponte, the turbulent possessor of the latter see, arrogantly took his seat at the Cardinal's right hand. Upon which the domestics of Richard, the mild and amiable Archbishop of Canterbury, took him thence by force, and in the ensuing scuffle he was beaten, and turned out of the assembly, with his episcopal robes sadly rent. Now this Richard was a Benedictine Monk, and Prior of the Monastery of St. Martin's, Dover; who was elected to the See of Canterbury on the death of Thomas à Beckett, in 1174. 'He was a man,' says Bishop Godwin, when writing his memoirs, 'very liberal, gentle, and passing wise;' and, what gives him great honour in *my* sight, he was the very Prelate whom Leland mentions in the passage I quoted, as subscribing so nobly to the foundation of London Bridge. And yet, 'tis strange, that only in his *'Itinerary,'* and in Stow's *'Survey,'* volume i. page 58, is this donation recorded; for even in the best and most splendid edition of Bishop Godwin's volume, *'De Præsulibus Angliæ Commentarius,'* by William Richardson, Canon of Lincoln, Cambridge, 1743, folio, page 79, the old Citizen is referred to at note *y*, as his authority for the fact. I cannot omit now giving you the blazon of this Prelate's own arms, as they appear in that noble illuminated copy of Archbishop Parker's work, *'De Antiquitate et Privilegiis Ecclesiæ Cantuariensis cum Archiepiscopis ejusdem 70,'* Lambeth, 1572, folio, page 123, which is estimated to be fully worth its weight in gold. This truly valuable volume was presented by our late good King George the Third to the British Museum, and formerly belonged to Queen Elizabeth. The arms, however, were Azure, three Mullets in bend, between two Cottises Argent; and whenever you turn to this volume, on which the ancient Art of Illuminating shed its latest rays, I pray you fail not carefully to inspect it: for you will find it a copy of that edition printed at his own palace, by John Day; with many leaves impressed on vellum, and the whole of the book carefully ruled with red-ink lines, the initials coloured and gilded, and all the Armorial Ensigns, with the Frontispiece, excellently well emblazoned. And I pray you also, forget not well to note the binding; since a richer, or more fancifully embroidered covering there are few tomes which can exhibit. The ground of it is green velvet, intended to represent the *vert* of a park, and it is surrounded by a broad border of pales with a gate, worked in brown silk and gold twist; whilst within are trees, flowers, shrubs, tufts of grass, serpents, hinds, and does, all executed in richly coloured silks, and gold and silver wire. At the back are the Queen's badges of red and white roses; the edges of the leaves are gilt, and the volume was once secured by ribbons of crimson silk.

"Of this most splendid book I must, indeed, yet add another word, that it may be estimated as it so well deserves. Dr. Ducarel, in his account of that astonishing copy of it which is deposited in the Archiepiscopal Palace at Lambeth, says, 'It was first printed at Lambeth by John Daye in 1572; and so small a number were then published, that, except this complete copy, there is but one extant in England, known to be so, which is preserved in the Public

Library of Cambridge, as I am informed.' See his Letter of July the 15th, 1758, addressed to Archbishop Secker, which is inserted in the Rev. H. J. Todd's *'Catalogue of the Archiepiscopal Manuscripts in Lambeth Palace.'* London, 1812, folio, page 242, Art. 959.

"The life of Archbishop Richard, which this book contains, is nearly the same as that related by Francis Godwin, Bishop of Landaff; and before I leave speaking of this early and Reverend patron of London Bridge, let me endeavour to clear his memory from something like a stain which attaches to it. He received the Archbishop's Pall, immediately after the death of a man of unconquerable spirit and insurmountable pride, for you will remember that he was successor to Beckett: and, perhaps, it was the strong contrast afforded by his yielding and quiet disposition, which has made some suppose that he did nothing worthy of memory. I am, however, myself rather surprised at the manner of his decease, when it is allowed by all his biographers, that he was a man so charitable, of such benefit to the revenues of the church, and was so liberal both to the poor, the nation, the King, and even the Pontiff himself. The story of his death is related by Gervase of Dover, by Henry Knyghton, the Canon of Leicester, and in the Chronicle of William Thorne, the Monk of St. Augustine's, Canterbury; but I shall recite it to you from the old English edition of Francis Godwin's *'Catalogue of the Bishops of England, from the first planting of the Christian Religion in this Island:'* London, 1615, 4to. page 96. 'The end of this man,' says the Prelate, 'is thus reported, how that being a sleepe at his Mannor of Wrotham, there seemed to come vnto him a certaine terrible personage'—Knyghton and Thorne say 'the Lord appeared vnto his sight,'—'demaunding of him, who he was; whereunto, when for feare, the Archbishop answered nothing, Thou art he, quoth the other, that hast destroyed the goods of the Church, and I will destroy thee from off the earth: this having said, he vanished away. In the morning betime, the Archbishop got him up, and taking his iourney toward Rochester, related this fearfull vision vnto a friend of his by the way. Hee had no sooner told the tale, but hee was taken suddenly with a great cold and stifenesse in his limmes, so that they had much adoo to get him so farre as Haling, a house belonging to the Bishop of Rochester. There he tooke his bed, and being horribly tormented with the cholike, and other greefes, vntill the next day, the night following, the 16th of February, hee gaue vp the ghost, anno 1183.'

"Though such was his untimely end, yet his being so great a benefactor to the original building of old London Bridge, ought to make his name revered by every true-hearted Citizen of London; and, indeed, Bridge-building has been thought by some to be an act of real piety, witness those rude old verses printed in Leland's *'Itinerary,'* volume vii. part I. Marginal folio 64 b, page 79, which were composed on the erecting of the Bridge at Culham, in

Oxfordshire, and hung up by Master Richard Fannand, Ironmonger, of Abingdon, in the Hall of St. Helen's Hospital.

'Off alle werkys in this worlde that ever were wrought,
Holy Chirche is chefe, there children been chersid.
For by baptim these barnes to blisse been ybrought,
Thorough the grace of God, and fayre refresshed.
Another blessid besines is Brigges to make,
Where, that the pepul may not passe after greet showers;
Dole it is to drawe a deed body out of a lake,
That was fulled in a fount stoon, and a felow of oures.
King Herry the fifte, in his fourthe yere,
He hathe yfounde for his folke a Brige in Berke schyre,
For cartis with carriages may goo and come clere,
That many Wynters afore were mareed in the myre.
And some oute of ther sadels flette to the grounde
Went forthe in the water wist no man whare;
Fyve wekys after or they were yfounde,
Ther kyn and ther knowlech caught them uppe with care.'

"By this then, you see there is much virtue in your Bridge-builder. The names of all the Benefactors to London Bridge, indeed, were fairly painted on a tablet, and hung up in St. Thomas's Chapel, which stood upon the middle of it; and, doubtless, the donation of King Henry II. would be found there recorded, if that grateful testimonial were yet in existence. The King's gift, however, is supposed to have been, in fact, the gift of the people, being the produce of a tax upon wool; and hence arose that absurd tradition, which the commonalty invented to make a wonder of the matter, that 'London Bridge was built upon woolpacks,' I am, indeed, inclined to think that the measure was not very popular; for the people of England seldom failed to complain of any additional duty placed upon that commodity; and of this you find some reliques in Lord Coke's Commentary on the 30th Chapter of the '*Magna Charta*' of King Henry III., contained in his '*Second Institute*,' pages 58, 59. He is there speaking, you know, of the taking away of evil tolls and customs, and he observes, that some have supposed that there was a tribute due to the King by the Common Law, upon all wools, wool-fells,—that is, the undressed sheep skins,—and leather, to be taken as well of the English as of strangers, known by the name of *Antiqua Custuma*. This amounted to half a mark, or 6*s*. 8*d.* for every sack of wool of 26 stone weight; and a whole mark upon every last of leather. But even this his Lordship also endeavours to prove a recent custom, by a Patent Roll from the Exchequer, of the 3rd of Edward I., A. D. 1274, which states, that the Prelates, Chiefs, and the whole Common Council of the kingdom, had consented to grant this new custom of wool to him, and to his heirs. Now, even the words '*novam consuetudinem*' may signify only a revival of the ancient tax, for some specific cause; as it might have lain dormant since the days of building London Bridge; thus having reference to a new occasion, and not to the date. But shortly previous to the final confirmation of the Great and Forest Charters, however, in the 25th of Edward I., 1296, the King set a new toll of forty shillings upon every sack of wool, without the consent of his Parliament; which the Commonalty felt to be a very heavy imposition. Against this they petitioned, and in the aforesaid '*Confirmationes Chartarum*,' Chapter vii. it was provided that such things should be abolished, and not taken, but by common consent and good will; excepting the customs before granted. There appears to me, however, even a still nearer connection between the Duties raised for the building of London Bridge, and the xxiii. Chapter of the '*Magna Charta*' of King John, for you there find that 'No City, nor Freeman, shall be distrained to make Bridges or water-banks, but such as have of old been accustomed to do so:' from which it is evident, that the taxation was general, and that this instrument was to make it particular; though, according to Lord Coke's exposition, there was nothing gained by it: for, in his '*Second Institute*,' folio 29, he says, that in the reigns of Richard I. and John, fictitious exactions were made in the names of Bridges, Bulwarks, and the like, but that neither the erection, nor the paying for them, was abolished by this act, since they could not be erected but by the King himself, or by an Act of Parliament.—But Mr. Barbican!—You doze, worthy Sir!"

"Why truly, Mr. Postern," said I, rubbing my eyes, "Tax-gathering is always dull work; and I verily thought we'd lost sight of the Bridge in the paying for it. You're as minute with all your authorities, as a Flemish painter that marks every hair on a cat's back, and I can turn over your old dull authors in my own dusty book-room."

"I must acknowledge," said my visitor, "that such details are rather dry; but you very well know, my good friend, as Father Le Long said, 'Truth is so delightful, that we should consider no labour too great to obtain it:' and, indeed, I wished to bring before you some circumstances which lie widely scattered, although they, nevertheless, most excellently illustrate the story, and I would do all honour to the memory of the worthy Peter of Colechurch."

"Really, Sir," answered I, "if his blessing be worth having, it ought to rest upon your head; for had you been Peter of Colechurch himself, ten times over, you could scarcely have taken more pains with your history: and so,—here's your health, and his, Mr. Barnaby."

"My best thanks to you, my honoured friend," replied Mr. Postern, "and I'll shortly repay your attention by a piece of a more brilliant description; for having once got the Bridge built, and paid for, we'll take a look at the picturesque old edifice itself, and at some of the many gorgeous sights and interesting scenes which took place upon it: indeed it shall go hard but what I'll find you amusement. The building, then, which the never-to-be-forgotten Peter of Colechurch began, took as long to complete as Solomon's Temple, for thirty and three years were employed in erecting it. Ere that period, however, the charitable Priest who designed it, the learned Architect and wise builder who watched its progress, went the way of all flesh; as we shall find hereafter, in 1205, and not, as Maitland erroneously says, in the third of King John, A. D. 1201, though he also supposes that he might then be worn out by age or fatigue, since in the Patent Rolls of the Tower of London, of that year, M. 2, No. 9, is the following Letter Missive of the King to the Mayor and Citizens of London, recommending a new Architect. For other references you may consult Maitland's History, page 45; Thomas Hearne's edition of the *'Liber Niger Scaccarii,'* London, 1771, octavo, volume i. page *470, where it is printed in the original Latin; and the *'Calendarium Rotulorum Patentium in Turri Londinensi, Printed by Command,'* London, 1802, folio, page 1, column 1. The Letter is as follows:—

"'John, by the Grace of God, King of England, &c. to his faithful and beloved the Mayor and Citizens of London, greeting. Considering how the Lord in a short time hath wrought in regard to the Bridges of Xainctes and Rochelle, by the great care and pains of our faithful, learned, and worthy Clerk, Isenbert, Master of the Schools of Xainctes: We therefore, by the advice of our Reverend Father in Christ, Hubert, (Walter) Archbishop of Canterbury, and that of others, have desired, directed, and enjoined him to use his best endeavour in building your Bridge, for your benefit, and that of the public: For we trust in the Lord, that this Bridge, so requisite for you, and all who shall pass the same, will, through his industry, and the divine blessing, soon be finished. Wherefore, without prejudice to our right, or that of the City of London, we will and grant, that the rents and profits of the several houses which the said Master of the Schools shall cause to be erected upon the Bridge aforesaid, be for ever appropriated to repair, maintain, and uphold the same. And seeing that the requisite work of the Bridge cannot be accomplished without your aid, and that of others, we charge, and exhort you, kindly to receive and honour the above-named Isenbert, and those employed by him, who will perform every thing to your advantage and credit, according to his directions, you affording him your joint advice and assistance in the premises. For whatever good office or honour you shall do to him, you ought to esteem the same as done to us. But, should any injury be offered to the said Isenbert, or to the persons employed by him, which we do not believe there will, see that the same be redressed so soon as it comes to your knowledge. Witness myself, at Molinel,'—in the Province of Bourbon, in France,—'the eighteenth day of April.' 'A Letter,' adds Hearne, on page *471, 'of the same form, was written to all the King's faithful subjects constituting the realm of England;' and the instrument itself is also to be found at length in the original Latin, in Sir Symonds D'Ewes' extracts from the Records, Harleian MSS. in the British Museum, No. 86, page 1 a.

"It is, however, by no means clear, notwithstanding this Royal Writ, that Isenbert was employed by the Citizens to complete the building of London Bridge; indeed, the Rev. John Entick, in his edition of Maitland's *'History of London,'* volume i. page 45, imagines quite otherwise, because he found that King John, in the seventh year of his reign, 1205, three years, as *he* says, before the Bridge was finished, granted the custody of it to one Friar West, taking it from the Lord Mayor, and obliging the City to apply certain void places within its walls to be built on for its support. Strype also quotes the former instrument as being yet preserved in the *'Rotuli Clausi,'* or Close Rolls, in the Tower, 7 John, c. 19, for you know it was a private instrument, and therefore sealed up, and directed to the persons whom it specially concerned.

"But now let us see how far this supposition is founded in truth. In the first place, the reference to the Close Rolls is erroneous, for the writ is to be found on the 15th Membrane, there being no such article as c. 19; and, in the next place, there was no such person as Friar West, for the title of Friar was not in use until the fourteenth century, and the person referred to was called *Wasce*, though the name of West has been copied and re-copied, and the error thus perpetuated *ad infinitum*. The actual words of the writ are, in English, as follow.

"'The King to Geoffrey Fitz Peter, &c.'—Chief Justice of England.—'We will that Brother Wasce, our Almoner, and some other lawful man of London, provided by you and the Mayor of London, be Attorney for the custody of London Bridge. And, therefore, we command you that they give the whole to these men, like as Peter, the Chaplain of Colechurch, possessed the same from them. Witness for the same, the Prior of Stoke, at Marlebridge, the 15th day of September.' Notwithstanding this instrument, we hear no more of Frater Wasce, nor of Isenbert of Xainctes, but are told by Stow, page 58, without his referring to any other authority, that 'this work, to wit the Arches, Chapel, and Stone Bridge over the Thames at London, having been thirty-three years in building, was, in the year 1209, finished by the worthy Merchants of London, Serle Mercer, William Almaine, and Benedict Botewrite, principal masters of that work.'

"This new Bridge consisted, then, of a stone platform, erected somewhat westward of the former, 926 feet long, and 40 in width, standing about 60 feet above the level of the water; and containing a Drawbridge, and 19 broad pointed arches, with massive piers varying from 25 to 34 feet in solidity, raised upon strong elm piles, covered by thick planks, bolted together. Such was the FIRST STONE LONDON BRIDGE, commenced by PETER OF COLECHURCH, A. D. 1176.

"Deeply as I venerate the memory of the great builder of that Bridge, which continued for so many centuries the wonder of Europe, yet I must not omit to notice to you, that many persons have grievously condemned his labours; the principal objections to which are summed up in the *Londinium Redivivum*,' of Mr. James Peller Malcolm, London, 1802-1807, 4to. volume ii. page 386, where he thus heavily censures that erection. 'Whatever were the pretensions of Peter of Colechurch to eminence as an Ecclesiastical Architect, I think any person who views Vertue's print of London Bridge, as it stood in 1209, will allow that he was a very bad Civil Engineer. He seems to have delighted in the number of his piers, which amounted to nineteen; and he was so ignorant of the true principles by which he should have been governed, that the centre was swelled into a Chapel, reducing the adjoining arches to half the diameter of the remainder. Indeed, it is wonderful that those piers maintained their situation, when we reflect how the torrent now rushes through, hurling heavy laden barges along as if they were feathers on the stream, when every practicable remedy to enlarge them has been applied.'

"An Architect of nearly an hundred years since, however, has considered these objections with somewhat more of mathematical proof; and what is better, even whilst he admits their full force, he still venerates the memory, and dares to applaud the public spirit, of the blessed Peter of Colechurch. You will readily guess that I allude to Master Nicholas Hawksmoor's '*Short Historical Account of London Bridge, with a proposition for a New Stone Bridge at Westminster*,' a quarto pamphlet of 47 pages, and 5 folding Copper-plates, originally published in the year 1736, for two shillings. The Author observes, at page 9, that the whole breadth of the River from North to South is nearly 900 feet, and that in his time there were eighteen solid piers of different dimensions, varying from 34 to 25 feet in thickness. According to this disposition, he argues, 'the greatest water way is when the tide is *above* the sterlings, which is 450 feet, and, considering the impediments, it is not half the width of the River for the water to pass; but when the tide is fallen *below* the sterlings, the water-way is reduced to 194 feet,—which is during the greatest part of the flux and reflux of the tide,—and the river of 900 feet broad, is forced through a channel of 194 feet, which is not a quarter of the whole.' We can at last, however, hardly judge of the Bridge of Peter of Colechurch with any degree of fairness, for that great benefactor of London died before he completed his *Pontificate*, as I may jocularly call it; and the author whom I last quoted, very candidly observes of him, that he, perhaps, 'did not intend to add those immense Sterlings that have so much obstructed the River's passage betwixt the Stone piers,' and which, after all, are the great cause of the evil: for, says the same person, at page 13, when answering the common objection to altering London Bridge, on account of the expense attending it, 'I have heard some masters of Hoys and Lighters say, that a Tonnage would willingly be paid for such a conveniency and security of their goods and vessels; and, as I have heard, an offer *was* made to pay Tonnage, if the Drawbridge had been opened, when the City last repaired it, to avoid the losses they suffered frequently by the Sterlings.' 'It is very probable,' continues the same authority, 'that the Sterlings were made afterwards, to keep the foundation of the piers from being undermined;—or, perhaps, these Sterlings might be increased after some damages that befell the piers, by the great quantity of ice which might be stopt by the narrowness of the arches; and those that intended to make the legs more secure, used such means as rendered them the less so, by the violent rapidity which they gave to the River so restrained,' In addition to this, he also attempts an apology even for that very part of Peter's Bridge, which has been the most condemned; having, perhaps, designed, says Mr. Hawksmoor, 'by the narrowness of his arches, to restrain the ebbing of the tide, the better to preserve the navigation of the River above the Bridge, though it would not have any great effect if the Sterlings were taken away,' considering 'that if the River had its free course, it would ebb away so fast, that there would be scarce any navigation above the Bridge, a little time after high-water.' This pamphlet also contains a defence of the Great Pier, which so violently excited the censure of Malcolm, who thought a Church on a Bridge was thrown away; for at page 12, he states that it might be intended 'firstly to be a steadying of the whole machine, instead of making an angle, as it is in the famous Bridge at Prague, and in some of the Bridges in France; so that this fortress was placed in the middle of the Bridge, to stem the violence of the floods, ice, and all other accidents that might be forced against it. Secondly,—that if by any accident of the ice or flood, or undermining any of the legs,'—he means the piers, but Hawksmoor frequently uses this very ungraceful epithet,— 'some of the arches might fall, as five did, Anno 1282, yet, by the help of this great buttress,—though this damage was done on one side,—the arches on the other side stood firm, so that there was less expense, and greater encouragement to make the repair. The third reason was, that he had an opportunity to shew his piety, having a situation for erecting a Chapel, which was done, and his body deposited in it.'

"At the great repair of London Bridge, which took place between 1757 and 1770, several additional arguments were brought forward against the original edifice; of which Mr. Robert Mylne, in his Answers to the Select Committee of the House of Commons, for improving the Port of London, dated May the 15th, and October the 30th, 1801, printed in the Fourth Report of that Committee, states the following particulars. 'The houses,' says he, 'being then taken down, and the sides of the Bridge being dismantled, the internal masses of its great bulk were found little better than rubbish, and of bad mason-work, &c. without active exertion, or even inert resistance. The original Piles, under the original stone-work of a very narrow Bridge, between the two modern sides and extreme parts, by cutting into the sides of the piers, and by one old being opened up, and totally removed, have been found composed of Sapling Oak and some Elm, carelessly worked, neither round nor square, but much decayed.'

"And now, worthy Mr. Barbican, having told you some of the objections to, and apologies for, the Bridge of the venerable Peter of Colechurch, before we ascend to the parapet, to examine the buildings which stood upon it, let me observe to you, that there are engraved Ground-plans of this Bridge, in George Vertue's prints, which I shall mention more particularly hereafter, and also in Hawksmoor's tract from which I have so largely quoted."

Here let me for a moment interrupt the narrative of Mr. Postern, by stating that on the next page the Reader has a reduced copy of the interesting plan last mentioned, to which are subjoined Hawksmoor's own measurements, and some additional particulars, also taken from Vertue; on the accuracy of every part of which, we have the best authority for placing the most complete reliance.

GROUND PLAN OF THE FIRST STONE BRIDGE AT LONDON: COMMENCED A. D. 1176, AND COMPLETED A. D. 1209.

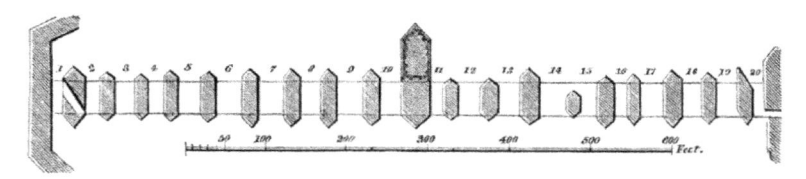

DIMENSIONS AND REFERENCES.
COMMENCING AT THE CITY, OR NORTH END.

	Feet.	Inches.
Breadth of First Arch	10	—
——————— Pier	30	—
——————— Second Arch	15	—
——————— Pier	18	—
Length of Second Pier	47	6
Breadth of Third Arch	25	—
——————— Pier	17	—
Length of Third Pier	41	6
Breadth of Fourth Arch	21	—
——————— Pier	18	—
Length of Fourth Pier	47	6
Breadth of Fifth Arch	27	—
——————— Pier	21	—
Length of Fifth Pier	47	6
Breadth of Sixth Arch	29	6
——————— Pier	21	—
Length of Sixth Pier	54	—
Breadth of Seventh Arch	29	6
——————— Pier	21	—
Length of Seventh Pier	54	—
Breadth of Eighth Arch	26	—
——————— Pier	21	—

	Feet.	Inches.
Length of Eighth Pier	54	—
Breadth of Ninth Arch	32	9
——————— Pier	21	—
Length of Ninth Pier	54	—
Breadth of Tenth Arch	25	6
——————— Centre Pier	36	—
Length of Centre Pier	95	—
Extreme Length of ditto	125	—

VERTUE *makes the extreme length of this Pier but 115 feet only.*

	Feet.	Inches.
Breadth of Chapel on the Centre Pier	20	—
Length of ditto	60	—
Exterior height from the Water	about 110	—
Breadth of Eleventh Arch	16	—
——————— Pier	21	—
Length of Eleventh Pier	37	—
Breadth of Twelfth Arch	24	6
——————— Pier	21	—
Length of Twelfth Pier	38	—
Breadth of Thirteenth Arch	25	8
——————— Pier	27	—
Length of Thirteenth Pier	50	—
Breadth of Drawbridge, or Fourteenth Arch	29	4

VERTUE *makes this space 30 feet broad.*

	Feet.	Inches.
Breadth of Fourteenth Pier	17	—
Length of Fourteenth Pier	26	—
Breadth of Fifteenth Arch	22	10
——————— Pier	26	—
Length of Fifteenth Pier	47	7
Breadth of Sixteenth Arch	21	10
——————— Pier	15	—
Length of Sixteenth Pier	46	—
Breadth of Seventeenth Arch	29	4
——————— Pier	25	—
Length of Seventeenth Pier	46	—
Breadth of Eighteenth Arch	24	—
——————— Pier	17	—
Length of Eighteenth Pier	46	—
Breadth of Nineteenth Arch	27	—
——————— Pier	17	—
Length of Nineteenth Pier, North Side	49	—
Breadth of Twentieth Arch	15	—

The Piers and Arches were both measured from the squares of the latter, the triangular ends being left un-noticed, excepting in the instance of the Great Pier. The length of the whole Bridge was 926 feet; its height, 60; and the breadth of the Street over it, 40 feet.

"Let us now then, my good Sir," continued Mr. Postern, "ascend to the Platform or Street of the old London Bridge, erected by Peter of Colechurch, and look at the buildings which stood upon it; the most celebrated of which was the famous Chapel dedicated to St. Thomas à Becket, the Martyr of Canterbury, whence it was familiarly called St. Thomas of the Bridge. This was erected upon the Tenth, or Great Pier, which measured 35 feet in breadth, and 115 from point to point; whilst the edifice itself was 60 feet in length, by 20 feet broad, and stood over the parapet on the Eastern side of the Bridge, leaving a pathway on the West, about a quarter of the breadth of the Pier, in front of the Chapel. The face of the building itself was forty feet in height, having a plain gable, surmounted by a cross of about six feet more; whilst four buttresses, crowned by crocketted spires, divided the Western end into three parts. The wide centre contained a rich pointed-arch window, of one mullion, with a quatrefoil in the top; and the two sides were occupied by the entrances to the Chapel from the Bridge-Street, each being ascended by three steps. Such was the general appearance of the WEST FRONT OF THE CHAPEL ON LONDON BRIDGE.

"The interior of this edifice consisted of two stories, both consecrated to sacred purposes, and greatly resembling each other in their appearance. The Upper Chapel was lofty, being supported by fourteen groups of elegant clustered columns, and lighted by eight pointed-arch windows divided by stone mullions into a double range of arches, surmounted by a lozenge. Beneath each of the windows were three arched recesses, separated by small pillars; and the roof itself was also originally formed of lofty pointed arches; though, when this magnificent fane was transformed into a warehouse, a wooden ceiling, with stout beams crossing each other in squares, was erected, which cut off the arches where they sprang from the pillars, and divided into two parts the INTERIOR OF THE UPPER CHAPEL OF ST. THOMAS.

The Eastern extremity of this building formed a semi-hexagon, having a smaller window in each of its divisions, with richly carved arches under them, corresponding with the series already mentioned on the side: and the architectural lightness and elegance of the whole, meriting the highest encomium. Beneath this principal edifice, was a short descending passage, having, on the left hand, a stone basin cut in a recess in the wall, for containing Holy Water, and leading, through the solid masonry of the Pier, into the LOWER CHAPEL OF ST. THOMAS, which was constructed in the Bridge itself.

"This CRYPT was entered both from the upper apartment and the street, as well as by a flight of stone stairs winding round a pillar, which led into it from the nearest Pier: whilst in the front of this latter entrance, the Sterling formed a platform at low water, which thus rendered it accessible from the River. The Lower Chapel, which—even decorated as *that* was, in my estimation, very far exceeded the upper one in architectural beauty,—was about 20 feet in height, and its roof supported by clustered columns, similar to those I have already described; from each of which sprang seven ribs, the centre, and the two adjoining it in every division, being bound by fillets with roses on the intersections; whilst the great horizontal ribs had clusters of regal and ecclesiastical masks, producing an effect little to be expected in such a structure, in such a situation; though I may trust to your correct taste, my good Mr. Barbican, for duly appreciating it. There was also a rich SERIES OF WINDOWS IN THE LOWER CHAPEL,

which looked on to the water, similar in character to, though much smaller than, those above: whilst the floor was beautifully paved with black and white marble; for in this place did the pious Architect propose to rest his bones. His monument, remarkable only for its plainness, was formed, according to

Maitland's '*History*,' page 46, under the Chapel staircase, in the middle of the building; and it measured seven feet and an half, by four in breadth. There was, indeed, neither brass plate, nor inscription, nor carving found about the sepulchre, when Mr. Yaldwin, the inhabitant of the Chapel in 1737, then a dwelling, and warehouse, discovered the remains of a body in repairing the staircase; though, from the '*Annals of Waverley*,' page 168, we know that the reliques of Peter were certainly entombed in this place. 'In 1205,'—runs the passage,—'died Peter the Chaplain of Colechurch, who began the Stone Bridge at London, and he is sepultured in the Chapel upon the Bridge.' By this entry then, we are assured that he lay there; and as for an epitaph, was not the whole edifice an everlasting catafalco to his memory, which should speak for all times? How finely, indeed, might we apply to him that inscription, which the son of Sir Christopher Wren composed for his father's burial-place in St. Paul's,—'He lived, not for himself, but for the public! Reader, if you seek his monument, look around you!'

"And now, before we enter upon an examination of the bed of the Thames at London Bridge, and consider whether the River were turned, as Stow thinks, to admit of its erection, let me cite you some ancient authorities concerning St. Thomas's Chapel. The first of these shall be the '*Itinerary of Symon Fitz Simeon, and Hugo the Illuminator*,' both of whom were Irish Monks, of the Order of Friars Minors, who visited London on their pilgrimage to Palestine, in 1322. 'This flux and reflux,'—say they, at pages 4, 5,—'continues to the sea from the famous River named Thames, upon the which is a Bridge, filled with inhabitants and wealth; and in the midst of them is a Church dedicated to the blessed Thomas, Archbishop and Martyr, which is well served continually.' About the year 1418, also, William Botoner, a Monk of Worcester, of the Parish of St. James in Bristol, who then travelled from that City to St. Michael's Mount in Cornwall, in his '*Itinerarium*,' pages 301, 302, thus spake of London Bridge and the Chapel. 'The length of the Chapel of St. Thomas the Martyr, upon London Bridge, is about twenty yards; having an under Chancel in the vault, with a choir, but the length of the nave of the said Chapel contains fourteen yards. The width of the middle steps is one yard. The length of the Bridge on the South, from the posts to the first gate newly founded by Henry the Cardinal, unto the two posts erected near the Church of St. Magnus, consists of five hundred of my steps. *Item*: there are five great windows on one side,'—of the Chapel,—'each of which contains three panes:' or rather divisions. Of these Itineraries I will observe nothing farther, than that they were published from the original Manuscripts in Corpus Christi College, Cambridge, by James Nasmith, the Editor of Tanner's '*Notitia Monastica*;' in 1778, octavo; under the title of '*Itineraria Symonis Simeonis, et Willielmi de Worcestre*.'

"Of this Chapel, and also of the first Stone Bridge, there are two large folio engravings, taken and published, by George Vertue, in 1744-48, which, after his decease, were, with many of his other plates of Antiquities, presented by his widow to the Antiquarian Society in 1775. The first engraving measures 18¼ inches by 20 inches and ⅜, and contains 'A View of the West Front of the Chappel of St. Thomas, on London Bridge; also the Inside View from West to East of the said Chappel, as it was first built An°. 1209:'—and also 'London Bridge as it was first built, An°. 1209:'—a Ground plan, and some measurements of the same, and a short Historical account of the structure, drawn up by Sir Joseph Ayloffe, Bart. Vice-President of the Society of Antiquaries. The publication line states, that it was 'drawn, engrav'd, and publish'd by G. Vertue, in Brownlow-Street, Drury-Lane, 1748.' A second edition was printed by the Society, in 1777.

"The other plate contains 'The Inside Perspective View of the Under Chappel of St. Thomas within London Bridge, from the West to the East end,' and beneath it: the 'Inside South View of the Under Chappel from East to West, representing the manner and form of this rare piece of Ancient Architecture, thus drawn and transmitted to posterity, by G. V., Antiquary, 1744. Published and sold by G. Vertue, in Brownlow-Street, Drury-Lane, 1747' This plate, which measures 18¼ inches by 20, contains a few additional historical notes, by Sir Joseph Ayloffe; and a reduced copy of the lower View was engraved in the 23d volume of the *'Gentleman's Magazine,'* for October, 1753, page 520. I must observe, also, that, in the large interior View on that plate of Vertue last-mentioned, there are introduced the portraits of the learned Samuel Gale, and the eccentric Dr. Ducarel. The former, by whose patronage and assistance Vertue produced these prints, is standing on the left hand, holding a plan of the Chapel, and listening to an outlandish-looking man, designed for Peter of Colechurch; whilst the latter Antiquary is employed in measuring. You find this information given from Gale's own lips, in that monument of labour, the *'Literary Anecdotes of the Eighteenth Century,'* by John Nichols, volume iv. London, 1812, 8vo. page 552, and volume vi. part I. page 402. I shall close this notice of these most ancient views of London Bridge, by observing to you, that there is a view and a ground-plan of it, with measurements, engraved by Toms, on the second plate in Hawksmoor's work, already cited.

"Let me remark to you, however, Mr. Barbican, as touching the Chapel which I have thus described to you, that the custom of erecting Religious Houses on Bridges, is certainly of great antiquity. A notable instance of this kind was on the Bridge at Droitwich, where the road passed through the Chapel and separated the congregation from the reading-desk and pulpit. Another famous Bridge Chapel is also to be found erected over the River Calder, at Wakefield, in the West Riding of Yorkshire; of which, a folding view, by W.

Lodge, is inserted in the *'Ducatus Leodiensis'* of Ralph Thoresby, London, 1715, folio, sometimes placed at page 164. This beautiful fane, you know, was built by King Edward IV. in memory of his father, Richard, Duke of York, who was killed in the battle fought near Wakefield, on December the 31st, 1460. The Bridge Chapel, however, though extremely rich in its architecture, was not so singular as our's at London, since it was not built *in* the pier, and descending even to the water's edge, but *upon* the pier, and the platform of the Bridge itself. Somewhat like our shrine of St. Thomas, however, as it belonged to the poor of the town, it was, about 1779, converted into a dwelling-house, and let at a small annual rent to a retail dealer in old clothes! as that industrious Antiquary, Richard Gough, tells us, in his *'British Topography,'* London, 1780, 4to. volume ii. page 437, note, r. 'To what base uses may we not return, Horatio!' The edifice which had been erected for Monks to chaunt forth their *Requiescats* in solemn procession; the shrine which had been endowed for the sweet repose of a warrior's soul; the—"

"I'll tell you what, Mr. Barnaby Postern," said I, starting up, "you'll contribute to *my* sweet repose, unless you leave wandering in Yorkshire, and return again to London Bridge: what have we to do with a bead-roll of all the Bridge Chapels that are scattered through England? I desire to know but of one; for, by its having existed, we are sure that there might have been some sort of custom for their erection; and, as old Chaucer saith,

'Experience, though none auctoritye
Were in this world, is quite enough for me.'"

"True, Sir, true," said the mild old Antiquary; "you have once more brought me back to my starting-post; for I own that I am too apt, when discoursing upon one subject, to branch out into others which seem to illustrate, or are in any degree connected with it. You will, however, I dare say, allow me to remark, that Plutarch denies the derivation of the word Pontifex from the old Roman custom of sacrificing on Bridges, which might, nevertheless, be the origin of Chapels being built upon them. He mentions this in his Life of Numa Pompilius, in his *'Vitæ Parallelæ,'* best edition, by Augustine Bryan, and M. du Soul, London, 1729-24, 4to. volume i. page 142. The Greek passage begins, 'Νουμᾶ δὲ και τὴν των αρχιερεων,' &c., and the Latin, *'Jam etiam sacerdotum;'* but I shall give you the excellent modern English version of Dr. Langhorne, in his very popular translation of the old Classic, from the edition of Mr. Archdeacon Wrangham, London, 1813, 8vo. volume i. pages 181, 182: 'To Numa,' says the passage, 'is attributed the institution of that high order of priests, called *Pontifices*; over which, he is said to have presided himself. Some say, they were called *Pontifices*, as employed in the service of those powerful gods that govern the world; for *potens*, in the Roman language, signifies powerful. Others, that they were ordered by their law-giver to perform such offices as were in their power, and standing excused when there was some great impediment. But most writers assign a ridiculous reason for the term, as if they were called *Pontifices*, from their offering sacrifices upon the Bridge, which the Latins call *Pontem*; such kinds of ceremonies, it seems, being looked upon as the most sacred, and of the highest antiquity. These Priests, too, are said to have been commissioned to keep the Bridges in repair, as one of the most indispensable parts of their sacred office.' Plutarchus, the author of this, you remember, died about A. D. 140; and the period of which he wrote, was about 630 years before the birth of Christ. That giant of learning, also, John Jacob Hoffmann, denies that the word *Pontifex* had any thing to do with a Bridge; as you may see discussed at considerable length, in his '*Lexicon Universale*,' Leyden, 1698, folio, volume iii. page 836, column 2, where he says, it is compounded of *posse* and *facere*, that is to say, such persons as are *able to do* the thing, or sacrifice: but as the article is equally long, erudite, and curious, I refer you to the original.

"And now we come to speak of Stow's singular hypothesis, that the River Thames was turned in its current, during the erection of the first Stone Bridge at London. He states this in his '*Survey*,' volume i. page 58, where he also says, that the course of the stream was carried through 'a trench cast for that purpose; beginning, as it is supposed, East about Rotherhithe, and ending in the West about Patricksey, now termed Battersey.' Strype, the last, and, perhaps, the best Editor of our old Metropolitan Historian, on the page above cited, seems inclined to support this idea; for he says, 'It is much controverted whether the River Thames was turned, when the Bridge over it was built, and whether the River was more subject to overflow its banks anciently than at present; and from all that hath been seen and written upon the turning of the River, it seems very evident to me, that it *was* turned while the Bridge was building, and that it is more subject to overflow its banks now, than it was formerly; for the channel of the River must have been deeper than it is now, or the Palace of Westminster would never have been built where the Hall and the rest of its remains are now situated. Is it to be supposed that any Prince would have built a Palace, where the lower rooms were liable to be overflowed at a spring-tide, as we see the Hall has been several times of late years, and the lawyers brought out on porters' backs? The reason whereof is, that the sands have raised the channel, and, consequently, the tides must rise higher in proportion, than they did formerly; and unless some care is taken to cleanse the River, the buildings on the same level with the floor of Westminster-Hall, will not be habitable much longer, as the sand and ouse are still daily increasing, and choking up the bed of the River.' Nicholas Hawksmoor, also, on page 8 of his work, which I have already quoted, says, that 'many skilful persons have thought that the River Thames was not turned, but that the flowing of the tides was then different, and that the water did not rise so high at the Bridge; for the Thames might heretofore overflow the marshes near the sea, and have a greater spreading; which being now restrained by the bank, called the wall of the Thames, into narrower limits, and the water which comes from the sea into the mouth of the Thames during the flood, not being received by the marshes, must come up into the country, and so swell the tide higher at London than it usually did. The celebrated Sir Christopher Wren was of opinion, that when the foundation of London Bridge was laid, the course of the River was *not* turned, but that every pier was set upon piles of wood, which were drove as far as might be under low-water mark, on which were laid planks of timber, and upon them the foundation of the stone piers: the heads of the said piles have been seen at a very low ebb, and may be so still when some of the chalk or stone is removed to mend the Sterlings.'

"Maitland, and his Editor Entick, are also both opposed to the idea that the River was turned during the erection of London Bridge, as they evince on page 46 of their '*History*;' where they ground their objections to it on the following arguments. Firstly, it is supposed that the vestiges of Knute's Canal—which, as we have seen, took the same course as Stow supposes the River to have taken,—might have deceived him; a reason also adopted by Hawksmoor, in the place I last cited. Secondly, the charge of such an immense work is next objected to; as the cost of the ground intended for the trench, the embankment of it, and the damming off the River itself, must have amounted to at least treble the sum which would otherwise have been required to erect the Bridge. The total silence of those Historians who mention the construction of London Bridge, upon the subject of so great a work as the turning of the River, is next insisted upon: and, finally, the length of time which the building occupied,—thirty-three years,—is adduced as alone sufficient to overthrow the whole hypothesis. 'For,' adds the author, 'had the people concerned in erecting it, had dry ground to have built upon, it might have been finished in a tenth part of the time, and in a much more durable manner.' Maitland then proceeds to state, that, in 1730, he surveyed the Bridge, in company with Mr. Bartholomew Sparruck, the Water-Carpenter of the same; and that he observed in many places,—where the stones were washed from the sterlings,—the mighty frames of piles whereon the stone piers or pillars were founded; the exterior parts of which, consisted of huge piles driven as closely together as art could effect. 'On the tops of these,' he continues, 'are laid long planks, or beams of timber, of the thickness of ten inches, strongly bolted; whereon is placed the base of the stone pier, nine feet above the bed of the River, and three below the sterlings; and on the outside of this wooden foundation,—and for its preservation,—are drove the piles called the sterlings.' He then goes on to observe, that Mr. Sparruck informed him, that he and the Bridge-Mason had frequently taken out of the lowermost layers of stones in the piers, several of the original stones, which were laid in pitch instead of mortar; and that from this circumstance they imagined, that all the outside stones of the piers, as high as the sterlings, were originally bedded in the same material, to prevent the water from damaging the work. This labour was, he thinks, continued at every ebb tide, until the piers were raised above high-water mark; and hence he argues, that if the Thames had been turned, there would not have been any occasion for the use of pitch, and that Plaster of Paris was not then in use in this country. These are the principal heads of the dispute concerning the turning of the River: to which I only add my own settled conviction, that *the course of the Thames was not altered.*"

"But pray, my worthy friend," said I, as he concluded, "what other buildings stood upon the Bridge built by Peter of Colechurch, besides the Chapel of St. Thomas?"

"That is a point," replied he, "upon which Antiquaries are very far from being decided: for whilst some assert, with Sir Joseph Ayloffe in his account of the Bridge attached to Vertue's prints, that, at first, there were no houses upon it, and that it was only plainly coped with stone until 1395,—late in the reign of Richard II.,—others argue that it was built upon to some extent two centuries before, and, indeed, there is proof of this being the case in the reign of King Edward I., as I shall shew you anon. Stow, in his '*Survey*,' volume i. page 22, says that the Bridge Gate, which was erected at the Southwark end, was one of the four first and principal gates of the City, and stood there long before the Conquest, when there was only a Bridge of timber, being the seventh and last mentioned by Fitz-Stephen. Maitland, at page 30 of his first volume, when he comes to speak of the same erection, denies not only the truth, but even the probability of Stow's assertions; and, indeed, Stephanides himself says only at page 24, 'On the West,'—that is of London,—'are two Castles well fortified; and the City wall is both high and thick with seven double gates, and many towers on the North side, placed at proper distances. London once had its walls and towers in like manner on the South, but that vast River, the Thames, which abounds with fish, enjoys the benefit of tides, and washes the City on this side, hath, in a long tract of time, totally subverted and carried away the walls in this part.' The Latin of this passage commences at '*Ab Occidente duo Castella munitissima*,' &c. Maitland then goes on to argue, that Fitz-Stephen could have no regard to a gate on the South, there being no wall remaining; 'whereas,' says he, 'on the contrary, it is manifest that his seven gates were in the continued wall on the land side.'

"It is probable, however, that, at a very early period after its erection, towers were reared upon London Bridge, for there was one standing at each end; but of these I shall speak more largely under future years: remarking only, that it is by no means impossible for a Watch-tower and gate to have stood upon the Bridge, even from its very first erection, seeing that it was, as it were, a new key to the City. A sort of Barbican, Mr. Geoffrey, such as you derive your name from; for you remember the essential importance which such buildings were of, and how Bagford speaks of them in his Letter to Hearne, which I have already quoted, page lxii. 'Here,' says he, 'they kept Cohorts of Souldiers in continual service'—for your Barbican Tower was of Roman invention,—'to watch in the night; that if any sudden fire should happen, they might be in a readiness to extinguish it, as also to give notice if an enemy were gathering or marching towards the City to surprise them. In short, it was a Watch-tower by day; and at night, they lighted some combustible material on the top thereof, to give directions to the weary traveller repairing to the City, either with provision or on some other occasion.'

"But to pass from probabilities to certainties, let us now, having got the Bridge fairly built of stone, consider the many events and changes which it hath experienced, from its infancy in the thirteenth Century, to its old age in the nineteenth: and so, my excellent auditor, Here begin the Books of the Chronicles of London Bridge.

"That sorrowful exclamation, 'No sooner born than dead!' may well, at the period at which we are now arrived, be uttered over this scarcely completed edifice; for in the night of the 10th of July, 1212, within four years after its being finished, a dreadful conflagration took place upon it. Stow, at page 60 of his '*Survey*,' cites the Book of Dunmow, William de Packington, and William of Coventry, as his authorities for that excellent account of it which I shall presently repeat to you. Let me, however, first observe, that Packington was Secretary and Treasurer to Edward the Black Prince, in Gascoigne, about 1380. For *William* of Coventry, I conceive that we should read *Walter* of Coventry; because the former, who wrote about 1360, is celebrated in page 148 of Bishop Nicolson's '*Historical Libraries*,' already cited, as the Author of a work 'concerning the coming of the Carmelites into England.' Walter, on the contrary, at page 61, is mentioned as having compiled three books of Chronicles, about the year 1217, which yet remain in Manuscript in Bennet College, Cambridge. The '*Chronicle of Dunmow*,' which is the other authority quoted by Stow, is now to be found only in a small quarto volume in the Harleian Library of Manuscripts, No. 530, article ii. page 2 a. It consists of a miscellaneous collection of notes, in the hand writings of Stow, Camden, and perhaps Sir Henry Savile; transcribed upon old, stained, and worn-out, paper. The notice of this great fire is very brief, and, with the heading of the extracts, runs thus: '*Collectanea ex Chronico de Dunmowe.*'—'1213. London was burned and the Brydge also, and many peryshed by violence of the fyre.' Stow's own account, however, is the most interesting extant, and is as follows. 'The Borough of Southwark,' says he, 'upon the South side of the River of Thames, as also the Church of our Lady of the Canons there,'—that is to say the Church of St. Mary Overies, which changed its name upon being re-founded, in 1106, for Canons Regular, by William de Pont de l'Arche, and William D'Auncy, Norman knights,—these 'being on fire, and an exceeding great multitude of people passing the Bridge, either to extinguish and quench it, or else to gaze and behold it; suddenly the North part, by blowing of the South wind was also set on fire; and the people which were even now passing the Bridge, perceiving the same, would have returned, but were stopped by the fire: and it came to pass, that as they stayed or protracted the time, the other end of the Bridge also, namely, the South end was fired; so that the people, thronging themselves between the two fires, did nothing else but expect present death. Then there came to aid them many ships and vessels, into which the multitude so unadvisedly rushed, that the ships being thereby drowned, they all perished. It was said, that through the fire and shipwreck, there were destroyed above three thousand persons, whose bodies were found in part or half burned, besides those that were wholly burned to ashes, and could not be found.'

"Such is Stow's account of this melancholy event, which is best confirmed by the '*Annals of Waverley,*' page 173; but they state also, that under this year, '1212, London, about the Bridge, was great part burned, together with the Priory of Southwark.' Now, if we might credit the '*Historiæ Angliæ*' of that wily, but elegant Italian, Polydore Vergil, we might be sure, that even at this period, London Bridge was built upon: '*Ipso illo anno,*' says he, at page 276 of his book, setting out, however, with an erroneous date, 'In that same year'— 1211,—'all the buildings that were erected upon London Bridge, were, even upon both sides, destroyed by fire: the which is esteemed a place of wonder.' Polydore Vergil, you know, was an Historian of the reign of King Henry VIII. so we shall refer to him hereafter; and his work, now cited, was written at that Monarch's request, so late as about the year 1521. It is esteemed chiefly for its elegant diction; and the best edition of it is considered to be that printed at Leyden, in 1651, octavo; though the foregoing reference is to the last impression of the Basil folio, A. D. 1570.

"There does not appear, however, to have been any very effectual or speedy order taken for the restoration of London Bridge; for in the '*Rotuli Clausi,*' or the Close Rolls, of the 15th Year of King John, 1213, Membrane the 3rd, is the following entry. 'It is commanded to the Mayor and Sheriffs of London, that the halfpence which are now taken of foreign Merchants, shall be given to the work of London Bridge. Witness Myself at the Tower of London, on the 18th day of December, in the 15th year of our reign.'—You will find the Latin of this printed in the second impression of Thomas Hearne's edition of the '*Liber Niger Scaccarii,*' London, 1771, 8vo. volume i. page *471; and the original record may be seen in the Tower of London, written in so small, delicate, and abbreviated a character, that it hardly makes two lines on the narrow parchment roll. And now that we are speaking of the repairs of London Bridge, I should observe, that they are closely connected with the history of the Bridge-House and Yard in Tooley Street, Southwark; since Stow tells you in his *'Survey,'* volume ii. page 24, that they were so called and appointed, as being 'a storehouse for stone, timber, or whatsoever pertaineth to the buildings or repairing of London Bridge.' He adds too, that this House 'seemeth to have taken beginning with the first foundation of the Bridge either of stone or timber;' and that it is 'a large plot of ground on the bank of the River Thames, containing divers large buildings for the stowage' of materials for the repairs of London Bridge. Of events which particularly concern this place, I shall, however, speak more fully in their proper order of time.

"In the year 1235, you will recollect that Isabel, third daughter of King John, by his third Queen, Isabella of Angoulême, was sent with great splendour into Germany, to marry the Emperor Frederick II. She was attended by William Brewer, Bishop of Exeter, and a Privy Councillor to King Henry III., and also by the Archbishop of Cologne, the Imperial proxy, who had pronounced her Empress. Upon this occasion, according to the customs of the ancient Norman Law and the Feudal System, the King received an aid to furnish her dowry, of two marks out of every Knight's Fee;—that is to say, as it is usually accepted, £1. 6s. 8d. from every person who possessed an estate of £20. per annum, which was granted by the Common Council of the kingdom. This rather uncommon aid, you find certified in Thomas Madox's *'History and Antiquities of the Exchequer of the Kings of England,'* London, 1711, folio, page 412; and in the voluminous collections of that eminent Antiquary, now preserved with Sir Hans Sloane's Manuscripts in the British Museum, No. 4563, page 181 b, is the following very curious document, which connects this circumstance with the history of London Bridge. 'To be remembered concerning the payments of Purprestures'—fines for enclosing and damaging of Land—'and of Escheats'—accidental returns of estates to their principal owners,—'It is commanded to the Sheriffs, that they get all the arrears of all the above rents, and the issues of all Purprestures and Escheats; *excepting the rents of London Bridge*, and the remainder of the amerciaments belonging to the Circuit of W. of York,'—most probably Walter Grey, then Archbishop of York, and Lord Chancellor,—'as well in the County of Middlesex as at the Tower, and all the deficiencies (of the aid) for marrying the King's sister, and for the passing over this sea into Gascony.' In the Exchequer Rolls of the 32nd of Henry III., A. D. 1247, 12 a.

"Towards the latter end of the year 1248, King Henry vainly endeavoured to collect from his Barons, a sum sufficient to enable him to recover certain provinces in France; upon which, he offered a portion of his plate and jewels for sale to the Citizens of London, by whom they were bought. The King, displeased at finding they readily procured money for such a purpose, and yet pleaded poverty whenever he solicited a supply, resolved upon retaliation; and, to that end, kept his Christmas in the City, forced the inhabitants to present him with divers costly New Year's gifts, and established a Market at Westminster, to last for fifteen days, beginning on the 13th of October, during which time all other fairs were suspended, and, in London itself, all commerce was prohibited. I think too, that we may trace the effects of Henry's anger yet farther; for, in the Patent Roll of the 34th year of his reign, 1249, Membrane the 5th, is the following writ.

"'Of taking the City of London into the hands of our Lord the King. The King, &c. to his faithful W. de Haverhull, his Treasurer; Peter Blund, Constable of the Tower of London; and Ernald Gerandin, his Chamberlain: Greeting. We command that without delay, you take into your hands our City of London, with the County of Middlesex, and London Bridge in like manner: so that the issues of the same be answered for to us at our Exchequer at our pleasure. And all the aforesaid shall be in safe custody, until the receipt of another mandate from us. In testimony of which thing, etcætera, Witness the King at Merton, on the 20th day of May.' The original of this is of course in the Tower.

"In the same National depository of invaluable records, Mr. Geoffrey, there is, in the Patent Rolls of the 37th of Henry III.—1252,—Membrane the 4th, an entry entitled 'A Protection for the Brethren of London Bridge, concerning the charitable gifts collected for the reparation of the said Bridge.' This, like the foregoing instrument, has not, as I can remember, ever been printed; and, translated into English, it is as follows. 'The King to the Archbishops, &c. Greeting. Know ye that we engage for the protection and defence of our Brethren of London Bridge, and their men, lands, goods, rents, and all their possessions. And therefore we command, that they, the Brethren, and their men, lands, goods, rents, and all possessions, in their hands, ye should hold protected and defended. Nor shall any bring upon them, or permit to be brought upon them, any injury, molestation, damage, or grievance. And if it be that any thing hath been forfeited by them, amendment shall be made without delay. And we also desire of you, that when the aforesaid Brethren, or their Messengers, shall come to you for your alms for their support, or for that of the aforesaid Bridge, ye shall courteously receive them, and cause them to be so received in all your Churches, Towns, and Courts; and that ye will bestow upon them of your goods according to your charity and the sight of our precept, the alms which they desire. So that in reward thereof ye may be worthy of all the blessings of mercy, and our special thanks shall be due unto you. In testimony of which thing, &c. Witness the King at Portsmouth, the fifteenth day of July.'

"Really," said I to Mr. Postern, as he concluded the last Charter, "your memory, Mr. Barnaby, is little less than miraculous! Why, it must be like a chain cable, to hold together the contents of all these musty Patent Rolls, with their endless repetitions. I myself am called by my intimates, '*Memory Barbican*,' and I can recollect events and stories indifferently well; but *you!* you remind me of the Wandering Jew, who has lived eighteen hundred years, and never forgot any thing in his life!"

"Ah! my good Sir," answered the Historian of London Bridge, "if my memory were equal to your praise of it, it were, indeed, worth boasting of; but in my broken narrative I can shew you but here and there an isolated fact, whilst to the greater part of the story, we are obliged to say with *Master Shallow*, 'Barren! Barren! Beggars all! Beggars all!'"

"Take a draught out of the fragment of Master Shallow's fat friend here," returned I, pointing to the Sack Tankard, "and set out afresh, my old kinsman; but pray let us have the spur on the other leg now, and give us a little History to lighten our Law; with which request,—Here's my service to you!" Mr. Postern bowed as I drank, and after having followed my example, thus continued.

"You must doubtless remember, my good Sir, that during those unhappy Baronial wars which lasted nearly the whole of the extended reign of Henry III. it was supposed that Queen Eleanor of Provence opposed the Sovereign's agreeing to the Barons' demands; and that in revenge for this, how very uncivilly the Citizens treated her at London Bridge. Matthew of Westminster tells the story under the year 1263, in his '*Flores Historiarum.*' London, 1570, folio, Part ii. page 315; and he, as you will recollect, was a Benedictine Monk of Westminster, who flourished, as Bishop Nicholson supposes in his '*Historical Libraries*,' page 66, about the year 1307, when his history ends. The event to which I allude was, that as the Queen was going by water to Windsor, just as her barge was preparing to shoot the Bridge, the populace intercepted her progress, attacked her with vehement exclamations and reproaches, and endeavoured to sink her vessel, and deprive her of life by casting heavy stones and mud into her boat. Upon this, she was compelled to return to the Tower, where the King had garrisoned himself, as the City had declared for the Barons, whence she was removed to the Bishop of London's Palace, at St. Paul's. It was in the latter end of the same year, that Simon de Montfort, the sturdy Earl of Leicester, and the Baronial leader, marched his forces through the County of Surrey towards London, in the hope that his friends, Thomas Fitz-Richard, then Lord Mayor, Thomas de Pynlesdon, Matthew Bukerel, and Michael Tony, with whom was connected an immense multitude of the common rabble, would open the Bridge Gates to him. When the King, however, became acquainted with the Earl's design, he left the Tower, and encamped with his troops about Southwark, to oppose his passage. As the Earl of Leicester relied more upon the assistance of the Citizens, than on the valour of his own soldiers, he vigorously attacked the King's troops, expecting that the Londoners would favour his entrance. Henry, however, had still several adherents in the City; and, indeed, Thomas Wikes, in his *'Chronicon,'* page 58, as it is printed in volume ii. of Gale's *'Scriptores,'* already cited, tells us that the Baronial party in London was composed of the meanest and most worthless, whom the wisest and eldest endeavoured to controul. During the fight, therefore, some of the Royalists, and especially one John Gisors, a Norman, perceiving that the City was in motion to assist De Montfort, locked up the Bridge Gates, and threw the keys into the Thames. So prompt an action had nearly proved fatal to the Earl of Leicester, who had approached the Bridge with only a few soldiers, lest his designs should be discovered; but at length the Gates were broken open, the Citizens rushed out in multitudes to his rescue; King Henry was obliged to retreat, and De Montfort entered the City. By this event we are informed that there certainly *did* exist a Bridge Gate in the year 1264; and the historians by whom the fact is related, are Matthew of Westminster, whose *'Flowers of Histories'* I have already quoted, of which book, see page 317; and the *'Chronicon'* of Thomas Wikes, a Canon Regular of Osney, near Oxford, which concludes with the year 1304.

"It would seem almost certain that, at this period, the keeping of London Bridge, with all its emoluments, was in the possession of the Brethren of St. Thomas of the Bridge; and the idea is somewhat supported by the Protection to which I referred you but a short time since. There is, however, in the Patent Rolls preserved in the Tower of London, of the 50th of Henry III.—1265,—Membrane the 43rd, the following instrument.

"'For the Hospital of St. Catherine, concerning the Custody of London Bridge, with all the rents thereof for the space of five years.

'The King to the Brethren and Chaplains ministring in the Chapel of St. Thomas upon London Bridge, the other inhabitants upon the same Bridge; and to all others to whom these letters shall come, Greeting: Know ye, that we commit unto the Master and Brethren of the Hospital of Saint Catherine near to our Tower of London, the Custody of the aforesaid Bridge with all its appurtenances, as well the rents and tenements thereof, as of others which belong to the aforesaid Bridge, within and without the City: to have and to hold by the said Master and Brethren for the space of five years. Yet so that out of the aforesaid rents, tenements, and other goods of the aforesaid Bridge, the repair and support of the Bridge is to be looked for, and to be done, from henceforth from that place as it shall be able, and as it hath been accustomed. And therefore we command you, that to the said Master and Brethren, as well as to the keepers of the aforesaid Bridge, all things belonging to that custody be applied, permitted, and paid, until the term aforesaid. Witness the King at Westminster, on the sixteenth day of November.' The Latin of this writ you find printed in Hearne's '*Liber Niger*,' which I have before quoted, volume i. page *471; and it affords us certain proof of the early existence of dwellings on London Bridge.

"I will but remark in passing onwards, that Madox, in his '*History of the Exchequer*,' already cited, page 534, quotes a Roll to shew that in the 52nd year of King Henry III.—1267,—Walter Harvey, and William de Durham, Bailiffs of the City of London, accounted to the Crown for the sum of £7. 0s. 2½d. being the amount of the Custom of Fish brought to London Bridge Street, and other Customs also taken there. The term for which the Hospital of St. Catherine was to enjoy the custody of London Bridge, wanted, however, more than a whole twelvemonth of its completion, when a new Patent was issued by Henry III. in 1269, the 54th year of his reign, granting it to his Queen Eleanor of Provence. It is entitled, 'The King gives to Eleanor, Queen of England, the custody of London Bridge, with the liberties;' and you will find it the third article on the 4th Membrane, in the Patent Roll for the above year: the Latin is printed by Hearne in the place which I last cited, page *472, and the writ in English is as follows:"

"'The King to all etcætera, Greeting. Seeing that some time since we would have granted to our most dear Consort Eleanor, Queen of England, the Custody of our Bridge at London, with the liberties and all other things belonging to that Bridge, to have for a certain term: We, therefore, do grant to the same Queen, out of our abundant grace and will, the custody of the Bridge aforesaid, with the liberties and all other things belonging to that Bridge, to be considered from the Feast of All Saints,'—1st of November—'about to arrive; and from the same Feast of All Saints, until the full end of the six years next approaching, and following. In testimony of which thing, etcætera, Witness the King, at Woodstock, on the 10th day of September.'"

"And pray, Mr. Barnaby Postern," said I, in a drowsy kind of voice, for I was almost tired at sitting so long silent, "did the Queen enjoy the whole of her term, or was the custody of London Bridge again otherwise disposed of?"

"You bring me, worthy Mr. Geoffrey," answered he, "by your very seasonable question, to speak of a matter in which the Citizens of London obtained a great triumph on behalf of their Bridge. It is somewhat singular, that Stow, at page 60 of his '*Survey*,' volume i. has very hastily, and, in my poor mind, very imperfectly, related this matter; whilst Maitland, on page 48 of his '*History*,' volume i. has told it still less circumstantially. I shall therefore, my good friend, take the freedom to put the proceedings between the Queen and the Citizens in somewhat more particular a form, illustrating them by the very records from whence we derive our information; for to these let me say, that neither of the authors whom I have mentioned give you any reference.

Previously to commencing, however, I must entreat you to bear with me, Mr. Barbican, if my proofs cited from the ancient Rolls of the Kingdom be dull and formal; and to remember that they are often the only *fragmenta* we possess of past events. Tracing of local history is like endeavouring to follow the course of a dried-up river: a rude channel here and there presents itself; some mouldering ruin, once the abutment of an ancient Bridge, or———"

"Mr. Postern," said I, taking up the Tankard, and interrupting him, "once more, here's your health, and I wish you safe out of your wilderness: keep to one thing at a time, man, leave your dried-up river, and 'turn again Barnaby,' to the dispute between Queen Eleanor of Provence, and the Citizens of London, concerning yonder Bridge."

"In good time," continued my visitor, "you have brought me back again. And now, I would first request you to remember, that King Henry III. died at London, on the 16th of November, 1272; Prince Edward his son then being in the Crusade in Palestine; whence, however, he returned to England in July, or August, 1274. Now, almost the whole of the reign of Henry III. had been disturbed by the truculent Barons contending with him for the final settlement of Magna Charta; and these Civil Wars had very naturally produced numerous abuses with respect to the Estates of England, such as the Nobility assuming almost regal rights, imposing heavy tolls, and the officers of the Crown using divers exactions under colour of the law. Such was the state of English affairs at the return of King Edward I., and it was one of the first acts of his reign—as the '*Annals of Waverley*' tell us on page 235,—to enquire into the state of the revenues, privileges, and lands of the Crown; as well as to examine into the conduct of the sheriffs and officers, who had at once defrauded the Sovereign and oppressed his subjects. For this purpose, as the next circuit of the Justices Itinerant was not expected for six years then to come,—as they generally travelled it but once in seven,—the King issued his Letters Patent under the Great Seal, dated from the Tower of London, on the 11th of October, 1274, appointing Commissioners for each County in England, to make this important inquisition. They were instructed to summon Juries to enquire on oath the answers to thirty-five Articles, examining into the King's rights, royalties, and prerogatives, and into the extent of all frauds and abuses; the most full and ample instructions being given them for their conduct. The returns and answers to these enquiries constitute that interesting body of Records denominated the '*Hundred Rolls*,' which are preserved in the Wakefield Tower, in the Tower of London: though, before we make any references to these, let me remark, that you will find their history, nature, and extent, fully described in the '*Reports from the Select Committee, appointed to enquire into the State of the Public Records*,' 1801, folio, pages 54, 57-62; and '*Rotuli Hundredorum Tempore Henrici III. et Edwardi I. in Turri Londinensi, et in Curiâ receptæ Scaccarii Westmonasteriensi*, *asservati.*' London, 1812-18, 2 volumes, folio. The original Patent Commissions, and Articles of Enquiry, are also still preserved in the Patent Rolls in the Tower, of the 2nd of Edward I., Membrane the 5th: by which we are informed, that Bartholomew de Bryaunton, and James de Saint Victoire, were appointed Inquisitors for the Counties of Kent, Surrey, Sussex, and Middlesex, and for the City of London: and that their enquiries for the latter place commenced in the 3rd year of King Edward I., 1274-75. On the first Membrane of the Roll for London it is stated, that twelve Jurors of Basinghall, or as it is often called Bassishaw Ward, gave the following evidence concerning London Bridge, for the original Latin of which see the '*Rotuli Hundredorum*,' which I have already quoted, volume i. page 403, column 1.

"'When they enquired concerning the Rents of the Citizens and Burgesses, &c.—They said that the custody of London Bridge, which is wont to belong only to the City, is alienated by the Lady Queen, Mother of Edward our King; and the Keepers of the said Bridge appointed by the same Lady Queen, expend but little in the amending and sustaining of the said Bridge. Whence danger may easily arise, very much to the damage of the King and of the City.' This is the second Inquisition quoted by Stow, on page 60. On the third Membrane of this same Roll, containing the inquisition made in the Ward of William de Hadestok, or Tower Ward, the Jurors said that 'the Lady Queen Eleanor, Mother of our Lord the King, is now possessed of the Bridge of London, who keeps it badly, and that it was belonging to the City of London:' and also that the custody had been alienated 'from the Battle of Evesham,' August the 4th, 1265, as I have already shewn you, until the time of the inquisition. See page 405, column 1, of the '*Hundred Rolls*' before cited.

"The Jurors of the Ward of Fori, or Fore-street, page 406, column 2 of the same book, and Membrane 4 of the original Roll, 'said that London Bridge had been for a long time in the hands of the City and Citizens of London, and that such had been always accustomed by general consent, to be made keepers of the common Bridge of our Lord the King, and of his City, and of all passers over it; and now,' they continued, 'the aforesaid Bridge is in the hands of the Lady the Queen, and they know not by what warrant. They said also, that the same Bridge is greatly and perilously decayed through defect of keeping, which is to the great peril of our Lord the King and his City, and all passing over it.' The evidence of the Jurors of the Ward of Walter le Poter, was to the same effect: and you will find it on Membrane 5 of the Roll, and on page 408, column 2, of the printed copy. A similar reply was also returned from the Ward of Peter Aunger, see Membrane 6, and page 410, column 1: from Coleman Street Ward, Membrane 7, page 412, column 1: and from the Ward of John de Blakethorne, Membrane 9, page 414, column 2; where, however, it is added, that 'the Bridge of London, which was formerly in the custody of the whole Commonalty to be repaired and re-edified, is now under that of Brother Stephen de Foleborn for the Queen Mother.'

"The verdict of the twelve Jurors of the Ward of John Horn, also testifies the Queen's possession of London Bridge, see Membrane 11, and page 416, column 2: but from Queenhithe Ward, or that of Simon de Hadestok, Membrane 13, and page 419, column 1, we learn that the Jurors 'said that the Lord King Henry took the Bridge of London into his own hands, presently after the Battle of Evesham, and delivered it into the hands of the Lady the Queen, Mother of the Lord the King, who hath it now; and that to the great detriment of the Bridge, and the prejudice of all the people; it is also now nearly in a falling state, through defect of support.' On Membrane 14, and page 420, column 1, the Jurors of the Ward of John de Northampton,— which is, by the way, the first Inquisition, so vaguely referred to by Stow, at page 60 of his *Survey*,'—depose to the same effect; as do those of the Ward of Thomas de Basing, Membrane 15, and page 421, column 1; the latter adding only, that when the Bridge was held by the City, it was delivered to two honest Citizens to keep, saving the rents of their custody. The only information we gain from the Jurors of the Ward of Dowgate, Membrane 16, and page 422, column 2, is, that Brother Stephen, Bishop of Waterford, was custodier for Queen Eleanor, whilst their evidence on the Bridge dilapidations is quite as full as that of the other Wards.

"Such were the chief answers to the inquisitions concerning London Bridge, in the reign of King Edward I.; I say the chief, for there are yet several others, which, for the most part, are but abridged repetitions of those already cited. Indeed, they are recorded upon a different Roll, which is kept in the Chapter House, at West-Minster; and you may see their contents in the printed copies of the *Hundred Rolls* to which I have so often referred you, volume i. pages 425-432."

"Well, Master Postern," said I, when my narrator came to this breathing place, "and how did King Edward and his Commissioners act upon this evidence against Queen Eleanor of Provence? Were they not of the mind of *Dogberry* as it regarded the answers of the Citizens; "Fore God! they are both in a tale,' seeing that nearly all of them swore alike?"

"I cannot, now," answered Mr. Postern, "call to mind any historical proof that the custody of London Bridge was immediately restored to the Mayor and Citizens, though Maitland states, at page 48 of his *History*,' but without quoting any authority, that the Citizens did not cease to prosecute their suit by *Quo Warranto*, until they regained their ancient rights and privileges. Now the fact is, it is by no means certain that there was any such suit ever commenced as it concerned the Bridge; for the inquisition was first commanded by the King, and the Citizens had only to answer concerning the ancient possession and present state of their property, part of which they stated had been alienated by the King to the Queen Mother, adding also, '*et nesciunt quo Warranto,*' they knew not by what warrant, or right. This, probably, was the phrase which led Maitland astray; added to which, he cites at page 104 the *Quo Warranto* Bag of the 3rd year of Edward I. No. 4, in the Exchequer, containing the complaints of the Citizens concerning levies unjustly made.

"It was, however, not the City of London only that presented and complained of alterations in the Bridge customs; for in Messrs. Manning and Bray's '*History and Antiquities of Surrey,*' London, 1804-14, folio, volume iii. page 548, there is the following entry. 'At an Assize at Guildford, in Surrey, in the Octave of St. Michael,'—that is to say within the eight days succeeding the 29th of September,—'in the 7th of Edward I. 1278—79, before John de Reygate and other Justices Itinerant. There came twelve for the Burgesses of Southwark. They present that a certain part of London Bridge, about the great gate of the Bridge, with the houses and buildings standing on that part, used to belong to the Burgh of the King, of Southwark, where the King used to have of rents of Assize,'—namely, fixed rents which could never be increased,—'yearly 11*s.* 4*d.*; and of the customs of things there sold, 16*s.* and one halfpenny, till fourteen years ago, in the time of King Henry III., when the Mayor and City of London appropriated it to the City:—the King to be consulted. Also they present that the Keeper of London Bridge holds a messuage which formerly belonged to Reginald de Colemille, who then held the same in Chief,' immediately from the King, 'by the rent of one penny farthing: and that Milo le Mareschall holds in Chief of the King two messuages which were formerly the property of Godefride de Marberer, and Henry le Mareschall, and pays yearly two pence halfpenny.' The '*Assize Pleadings,*' or Rolls, containing these particulars, were written in consequence of inquisitions into the damages and alienations of the King's property, during the reign of King Henry III., as I have already remarked with regard to the Hundred Rolls: the original pleadings are preserved in the Tower of London, and in the Court of the Receipt of the Exchequer, in the Chapter House at Westminster. Such were the ancient rents of the houses on London Bridge; to which I may add, that a Fruiterer's Shop, two yards and a half and one thumb in length, and three yards and two thumbs in depth, was let on a lease from the Bridge-master, at a rental of twelve pence.

"We well know, Mr. Barbican, that in the olden time, Bridges were applied to many purposes which now seem altogether foreign to such edifices. The celebrated Du Cange, you will recollect, in his '*Glossarium ad Scriptores Mediæ et Infimæ Latinitatis,*' Paris, 1733-36, folio, volume ii. page 67, tells us, that Philip the Fair, King of France, ordained in 1304, that the public Exchange, or Bankers' Money Table for Paris, should be held upon the Great Bridge there, between the Church of St. Leufred and the Great Arch, as it was anciently accustomed to be. You may remember, also, that Bridges were once considered as Funeral Monuments, for Olaus Wormius, in his *'Monumentum Danicorum,'* Hafnia, 1643, folio, page 523, when speaking of the Island of Foesoe, observes, that there was erected a Bridge at the costs of two or three persons, as well to preserve their own names to posterity, as to commemorate that of Jotheimnt who converted them to Christianity. He adds also, that the word *Bru*, which is unquestionably the most ancient etymon of the term Bridge, signifies that coronal of stone with which the large burial-places, or *tumuli*, in fields, were encircled. With what great propriety then, did the blessed Peter of Colechurch confide his fame to, and rest his most excellent bones, in London Bridge!

"Such, then, being the purposes to which Bridges were once appropriated, we are not to wonder that a Market formerly existed upon that of London; although the circumstance is marked only by the order for its removal, which we find mentioned by Maitland in his *'History,'* volume i. page 104, in the following terms. 'In the fifth year of this King's reign,' that is to say Edward I. 1276,—'it was ordained, that there should not be kept a Market on London Bridge, nor in any other place, except those appointed for that purpose: also that no person should go out of the City to Southwark to buy cattle, or any wares which might be bought in the City, under the penalty of the forfeiture of the thing bought. This is the first Ordinance of the Common Council we find on record, concerning the regulation and appointment of Markets in this City.' The margin of Maitland's work states that he derived this information from the book entitled *'Liber Albus,'* preserved in the Record Chamber of the City of London, folio, 130 a. Now this same White Book, which I imagine to have been so called from its having once had a cover of cream-coloured calf, was a most curious and elaborate work, compiled, as it is supposed by Strype, by one J. Carpenter, who was Town Clerk in the reign of Henry V., and a great benefactor to the City. It is dated November 5th, 1419, in the Mayoralty of Master Richard Whyttington, and the 7th year of the Reign of Henry V. and 'it contains laudable customs not written, wont to be observed in the City, and other notable things worthy of remembrance here and there scatteringly, not in any order written.' Some of these memoranda, as the Latin Prologue to the volume sets forth, are short indexes to the contents of other City Books, Rolls, and Charters, which are cited by their names, or marks; and in the 4th Book, folio 70 a, there is a reference to another record marked A, page cxxx., concerning the market on London Bridge, which was probably the occasion of Maitland's marginal note, as the *'Liber Albus Transcriptum,'* itself, has not in any part of it a page numbered 130. The volume then, in which this very ancient order of the Common Council is really contained, is a small folio of a moderate thickness, cased in boards, covered with white leather, having a coating of rough calf over it. The outside is garnished with bosses and clasps, now black with age; and in the centre, a metal border holds down a piece of parchment, on which is written in Latin the title of the volume, in a clear black letter, guarded by a plate of horn: informing us that it was begun in the 4th year of the reign of Edward I. 1275, and finished in his 22nd year, 1293. The leaves are of parchment, with the contents written in a small Court-hand in Latin; and on folio 130 a, is this entry. 'Also that no Market place shall be kept upon London Bridge, nor in any other place excepting the appointed stations.' On the preceding folio, namely 129 b, there is also this farther order concerning the Bridge: 'Item, that no regraters,'—that is to say those who both bought and sold in the same market or fair,—'shall come from below London Bridge, for the buying and preparing of bread in the City; because the Bakers of Southwark are not permitted by the statutes of our City, to come from without the City.' Before I quit these venerable records of London, I must observe to you that they contain an almost infinite number of very curious memoranda concerning London Bridge, which would occupy no trivial time, either to collect or relate; since in the same *Liber Albus* are numerous references to such particulars, see 'for a taste now,' as *Touchstone* saith, the articles entitled 'Of the Customs of the Bridge, Part I. folio xii. a;'—'of the Fees'—of Fish,—'of the Bridge Bailiff, folio xii. b;'—'concerning the keeping, rent, and course, of the water under the wall,'—Wall-brook;—'of the cleansing of Fleet-ditch, and of the Bridge of London, and the roads about London,' book iv. page 16 a; 'That the Quays and house of St. Botolph be built and repaired by the keepers of the Bridge, volume E. folio cxxv.;' and 'Writ for the keepers of the Bridge against the Parson of Wolchurchaw, concerning the stalls on the same. Volume G. folio clviii.' Such are a few of the very many historical notices relating to London Bridge, preserved in the Civic Records; 'Books,' says Strype, in the interesting Preface to his first edition of Stow's Survey, London, 1720, never afterwards reprinted,—'Books, that contain such a treasure, as, notwithstanding what Mr. Stow, as well as others, have extracted thence, and published, many other things in vast variety still remain there unprinted,' and, we may almost add, unknown. Alas! my good Sir, can we wonder at the paucity of historical narrative, when we reflect how often its very sources are undiscovered? Too many of our topographers, 'content to dwell in decencies for ever!' flatter each other, and copy each other's errors; but how seldom do we see one, who, diving deeply into the broad stream of Antiquarian lore, brings up———"

"Mr. Postern," said I, with some warmth, "this is actually intolerable; there is really nothing but what serves you for a Jack o'lanthorn to go astray by. Whether it be a book, or a bit of musty morality, which has nothing at all to do with the matter, away go you over hedges and ditches, and through a thousand thickets and sloughs, rather than keep the straight road; and dragging me along with you, over the boots in mire. I think, on the whole, indeed, that my estate is gracious that you have not *all* the Bridge Records at command, for then should I be overwhelmed, and *you* be ten times more wearisome. Come back then, my good Sir; do pray come back again, and finish the reign of Edward I., as it was connected with the history of London Bridge."

"I own," answered Mr. Postern, in his usual undisturbed manner, "that your patience is somewhat tried by these details; but ever remember, Mr. Barbican, I pray you, that our ancient Charters, with all their barbarisms and tautology, our old Latin Chronicles, with all their monkish fables and rudeness, our brief Patent Rolls, with all their dryness and seeming want of interest,—ever remember that these are the sure foundations on which all History is built. Simple truth was, in general, the only aim of the first Chroniclers, to which later ages have added grace of style, vividness of description, and interest of narrative, to adorn their antique fidelity and plainness.

"But to proceed.—We are not made acquainted, Sir, with any particulars of the repairs which followed these inquisitions concerning London Bridge; but in the 9th year of King Edward I.—1280,—there was the following Patent issued for its support: the original of which is preserved with the other Patent Rolls in the Wakefield Tower, in the Tower of London, 9th Edward I. Membrane 25-27; a copy of the Latin is printed in Hearne's '*Liber Niger*,' which I have already quoted, volume i. page *472; and English translations are to be found in Stow's '*Survey*,' volume i. page 59; and Maitland's '*History*,' volume i. page 47. The words of the Patent were these.

"'Concerning the Relief and Reparation of the Bridge of London.

'The King to all his Bailiffs, and his faithful subjects, to whom, &c.—these presents shall come,—Greeting. It hath been lately represented unto us, and it grieves us to see, that the Bridge of London is in so ruinous a condition; to the repair of which unless some speedy remedy be put, not only the sudden fall of the Bridge, *but also the destruction of innumerable people dwelling upon it, may suddenly be feared.*'—I pray you to take notice of this expression, my good Sir, because it is an undeniable proof of the very early occupation of the platform of London Bridge by residences.—'And that the work,' continues the Patent, 'which may now be helped by some before it fall, may, for want of a supply, come to the expense of a damage not to be repaired; Wherefore we, who are bound to take care of, and, by all gentle means, to provide for both the public and private good, and with affection specially to embrace those whom we perceive to be in want of our assistance, and to receive them under our Royal protection; We command and require you, that when the keepers of the said costly work of the Bridge aforesaid, or their messengers, who are under our especial protection and license, shall come to you to collect everywhere throughout our realm aids for the said work from pious devotion, you do admit them friendly through the contemplation of God, in respect of Charity, and for evidence of devotion in this behalf: not bringing on them, nor permitting to be brought upon them, injuries, molestations, damage, impediment, or grievance: and if any damage be done them, that ye make them amends without delay. And when ye shall be required by the aforesaid keepers, or their messengers, to help in the reparation of the aforesaid Bridge, ye will cheerfully contribute somewhat of your goods thereto, according to your abilities. And let each of you endeavour to outrun the other in such memorable works of Charity, for which ye must have merit with God, and shall gain thanks of us. In testimony of which thing, Witness the King, at Walsingham, on the eighth day of January.

"'And it is also commanded to the Archbishops, Bishops, Abbots, Priors, Rectors, and to all other Ministers of the Holy Mother Church, to whom these presents shall come, that when they, the keepers of the costly work of the Bridge aforesaid, or their messengers, who are under our especial protection and license, shall come to you to gather supplies for the said work, everywhere throughout your Dioceses, Rectories, or other jurisdictions whatsoever, from the pious and devout, you do admit them from the contemplation of God, the regard of Charity, and for evidence of devotion in this matter. Admitting them to excite the people by their pious persuasions, and charitably to invoke the assistance of their alms for the repair of the Bridge aforesaid. Not bringing upon them,'—and so forth to the end, as before.

"And, because, says Stow, when he has finished this instrument, 'because these voluntary alms and charitable benevolences were not like to bring in the whole charge of the business, therefore the next year, *viz.* the 10th of Edward I., Anno 1281, the same King issued out other Letters Patents for taking Customs of all commodities for the same in London, and that for a certain term of years.' These grants are also in the Tower, and the first occurs in the Patent Roll of the 10th of Edward I. Membrane the 18th; for you must remember that the earliest articles are the highest in number on the Roll, which counts from bottom to top, though the printed Calendar, or Index, reverses this order. The Latin text of King Edward's Patent is in Hearne, as before, page *474, and the translation of it is as follows.

"'Concerning the Reparation of London Bridge.

'The King to his Mayor of London, Greeting: Because of the sudden ruin of the Bridge of London, we command you to associate with you two or three of the more discreet and worthier Citizens of the City aforesaid, to take, until our Parliament after Easter next approaching, in supply of the reparation of the Bridge aforesaid, the Customs hereafter written; namely, of every man crossing the water of Thames, or going over the aforesaid Bridge of London upon either side, one Farthing; both unto Southwark, and from Southwark unto London, by reason of the deficiency of repair of the Bridge aforesaid: Of every Horseman so crossing the same, one penny; and for every pack carried on a horse, so crossing over the same, one halfpenny. But we command, in the mean time, that not any thing be taken on the same on this occasion, excepting for the supply of the repairs of the Bridge aforesaid. In testimony of which, &c. Witness the King, at Cirencester, the Fourth day of February.'

"Before the appearance of the new Patent confirming the foregoing, there was, however, issued that grant to which I have already shewn you that Maitland has a reference; and which is to be found recorded on the Roll of the same year as the preceding, Membrane the 11th. Stow also refers to it; and Hearne, on page *475, prints it in the original Latin; in English it ran thus.

"'That the Mayor and Commonalty of London have power to rent three waste portions of land in divers places in London for the support of London Bridge.—The King to all to whom these presents shall come. Whereas by the testimony of our beloved and faithful Ralph de Hengham, and William de Brumpton, and of others worthy of credit, we have been informed, that it is not to our damage, nor to the hurt of our City of London, if we grant unto our beloved Henry le Waleys, the Mayor, and the Commonalty of the same City, that those vacant places adjoining the wall of the Church of Wolchurch, on the Northern side of the Parish of Wolchurch; and that the other waste places adjoining the wall of the Churchyard of the Church of St. Paul, on the Eastern side, between the Gate of St. Augustine, and the Street of West-Cheap: of which places one half lieth in the Parish of St. Augustine, and the other half in the Parish of St. Michael, at the Corn-Market; and that the other empty places adjoining the wall of the aforesaid Burial-place of the Church of St. Paul, on the Northern side, between the great gate of the said Burial-place, over against the aforesaid Church of St. Michael; also the other gate in the same wall towards the West, over against the narrow way of Ivy lane, that they may build thereon, and rent them for the support of the Bridge at London. We grant for us, and for our heirs, to the aforesaid Henry, and the Commonalty, that the places aforesaid may be built upon and rented for the benefit of them, and of the same City, as they shall see greater cause to expedite them: and they, the said buildings and rents, are to be held of them and of their heirs for ever, for the support of the aforesaid Bridge, without occasion or impediment, of us and of our heirs, our Justices and our Bailiffs whomsoever. In testimony of which thing, Witness the King, at Hartlebury, the 24th day of May.'

"And now I am to remind you, Mr. Barbican, that the Parish Church of St. Mary Woolchurch stood, until after the Fire of London, on that spot of ground once occupied by the Stock's Market, and now by the Mansion-House; and a part of those waste places, which adjoined to St. Paul's Church Yard, was situate on the Eastern side of that street which we at present term Old 'Change, because of the Royal Exchange for the receipt of coined bullion, which was once kept there. The Street of West-Cheap, mentioned in the foregoing grant, was our modern Cheapside; and St. Austin's Gate stood on the Northern side of Watling-street, forming the South-East end of Old 'Change. Stow tells us, in volume i. of his '*Survey*,' page 637, that in consequence of the preceding license of Edward I. Henry Walleis built one row of houses on the Eastern side of Old 'Change, the profits of which belonged to London Bridge. The other portion of those vacant pieces of ground lay in the Parish of St. Michael *ad Bladum*, as the Latin original hath it, which is to say St. Michael at the Corn, or, corruptly speaking, St. Michael Quern, because there was formerly a Corn-Market on the site of it; and its famous Church, which was never rebuilt after the fire, stood, as Stow tells you, page 684, where Newgate Street and Pater Noster Row, 'like two rivulets joining into one, fall into Cheapside.' These vacant spaces, therefore, that were given to London Bridge were in Pater Noster Row; the houses in which, says Stow, page 664, 'from the first North gate of St. Paul's Church Yard, unto the next gate, were first built without the wall of the Church Yard, by Henry Walleis, Mayor, in the Year 1282. The rents of those houses go to the maintenance of London Bridge.' This estate, as the deed informs us, lay over against, or to the South of, the *Venella*, that is to say the narrow Street or Way, which, even in 1281, was called Ivy Lane.

"This year was, indeed, prolific in Royal Grants, for the benefit of London Bridge; for, in support of that gift of Customs to be taken upon it, which I have already recited, King Edward also issued the following instrument which stands on the Patent Rolls of the 10th of his reign, Membrane the 9th: You will find a copy of the Latin in Hearne, page *476; and translations of it are in Stow, volume i. page 59, and in Maitland, volume i. page 47.

"'Concerning the Customs taken for the Repair of London Bridge.

'The King to his Mayor of London. When lately, by reason of the sudden ruin of London Bridge, we commanded you, that associating with you two or three of the more discreet and loyal Citizens of the aforesaid City, ye should take, until our Parliament after Easter next past, in supply of the reparation of the Bridge aforesaid, a certain Custom, as in those Letters Patents which we have caused to be made from that time to you, is more fully contained. We, being willing that the taking of the said Customs be continued longer, command you, that from the Feast of St. Margaret the Virgin, next coming,'—namely, the 20th of July,—'unto the end of the Three

Years next following completed, ye take the underwritten Custom of the aforesaid Bridge. That is to say, of every man on foot, bringing merchandise or other saleable goods, and crossing the Bridge aforesaid, and betaking himself to other parts, one Farthing: of every Horseman, crossing that Bridge, and betaking himself to other parts with merchandise or other saleable things, as aforesaid, one Penny: of every Pack carried on a horse, and passing over that Bridge, one Halfpenny. Nor will we, in the mean time, that any thing be there taken on this occasion, but for the supply of the reparation of the said Bridge. But the aforesaid term of Three Years being completed, let the above-mentioned Custom cease and become void. In testimony of which thing, &c. for the aforesaid term of Three Years, this may last. Witness the King, at Chester, the Sixth day of July.'

"It is, however, worthy of remark, Mr. Geoffrey, before I pass downwards to another Year, that both Stow, at page 60, and Maitland, page 47, speak of this as the first Grant of Customs to London Bridge, and allude to that which I before rehearsed, as the second; when the months in which they were issued, are no less distant than February and July, independent of the direct reference which this latter deed has to the commencement and terms of the former. The mistake has probably arisen from the peculiarity of numbering the skins on the Patent Roll, counting from the lowest end of it, which I have already mentioned to you, since the first instrument is on the eighteenth Membrane, and the latter on the ninth.

"My next notice of London Bridge is of a nature far less happy than are these Patents for its support, for the Christmas of 1281 proved a most fatal season to it; since Stow, in his '*Annals*,' edited by Edmund Howes, London, 1631, folio, page 201, tells us, though without mentioning his authority, that 'from this Christmas till the Purification of Our Lady, there was such a frost and snow, as no man living could remember the like; where-through, five arches of London Bridge, and all Rochester Bridge, were borne downe, and carried away with the streame; and the like hapned to many bridges in England. And not long after, men passed over the Thames betweene Westminster and Lambeth, and likewise over the River of Medway betweene Stroude and Rochester, dry-shod. Fishes in ponds, and birds in woods, died for want of food.' It would appear as if this devastation had not been very quickly repaired, for, when added to the former ruinous state of the Bridge, the complete demolition of more than a fourth part of it, made it not only a very lamentable, but almost hopeless undertaking. Then, too, the very recent repetitions of grants for its repair and support, rendered the same course nearly impracticable, though old Stow tells us, in his '*Survey*,' volume i. page 61, that 'in the year 1289, the Bridge was so sore decayed for want of reparations, that men were afraid to pass thereon; and a subsidy was granted towards the amendment thereof. Sir John Britain being Custos of London,

Anno 1289, a great collection, or gathering, was made of all Archbishops, Bishops, and other ecclesiastical persons, for the reparations of London Bridge.' Of the writs for such collections I have, perhaps, already given you sufficient specimens.

"Several years now passed, unmarked in our Bridge Annals but by the renewal of those various tolls, of which, but a short time since, I related to you the particulars; which circumstances not only too fatally prove into how lamentable a state of decay our venerated edifice had then fallen; but what is infinitely worse, those repeated Royal grants and tolls as plainly indicate the dearth of that public spirit, which had erst lived in the glorious Peter of Colechurch. I will but observe then, that Stow, at page 60 of his '*Survey*,' and Maitland, who probably merely copied him, at page 47 of his '*History*,' both record the fact, that in the 27th and 30th Years of King Edward I., namely in 1298 and 1301, the same tolls and customs were continued for the repair of London Bridge. You will find the former of these grants entered on the Patent Roll for the proper year, in the Tower, under the title of '*Pontage for London*,' Membrane 29; but as the instrument is of some considerable length, I shall prefer giving you a similar shorter one hereafter, being the last Pontage Patent issued by that King.

"And now, Mr. Barbican, we come to speak of a new matter connected with London Bridge, and a singularly curious one it is, inasmuch as it shews the great antiquity and power of the Bridge Master; but for the better illustration of it, have patience with me, I pray you, for a few moments, whilst I recall to your memory a point of legal history to which it is collaterally related. In the times of our Saxon ancestors, you may recollect one superior Court of Judicature, called the *Wittenagemote*, or General Council of Wise Men, was sufficient for the whole Kingdom. When William I., however, came to be Sovereign, he contrived to separate from it the Ecclesiastical and Judicial authority, by establishing a new and permanent Court in his own Palace, called in history by the various names of *Curia Regis*, the King's Court, and *Aula Regia*, or *Aula Regis*, the King's Hall. This was divided into several different departments, the principal of which were composed of the King's great Officers of State, who were resident in his Palace. Thus, the Lord Marshal generally presided in affairs relating to honour and arms, and the military and national laws; the Lord Chancellor kept the King's Seal, and had cognizance of all instruments to which it was attached; the Lord Treasurer was the chief authority in all matters concerning the Revenue; and certain persons well acquainted with the Laws, called the King's Justices, assisted by the Greater Barons of Parliament, formed a Court of Appeal in difficult cases, over which presided the Chief Justiciary of all England. For a considerable time this universal Court was bound to follow the King's household in all its progresses and expeditions, to the great delay of equity, and the extreme trouble of the people; so that in the articles of petition, which preceded the '*Magna Charta*' of King John, Section 8, it was solicited that Common Pleas, or causes, should no longer follow the King's Court, but be held in some certain and permanent place. This article was one to which John consented more readily than to any other in his Great Charter, as the power of the Chief Justiciary being already very considerable, he readily confirmed it by Chapter xvii. of his grant. This officer's place, however, was even then but little altered, as he remained in Westminster Hall, where the *Curia Regis* had originally sat; and in the same building a Court of Common Pleas was established, for the determination of all causes concerning land, and injuries between subject and subject. The other departments of the *Aula Regia*, naturally beginning to decline, soon after this separation, King Edward I. then new modelled the whole judicial polity of England, by dividing it into other Courts.

"Now, Sir, my intention in bringing to your memory these historical memoranda, is, to remind you that abstracts of written proceedings of these Courts, sometimes called the *Placita Rolls*, or Rolls of Pleas, are yet preserved, recorded in Law Latin in a current Court-Hand full of contractions, some being in the Tower of London, and others in the Chapter House at Westminster. These Rolls contain pleadings as well made in the ancient *Curia Regis*, as in the Courts subsequently erected; though, those of the reigns of the First and Second Edwards are chiefly of pleas in the King's Bench, which is the last fragment of the King's Hall, because it *may* be removed with the Sovereign's person, wherever he goes; and, although he be not actually present, yet he is still supposed to be so, since the style of the court is yet '*coram ipso Rege*,' before the King himself. Now, a collection of abstracts from the Placita Rolls of the various Courts, having been made, and the contents being thus of a very miscellaneous character as to their original time and place, it has been printed by order of the Commissioners of Records under the title of '*Placitorum Abbreviatio*,' or Abstracts of the Pleadings preserved in the Chapter House at Westminster, London, 1811, folio.

"In this volume then, on page 316, column 2, we find it stated, that during Easter Term, in the sixth of the reign of King Edward II.,—that is to say 1312,—there were pleadings before the King, at Westminster, concerning the property of the Master of London Bridge, in certain Mills on the River Lee in Essex; but as these pleadings refer to an Inquisition originally made in the time of Edward I., the present will be the most proper period to describe and translate them. Stow mentions the circumstance, when speaking of the office of Bridge-Master, in his '*Survey*,' volume ii. page 25, in the following terms. 'The Keeper of the Bridge House had, in ancient times, an interest in certain Mills upon the River Lee, near Stratford; and the Master of St.

Thomas of Acres,'—now Mercers' Chapel, in Cheapside,—'had a title to other mills there. For, as it appears by an old Inquisition, taken in the time of King Edward the First, there was a *Calcetum*—*i. e.* a chalk causeway—on the North, near Stratford, which was made by Queen Maud, through which there were three trenches made for three courses of water to run, for the use of several mills, partly belonging to the Master of St. Thomas, and partly to the Bridge Master: over which were three wooden bridges made by the said Masters. This is manifest by an extract out of an ancient Inquisition taken at Stratford at Bow, before Roger Brabanzon and others, in Anno xxxii°.'—we shall presently find that this ought to have been xxxi°.—'*Regis Edwardi filii Regis Henrici*, &c.—the purport of which is, that there were three mills made upon this chalk causeway Northward; one a Fuller's Mill, and the site of another mill belonging to the Master of St. Thomas of Acre: and two other Mills, called Sayen's Mill, and Spileman's Mill; the one a Water Mill, and the other a Fuller's Mill, both held by the Keeper of London Bridge. From which mills came three courses of water in three trenches, made cross the chalk causeway by the said Master and Keeper. Beyond which trenches were made three wooden bridges in that said causeway by the said Master and Keeper, which greatly wanted repair.' Now, Sir, I have already shewn you that in Easter Term, in 1312, these pleadings of 1302-3 were renewed against the Bridge Keeper, and the Master of St. Thomas of Acres, by John de Norton, the King's Attorney General, who charged them to repair the Bridges, according to the said presentment. The pleadings of 1312 are recorded on Roll 95; and as the form in which they are written is full of curious historical matter, I shall give you a translation of the instrument at length.

"'Middlesex and Essex. Our Lord Edward, the King's Father, in the 31st year of his reign,'—namely, 1302, in which you see, this record, on authority we cannot doubt, differs from Stow,—'commanded Roger de Brabanzon, William de Beresford, Roger de Hegham, and Stephen de Gravesend, that they should enquire who ought to repair the Bridges and Chalk Causeway in the King's Street between Stratford atte Bowe, and Hamme Stratford; and concerning the deficiencies of support, and repairs of the same, which, from that Inquisition taken by a jury, namely, by twelve for the County of Essex, and by twelve others for the County of Middlesex,' standeth thus:—'They said that the Ferry over the water of Luye, or Lee, at Stratford atte Bowe, was anciently accustomed to be in that place called Oldeforde, which is one league distant from the place of both Bridges and the Causeway, that now are near together; at which Ferry, many crossing over from various places have been plunged in the water and in danger. And when, afterwards, such great danger came to be made known to the Lady Matilda, then Queen of England, Consort of our Lord Henry the First, King of England, she, moved by her piety, commanded it to be examined how both the Bridges and the Causeway could be made better, and more convenient, for the utility and easement of the country, and the passengers over them. The which was done by the said Queen, who also caused two Bridges to be built; namely, the Bridge over the water of Lee at the upper end of the town of Stratford atte Bowe,'—which you remember Stow says, in his '*Survey*,' volume i. page 58, in the margin, and elsewhere, was 'the first arched Bridge in England, and gave name to the Town, for that it was shaped like a Bow:'—'and another Bridge over another trench of the same water towards Essex, which is called Channelesbrigge. And also one Chalk Causeway between the said Bridges, so that all passengers going over it, may well and securely cross the same. And, forasmuch as the said Queen desired, that the reparation and support of the aforesaid Bridges and Chalk Causeway should from that time be imposed, so, out of her charity, she bought those lands, rents, meadows, and one water-mill, which is called Wiggemulne, and assigned and commanded them to be for the repair and support of the Bridges, and the Chalk Causeway aforesaid. And because she believed that their repair and support would be better done by religious men, if they were thenceforward laid upon them, than by secular persons, lest that such secular persons themselves, or their heirs, should, in the course of years, be wanting, to preserve them: nor was there then any Religious House near to the aforesaid Bridges and Chalk Causeway, but the Abbey of Berkinggs, the Abbey of Stratford not yet being founded; so that the aforesaid lands, rents, meadows, and mill, with their appurtenances, were then given to the Abbess of Berkinggs and her house: so that she and her successors, &c. should for ever sustain and repair the said Bridges. But afterwards, Gilbert de Mauntfichet founded the Abbey of Stratford, &c.'—that is to say about 1135,—'And a certain Abbot of the same house bought the lands, &c. from the aforesaid Abbess, because they were near his Abbey, and lying, in situation, commodiously for his house, that is to say, however, undertaking, for himself and his successors, &c. the repair of the Bridges, and Chalk Causeway aforesaid, for the Abbess herself, &c. and farther giving to the same four marks of silver,'—£2. 3s. 4d.—'by the Year, &c. And so they were found, by the same Inquisition,'—cited at the beginning of this instrument,—'to be decayed, and who ought to repair the said Bridges and Chalk Causeway? Upon which Inquisition, our Lord the King caused his writ to issue, &c.; and upon this precept it is shewn that the Abbot aforesaid, the Master of the House of the Blessed Thomas of Acre, and the Keeper of London Bridge, made their appearance to answer why the Bridges were not repaired, &c. When the Jurors came, therefore, between the King and the Abbots, they said that the said Abbot was not held to repair, excepting the Bridge called Channelesbrigge, and that none of his predecessors have, at any time, repaired the said Bridges and Chalk Causeway, and that not any of the lands or tenements held by him have been accustomed to make reparations, or support them:—therefore the Abbot was dismissed without a day. But another of the Jurors has found that it is the said Abbess who ought to repair the Bridges. And at length,'—that is to say in 1315,—'an agreement was made between the said Abbot and Abbess, in the presence of the Earl of Hereford and Essex, and Chancellor of England; also Chief Justice, Chief Baron, and Escheater of our Lord the King on this side Trent, and it was enrolled that the said Abbot obliges himself, and his successors, to repair for ever: for which the said Abbess gives to the said Abbot two hundred pounds, yet saving to her the annual four marks.' See the Pleadings before the King at Westminster, in Easter Term, 6 Edward II., Roll 95.

"After this very long, though curious document, I have nothing farther to observe on the connection of the Bridge Master of London, and his Mill and Bridge on the River Lee, than that, although he at first traversed, as the Lawyers say, or denied his right to repair them, yet, in 1315, the original claim was confirmed against his denial, as is asserted by Stow, in his '*Survey*,' volume ii. page 25."

"Methinks, Mr. Barnaby Postern," said I, "that before you entirely quit the connection of the Lee River and London Bridge, it would not be irrelevant to speak somewhat of that *Cantiuncula*, that little song, or, as I may properly call it, that *Lallus*, for it is truly a nurse's song, in which they are both united."

"You say well, Sir," answered my visitor; "and seeing that I have already spoken somewhat at length, 'shall I,' as Izaak Walton says, 'have nothing from you, that seem to have both a good memory, and a cheerful spirit?' Come, then, my honoured kinsman, do you relate what hath been written and collected concerning that same *Cantiuncula*; nor deem that any fragmenta, touching the history of London Bridge, can be uninteresting; wherefore, doubt not but your narrative will be to me like that which Adam made to Raphael:—

'Nor are thy lips ungraceful, Sire of men,
Nor tongue ineloquent.—
But thy relation now; for I attend,
Pleased with thy words no less than thou with mine.'"

"After the deep reading and extensive knowledge," returned I, "which you, Mr. Postern, have displayed in your discourse, it is unfortunate for me to have to speak upon a subject, where I am no less perplexed by the paucity of materials, than by my own ignorance of many which may be in existence. For you must know, my fellow-antiquary, that searching out the origin and history of a ballad, is like endeavouring to ascertain the source and flight of December's snow; since it often comes we know not whence, is looked upon and noticed for awhile, is corrupted, or melts away, we know not how, and thus dies unrecorded, excepting in the oral tradition or memory of some village crones, who yet discourse of it. However, Sir, to proceed methodically, I will first give you the words of this very popular song; then the customs and history connected with it; and, lastly, the musical notation to which it is most commonly sung.

"One of the most elegant copies of this ballad you will find in the late Joseph Ritson's rare and curious volume, entitled, '*Gammer Gurton's Garland: or the Nursery Parnassus. A choice collection of pretty Songs, and Verses, for the amusement of all little good children who can neither read nor run.*' London, 1810. 8vo. Part i., page 4; where it is called 'The celebrated song of London Bridge is broken down;' and is as follows:

'LONDON BRIDGE is broken down,
Dance o'er my Lady Lee;
London Bridge is broken down,
With a gay lady.

How shall we build it up again,
Dance o'er my Lady Lee;
How shall we build it up again?
With a gay lady.

Silver and gold will be stolen away,
Dance o'er my Lady Lee;
Silver and gold will be stolen away,
With a gay lady.

Build it up with iron and steel,
Dance o'er my Lady Lee;
Build it up with iron and steel,
With a gay lady.

Iron and steel will bend and bow,
Dance o'er my Lady Lee;
Iron and steel will bend and bow,
With a gay lady.

Build it up with wood and clay,
Dance o'er my Lady Lee;
Build it up with wood and clay,
With a gay lady.

Wood and clay will wash away,
Dance o'er my Lady Lee;

Wood and clay will wash away,
With a gay lady.

Build it up with stone so strong,
Dance o'er my Lady Lee;
Huzza! 'twill last for ages long,
With a gay lady.'

"In that treasury of singular fragments, the *'Gentleman's Magazine,'* for September, 1823, volume xciii., page 232, there is another copy of this ballad, with some variations, inserted in a Letter, signed M. Green, in which there are the following stanzas, wanting in Ritson's, and coming in immediately after the third verse, 'Silver and gold will be stolen away;' though it must be observed, that the propositions for building the Bridge with iron and steel, and wood and stone, have, in this copy also, already been made and objected to.

'Then we must set a man to watch,
Dance o'er my Lady Lea;
Then we must set a man to watch,
With a gay La-dee.

Suppose the man should fall asleep,
Dance o'er my Lady Lea;
Suppose the man should fall asleep,
With a gay La-dee.

Then we must put a pipe in his mouth,
Dance o'er my Lady Lea;
Then we must put a pipe in his mouth,
With a gay La-dee.

Suppose the pipe should fall and break,
Dance o'er my Lady Lea;
Suppose the pipe should fall and break,
With a gay La-dee.

Then we must set a dog to watch,
Dance o'er my Lady Lea;
Then we must set a dog to watch,
With a gay La-dee.

Suppose the dog should run away,
Dance o'er my Lady Lea;
Suppose the dog should run away,
With a gay La-dee.

Then we must chain him to a post,
Dance o'er my Lady Lea;
Then we must chain him to a post,
With a gay La-dee.'

"I pray you, do not fail to observe in these verses, how singularly and happily the burthen of the song often falls in with the subject of the new line: though I am half inclined to think, that the whole ballad has been formed by many fresh additions, in a long series of years, and is, perhaps, almost interminable when received in all its different versions. Mr. Green, in his letter which I last quoted, remarks that, the stanzas I have repeated to you are 'the introductory lines of an old ballad, which, more than seventy years previous, he had heard plaintively warbled by a lady, who was born in the reign of Charles the Second, and who lived till nearly that of George the Second.' Another Correspondent to the same Magazine, whose contribution, signed D, is inserted in the same volume, December, page 507, observes, that the ballad concerning London Bridge formed, in his remembrance, part of a Christmas Carol, and commenced thus:

'Dame, get up and bake your pies,
On Christmas day in the morning:'

'The requisition,' he continues, 'goes on to the Dame to prepare for the feast, and her answer is

'London Bridge is broken down,
On Christmas day in the morning.'

'The inference always was, that until the Bridge was rebuilt, some stop would be put to the Dame's Christmas operations; but why the falling of a part of London Bridge should form part of a Christmas Carol at Newcastle-upon-Tyne, I am at a loss to know.' This connection has, doubtless, long since been gathered into the 'wallet which Time carries at his back, wherein he puts alms for oblivion;' though we may remark, that the history and features of the old Bridge of that famous town had a very close resemblance to that of London; as you may find upon reading the Rev. John Brand's *'History and Antiquities of the Town and County of the Town of Newcastle-upon-Tyne.'* London, 1789. 4to. volume i., pages 31-53. The chief points of resemblance between these two

Bridges, were, that both were founded in the hidden years of remote antiquity; that in each instance wooden Bridges preceded the stone ones; that to each was attached a Chapel dedicated to St. Thomas; that continual dilapidations and Patents for repair characterised each; that both formed a street of houses, having towers, gates, and drawbridges; and, finally, that in 1771, a violent flood reduced the Bridge of Tyne to the same hapless state as erst marked that of London, when ruinated by the terrible fire of 1757. Such, Mr. Postern, are the words, and such are the very few historical notices that I am able to give you, of a song, of which there is, perhaps, not a single dweller in the Bills of Mortality, who has not heard somewhat; and yet not one of whom can tell you more concerning it, than that they have heard it sung 'many years ago,' as the gossiping phrase is. If one might hazard a conjecture concerning it, I should refer its composition to some very ancient date, when London Bridge lying in ruins, the office of Bridge Master was vacant; and his power over the River Lee—for it is doubtless that River which is celebrated in the chorus to this song,—was for a while at an end. But this, although the words and melody of the verses be extremely simple, is all uncertain; and thus, my good Sir, do general traditions float down the stream of Time, without any fixed date; for none regard them as of value enough to record, whilst they are yet known in all their primitive truth. Oh! how many an interesting portion of History has been thus lost! How many a———"

"I am glad," interrupted my visitor at this part of my apostrophe, "to find that I am not the *only* Antiquary who is apt to be led away from narrative to rhetoric; and who is sometimes induced to declaim when he set out to describe. But you were speaking of the melody to this song, Mr. Barbican; now I would fain hear it, if it live in your memory."

"Give me a draught of sack," said I, taking up the tankard, "and you shall hear it, as well as my feeble voice, now 'turning again to childish treble,' Mr. Postern, hath the skill to chaunt it. But look for nothing fine, Mr. Barnaby: here are none of Von Weber's notes; and, indeed, I know of nothing which so well characterises it, as that fine description of a popular ballad in *Twelfth Night*:—

'Mark it, Cesario, it is old and plain;
The Spinsters, and the Knitters in the sun,
And the free maids that weave their thread with bones,
Do use to chaunt it———'"

"Come, my good Sir," replied Mr. Postern, "no more words on't, but sing, I pray you."

"Then listen," answered I, clearing my throat to reach the treble C, with which the melody commences; "but you must sing a part of it, as it stands in this paper, Master Barnaby, for it begins with the chorus; and so here follows the ancient Music to the Song and Dance of London Bridge is broken down."

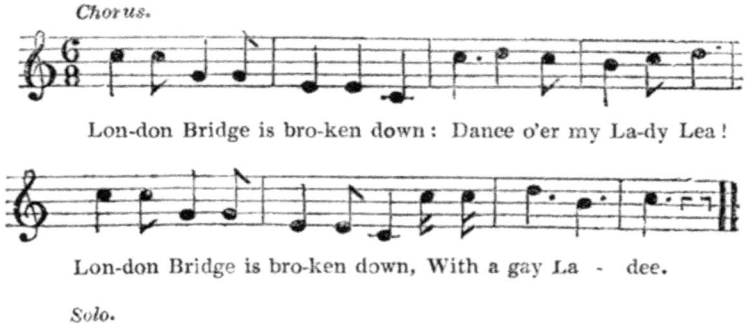

Chorus.

Lon-don Bridge is bro-ken down:
 Dance o'er my La-dy Lea!
Lon-don Bridge is bro-ken down,
With a gay La-dee.

Solo.

How shall we build it up a-gain?
Dance o'er my La-dy Lea!
How shall we build it up a-gain?
With a gay La-dee.

"A choice piece of simple melody, indeed," said Mr. Postern, as I finished the last strain of the solo, "and, certainly, from its extreme plainness, not unlikely to be of some considerable antiquity; but you called it also a dance, Mr. Barbican; pray was it ever adapted to the feet, as well as to the tongue?"

"You shall hear, Sir," returned I, "for I learn from a Manuscript communication, from a Mr. J. Evans, of Bristol, which has been most kindly placed in my hands by the venerable proprietor of the *'Gentleman's Magazine,'* and which enclosed the notes of the tune we have now concluded; that 'about forty years ago, one moonlight night, in a street in Bristol, his attention was attracted by a dance and chorus of boys and girls, to which the words of this ballad gave measure. The breaking down of the Bridge was announced as the dancers moved round in a circle, hand in hand; and the question, 'How shall we build it up again?' was chaunted by the leader, whilst the rest stood still.' The same correspondent also farther observes, that it is possible some musical critics may trace in these notes sundry fragments that have sailed down the stream of Time, beginning with *'Nancy Dawson,'* and *'A frog he would a wooing go;'* though the Lament of London Bridge is certainly far, very far, anterior to the latter. I cannot, however, imagine, that the air of our ballad has more than a very distant consanguinity with either; for the melody of Nancy Dawson is generally supposed not to be more than sixty years old, about which time its heroine flourished; and the metre of that worthless song is perfectly different, each verse having eight lines instead of four. Now, when Isaac Bickerstaff produced his Opera of *'Love in a Village,'* he composed his 14th air, in the last Scene of the first Act, to that very tune; for there the Housemaid commences the Finale, and thus it runs:

'I pray ye, gentles, list to me,
I'm young, and strong, and clean, you see,
I'll not turn tail to any she,
For work, that's in the county:
Of all your house the charge I'll take,
I wash, I scrub, I brew, I bake,
And more can do than here I'll speak,
Depending on your bounty.'

"Thus, you observe, my good Sir, that the verse has no resemblance at all; and the only similitude of the music lies in a very few notes in the second and third bars of the first and fourth lines. The Adventures of the Frog who went a courting is certainly much more like the ballad of London Bridge; but, in addition to its variations in the latter part, it is quite a modern composition, and, therefore, cannot illustrate the antiquity of that other song, of which it is itself merely a musical parody."

"My hearty thanks are due to you, Mr. Geoffrey Barbican," began Mr. Postern, as I concluded; "I have to thank you very heartily for the agreeable manner in which you have contrived to carry on the history of London Bridge, whilst I have breathed from continuing my duller detail: and now, let me observe, that having brought you down to the 31st year of the reign of

Edward I., 1302, I shall give you a translation of what was, perhaps, his last and fullest Charter to London Bridge, in the form of a Patent of Pontage, or Bridge Tax, granted in 1305, the 34th year of his sovereignty; which is curious, inasmuch as it enumerates so many of the articles of commerce in that day. The original is, of course, in the Tower, in the Patent Rolls for that year, membrane 25, entitled 'Pontage for London;' and the Latin you may see in Hearne's '*Liber Niger,*' already cited, volume i., page *478: the English, no very easy matter to discover, is as follows.

"'The King to his beloved the Mayor and Sheriffs, and to his other Citizens of London,—Greeting. Know ye, that in aid of repairing and sustaining the Bridge of London, we grant that from the day of making these presents, until the complete end of the three years next following, the underwritten customs shall, for that purpose, be taken of saleable goods over the Bridge aforesaid, and of those which cross under the same, that is to say:—of every *poise*, or weight of cheese,'—namely, 256 pounds,—'fat of tallow, and butter for sale, one penny. Of every poise of lead, for sale, one farthing. Of every hundred of wax for sale, two pence. Of every hundred of almonds and rice for sale, one penny. Of every hundred of barley corn for sale, one penny. Of every hundred of pepper and ginger, cotewell and cinnamon, Brazil-wood, frankincense, quicksilver, vermillion and verdigrease for sale, two pence. Of every hundred of cinior, alum, sugar, liquorice, syro-montanian aniseed, pion, and orpiment for sale, one penny. Of every hundred of sulphur, orchel, ink, resin, copperas, and calamine stone for sale, one farthing. Of every great frail of figs and raisins for sale, one halfpenny; and of every smaller frail, one farthing. Of every pound of dates, musk nuts, mace, the drug cubebs, saffron, and cotton for sale, one farthing. Of every store butt of ginger for sale, one penny. Of every hundred weight of copper, brass, and tin, for sale, one halfpenny. Of every hundred weight of glass for sale, one farthing. Of every thousand of the best *Gris*, or grey squirrel skins dressed,'—the famous Vaire fur you remember,—'for sale, twelve pence. Of every thousand of red skins dressed, for sale, six pence. Of every thousand bark-skins for sale, four pence. Of every hundred of rabbits for sale, one halfpenny. For every *timbria*'—an ancient Norman law phrase, signifying a certain number of precious skins,—'of wolves' skins for sale, one halfpenny. For every *timbria* of coats for sale, one halfpenny. For every twelfth gennet-skin for sale, one halfpenny. For every hundredth sheep-skin of wool for sale, one penny. Of every hundredth lamb-skin and goat-skin for sale, one halfpenny. Of every twelfth *alicum*,'—a kind of vest with sleeves,—'for sale, one penny. Of every twelfth *Basane*,'—this old Norman word, you know, meant either a purse, or shoe, or any thing made of tanned leather,—'for sale, one halfpenny. Of every quarter of woad,'—the famous blue dye,—'for sale, one halfpenny. Of every *dole*,'—a Saxon word signifying a part or portion,—'of honey for sale, six pence. Of every dole of wine, six pence. Of every dole of corn, crossing over the Bridge, the same going into countries beyond the sea, one penny. Of every bowl of salt for sale, one penny. Of every mill-stone for grinding, for sale, two-pence. Of every twelfth hand-mill for sale, one penny. Of every smith's mill for sale,'—perhaps a forge or a grindstone,—'one farthing. Of every dole of ashes and of fish for sale, one halfpenny. Of every hundredth board of oak, coming from parts beyond the seas for sale, one halfpenny. Of every hundred of fir boards, coming from parts beyond the seas for sale, two pence. Of every twenty sheafs of wooden staves and arrow heads, for sale, one halfpenny. Of a quarter of a hundred of pountandemir for sale, one penny. For all horses laden with serge, stuff, grey cloth and dyed cloth for sale, one penny. Of every hundred ells of linen cloth, coming from parts beyond the seas, for sale, one penny. Of every twelfth poplorum,'—mantle or carpet,—'for sale, one halfpenny. Of every silk or gold cloth, for sale, one halfpenny. Of all satins and cloths worked with gold, two pence. Of every twelfth piece of fustian for sale, one penny. Of every piece of sendal,'—thin Cyprus silk,—'embroidered, for sale, one farthing; and of every other two sendals for sale, one farthing. Of every pound of woven cloth coming from parts beyond the seas, six pence. Of every hundred pounds weight of *Bateria*,'—beaten work of metal,—'namely, of basins, platters, drinking pots, and cups, for sale, one penny. Of all Flanders cloth bound, and embroidered, for sale, two pence. Of every *Estanford*,'—a species of cloth made at Stanfort,—'for sale, from the same parts, one penny. Of every twelfth pair of nether-stocks, for sale, coming from the same parts, one halfpenny. Of every hood for sale, one penny. Of every piece of Borrell,'—coarse cloth,—'coming from Normandy, or elsewhere, one halfpenny. Of every twelfth Monk's cloth, black or white, one penny. Of every trussell cloth,'—perhaps a horse-cloth—'for sale, the same coming from parts beyond the seas, eighteen pence. Of all English dyed cloth and russet for sale, excepting scarlet, crossing the Bridge for the selling of the same, two pence. Of all scarlets for sale, six pence. Of all thin, or summer cloth, for sale, coming from Stamford or Northampton, or from other places in England, crossing the same, one penny. Of every twelfth *chalonum*,'—which is to say, a carpet or hangings,—'set for sale, one penny. Of every pound of other merchandise for sale, crossing the same, and not expressed above, four pence. Of every ship-load of sea-coal for sale, six pence. Of every ship-load of turf for sale, two pence. Of every scitata of underwood for sale, two pence. Of every small boat-load of underwood for sale, one penny. Of every scitata of hay for sale, two pence. Of every quarter of corn for sale crossing the same, one farthing. For two quarters of white corn, barley, mixed corn, pease, and beans, for sale, one farthing. For a quarter of a *seme*,'—a horse load, or eight bushels—'of oats for sale, one penny. For two quarters of groats, and brewers' grains for sale, one farthing. For every horse for sale, of the price of forty shillings and more, one penny. For every horse for sale, of a price less than forty shillings, one halfpenny.

For every ox and cow for sale, one halfpenny. For six swine for sale, one halfpenny. For ten sheep for sale, one halfpenny. For five bacon hogs for sale, one halfpenny; and for ten pervis for sale, one halfpenny. Of every small boat which works in London for hire, and crosses by the same, one penny. Of every cart freighted with fish for sale, crossing the same, one penny. For the hull of every great ship freighted with goods for sale, excepting these present, crossing by the same, two pence. For the hull of every smaller ship freighted with the same goods, excepting these present, one penny. For every little boat loaden, one halfpenny. For every twelfth salted salmon for sale, one penny. For twenty-five milnell for sale, one halfpenny. For one hundred salted haddocks for sale, one halfpenny. For one hundred salted mackerel for sale, one farthing. For every thousand of salted herrings for sale, one farthing. For every twelfth salted lamprey for sale, one penny. Of every thousand salted eels for sale, one halfpenny. Of every hundred pounds of large fish for sale, one penny. Of every hundred pieces of sturgeon for sale, two pence. For every hundred of stockfish, one farthing. For every horse-load of onions for sale, one farthing. For every horse-load of garlick for sale, one farthing. And of every kind of merchandise not here mentioned, of the price of twenty shillings, one penny. And, therefore, we command you, that the said customs be taken, until the aforesaid term of three years be completed; but at that term, the aforesaid customs shall cease, and be altogether taken away. In which, &c. for their lasting the term aforesaid, Witness the King, at Winchester, the seventh day of May. By writ of Privy Seal.'

"Such, Mr. Geoffrey Barbican, is a tolerably exact translation of this long and very curious Patent of Pontage for London Bridge; but a perfect rendering of it into English is a matter attended with more than usual difficulty; since it is composed of so many barbarous Anglo-Norman nouns, with Latin terminations attached to them; of quaint legal phrases, of which Fortescue and Rastall must be the interpreters; and of numerous articles of which both the names and the nature are to us almost utterly unintelligible. However, Sir, I here give it you to the best of my poor skill; and in doing so, let me add to it the apologetical words of your namesake and fellow citizen, the amiable old Chaucer;—'Now pray I to them all that hearken this treatise, or rede, that if there be any thing that liketh them, that thereof they thank Him, of whom proceedeth all wit and goodness. And if there be any thing that displease them, I pray them also that they arrette it to the default of mine unknonnyng, and not to my will, that would fain have said better if I had knowing.'"

"Doubtless, Mr. Postern," answered I, "my civilities are at the least due to you, for the labour you bestow upon me; but yet I must be so plain as to tell you, that your Pontage Patent reminded me mightily of a Table of Tolls at a Turnpike-Gate, whereon we read 'For every horse, mare, gelding, or mule, laden or unladen, not drawing, two pence,' So again, and again, I say, let me have stories, man! I want stories! 'for,' as Oliver Goldsmith said of old to the Ghost of *Dame Quickly*, 'if you have nothing but tedious remarks to communicate, seek some other hearer, I am determined to hearken only to stories.'"

"Be of a sweet temper, however you may be disappointed, Mr. Geoffrey," replied the old Gentleman; "if I possessed the wit either of honest Oliver, or the Ghost of Mistress Quickly, you should, indeed, be entertained; but, seeing that we lack humour, we must make it up in the real, though somewhat dull, formula of past days. This time, I have, however, a romantic scene for you *in petto*, and even now we have arrived at a point of the history of London Bridge, which, when skilfully managed, with a little fiction, has drawn tears from many an eye, and awakened an interest in many a heart: I mean the capture and death of the brave and unfortunate Sir William Wallace.

'Joy, joy in London now!
He goes, the rebel Wallace goes to death;
At length the traitor meets a traitor's doom.
Joy, joy in London now!'

"It was after the return of the fourth expedition of King Edward I. into Scotland, about the beginning of August, 1305, that London Bridge was defaced, by the placing upon it the trophies of his vengeance. Matthew of Westminster, in his *'Flowers of Histories,'* which I have already cited to you, tells the sorrowful story of Sir William Wallace's execution, in his Second Book, page 451; beginning at *'Hic vir Belial,'*—for he treats the Scottish hero with but little reverence,—and in plain English thus runs the narrative. 'This man of Belial, after innumerable crimes, was at last taken by the King's officers, and, by his command, was brought up to be judged by himself, attended by the Nobles of the kingdom of England, on the Vigil of St. Bartholomew's day,'—the 23rd of August,—'where he was condemned to a most cruel, yet most worthy death. Firstly, he was drawn at the tail of a horse through the fields of London, to a very lofty gibbet, erected for him, upon which he was hung with a halter; afterwards, he was taken down half dead, embowelled, and his intestines burned by fire; lastly, his head was cut off, and set upon a pole on London Bridge, whilst the trunk was cut into four quarters. His body, thus divided, was sent into four parts of Scotland. Behold! such was the unpitied end of this man, whom want of pity brought to such a death!'

"The head of the gallant but ill-fated Wallace was not, however, the only ghastly spectacle upon London Bridge; for the Catalogue of the Harleian Manuscripts, under the Number 2253, has the following notice at article 25:—'*A long Ballad against the Scots, many of whom are here mentioned by name, as* also many of the English, besides the King and Prince. But, particularly of William Walleys, taken at the Battle of Dunbar, A. D. 1305, and of Simon Frisell,—or Fraser,—taken at the Battle of Kyrkenclyf, A. D. 1306, both of whom were punished as traitors to our King Edward I. and their heads set among others of their countrymen upon London Bridge.' The passage which immediately concerns our purpose, you will find at folio 61 a, and, in its own rude dialect, thus it runs:—

"'With feters and with gyues ichot he wos to drowe,
Ffrom the tour of Londone that monie myght knowe,
Jn a curtel of burel aselkethe wyse
Thurh Cheepe;
And a gerland on hys heued of the newe guyse:
Monimon of Enge*lond*—for to se Sy*mond*
Thideward con lepe.
Tho he com to galewes, furst he wos an honge,
Al qc. beheued, thah him thohte longe;
Seththe he was yopened, is boweles ybrend,
The heued to londone brugge wos send
To shonde;
So ich ever mote *the*—sum while wende he
Ther lutel to stonde.
He rideth thourth the site as J tell may,
With gomen and with solas that wos here play,
To londone brugge hee nome the way;
Moni was the wyues chil' that ther on loketh a day,
And seide alas!
That he was i*bore*—and so villiche for*lore*
So feir mon as he wos!
Now stont the heued above the tubrugge,
Fast bi Waleis soth for to sugge.'

"Now, Mr. Geoffrey Barbican, as these barbarous rhymes are but just intelligible, even to an Antiquary, by a very careful reading and consideration, you will, I dare say, excuse me, if I give you a paraphrase of them in modern prose; which would be expressed somewhat in this manner.—With fetters and with leg-irons I wot that he was drawn from the Tower of London that many might know it; dressed in a short coat of coarse cloth, through Cheapside, having on his head a garland of the last fashion; and many Englishmen, to see Simon Frisel, began to run thither. Then was he brought to the gibbet, and first being hung, he was also beheaded, which he thought it long ere he endured it. After, he was opened, and his bowels burned; but his head was sent to London Bridge, to affright beholders: so ever might I thrive, as that once he little thought to stand there. He rides through the City, as I may well tell you, with game and gladness around him, which was the rejoicing of his enemies, and he took the way to London Bridge. Many were the wives' children that looked upon him, and said, Alas, that he was born! and so vilely forsaken, so terrible a man as he was! Now the head stands above the Town bridge, close to that of Wallace, truly to say.

"Such is this ballad account of the matter; and, in quitting my notice of the manuscript that contains it, I have but to say that, it is written on old discoloured parchment, in a square gothic text, the ink of which is turned brown by time, with many contractions, and much vile spelling; and that its other contents are all exceedingly curious and valuable; and, as the '*Harleian Catalogue*,' volume i., at page 585, tells us, they are 'partly in old French, partly in Latin, and partly in English, partly in verse, and partly in prose.' You will find, however, the whole of this long Poem printed in the late Joseph Ritson's interesting volume, entitled, '*Ancient Songs from the time of King Henry the Third to the Revolution*,' London, 1790, 8vo., pages 5-18. Maitland himself also relates the fate of Sir William Wallace, at page 109 of his '*History*,' verifying his narrative by references to several of the Cloisteral Historians; nor does there, I believe, exist any earlier notice of the Tower on London Bridge having been used for the terrific purpose of exhibiting the heads of such as were executed for High Treason, which procured for it the name of Traitors' Gate. You will remember I have already proved that edifices were standing upon London Bridge at a very early period; and, were it required, here is an additional proof of it, not to be disputed. Stow, when he is speaking of the Towers upon the Bridge, in his '*Survey*,' volume i., pages 61 and 64, gives us not a word concerning their age, so of that I must treat hereafter, when we come down to the years in which they were repaired, or rebuilt; and I will, therefore, here remark only, that the heads were at this time erected on a Tower at the North end, and that they were not removed to the Southern extremity, where they so long remained, until about the year 1579.

"I am for *your* sake, my good friend, truly sorry that my next notice of London Bridge must be another Patent Roll, of the 14th year of King Edward II.,—1320,—Part the First, Membrane the 19th; but, it shews, at any rate, the state of the edifice in that year: and you will find it referred to in Stow's '*Survey*,' volume i., page 60; in Maitland's '*History*,' volume i., page 47; in the original Latin in Hearne's '*Liber Niger*,' volume i., page *477; and in English it ran as follows.

"'Concerning the subsidies of the Messengers for the work of the Bridge of London, complaining to be admitted.

"'The King to the Archbishops, Bishops, Abbots, Priors, Rectors, and all other Ministers of the Holy Mother Church, to whom these presents shall come,—Greeting. Seeing that, even now, so many evils,—not only in the loss of goods, but that innumerable bodies of men are in peril through the ruin of the Bridge at London,—are likely soon to come to pass, if that they should not be taken away: we, being willing to provide against this kind of dangers, and to take care of the public and private interests, do desire you, when the keepers of the costly work of the Bridge aforesaid, or their messengers, whom we undertake specially to protect and defend, shall come to collect every where throughout your Dioceses, Rectories, or any other of your jurisdictions, aids for the said work from the pious and the devout, you do, in friendship, admit them, from the contemplation of God, the regard of charity, and for evidence of devotion in this matter: admitting them to excite the people by their pious persuasions, and charitably to invoke the assistance of their alms for the reparation of the Bridge aforesaid. Not bringing upon them, nor permitting to be brought upon them, any injuries, molestations, damage, impediment, or grievance. And if any thing shall have been forfeited by them, amends shall be made without delay. In testimonial of which, &c. Witness the King, at Langele, the Thirteenth day of August.'

"A much more curious instrument than this, however, is recorded on the Patent Rolls of the 17th Year of Edward II.,—1323,—Part the Second, Membrane 9; inasmuch as it particularises several parts of the Bridge property in the ancient Stocks Market, of which we should now be without the knowledge, if it had not been for the careful enumeration of them which is here contained. You will see, that this confirmatory instrument has particular reference to one which I have already rehearsed to you, and that it is of that kind, commonly called an *Inspeximus*, from the Latin word used in their commencement, meaning, 'we have seen,' because the words of the original Charter are there repeated. This Patent is entitled 'For the Keepers of the Bridge of London;' the original Latin may be seen on page *482 of Hearne's '*Liber Niger*,' volume i.; and the English of it runs in the following terms.

"'The King to all to whom, &c. Greeting. We have seen a Charter belonging to the Mayor, Aldermen, and Commonalty of the City of London, written in these words.—'To all the faithful in Christ to whom these present letters shall come, Hamo de Chiggewell, Mayor, the Aldermen, and the whole Commonalty of the City of London, Greeting:' Know ye that as the Lord Edward, formerly King of England, of famous memory, father of our Lord the King that now is, in the tenth year of his reign, granted for himself and his heirs, to Henry le Waleys, then Mayor, and the Commonalty of the City aforesaid, that those places contiguous to the wall of the burial-place of the Church of Wolchurch, on the North part of the Parish of the same Church, should be built upon and rented for the support of the Bridge of London, according as they should see to be expedient for their commodity, and that of this great City; and that the said places, so built upon and rented, should be held by themselves, and their heirs, for the support of the Bridge aforesaid, for ever, even as in the aforesaid letters is fully contained. And the before-mentioned Henry, the Mayor, and the Commonalty of the City aforesaid, for the common profit of their City, have built and constructed that house upon the places aforesaid, and have called it the Stokkes, and they have ordained the same for the Butchers and Fishmongers selling therein, as in a place situated nearly in the midst of the City; and the rents from the stalls are assigned for the increasing and support of the aforesaid Bridge. For the Stalls of the Butchers, and of the Fishmongers, may not be permitted, excepting, namely, in the broad way of Bridge Street, of East Cheap, and in the way of Old Fish Street, and the Butcher Row on the West, in the Parish of St. Nicholas; even as it was anciently accustomed to be, according to the ordinance and disposal of the aforesaid Henry, and the then Common Council of the City aforesaid, as in this part we have seen fully to be preserved: at which time the Butchers and Fishmongers sold their flesh and fish in the same, and in none other of the contiguous places and neighbourhoods, excepting the streets before mentioned, and the rents of the said stalls were carried to the keepers of the said Bridge, who, for a time, returned them in aid of the support of the said Bridge. But we, the aforesaid Mayor and Aldermen, lately receiving the complaint of John Sterre and Roger Atte-Wynne, Keepers of the Bridge aforesaid, that the Butchers and Fishmongers of the City aforesaid, who ought to stand to sell their flesh and fish in the place aforesaid, have accustomed themselves to diminish the rents of the aforesaid, contriving another stall for selling their flesh and fish, at the top of King Street, and in other contiguous places and neighbourhoods without the house aforesaid, that such persons for stalls existing within the house aforesaid, pay nothing, against the ordinance in this article formerly provided; and by their own authority they have prepared, and have sold their flesh and fish; by which the rents aforesaid, on which, in great part, the maintenance of the aforesaid Bridge exists, will be immensely reduced. Upon which the said keepers supplicate us for their remedy, to be by us applied. And we having considered this, whether that such kinds of sales may any longer be tolerated in the Bridge aforesaid, and in the aforesaid City, as, to all crossing by that Bridge, peril and damage may manifestly happen: and also this, that our Lord the King, by his writ, hath given it in command, that those things which in the premises are least according to custom, and against the aforesaid ordinance, should be attempted to be corrected and amended, and in their original state rebuilt,—we should build. And being willing to provide against such kinds of damages and perils, and to be obedient in all things to the commands of our Lord aforesaid, we have caused to be called before us the Butchers and Fishmongers aforesaid, and also those that have sold their flesh and fish in other contiguous places and neighbourhoods, without the house aforesaid, against the aforesaid ordinance; and in the discourse which we have held, there was nothing which they have said in this matter, nor have known to be said, by which the said ordinance ought to be invalidated, but they have petitioned that the ordinance and agreement formerly made in this article, might be observed. We therefore looked at the ordinance for this kind of sales, and the ancient customs, and saw the agreement of the aforesaid Henry le Waleys, then Mayor, concerning this kind of sales, made and ordained by the consent of the whole Commonalty; and by our general consent, and that of the whole Commonalty aforesaid, we have agreed, and granted, that the aforesaid ancient ordinances and agreements concerning this kind of sales, be, for the future, firmly and permanently established: so that if any shall have offended, or have spoken against the aforesaid ancient ordinances and customs, they shall, firstly, lose the thing exposed for sale; and, secondly, they shall lose the liberty of the aforesaid City, according to the laws and customs of the same City, as hath been anciently accustomed to be done. And because it is useful that we revolve excellent things which are departed, and ancient things lying obscured to lead into light, that by the same the memory of perishable matters may be recalled to sense, and offenders themselves be made to abstain from evil actions on account of their perpetual memory, for the strengthening of these presents we have caused to be attached to them the Common Seal of our City aforesaid, under the custody of the aforesaid keepers, and of the succeeding keepers, who, for the time, have been, and are for ever to be preserved. Given in Guildhall, London, before the Mayor, Aldermen, and Commonalty aforesaid, on Saturday next after the Feast of Saint Valentine,'—February the 14th,—'in the seventeenth Year of the reign of King Edward the son of King Edward.—We have also granted and confirmed the ordinances, agreements, contracts, and grants aforesaid, and all other things contained in the aforesaid writing, having established and acknowledged them for us and our heirs, so much as in us lies, as the aforesaid writing may fairly witness. In testimony of which, &c. Witness the King, at the Tower of London, the 16th day of June. For a fine of ten marks:'—that is to say the sum of £6. 13*s*. 4*d*.

"Before entering upon the tumultuous reign of Richard II. I must observe to you, Mr. Barbican, that in the Patent Roll for the 42nd of Edward III.—1368,—Membrane 21, there is a sort of memorandum of a transfer of a piece of ground from the Friars Minors for the support of London Bridge, the title of which is couched in the following terms: 'The Guardians of the Friars Minors of London remit for ever to the Mayor, &c. of London, one portion of land on the Southern side of the Church within Newgate, in London, for the support of the Bridge at London, they giving for the same, to the Abbot of Westminster, the sum of four shillings, the which is contained in divers covenants: the King hath confirmed it.'

"Well!" said I to Mr. Postern, on his conclusion of these Patents, "this succession of your dull and never-ending Charters would weary the patience of the most phlegmatic Dutch Lawyer that ever studied at Leyden. Come there any more of them, my honest friend? or may we yet look out for land, after so long tossing in the wide sea of the Tower Records?"

"Tranquillise your perturbed feelings, my good Sir," replied Mr. Barnaby, "for we are now drawing very rapidly towards that time, when we can give only mere facts, and descriptive scenes of history, unsupported by any of those curious and unquestionable proofs which these evidences furnish. Not but that there are, doubtless, yet many scores of most interesting papers and Charters concerning this Bridge, preserved in the Close Rolls, the '*Rotuli Chartarum*,' the Patent Rolls, and the vast body of the Records of this kingdom: but life is too short, and the search would be too long, to discover them all; though I would, for your sake, that I knew them better, and could delight your ears with their recital."

"God forbid! Mr. Postern," ejaculated I, "that you should bestow all your tediousness upon me! for truly, from that which you have recited, I have some conception of what the whole must be; and I would rather entreat you now to pass on to some of those same 'facts, and descriptive scenes of history,' which you seem to undervalue so much, because they do not drag a wearisome Patent Roll after them. Therefore once more, Master Barnaby, I say, give me a tale."

"Well," returned he, "as we have now arrived at rather an eventful period, perhaps you will begin to be more gratified; and here let me remark that the gate of London Bridge being so advantageous, as well as so immediate, an entrance into the very heart of the City, was too often the favourite passage by which the rebels of ancient days marched into the bowels of our hapless land. I have already given you one instance of this, in speaking of the Baronial Wars of the days of King Henry III.; and now, when we have arrived at the Year 1381, the 5th of Richard II., we find another melancholy instance of it in the insurrection of Wat Tyler. Stow notices this but very slightly in his '*Survey*,' volume i., page 61; though in his '*Annals*,' to which he there refers, page 283, he gives a much more full account of their proceedings on London Bridge, taken chiefly from the '*Chronicle*' of Thomas Walsingham, a native of Norfolk, and a Monk of St. Albans Abbey, who lived in the time of Henry VI., and died in 1440; his history commencing at the end of the reign of King Henry III. His principal work, entitled '*Chronica Thomæ Walsingham, quondam Monachi Sancti Albani*,' will be found in William Camden's '*Anglica, Normannica, Hibernica, Cambrica, a Veteribus Scripta*,' Frankfurt, 1603, Folio; where, on page 249 you will find his account of it; but, however, we'll take the English one of old Stow, from the page which I have already cited.

"'On which day,' says he, meaning Thursday, the Feast of Corpus Christi,—or June the 13th,—'also in the morning, the Commons of Kent brake downe the stew-houses neare to London Bridge, at that time in the hands of the frowes of Flanders, who had farmed them of the Mayor of London. After which, they went to London Bridge, in hope to have entred the Citty; but the Maior,'—the famous Sir William Walworth, you remember,—'comming thither before, fortified the place, caused the Bridge to be drawne vp, and fastened a great chaine of yron a crosse, to restraine their entry. Then the Commons of Surrey, who were risen with other, cried to the Wardens of the Bridge to let it downe, whereby they mought passe, or else they would destroy them all, whereby they were constrained for feare to let it down, and give them entry, at which time the religious present,'—perhaps he means the Brethren of the Bridge,—'were earnest in procession and prayer for peace.'

As this fragment of History brought to my recollection a point of Heraldical enquiry, which I had long considered, I here interrupted my visitor, in the following words.

"I cannot, Mr. Barnaby Postern, turn from the days of that most notorious rebel, Wat Tyler, without briefly noticing the dispute concerning the Armorial Ensigns of our goodly City, which claim to have had an honourable augmentation arising from the gallantry of the Lord Mayor of that period. If rhyme might pass for reason and argument, we should then be assured of the origin of the City's Dagger, from the evidence afforded by those verses, which are inscribed beneath Walworth's effigy in the Fishmongers' Hall, above us; and which run—

'Brave Walworth, Knight, Lord Mayor, yet slew
Rebellious Tyler in his alarmes;
The King therefore did give in lieu
The dagger to the City's Arms.

In the fourth Year of Richard II., Anno Domini, 1381.'

"This, however, can stand for nothing, and the arguments for, and against, the popular reason for the introduction of the weapon, are best learned from the ancient English Chronicles and Historians of London. The principal Authors who assert that King Richard added the Dagger to commemorate the loyal valour of Walworth, are Richard Grafton, in his *'Chronicle at large, and meere History of the Affayres of Englande, and Kinges of the same,'* London, 1569, folio, page 340; in the Margin: Raphael Holinshed, in his *'Chronicles of England, Scotland, and Ireland,'* London, 1586, volume ii., page 436: John Speed, in his *'Theatre of the Empire of Great Britaine,'* London, 1611, folio, volume ii., page

596; and Sir Richard Baker, in his *'Chronicle of the Kings of England,'* London, 1733, folio, page 140.

"Such are the assertors of this very common legend; and the evidence against it, is given, firstly by old Stow, in his *'Survey,'* volume i., page 506, at that part of it where he is treating of Walworth's Monument, in the Church of St. Michael, Crooked Lane. He there states, you know, that, in the fourth Year of King Richard II.,—1380,—it was determined, in a Court of the Aldermen and Common Council of the City, that the old seal of the Mayoralty of London should be destroyed, and a new one, engraven with greater skill, then be provided. The device upon the new seal consisted of the effigies of the Saints Peter and Paul, with the Blessed Virgin above them, supported between two Angels, under as many tabernacles. Beneath the feet of the Saints were the Armorial Ensigns of the City, supported by two Lions, and two Serjeants at Arms. Now, Stow's deductions from this fact are, firstly, that as the Mayor is not called by any title of Knighthood in this Seal, it was made before he received that dignity, and, therefore, before his gallant action in Smithfield, or, the augmentation could have been made to the City Arms. Secondly, he argues, that the Arms were the same in the old seal as in the new, and that, consequently, the weapon was not the dagger of Walworth, but the sword of St. Paul; for when the turbulent Robert Fitz-Walter was Banner-bearer to the City of London, his standard was red, charged with the image of St. Paul in gold, holding a sword, which, together with the head, hands, and feet of the effigy, was silver. These particulars you will also find in Stow's *'Survey,'* volume i., page 65; and such is the attempt of this worthy historian to prove the weapon to have been the sword of St. Paul's Martyrdom, at *Aquæ Salviæ*, on the 29th of June, A. D. 66. Now, since that holy Martyr is oftentimes called, by the more ancient writers, 'the titularie patron of London,' and since her chiefest metropolitan fane was, so early as 610, dedicated to his ever-fragrant memory, there is nothing impossible, or even unlikely, in all this: and that it should have been so, certainly arises from the circumstance that 'Paul preached in the Islande of Britaine, which cannot be doubted; seeing both Sophronius, Patriarche of Jerusalem, and Theodoret, an ancient Doctor of the Chvrche, doe affirme and approve the same, saying that Fishers, Publicans, and the Tent-maker,'—St. Paul, see Acts xviii. 3,—'which brought the evangelical light unto all nations, revealed the same unto the Britaines.'

"The only authority adduced by Stow for the support of his novel hypothesis concerning the Dagger of London, is a Manuscript preserved in the City Chamber, and called *'Liber Dunthorne,'* from William Dunthorne, the name of its author. It is, in form, a large folio volume, written in a very fair, small, black law text, on vellum; and its contents are ancient Civic Laws, commencing with the series of the City Charters, in the first of which, granted by William I., the initial W contains an illumination of the effigy of St. Paul, as already described. I will add only, that this venerable register is bound in wood, covered with rough calf leather, and garnished with brass bosses and clasps, now black with age; whilst on the cover, under a plate of horn, surrounded by a metal frame, is a piece of parchment bearing the name 'Dvnthorne.'

"Notwithstanding, however, that the effigy of the most glorious Apostle St. Paul might be advanced into the banner of London, I think it still probable that the ancient Civic Armorial Ensigns were a White Shield bearing a Red Cross, having the first quarter either uncharged, or charged, as a distinction from the multitudes of places and persons which adopted the same insignia. For you may observe, that the Cross was anciently and commonly used by all Christians as their badge; some Heralds deriving its introduction from the Emperor Constantine the Great, and others from so holy a person as Joseph, the Son of Joseph of Arimathea; who, being the first preacher of Christianity in Britain, when dying, drew with his own blood a red cross on a white banner, and promised victory to its followers, whilst they continued in the Christian faith. There is also much mystical meaning in this plain, yet noble ensign; for 'the white shielde,' says a very ancient and interesting author, 'betokeneth purenes of life, and the crosse, the bludd that Christ shed for us, his especialle people of Englande.'—'King Arthur,' too, says John Bossewell, in his very rare and curious '*Workes of Armorie,*' London, 1597, small 4to., Part 2., page 22 a, 'that mightie Conquerour and worthie, had so great affection and loue to this signe, that he left his Armes which he bare before, and assumpted, or tooke to his Armes, as proper to his desire, a Crosse siluer, in a field vert; and on the first quarter thereof, was figured an Image of our Lady, with her Sonne in her armes. And bearing that signe, he did many marueiles in Armes, as in his books of Acts and valiant Conquests are remembred. Thus,' adds he, 'in olde time it may be perceiued what Princes thought of the Crosse.' Now, without believing this origin to its utmost extent, we may nevertheless learn thereby, of how great antiquity is the bearing of that most honourable Ordinary; 'whose godly observation,' says John Guillim, in his '*Display of Heraldry,*' best edition, by James Coats, London, 1724, folio, page 51, 'was in great use in the primitive Church; though, in later times, it hath been dishonourably entertained by two kinds of fantastics; the one, who so superstitiously doat on it that they adore it like their God; the other, who so unchristianly detest it, that they slander the most godly and ancient use thereof in our first initiating unto Christ, as if it were some devilish idol. But the true soldiers of such a captain, need not to be ashamed to bear his ensign.'

"There is also yet another historical reason given why the Red Cross of St. George should be so often adopted in England; for it is related, that when

Robert, Duke of Normandy, the son of our King William I., was prosecuting his victories against the Turks, and laying siege to the famous City of Antioch, A. D. 1098, it was almost relieved by a considerable army of Saracens. In this difficulty there appeared the beatific vision of St. Demetrius, St. Mercurius, and St. George, coming down from the mountains of Syria; the latter being clothed entirely in white, and bearing a Red Cross on his banner, and, at the head of an innumerable reinforcement; which miraculous interference not only reanimated the Christians, but also caused the infidels to fly, and the Crusaders to possess themselves of the City. This legend is related by Matthew Paris, a Monk of St. Albans, in the 13th century, in his *Historia Major*,' Paris, 1644, folio, page 29: and it consequently made St. George to become exceedingly famous at that time; and to be esteemed a patron, not of the English only, but of Christianity itself.

"So much, Mr. Barnaby, for the use of the Cross in our City Arms; and as to the distinction borne in the first quarter, there are some who hold the belief that the Roman letter L once occupied the place of the sword. This story appears to have originated with a Mr. William Smith, a Merchant of London, who was created Rouge Dragon Pursuivant of Arms, on October the 22nd, 1597. As he had travelled much on the Continent, and 'was honest, of a quiet conversation, and well-languaged,' the Officers of the Heralds' College solicited to have him joined to their society; and it was from the reminiscences of his former travels, that he was enabled to state the following particulars concerning the original distinction attached to the City Arms, wherein he opposes the hypothesis of Stow. 'The Aunceint Armes of the Cittie of London, as they stand in (the uppermost North Window of) our Lady Church at Andwerp, in which Church windowes stand the effigies of King Edward the Third, and all his children; with most of the Armes of the Corporate Townes of England at that tyme; and this standeth first, and hath an ould Roman L in the first quarter, which John Stowe tooke in an ould seale which he had seene, for a sword, afferminge thereby that it was the Sworde of St. Paule, patron of the saide Cittie: whereby he constantly affermed that they had aunciently soe borne it, and that it was no reward giuen by King Richard the Second, as our Chronicles reporte, for the seruice done in Smythfieeld against Watt Tyler ye Rebell, by William Wallworth, Maior of London, whoe slewe the sayd Tyler with his dagger; in memory whereof, say they, the dagger was added to the Cittie's Armes.' This passage you will find in two ancient Manuscript copies of Heraldical Collections for London, in the Harleian Library, No. 1464, page 1; and No. 1349, page 2 b; attended by sketches of the ancient and modern bearings, drawn in pen and ink, technically called *Tricks of Arms*. This same story, told in the very same words, with two rude sketches of the Arms in the margin, is also to be found in one of Philpott's Manuscripts, in the Library at the Heralds' College, marked P b. No. 22, page 10 a; where it is written on paper, in an ancient running hand about the year 1602; and, what is extremely singular, there does not appear to be any other entry of the City Arms in the books of that Office.

"Notwithstanding, however, as Strype tells us, in his most interesting *'Life of John Stow,'* prefixed to his *'Survey,'* volume i., page 15, that the worthy old Citizen, and Master Rouge Dragon, were well acquainted, and communicated their labours to each other, yet he says also, that Stow would not be persuaded concerning the Dutch blazon of the London Arms, but affirmed them to have been always the same. I have but two other proofs to bring forward concerning these bearings; and then I will no longer trespass upon your long-tried patience, but return back with all speed to our *memorabilia* of London Bridge.

"The first of these is, that in Mr. J. B. Nichols's *'Brief Account of the Guildhall of the City of London,'* London, 1819, octavo, we are told, at page 34, that in the Eastern Crypt of that building, the groinings of the roof meet in bosses carved with Armorial Ensigns; some being those of King Edward the Confessor, and others those of the City of London. 'It is worthy of remark,' adds the Author of this volume, in the same place, 'that the Arms of London represented in the bosses on the side aisles *have* the dagger, while all those in the centre aisle are *without* it.' I will make no other commentary upon this, than, that part of the crypt is said to have been built antecedent to the reign of King Richard II., or, probably, formed part of the ancient Guildhall, erected, as some suppose, in 1189; the present building being commenced, as Stow tells us in his *'Survey,'* volume i., page 558, in 1411, during the reign of Henry IV. The last evidence which I have to cite on this subject, is a small, but rare tract in the British Museum, entitled *'The Citie's Advocate in this Case, or Question of Honour and Armes; whether Apprenticeship extinguisheth Gentry?'* London, 1629, 4to. The Author of this volume is supposed to have been that John Philipot, or Philpott, whom I before mentioned, who was created Somerset Herald, on July the 8th, 1624, and who died on the 25th of November, 1645. He engraves both the banner of St. Paul, supported by an effigy of Robert Fitz-Walter, and the Arms as they are now borne, for the Ensigns of London; and states that they were 'a copy of that which an old imperfect larger volume at the Office of Armes containeth.' He cites this record in proof of Stow's veracity in explaining the weapon to signify the Sword of St. Paul; and adds that his effigy as 'titularie patron of London, aduanced itself into the standard, and upon the shield were those well-known armories of the crosse and weapon.' It is, perhaps, almost unworthy of mention, that Edward Hatton, in his *'New View of London,'* London, 1708, 8vo., volume i., in the inscription to the frontispiece representing the City Arms, blazons them 'Argent, a Cross Gules: on ye 1st quarter a sword (by some falsly called y^t of St. Paul, by others ye dagger of Sr. Wm. Walworth; but I take it to represent y^t of Justice) of ye 2nd:' this idea, however, is without the slightest support either in reason, history, research, or heraldry. Such is the chief evidence now extant concerning our Civic Ensigns, which you will find very fully and wittily considered, by a learned and facetious gentleman, an intimate of mine, in a paper signed R. S., printed in a periodical of much merit, entitled the '*New European Magazine*,' volume iv., May, 1824, pages 397-401.

"Mr. Barnaby Postern," said I, as I concluded this discourse on our Civic Heraldry, "I have spoken somewhat at length on this subject, partly on account of its great interest, and partly because you ever and anon remind me of the sentiment uttered by that talkative knave, *Gratiano*, in the '*Merchant of Venice*;' who says,—

'Well! keep me company but two years more,
Thou shalt not know the sound of thine own tongue!'

But, as we have now gotten through our wanderings for the present, let me recall to your mind that our Bridge history was brought down to the period when——"

"To the time," interrupted the Antiquary, "when the prompt courage and prudence of the youthful Richard, after the death of the rebel Tyler, the valour of the famous Henry Spencer, Bishop of Norwich, and the united efforts of the King's Armies and Councils, had succeeded in putting an end to one of the most extensive and dangerous insurrections ever known in England. During these turbulent times at home, the King's Ambassadors abroad had been vainly endeavouring to negociate a marriage between their Sovereign, and a daughter of the Duke of Milan. On the failure of which negociation, he demanded the hand of Anne of Luxemburg, daughter of the Emperor Charles IV., and sister to Wenceslaus, Emperor and King of Bohemia; with whom, on May the 2nd, 1381, his marriage was formally concluded at Nuremburg. I mention this only to remind you, to whom the Pageants were presented which I shall very speedily have to notice. Before, however, that we arrive at any events so entertaining as these, I must mention some other circumstances, and repeat to you another extract from a Patent Roll concerning the appointment of a Gate-Keeper to London Bridge, recorded in the eighth Year of King Richard II., A. D. 1385., Membrane the 22nd. It is addressed, 'For Walter Fesecock,' and in English runs in the following terms; the original Latin being printed in Hearne's '*Liber Niger*,' volume i., page *486.

"'The King to all to whom these presents shall come,—Greeting. Know ye, that of our special grace, and for the good service of our beloved Walter Fesecock, one of our Bargemen, we grant to the same Walter, for as much as in us lieth, the Officer of Gate-keeper of the Bridge of our City of London;

he being near to us, and paying to us a price not exceeding thirteen shillings and four pence by the year: that is to say, he is to have the said office, with the profits belonging thereto, for the term of his life; in the manner that John Chese, deceased, had the office aforesaid, by the grant of our most dear Lord and grandfather deceased. In testimony of which thing, Witness the King, at Westminster, on the eighth day of April. By Writ of Privy Seal.'

"I am next, Mr. Geoffrey Barbican, to speak of a famous action on London Bridge, which most authors who have written the history of that edifice, place five or six, and some even eight, years later, than it really happened; which I cannot imagine to have arisen from any other cause, than that of their carelessly following each other, or else copying Stow, in his '*Survey*,' page 61, without turning to the original ancient Author, whom he cites in the margin of his '*Annals*,' pages 312-313, as his authority for the fact. This memorable exhibition was a solemn Justing between an English and a Scottish Knight, as a display of the valour of their different countries; which was held on St. George's day, the 23d of April, 1390; and not, as Stow has most unaccountably stated, in the works which I have quoted, either in 1395 or 1396. The authorities with which I shall support my argument, are ancient, and some of them even contemporary; but we will first relate the plain story from the elegant Latin of Hector Boethius, a Scottish Historian, who was born at Dundee in 1470: the best edition of whose '*Scotorum Historiæ*' is that printed at Paris in folio, 1575; where, on page 335 b, the passage commencing '*Durante inter Anglos Scotosque pace publica*,' is, in English, to the following effect.

"'During the general peace between the Scots and the English, many of the English, who were of Knightly rank, and who excelled in military arts and prowess, frequented Scotland, and there also came many Scots into England; producing, on both parts, many honourable tournaments, to which mutual challenges were published. Of these feats, the most worthy of memory was accounted that victory on London Bridge, by David Lindesay, Earl of Crawfurd. An Englishman, the Lord Wells, was then the Ambassador of King Richard, in Scotland, and was attending at a solemn banquet, where many persons, both Scots and English, were discoursing upon courage and arms. 'Away with this strife of words,' said the Englishman; 'whoever would experience the valour of the English, let his name be declared, and also a time and place be appointed, wherever ye list, for a single passage of arms, and I am ready. I call on thee,' said he to David, 'who hast spent many words against me, and thou shalt have to just with me rather than all the rest.' 'Yea, truly,' said David, 'and I will do it blithely, if thou canst bring the King to consent to it.' The King agreeing, the Englishman made choice of the place, and, because it should be in another country, he selected London Bridge: David named the time, the holy St. George's day, because he was the chief patron of soldiers. Thereupon the Lord Wells returned to London, and

David provided himself with arms, as well as he might. As the day was approaching, he made a journey with thirty-two persons in his train, immediately to London,'—this, however, is an error, for there were but twenty-nine in all, as I shall presently shew,—'coming to King Richard, who received them with great honour.'

"Of the actual time when Sir David Lindsay came to England to engage in this passage of arms, we have the most authentic proof, in the original writs granted for his safe conduct, which are yet extant in that interesting body of Scots' Records, entitled '*Rotuli Scotiæ*,' or the Rolls of Scotland. These invaluable historical documents contain,—says the Rev. Thomas Hartwell Horne, in his excellent notices of them attached to the printed copies, published by the Commissioners of the Public Records, London, 1819, folio, volume ii., page 7,—'an important collection of Records, illustrative of the Political Transactions between England and Scotland.' They commence with the nineteenth year of King Edward I.—A. D. 1290,—and terminate with the eighth year of King Henry VIII.—1516. With the exception of two Rolls of 1339 and 1360, the 13th and 34th of Edward III., which are in the Chapter House at Westminster, all the remainder are deposited in the Wakefield Tower, in the Tower of London. The character in which they are written, of course, varies according to the different reigns, but it is, in general, a small and clear current Court-hand, with a moderate proportion of contractions; and their contents are composed of Treaties, Ransoms, Attainders, Grants, Licenses, and Passes of Safe Conduct for persons during war, some of which I am about to mention to you, as being proof of the Justing on London Bridge, in 1390. In the Second Volume then of the printed '*Rotuli Scotiæ*,' page 103, Column 1; or on Membrane 3 of the original Roll of the 13th of Richard II.,—1389-90 you will find the first of these instruments, a translation of which runs thus.

"'Safe conduct for David de Lyndesey, Knight, for the duel to be fought with John de Welles.

'The King to all and singular, our Sheriffs, Mayors, Bailiffs, Ministers, and faithful subjects, within and without our liberties, to whom these present letters shall come, Greeting. Know ye, that because our beloved and faithful John de Welles,—for the perfecting of a certain Passage of Arms within our Kingdom of England, against David de Lyndeseye, of Scotland, Knight, as he appears to have been calumniated by the said David,—he is petitioner to us for the security of the said David, with his followers and servants coming into our Kingdom aforesaid, for the cause aforesaid, and graciously to provide for their remaining here, and returning again to their own country. We therefore, inclined at the supplication and urgent request of our liegemen who are at this time assisting to us, do undertake for the coming of the said David, *with twenty and nine persons of his company and retinue, in armour, David himself being in the said number*, and twelve other Knights, with their Esquires, Varlets, and Pages also accounted, and with thirty horses, into our kingdom aforesaid, for the completing of the aforesaid Passage of Arms with the said John, from the sixth day of May next approaching; for the coming of the same, and for their cause of remaining, and for their going out and returning to their own parts: nevertheless upon condition, that if any of the aforesaid who may be outlaws to us or our kingdom, shall present themselves in our Kingdom aforesaid, under the colour and protection of the company of David, they shall not enter nor remain in our safe and secure conduct. We will also, that the said David be sufficiently armed for himself: with trusses'—most probably couches, or beds—'for himself, and also during the completing of the Passage of Arms aforesaid, to carry, conduct, and have such with him, to be used for him upon any attack. And therefore we command you, and all of you whatsoever, that the said David, with his men, arms, and horses aforesaid, with all their harness coming into our Kingdom aforesaid, in the manner and for the cause aforesaid, is, in remaining here, and in returning to his own country, to be in friendship, protection, and defence; not bringing upon them, nor permitting to be brought upon them, any injury, molestation, damage, or grievance. In testimony of which, this shall last from the first day of April next to come, for the two months then immediately following; to be accounted from the first day of the same. Witness the King, at Westminster, the twenty-second day of January. By Letter of Privy Seal.'

"And now, Sir, let us suppose the parapet of London Bridge decorated with rich hangings of tapestry and cloth of gold, such as we know it was customary to adorn those edifices with on occasions of rejoicing and triumph. The lists for a Justing, you remember, were sixty paces in length, by forty in breadth, but as the whole width of the Bridge was but forty feet, this rule, though made by Thomas, Duke of Gloucester, Uncle to Richard II., the King in whose reign we now are, must have been dispensed with; for, estimating the pace at two feet and an half, the measurement amounts to 150 feet by 100. The ground within the lists was to be paved with large stones, hard, level, and firm; and the entrances, which were commonly erected East and West, were to be fenced with bars, seven feet, or more, in height, that a horse might not be able to leap over them. At either end of the lists were erected the tents of the tilters, having their shields suspended over the entrances; which it was also customary to hang up at the windows of the houses where they lodged, at once to denote their residence, and to declare their Knightly intentions. We find, however, in that very curious and sumptuous work by Dr. Samuel Rush Meyrick, entitled '*A Critical Enquiry into Ancient Armour*,' London, 1824, folio, volume ii., page 59, *Note*, that he supposes that the lists for this Justing upon London Bridge, were without the centre paling between the Knights, called, in France, the double Lists, because, he imagines, one of the champions was overthrown by the concussion of their steeds.

"We will, however, now return to the account of this Justing given by Boethius; 'When the day of battle was come,' continues he, 'both parties being armed, were most honourably conducted to the Bridge, which was filled in all parts with noble spectators, with whom Richard was seated in an eminent place; though a great concourse of the common people also was collected, excited by the novelty of the event, and the fame of the champions. The signal being given, tearing their barbed horses with their spurs, they rushed hastily together with a mighty force, and with square-ground spears, to the conflict. Neither party was moved by the vehement impulse and breaking of the spears; so that the common people affected to cry out that David was bound to the saddle of his horse, contrary to the law of arms, because he sat unmoved, amidst the splintering of the lances on his helmet and visage. When Earl David heard this, he presently leaped off his charger, and then as quickly vaulted again upon his back without any assistance; and, taking a second hasty course, the spears were a second time shivered by the shock, through their burning desire to conquer. And now a third time were these valorous enemies stretched out and running together: but then the English Knight was cast down breathless to the earth, with great sounds of mourning from his countrymen that he was killed. Earl David, when victory appeared, hastened to leap suddenly to the ground; for he had fought without anger, and but for glory, that he might shew himself to be the strongest of the champions, and casting himself upon Lord Wells, tenderly embraced him until he revived, and the surgeon came to attend him. Nor, after this, did he omit one day to visit him in the gentlest manner during his sickness, even like the most courteous companion. He remained in England three months by the King's desire, and there was not one person of nobility who was not well-affected towards him.'

"This extended residence of Sir David Lindsay in England, is also proved by a renewal of his safe conduct, which was granted him in the following terms; the original instrument being recorded on Membrane 3 of the Roll for the Year already mentioned; and a copy is inserted on page 104, column 1, of the printed edition of the '*Rotuli Scotiæ*.'

"'Renewal of the Safe Conduct of David de Lyndeseye, Knight.

'The King to all and singular the Sheriffs, Mayors, Bailiffs, Officers, and our faithful subjects within and without our liberties, to whom these present letters shall come, Greeting. Know ye, that David de Lyndeseye of Scotland, Knight, hath lately come, by authority of our safe conduct into our Kingdom, for the perfecting of some certain passages of arms within the same, with nine and twenty persons in his company and retinue, David himself being of their number; and because he yet appears in our said Kingdom, and purposes for a short space of time to remain and continue within our Kingdom, some certain impediment and affairs of great importance touching his own person being in the mean while to be concluded: We, at the immediate request of David himself, to whom we are at this time graciously inclined, do undertake for the remaining of the said David, with the aforesaid twenty and nine persons of his society and retinue, David himself being accounted of their number, with their horses and harness, for the matter aforesaid; and afterwards for their returning into their own parts under our safe and secure conduct. Nevertheless, upon condition that if any traitors to us or our Kingdom, or any outlaws from the same, present them in our Kingdom under pretence and protection of David's company, they shall not enter nor remain therein. We will also, however, that the said David be sufficiently armed, with trusses for his own person, for the perfecting of the aforesaid passage of arms, to carry, conduct, and have with him, to be used for him upon any attack whatsoever. And therefore we will and command you, and all of you, that the said David, with his men, arms, and horses aforesaid, with all their harness, in our Kingdom, in the manner and for the cause aforesaid, is, in remaining, and afterwards in returning to his own countries, to be in friendship, protection, and defence,' &c. as before. 'In testimony of which, these presents shall last for the two months immediately following. Witness the King at Westminster, on the thirteenth day of May. By the King himself.'

"That I may the better complete the narrative of this Knight's residence in England, I will yet give you the translations of two writs more, recorded on the Second Membrane of the same Roll, and printed upon the same page as the last, Column 2.

"'Another Renewal of the same Safe Conduct.

'The King by his Letters Patents, which shall last from the first day of June next to come, for the two months then immediately ensuing, to be accounted from the first day of the same, undertakes for his safe and secure conduct, and for the King's special protection and defence to David Lyndesey, of Scotland, Knight, coming into the King's realm of England, with twenty and nine persons of his company and retinue, David himself being accounted in their number, to be confirmed in Towns by virtue of the license of the Mayors, Bailiffs, and Keepers of the same, on his entering and returning towards the countries of Scotland, with his familiar people, their horses, harness, and all goods whatsoever. Witness the King, at Westminster, on the twenty-fifth day of May. By Bill of Privy Seal.'

"We have lastly, in the following warrant, an authentic notice of his departure for Scotland.

"'Safe Conduct for the Scottish Ship for the carriage of the Armour of David Lyndesey.

'The King by his Letters Patents, which shall last from the first day of June next to come, for the two months then immediately ensuing, to be accounted from the first day of the same, engages for his safe and secure conduct, and for his special protection and defence to a certain vessel of Scotland, called Seinte Marie, Ship of Dundee, whereof William Snelle is Master, with twelve Mariners crossing the seas for trading, the said Master and Mariners not carrying with them any property or goods whatsoever, nor any illicit goods, or prohibited merchandise, out of the Kingdom of the King aforesaid, excepting only one complete Armour of War for the body of David Lyndesey of Scotland, Knight. Witness the King, at Westminster, the twenty-fifth day of May. By Letter of Privy Seal.'

"Such, then, are the particulars of this memorable event, as related by Boethius, and supported by proofs from the most undoubted records, which fix it in the Year 1390; illustrated also by the addition of some curious particulars from Stow's translation of the passage given in his '*Annals*,' which I have already cited; though it is far beyond my ability to give you either the elegance or strength of expression, which the original author has infused into his narrative. Now, for the time when this Justing took place, let me observe that Boethius does not mention any year; Stow has called it 1395 and 1396; Raphael Holinshed, who professed to have translated the Scottish Historian in the Second part of his '*Chronicles of England, Scotland, and Ireland*,' London, 1585-86, volume i., page 252, makes it 1398; and James Howell, whose account of London Bridge is a verbatim reprint of Stow's, in his '*Londinopolis*,' London, 1657, folio, page 22, sets it down as 1381. So far, then, all are at variance: but these are only the later and English Authors; whilst, on the other hand, we have the following positive assurance of John de Fordun, a Scottish Priest, who is said in 1377 to have dedicated his History of Scotland to the Cardinal Walter Wardlaw, Bishop of Glasgow; the best edition of whose work, '*Johannis de Fordun Scotichronicon*,' with the Continuation of Walter Bower, Abbot of St. Columb's Isle, in 1424, is that of Walter Goodall, Edinburgh, 1759, folio; where, in volume ii., book xv., chapter iv., page 422, is the passage to which I have alluded. 'In the same year, and on the 21st of the month,'—it commences, these being 1390, and April,—'the Lord David Lindesay is made first Earl of Crawfurd, a valiant Knight, and in all warlike virtues most highly commended; who, with other proofs of them, had a glorious triumph over the Lord Wells of England, in his days a most famous soldier, at London, in the presence of King Richard II., in the year 1390, in a warlike pastime with spears: of which proof of military prowess, the fame hath hitherto been widely celebrated throughout England.'

"The next authority which I shall adduce is that of Andrew of Wyntoun, a Scottish Chronicler, who was Canon Regular of St. Andrews, and Prior of the Monastery of St. Serf in Loch-leven; and who died about the year 1420. The best edition of his labours is that beautiful one, entitled '*The Orygynale Cronykil of Scotland, be Androw of Wyntown, Priowr of Sanct Serfis Ynche,*'—that is Isle,—'*in Loch levyn. Now first published with Notes and a Glossary, by David Macpherson,*' London, 1815, 8vo., 2 volumes. In the Second Volume of this work then, at page 353, the commencement of Chapter xi. reads thus,—

'Qwhen Schyr David the Lyndyssay rade
Til Lundyn, and thare Tourné made.

*A thowsand thre hyndyr and nynty yhere
Frà the Byrth of oure Lord dere*

The gud Lyndyssay, Schyr Dawy,
Of Glenesk the Lord mychty,
Honest, abil, and avenand,
Past on (safe) conduct in Ingland.'

"This Author, indeed, never mentions London Bridge, and assigns a different day for the encounter, as we read in the verses on the next page.

'Swà ewyn a-pon *the sext day
Of that moneth that we call May*,
Thai ilk forsayd Lordis tway,
The Lyndyssay and the Wellis thay
On horse ane agane othir ran
As thare taylyhè (*tally, a bond, or indenture to fight*) ordanyd than.
The Lyndyssay thare wyth manful fors
Strak qwyte the Wellis fra his hors
Flatlyngis downe a-pon the grene.
Thare all his saddile twm (*toom, empty*) was sene.'

"We have, however, sufficient authority for believing that this Justing did actually take place on St. George's day, for Hector Boethius states, on page 336 b. of his '*History,*' that because it was through the protection of St. George, on whose day Sir David, or rather Earl, Lindsay fought, he had gained this victory, he founded a Chantry, with a gift of 48 marks,—£32 yearly,'—for seven Priests, with divers Virgins, for ever to sing holy Anthems to the Saintly Soldier in the Church of Dundee. 'The which,' adds he, 'they did unto our time,'—that is, about eighty years afterwards—'not without singular commendations to the Earl.'

"The Poem also speaks of the use of other weapons than lances; and gives both Sir David Lindsay and King Richard a less degree of courtesy than we find mentioned elsewhere, as you will discover in the following passage.

'Qwhen all thare cursis on hors wes dune,
To-gyddyr thai mellayid on fute swne,
Wyth all thare wapnys, as by the taylyhè
Oblyst thai ware, for til assaylyhè.
Swà wyth thare knwys at the last
Ilk ane at othir strak rycht fast,
Swà of this to tell yow mare
The Lyndyssay fastnyd his daggare
In-till Wellis armowris fyne
Welle lauche (*a good depth*) and hym lyftyd syne
Sum thyng fra the earth wyth pyth;
And all (rycht) manful wertu wyth
Oppynly before thame all
He gave the Wellis a gret fall,
And had hym haly at his will
Qwhat evyr he wald have dwne hym til.
The Kyng, in his Swmere Castelle
That all this Towrne sene had welle,
Sayd, 'Lyndyssay, Cusyne, gud Lyndissay,
Do forth that thow suld do this day.'
As to be sayd, do furth thi dete,
Thare shall ná man here mak lete.'"

"Let *me* finish this story, Mr. Postern," said I, as he concluded his repetition of these old Scottish verses; "if it *be* to have a finish, and you do not really intend to keep me all night in the year 1390 for we must not, certainly, let two such champions pass without one word concerning their families and their Arms; nor leave without distinction the actual Sir David Lindsay, and Lord Wells, who were engaged in this very famous passage of arms. You must, I am sure, remember, Mr. Barnaby, that the immortal Sir William Dugdale, Garter King of Arms, hath, in his '*Baronage of England*,' London, 1676, folio, volume ii., page 11, a memoir of Lord Wells, very meet to be mentioned here. His Lordship was the descendant of Adam de Welles, who lived in the time of Richard I. and he had served in the wars in Flanders, France, and Scotland, under the Kings Edward III., and Richard II., and the valiant John, Duke of Lancaster. As he was ten years old at his father's death in 1360, he must have been about forty when he justed on London Bridge; and after having been summoned to Parliament from 1376 to 1420, he is supposed to have died in the following year, on the Tuesday next after the

Feast of St. Bartholomew the Apostle, which being Sunday, August the 24th, 1421, made it the 26th of the month. Andrew of Wyntown, whom you have quoted, says of this Lord, you remember, in his Chronicle, volume ii., page 354, alluding to the Justing on London Bridge:—

'For in all Ingelond afore than
The Welles was a commended man;
Manful, stoute, and of gud pyth,
And high of harte he was there wyth.'

"He bore for Arms, Or, a Lion rampant double queuée, Sable. Of Sir David Lindsay, of Glenesk, commonly called Earl of Crawfurd, you may see some notices with proofs, in *'The Peerage of Scotland,'* by Sir Robert Douglas, Edited by John Philip Wood, Esq., Edinburgh, 1813, folio, volume i., page 375. He married Catherine, fifth daughter of Robert II., King of Scotland, and his brother-in-law, Robert III., created him Earl of Crawfurd, April 21st, 1398; though Hector Boethius, on page 336 b of his *'History,'* denies this, saying:— 'There are who write, that the before-named David was created the first Earl of Craufurd by King Robert the Third; but because we discover by the witness of ancient volumes, that James his father,'—rather his uncle, who was created Baron of Crawfurd, January 1st, 1382,—'was made Earl by Robert the Second, we have followed a different manner in the history of this family.' Earl David was, however, twice a Commissioner and Ambassador to England, in 1404 and 1406; and it is probable that he died before 1412. The arms borne by the Lindsays were Gules, a fesse Chequé Argent and Azure; but his victorious banner has long since fallen a prey to a mightier conqueror: the lance and the falchion which struck down all before them, have been in their turn overcome by slow-consuming decay: the champion himself lives but in these scattered fragments; remembered only by descendants, or antiquaries; his tomb, and that of his rival, are alike unknown, and even if they could be traced,—

'The Knights are dust,
And their good swords are rust,
Their souls are with the Saints we trust!'"

I must own that I thought it a little uncivil in Mr. Barnaby Postern, as I finished these reflections with an air of great philosophical wisdom, to give a short dry cough, push the tankard towards me, and then to say, "Sorrow is dry, Mr. Geoffrey, and morality is musty; so do you take another draught of the sack, and I'll give you another chapter from the Chronicles of London Bridge."

"And now, Sir," recommenced my visitor, "that our history may not be without the mention of at least one strange fish, connected with London Bridge, let me tell you, that on Christmas day in the year 1391, as Stow tells us in his '*Annals*,' page 30 b, 'a Dolphin came forth of the Sea, and played himself in the Thames at London to the Bridge; foreshewing, happily, the tempests that were to follow within a weeke after; the which Dolphin being seene of Citizens, and followed, was, with much difficulty, intercepted and brought againe to London, shewing a spectacle to many of the height of his body, for he was tenne foote in length. These Dolphins are fishes of the sea, that follow the voices of men, and reioyce in playing of instruments, and are wont to gather themselves at musick. These, when they play in rivers, with hasty springings or leapings, doe signifie tempests to follow. The seas containe nothing more swift nor nimble, for oftentimes with their skips, they mount ouer the sailes of ships.' The original of this story is to be found, with many more particulars concerning Dolphins, in the '*Historia Brevis*,' of Thomas Walsingham, London, 1574, folio, the admirable edition by Archbishop Parker, page 380.

"As the political troubles which succeeded the appearance of this monster, were productive of a very sumptuous triumph upon London Bridge, I shall take the freedom to remind you, that King Richard being greatly attached to regal magnificence and banquets, naturally found his revenues very insufficient to support the splendours of his Court; for, as Walsingham and Knyghton, the best historians of the time, assert, he valued himself upon surpassing all the other Sovereigns of Europe in magnificence; they add that he daily entertained no less than six thousand individuals; that three hundred servants were employed in his kitchen alone; and that his Queen had an equal number of females in her service. To supply the means for this extraordinary splendour, he endeavoured to procure aid from the Citizens of London; and sent to borrow from them the large sum of £1000; but it then was an unhappy time in England, for a dreadful Plague and Famine had overspread the land, and they not only refused his Majesty's request, but, upon a Merchant of Lombardy offering to comply with it, they violently attacked, and almost slew him. This was early in the year 1392; and on the 25th of May following, the King, incensed to a very great degree, summoned a Parliament at Stamford, when the City Charter was seized; the Law Courts were removed to York; and the Mayor, Sheriffs, and principal Citizens, deposed and imprisoned; until, by the mediation of Queen Anne, the Bishop of London, and the Duke of Gloucester, the King's anger was in some degree pacified, and he consented to indulge the Londoners with an audience at Windsor. At this interview the Citizens, after submitting themselves to the King's pleasure, offered him £10,000 for the redemption of their privileges; but were dismissed in dejection and uncertainty; though when Richard was informed of their sorrow, he determined to proceed immediately to London, to re-assure them of his favour. It was upon this occasion, that the Bridge bore a very important part in the triumph; though the ceremony of receiving the King and Queen with great splendour and a considerable train, began at Wandsworth; where four hundred of the Citizens well mounted, and habited in one livery, entreated him to ride through his Chamber of London. At St. George's Church, in Southwark, the procession was met by Robert Braybrooke, Bishop of London, and his Clergy of the City, followed by five hundred boys in surplices, who attended them through the streets towards Westminster. When the train arrived at the Gate of London Bridge, nearly the whole of the inhabitants, orderly arranged according to their age, rank, and sex, advanced to receive it, and presented the King with a fair milk-white steed, harnessed and caparisoned in cloth of gold, brocaded in red and white, and hung full of silver bells; whilst to the Queen was presented a palfrey, also of white, caparisoned likewise in white and red. The other streets of London, too, put on all their bravery; the windows and walls being hung with cloths of gold, silver, and silk; the Conduit in Cheapside poured out floods of red and white wine; a child, habited like an angel, crowned the King and Queen with golden crowns, from a sumptuous stage covered with performers in rich dresses; a table of the Trinity wrought in gold, and valued at £800, was given to the King, and another of St. Anne to his consort; and truly I know of nothing which might so well express the splendours of that day, as the passage with which Walsingham concludes his notice of it. 'There was so much glory,' says he, 'so much pomp, so great variety of divers furniture provided, that to have undertaken it might have been a triumph to any King. For horses and trappings, plate of gold and silver, clothes of gold, silk, and velvet, ewers and basons of yellow gold, gold in coin, precious stones, and jewels so rich, excellent, and beautiful, were given to him, that their value and price might not easily be estimated.'

"This gorgeous scene took place on the 29th of August, and you will find my authorities for this account of it in Henry Knyghton's books '*De Eventibus Angliæ*,' printed in Twysden's '*Scriptores*,' already cited, page 2740; in Robert Fabyan's '*Chronicles of England and Fraunce*,' London, 1559, folio, volume ii., page 334; in Stow's '*Annals*,' page 307; and in Maitland's '*History*,' volume i., page 180. I will but observe, to finish this portion of history, that the Citizens redeemed their Charter by the payment of £10,000; and the King, by his Letters Patent, dated at Westminster, in February 1392-93, restored them to his favour; and so, observes Stow in his '*Annals*,' 'the troubles of the Citizens came to quietnesse; which troubles, the Dolphin in the Thames at Christmas last past, did happily signifie afar off.' Though Maitland, at page 180 of his '*History*,' volume i., most unaccountably makes the Dolphin appear the Christmas *after* this fine was paid.

"I can scarcely imagine, worthy Mr. Barbican, what could induce the accurate Stow,—and of course all other Authors of London history,—to remark, when speaking of the year 1395, our next eminent epoch in the Chronicles of London Bridge, that, because the Justing which we have already spoken of was, as he says, then holden upon it, such 'history proveth that at that time, the Bridge being coaped on either side, was not replenished with houses built thereupon, as since it hath been, and now is.' You will observe that this passage, which occurs in volume i., page 61, of his '*Survey*,' is no interpolation of later, or more unskilful, Editors, because it is to be found in the first black-letter edition of that most valuable work, 1598, small folio. Now, in most of his preceding pages he has been giving proofs of the Bridge being built upon at an early period to some extent; and I also, after him and others, have adduced to you abundant evidence that such was the case. I have shewn that the Gate and Towers were certainly as ancient as 1264; that in the Patent granted to Isenbert of Xainctes, in 1201, it is stated 'that the rents and profits of the several houses, which the said Master of the Schools shall cause to be erected on the Bridge, shall be for ever appropriated to repair, maintain, and uphold the same;' that in the Patent of relief granted by Edward I., in 1280, it is observed that the dilapidations of the Bridge may occasion not only its sudden fall, 'but also the destruction of innumerable people dwelling on it;' and that in the reign of the same Edward, the Assize Rolls mention the very rents and situations of houses then standing on London Bridge. All this, I imagine, might be received as fair and conclusive evidence that this part of the City was built upon and inhabited, long before 1395; to which let me add, that Richard Bloome, one of the continuators of Stow, observes, on page 62, when speaking of the dreadful conflagration of the Bridge in 1632-33, that some of the houses remained unbuilt until the year 1666, when the Great Fire of London destroyed all the new edifices. 'But,' rejoins he, 'the old ones at the South end, some of which were built in the reign of King John,'—and he died, you will remember in 1215,—'were not burnt.' It is, however, extremely probable, that London Bridge did not even in 1395 present that form of a continued street which was afterward its most celebrated and peculiar character. There were, I doubt not, several places open to the water, perhaps, as Stow says, 'plainly coped with stone;' and in one of these, it is most probable, that the Justing, which he erroneously mentions in that year, took place.

"Anne of Bohemia, the Queen of Richard II., dying in 1394, his sorrow for her loss was both passionately expressed, and deservedly bestowed; though, so early afterwards as in 1396, during an interview between him and that insane Monarch, Charles VI. of France, a truce was concluded betwixt the two Kingdoms for twenty-eight years, and Richard espoused Isabel, the French King's eldest daughter, although she was then under eight years of age; whence she was called 'The Little,' and the English Sovereign was about thirty. This marriage was solemnized by Thomas Arundel, Archbishop of Canterbury, in the Church of St. Nicholas, at Calais, on Wednesday, October the 31st, or rather the 1st of November, when Richard is said to have expended on the occasion, the immense sum of three hundred thousand marks, or in modern coinage £200,000. On the 2nd of November they sailed for England, and on arriving at Blackheath the Royal train was met by the usual procession of the Mayor and Aldermen of London, habited in scarlet, who attended the King to Newington, where he dismissed them, as he was to rest for a short time at Kennington. On the 13th, however, Richard and his Consort entered the City on their way to the Tower; when so vast a multitude was collected on London Bridge to see the young Queen pass, that nine persons were killed in the crowd, of whom the Prior of the Austin Canons at Tiptree, in Essex, was one, and a worshipful matron of Cornhill was another. John Stow is commonly cited as the authority for this circumstance, and it may be seen related in his '*Annals*,' page 315; though it is also to be found in '*The Chronicle of Fabian*,' London, 1559, small folio, page 338. Robert Fabian, as you must well remember, was, in 1493, an eminent Merchant and Sheriff of London, and died in 1512, about thirteen years previously to the birth of John Stow. You will also see the following notice of the event in the Harleian Manuscripts, No. 565, article 5, page 61 a, which consists of '*A Chronicle of English Affairs, and especially of those relating to the City of London, from the first year of King Richard I., 1189, to the 21st of Henry VI., 1442, inclusive*'—'In yis yere, a bouzte ye feste of Alhalwen, Isabell ye Kynges doughter of Fraunce was spoused to Kyng Richard at Caleys: whiche afterward on ye viij day of Januer was crowned Quene at Westm^r. At whos comynge to London, ye Priour of Typtre in Essex, with other viij persones vp on London bregge in ye gret prees weren crowsed to ye deth.' Now, as I shall hereafter frequently, have to cite this Chronicle for some particulars of events not to be found in any other Annals, I must observe that it is a small quarto, fairly written on parchment, in a current Court-hand of the time of Edward IV., and decorated with vermillion lines and ornaments.

"It was, you will recollect, in 1397, that Thomas of Woodstock, Duke of Gloucester, and uncle to Richard II., being charged with disaffection and conspiracy, was suddenly carried to Calais; in which confinement and exile he died, on the 24th of September in the same year, of an apoplectic fit, as some Historians relate, although the greater number charge Richard with his murder, and assert that he was smothered, or strangled: for he was rude and overbearing in his disposition, and usually opposed the King in most of his measures; censured his extravagant expenditure, and on several occasions is said to have reproached and upbraided him with great severity of language. On these accounts is the Duke's death charged upon the King, and his favourites; and you have a very curious and interesting examination of the circumstance, in Richard Gough's *'History and Antiquities of Pleshy, in the County of Essex,'* London, 1803, quarto, pages 85-123. The reign of this unfortunate Monarch was, however, nearly at a close; for, on the 29th of September, 1399, he resigned the ensigns of Royalty to the Duke of Lancaster, afterwards Henry IV., and in the formal accusation, consisting of 33 Articles, drawn up for his deposition, in the fourth he is charged with having caused the murder of the Duke of Gloucester. When these accusations were read over to Richard, and he had named his principal advisers in each action, it was Henry of Lancaster's care to discover the four Knights who actually strangled the Duke of Gloucester in the Castle of Calais; and having done so, he confined them in four separate prisons in London, 'and would not,' says Sir John Froissart, 'have taken twenty thousand nobles for their deliverance.' Sir Thomas Knolles, the Mayor, and the Citizens of London, were next acquainted with the Articles of Deposition, and the King's confession concerning the four Knights; when the crowds, which had assembled in the Guildhall, cried out with execrations against them, and loudly demanded their immediate condemnation. This very speedily followed, and old London Bridge, which has in its days witnessed so many scenes of blood, was appointed the place for the exhibition of their heads; but in giving you a short narrative of this execution, we can go to no better authority than to the Herodotus of his time, Sir John Froissart, who, as you will doubtless recollect, was born at Valenciennes in 1337, and was Priest, Canon, and Treasurer of the Collegiate Church of Chimay; he died about 1401, and his Chronicles of his own time were compiled from the most authentic sources.

"The French of that part of Froissart's Chronicles to which I have alluded, commences *'A donc se tirerent ensemble le Maire de Londres,'* &c., volume iv., chapter cxii.; but we shall take the excellent English of Colonel Johnes' translation, Hafod Press, 1803, quarto, volume iv., pages 663-664. 'The Mayor and Lawyers,' says he, 'retired to the judgment-seat, and the four Knights were condemned to death. They were sentenced to be brought before the apartment of the Tower of London in which King Richard was confined, that he might see them from the windows, and thence drawn on sledges by horses to Cheapside, each person separately, and there beheaded, their heads affixed to spikes on London Bridge, and their bodies hung upon a gibbet, and there left. When this sentence was pronounced, they hastened to execute it. Every thing being prepared, the Mayor of London, and the Lords who had assisted him in this judgment, set out from Guildhall with a large body of people, and came to the Tower of London, where they seized the four Knights of the King, Sir Bernard Brocas, the Lord Marclais, Master John Derby, Receiver of Lincoln, and the Lord Stelle, Steward of the King's Household. They were all brought into the court, and each tied to two horses, in the sight of all in the Tower, who were eye-witnesses of it as well as the

King, who was much displeased, and in despair; for the remainder of the King's Knights that were with him looked for similar treatment, so cruel and revengeful did they know the Londoners. Without saying a word, these four were dragged from the streets to Cheapside, and on a fishmonger's stall had their heads struck off, which were placed over the Gate on London Bridge, and their bodies hung on a gibbet. After this execution, every man retired to his home.'

"The fatal tragedy of the reign of King Richard II. was at length consummated by his murder at Pontefract Castle, February 14th, 1399-1400; for whether he died of grief, starvation, or by the weapon of Sir Piers Exton, his death cannot be called by any other name; though Henry of Lancaster was not yet so firmly seated on the throne as to prevent numerous insurrections throughout the realm, on behalf of the younger Edmund Mortimer, Earl of March, the legitimate heir to the crown. For about the year 1386, King Richard had appointed as his successor Roger Mortimer, the son of Edmond, second Earl of March, and Philippa his Countess, who was daughter and heiress to Lionel, Duke of Clarence, *third* son of King Edward III.: whereas Henry of Lancaster was the son of John of Ghent, who was only *fourth* son of that Monarch. One of the most famous of these insurrections, was that raised by Henry Percy, Earl of Northumberland, which was overthrown by Sir Thomas Rokeby, Sheriff of York, at Horselwood, on February the 19th, 1407-1408. In which encounter, Lord Thomas Bardolf,—who is a character in Shakspeare's '*Second Part of King Henry the Fourth*,'—was mortally wounded, and died soon afterwards; but being on the party of the Earl, his body was quartered as a traitor's, and set up at several places, with the Earl's, one of which was London Bridge. This you find identified by Thomas of Walsingham, in his '*Historiæ Angliæ*,' page 419; for there he says, with considerable pathos: 'The root of Percy dies in ruin wild! for surely this Nobleman was altogether the living stock of the Percy name; and of most of the various others who were lost in his defeat. For whose unhappy end the common people did not grieve the least; recalling that famous, glorious, and magnificent man, and applying to him the mournful song of Lucan, where he says,

'But not his blood, his wounds did not so move
Our grieving souls, or wake our weeping love,—
As that we saw, in many a town, appear
His aged head transfixed on a spear.'

PHARSALIA, ix. 136.

For his venerable head adorned with its silver locks, set upon a pole, was publicly carried through London, and regardlessly placed upon the Bridge.'

"Sir William Dugdale, in his '*Baronage*,' volume i., page 683, says that Lord Bardolf's head was erected over a gate at Lincoln; and this is partly supported by the Chronicle in the Harleian Collection, No. 565, page 68 a, which states that in the ninth year of Henry IV., 'the Erle of Northumberland and ye Lord Bardolf, which arysyn a yeynis ye Kyng, were taken in ye north cuntre, and be heded, and ye hed of ye forsaid Erle, and a quarter of ye Lord Bardolf, were sent to London, and sett vp on London Brigge.' Dugdale adds, however, from the authority of the Close Rolls, that Avicia, the widow of that Baron, was permitted by the King to take down his body and bury it.

"The only historical notice which I find connected with London Bridge, immediately succeeding the last unhappy story, is of a light and even trivial nature, being nothing greater than a dispute in the Bridge-Street, between Thomas of Lancaster, Duke of Clarence, and John of Lancaster, Duke of Bedford, the second and third sons of Henry IV., their followers and the Citizens. Stow, in relating this circumstance, in his '*Annals*,' page 338, makes no farther mention of the place than that they 'being in East-Cheape, in London, at supper, after midnight, a great debate hapned betweene their men and men of the Court, lasting an houre, till the Maior and Sheriffs, with other Citizens, ceased the same:' and Maitland adds, in volume i., of his '*History*,' page 185, that these Officers were, in consequence, summoned before Sir William Gascoigne, the Chief Justice, to submit themselves to the King's mercy on behalf of the Citizens. Richard Marlow, however, the then Lord Mayor, and John Law and William Chicheley, the Sheriffs, with the Aldermen, strenuously asserted their innocence, alleging that they had only done their duty in preserving the peace of the City; and the King being fully satisfied with this answer, the Corporation returned to London. I have only farther to remark, that Prince Thomas of Clarence was engaged in a similar fray in East-Cheap in the year previous to the present, namely 1407-8; and that it is to him that Shakspeare makes the dying King Henry deliver that noble speech in the '*Second Part of King Henry IV*.,' Act 4, Scene 4. We derive, however, such a character of John of Lancaster from Falstaff, that we wonder to find him either in East-Cheap or Bridge-Street; for in that very same dramatic history, and in the preceding scene, he says of him: 'Good faith, this same young sober-blooded boy doth not love me; nor a man cannot make him laugh;—but that's no marvel, he drinks no wine.' Here, then, close all the events of London Bridge which have come under my reading, in the year 1409.

"The Festival of St. Mary Magdalen, July 22nd, in the first year of Henry V., A. D. 1413, brings to us the recollection of a very ancient and curious Saxon law, namely that of Sanctuary: by which privilege, if a person accused of any crime,—excepting Treason and Sacrilege, in which the Crown and the Church were too nearly concerned,—had fled to any Church, or Church-

Yard, and within forty days after went before the Coroner, made a full confession of his crime, and took the oath provided in that case, that he would quit the realm, and never return again, without leave of the King, his life should be safe. At the taking of this oath he was brought to the Church-door, where being branded with an A, signifying Abjured, upon the brawn of the thumb of his right hand, a port was then assigned him, from which he was to leave the realm, and to which he was to make all speed, holding a cross in his hand, and not turning out of the highway, either to the right hand or the left. At this port he was diligently to seek for passage, waiting there but one ebb and flood, if he could immediately procure it; and if not, he was to go every day into the sea up to his knees, essaying to pass over. If this could not be accomplished within forty days, he was again to put himself into Sanctuary. These privileges of Sanctuary and Abjuration were taken away in 1624, by the Statute of the 21st of James I., chapter 28: but you will find the ancient law on these points fully set forth in William Rastall's *'Collection in English of the Statutes now in force,'* London, 1594, folio, under their proper titles, folios 2 a, 399 b, and also in Andrew Horne's learned work of *'La Somme, appellé Mirroir des Justices,'* London, 1624, 12mo., chapter 1, section xiii., page 102. Rastall, you will recollect, was Chief Justice of the Common Pleas under Queen Mary; and Horne was a Lawyer of great erudition and eminence, in the reigns of the First and Second Edwards.

"Well, Sir, having brought to your remembrance these ancient privileges, I am next to tell you that in 1413, a train of five abjurants of the realm crossed London Bridge on their way to Calais; having issued from a member of the famous Sanctuary of St. Martin's le Grand, which was founded by Ingelric, Earl of Essex, and his brother Girardus, in 1056, and confirmed by Pope Alexander II., and King William I., in 1068. For these facts I must refer you to Stow's *'Survey,'* volume i., pages 605-606; and to page 16, &c. of a modest little volume of much curious information by Mr. Alfred John Kempe, entitled *'Historical Notices of the Collegiate Church, or Royal Chapel and Sanctuary, of St. Martin's le Grand,'* London, 1825, 8vo. As for the circumstance which caused these worthies to fly their country, we have it set down in the following terms, in that Chronicle contained in the Harleian Manuscript, No. 565, folio 74 a. 'And in the same yere, on Seynt Marie Maudeleyn day,'—July 22nd.—'John Nyaunser, Squyer, and his men, sclowen Maist[r]. Tybbay, Clerk,'—Archdeacon of Huntingdon, and Chancellor to Joan, Queen of Henry IV.—'as he passyd thorugh lad lane. For the whiche deth the same John Nyaunser and iiij of his men fledden in to Seynt Anne's Chirche with inne Aldrich gate,'—that is to say, St. Anne in the Willows, as we now call it, though without exactly knowing why,—'And with inne the said Church they were mured vp. And men of diuers wardes wacched them nyzt and day. And y[e] forsaid John Nyaunser and his men for suoren the Kynges lond, and passyd through the Citee of London,'—on August the 21st,—'toward Caleys, in there schertes and breches,'—a purse about their necks,—'and ich of them a cross in ther hand.' Let me add, that you will also find this circumstance recorded in Stow's '*Annals,*' page 345."

"My worthy Mr. Postern!" exclaimed I, for I now began to grow exceedingly impatient, "I really can bear this no longer: you promise to give me a descriptive history of London Bridge, and here you tell me of nothing but a riot which took place in the street *near* to it, and of a troop of knaves which *probably* walked over it. Positively, my good Sir, it's too bad; and unless your story mend, why——"

"'It shall be mended, Mr. Barbican,'" answered the imperturbable Antiquary, in much the same tone of voice as that with which *Lope Tocho* calmed the enraged Muleteer, in the same words;—"'It shall be mended,' and our Chronicles too, Mr. Geoffrey; but sweeten your disposition, my good friend, I pray you. Remember, that an Antiquary may *ruffle* his shirt, but never his temper; for though I confess to you that the collateral events which I am obliged to introduce, are somewhat like—

'Rich windows that exclude the light,
And passages which lead to nothing:'—

yet, when we consider how little the tooth of Time hath left to us of continuous History, we should labour to supply that defect by joining all the fragments with which we meet, wherever they may be united to the principal, but still imperfect, chain. We are, however, now arrived at a period, which our Bridge Historians do in general pass over, with little information to their readers, and less labour to themselves; yet even here, although we have no pictorial delineations to refer to, yet, with a little research, we have enough of descriptive story to call up the very scenes before our eyes, and to bring the actors again living before us.

"The year 1415 is not only immortalized in History by the famous Battle of Agincourt, fought on the 25th of October, but even in the Chronicles of London Bridge it is a most memorable era, on account of the splendid Pageants which welcomed the victorious Henry V., as he returned over that edifice to his Palace at Westminster. About the middle of November, or, as some tell us, the 16th, the King embarked for England, bringing his principal prisoners with him; and you may remember, by the way, that his fleet being encountered by a violent storm, two of his ships were sunk, and all were in extreme danger. You will find a few particulars of these facts in Stow's '*Annals,*' page 351, and also in that Chronicle which I have so often quoted, in the Harleian Manuscript, No. 565; of which latter, the following are the words, from page 76 b.

"'Also in this yere, that is to say the xxviij day of Octobr., the Kyng com to his Town of Caleys, and was there til ye xvj day of Nouembr. And that same day ye King schypped fro his Town of Caleys toward Engelond: And he landed ye same day at nyzt, at Douerre, and com forth all ye woke after toward London. And ye fryday at nyzt, ye King come to Eltham, and there he lay all that nyzt; and on ye morwe was Satyrday, ye xxiij day of Nouembr. The Maire of London, and alle ye Aldermen, with all ye Craftes of London, reden euery man in reed, with hodes reed and white, and mette with ye Kyng on ye Blake heth comyng from Eltham ward, toward his Citee of London; and ayens his comynge was ordeyned moche ryalte in London: that is to weten, at London Bregge, at ye Conduyt in Cornhill, at the grete Conduyt in Chepe; and at ye Crosse in Chepe was mad a Ryall Castell with Angells and Virgynes, syngynge there jnne. And so ye Kyng and hise presoners of Frensshmen reden thorugh London vn to Westminster to mete.'

"It is fortunate for us Antiquaries, however, that we have still better descriptions of these Pageants, and especially of that exhibited on London Bridge; and if in relating them to you, I seem to speak over much upon one subject, I pray you to remember, as I said, how very slightly that subject—at least so far as concerns the Bridge,—has been treated by Historians in general; and how many of those who have pretended to write of this edifice, have omitted it altogether. Give me your patience, then, whilst I translate for you two curious accounts of those Pageants, which welcomed King Henry into the best and the greatest of Cities.

"The first which I shall cite, is, most probably, from the pen of an eye-witness, both of the King's valour abroad, and of his triumphs at home; since it is from a Latin Manuscript in the Cottonian Library, marked *Julius*, E. IV., Article 4, which the Catalogue at page 17 calls '*The Acts of King Henry V.: the Author, a Chaplain in the Royal Army, who saw them for himself.*' This Manuscript is written on paper, in a very small and fair current black-letter, full of contractions; and on page 122 b, the account of the Bridge Pageants runs thus. 'And therewith, about the hour of ten in the day, the King came in the midst of them all; and the Citizens gave glory and honour to God, and many congratulations and blessings to the King, for the victories he had brought them, and for the public works which he had wrought; and the King was followed by the Citizens towards the City, with a proper, but a moderate, protection. And for the praise and glory of the City, out of so many magnificent acts of the noble Citizens, some things worthy of note the pen records with applause. On the top of the Tower at the entrance of the Bridge, which stands, as it were, on going into the strength of the City, there stood on high a figure of gigantic magnitude, fearlessly looking in the King's face, as if he would do battle; but on his right and left hand, were the great keys of the City hanging to a staff, as though he had been Gate-keeper. Upon his right, stood the figure of a woman not much less in size, habited in the gown, tunic, and ornaments of a female, as if they had been meant for a man and his wife, who appeared favourers of the King, and desired that they might see his face, and receive him with many plaudits. And the towers about them were ornamented with halberts and the Royal Arms; and trumpeters stood aloft in the turrets, which were resounding with horns and clarions in winding and expanding melody. And in the front of the fortress this appropriate and elegant writing was imprinted, '*The King's City of Justice.*' And there appeared, on both sides, all the way along the Bridge, very little youths; and, also, on both sides, out of the stone-work before them, was a lofty column, the height of the smaller towers, made of wood, not less delicate than elegant, which was covered over with a linen cloth painted the colour of white marble and green jasper, as if it had been of a square shape, and formed of stones cut out of the quarries. And upon the summit of the column on the right side, was the figure of an Antelope rampant, having a splendid shield of the Royal Arms hanging about his neck, and in his right foot he held a sceptre extended, and offered it to the King. Upon the top of the other column was the image of a lion, also rampant, which carried a spear having the King's banner displayed upon the upper end, which he held aloft in his dexter claw. And across, at the foot of the Bridge, was erected the fabric of a Tower, the height of the aforesaid columns, and painted; in the midst of which, under a superb tabernacle, stood a most beautiful effigy of St. George, all in armour, excepting his head, which was adorned with laurel interwoven with gems, which shone between it like precious stones for their brightness. Behind him was a tapestry of cotton, having his Arms resplendently embroidered in a multitude of escutcheons. Upon his right was suspended his triumphal helmet; upon his left his shield of Arms of a correspondent magnitude; and he had his right hand upon the handle of his sword, which was girt about him. Upon the tower was raised an extended scroll, containing these words, '*To God only be honour and glory;*' and in front of the building, this congratulatory prophecy,—Psalm xlvi. 4.—'*The streams of the River make glad the City of God.*' and all the principal towers were gallantly adorned with the Royal Arms embossed upon them, or displayed in banners upon lances reared above them. In the house adjoining to the fortress behind, were innumerable children representing the English Priesthood, in radiant garments with shining countenances: others were like virgins, having their hair adorned with laurels interwoven with gold; and they continued singing from the coming in of the King, with modulation of voice and melody of organs, according to the words of this song in English.'

"I know very well that it is most common for the events of the reign of Henry V., to be cited from the '*History of his Life and Actions,*' written in Latin verse by Thomas, a Monk of Elmham, in Norfolk, in his time Prior of the Monastery of the Holy Trinity at Lenton, in the County of Nottingham. As that part of his Poem, however, which treats *'De adventu Regis ad Pontem Londoniarum,'*—concerning the King's entrance at the Bridge of London,—is considerably inferior to the account which I have already given you, I shall dispense with your labour in listening to it, and mine in translating it; and only observe to you, that an authentic copy of Thomas of Elmham's *'Historia de Vitâ et Gestâ Henrici V. Anglorum Regis,'* is preserved in the Cottonian Manuscript which I last cited, article 3, fairly written on parchment, in the small black text-hand of the latter part of the fifteenth century; and that the passage will be found at folio 101 b. Capitulum xliiii. I would remind you, also, that a printed edition of this work was published by Tom Hearne, Oxford, 1727, 8vo., which is not one of his most common books; the text was taken from several old Manuscripts, and the value of a large-paper copy fluctuates between four and six guineas. The next authority, therefore, whom I shall quote upon this subject, is supposed to have been the production of the justly famous old John Lydgate, who was in his days a very eminent English Poet; being born about 1375, and dying about 1461. He was a Monk of the Abbey of Bury, in Suffolk; and of these historical verses by him there is a Manuscript copy, written on parchment in an old Court-hand, ornamented with vermillion chorusses and lines, in No. 565, of the Harleian Manuscripts, in the British Museum. You will find them forming Articles 8 and 9 of that volume, and thus entered in the Catalogue, volume i. page 351. *'A Poem upon the Wars of King Henry the V. in France; and his return to England, after the battle of Agincoure; composed perhaps by John Lidgate.'*—*'The making of* (i. e. Poem upon) *the comynge of the Kynge* (Henry V.) *out of Fraunce, to London. By John Lidgate, the Monke of Bury.'* Such are the titles of these verses, from which I shall repeat to you all that concerns the King's entry at London Bridge; and, firstly, at page 111 b. the story runs thus, beginning at the second stanza of *'Passus Tercius.'*

"The Mayr of london was Redy bown,
With all ye craftes of that Cite
Alle clothyd in red, thorugh out ye town
A semely sight it was to se:
To ye black Hethe thanne rod he,
And spredde ye way on euery syde;
Xx^{ti} M^l. men myght wel se
Oure comely kynge for to abyde.
Wot ʒe right well that thus it was
Gloria tibi Trinitas.

The kyng from Eltham sone he nam,
Hyse presoners with hym dede brynge;
And to yᵉ Blake Heth ful sone he cam,
He saw london with oughte lesynge.
'Heill Ryall london,' seyde our kyng,
'Crist yᵉ kepe from euere care!'
And thanné zaf it his blessyng
And preied to Crist that it well fare.
Wot ȝe right well that thus it was,
Gloria tibi Trinitas.

The Mair hym mette with moche honour
With alle yᵉ Aldermen with oughte lesyng;
'Heyl,' seide yᵉ Mair, 'thou conquerour,
The grace of God with the doth spryng:
Heil Duk, Heil Prynce, Heil comely Kyng;
Most worthiest Lord vndir Crist ryall,
Heil rulere of Remes with oughte lettyng,
Heil flour of knyghthood now ouer all.'
Wot ȝe right well that thus it was,
Gloria tibi Trinitas.

'Here is come youre Citee all
Zow to worchepe, and to magnyfye;
To welcome zow bothe gret and small,
With zow euere more to lyue and dye.'
'Graunt mercy Sires,' oure kyng 'gan say,
And toward london he 'gan ryde;
This was vp on Seynt Clementys day
They welcomed hym on euery side.
Wot ȝe right well that thus it was,
Gloria tibi Trinitas.

The lordes of Fraunce thei 'gan say then,
'Jngelond is nought as we wene;
Jt farith by these Englyssh men,
As it doth by a swarm of bene:
Jngeland is lik an hyve with jnne,
There fleeres makith vs full evell to wryng,
Tho ben there arrowes sharpe and kene,
Thorugh oure harneys they do vs styng.'
Wot ȝe right well that thus it was,
Gloria tibi Trinitas.

To london Brygge thanne rood oure kyng,
The processions there they mette hym ryght;
'*Ave Rex Anglorum,*' thei 'gan syng,
'*Flos Mundi,*' thei seide, 'goddys knyght.
'To london Brigge whan he com right,
Vp on the gate ther stode on hy
A gyaunt, that was full grym of myght,
To teche the Frensshe men curtesy.
Wot ƺe right well that thus it was,
Gloria tibi Trinitas.

And at the Drawe brigge that is faste by,
Two toures there were vp pight;
An Antelope and a Lyon stondyng hym by,
Above them Seynt George oure lady's knyght.
Be syde hym many an Angell bright,
'*Benedictus*' thei 'gan synge;
'*Qui venit in nomine domini,* goddys knyght'
Gracia Dei with zow doth sprynge.'
Wot ƺe right well that thus it was,
Gloria tibi Trinitas."

"Thus finish Lydgate's verses, so far as they relate to these Pageants on London Bridge; but as they tell us nothing of the Royal display upon that occasion, let me remark to you, that we are told, in an Heraldical Manuscript in the Harleian Collection, No. 6079, folio 24 a, that 'At the cominge in of Kinge Henry the Vth out of Fraunce into Englande, his coursers were trapped wth trappers of partye colours: scilicet, one syde blewe velute embroudered wth Antellopes sittinge vpon stayres wth longe flowers springinge betwixt their horns.' Which trappings were, by the King's order, subsequently given to the Abbey of Westminster for the vestry, where they were converted into copes and other Ecclesiastical habits."

"But before you quite shut up your account of these Pageants, my good Mr. Postern," said I, as he came to a close, "let *me* say a word or two, touching those Royal supporters, which sat upon the columns on London Bridge; since there are many curious little points of Antiquity to be met with in the history of Heraldic bearings. The first use of an Antelope as a supporter to the King's Arms, is doubtfully hinted at in a Manuscript in the Harleian Library in the British Museum, No. 2259, as having been so ancient as the reign of King Richard II.; though we are much more certain that King Henry IV. entertained a Pursuivant named Antelope, and probably adopted such an animal as his dexter supporter, from the family of Bohun, Earl of Hereford and Essex, into which he married. The instance of a Lion also appearing as a supporter, is mentioned in Gough's '*Sepulchral Monuments,*' which you have already quoted, volume ii., part ii., page 68, from the information of John Charles Brooke, Esq., Somerset Herald, who says that when Henry V. became King, he bore on the dexter side of his Arms, a Lion rampant guardant, and on the sinister, an Antelope. We read also that he bore an Antelope and a Swan, and two Antelopes; and you may see all these excellently drawn and described in Mr. Thomas Willement's '*Regal Heraldry,*' London, 1821, 4to., pages 21, 28, 30, 33, and 36."

"Many thanks to you, Mr. Geoffrey Barbican," recommenced my visitor, "for this most opportune display of your Heraldical learning: and, in returning to London Bridge, I must observe, that as all history is but a record of the evanescent scenes of human life, it must, of course, be formed of all those strong lights and shades which are so very conspicuous in its original; and hence arises that striking contrast of events, which so frequently fills us with solemnity and awe. We retire, perchance, from a banquet to a prison, or from a triumph to an execution; at least, such is the nature of the next event which I find for our Chronicles, for the Towers of London Bridge usually claimed a portion in most of the victims of the axe and the scaffold. The principles of the Lollards, as they were invidiously called, were then rapidly spreading; and Sir John Oldcastle, commonly called the good Lord Cobham, was one of the most active leaders in the religious reform commenced by Wickliffe: as he was not only at a very considerable cost in collecting and transcribing his works, which he caused to be widely distributed, but he also maintained many of his disciples as itinerant preachers throughout the country. Oldcastle had, however, escaped from the power of the Clergy who had condemned him as a heretic, and confined him in the Tower; when King Henry being persuaded by them that he headed 20,000 Lollards for his destruction, he was attainted, and a large reward offered for his head: in confirmation of which Stow informs us, in his '*Annals,*' page 352, that on the 'viii day of October'—1416—'was a Parchment maker of Trill-melle Streete drawne, hanged, and headed, for that he had harboured Sir John Oldcastle:' and the Harleian Chronicle, No. 565, page 77 a, adds, that his head 'was set upon London Bridge for tretory.' Another obscure person, most probably concerned in the same unhappy society, is also recorded as coming to a similar end: for, 'John Benet, Woolman,' says Stow, in the place I last cited, 'who had in London scattered sceduls full of sedition, was drawne, hanged, and beheaded on Michaelmas-day:' and the Harleian Chronicle adds, that his head was also fixed upon London Bridge.

"Our next ceremonial procession over this edifice was the solemn and splendid funeral of King Henry V.; when that gallant Sovereign had departed this life, on Monday, the last day of August, 1422, at the Castle of Bois de Vinciennes, a short distance from Paris. That sumptuous spectacle is described in several places, although I do not find it mentioned either in the Life by Thomas of Elmham, or in that by Henry's Chaplain; but Stow, in his '*Annals*,' page 363, says that the Royal body arrived in London about the tenth of November, and so was conveyed by London Bridge through Cheapside, to the Cathedral Church of St. Paul, where funereal exequies were performed; and thence it was carried and interred in Westminster Abbey. As the corse advanced in rich and solemn procession over the Bridge, it was truly a magnificent and imposing spectacle. On a royal chariot, decorated with cloth of gold like a bed of state, was laid a figure exactly representing the late King, habited in a robe of purple velvet, lined with ermine; wearing an imperial diadem of gold and jewels on the head, and bearing in the hands, the regal sceptre, and the mound and cross. The face, which was painted exactly to resemble the life, was uncovered, and looking towards Heaven; and on the bed lay a covering of red silk beaten with gold. The chariot was drawn by six stout horses, richly harnessed, with heraldic devices upon their housings: thus, the first bore the Arms of St. George; the second, of Normandy; the third, those of King Arthur; the fourth, those of St. Edward the Confessor; the fifth, the coat of France, alone; and the sixth, those of France and England quarterly. When the chariot passed through any town of eminence, a rich and costly canopy was held over it, by some of its more honourable attendants; and it was surrounded by three hundred torchbearers habited in white; by five thousand men-at-arms on horseback in black armour, holding their spears reversed; and by a multitude of Lords bearing pennons, banners, and bannerolls; whilst twelve captains went before carrying the King's achievement. After the body followed the servants of the Household all in black; then came James I., King of Scotland, as Chief Mourner, with the Princes and Lords of the Royal blood, in mourning habits; and lastly, at the distance of two miles in the rear, followed Queen Katharine, no less honourably attended.

"We learn, also, from a very interesting history of King Henry V. in English, contained in the Harleian Manuscripts, No. 35, folio 138 a, that when the funeral 'should enter the Cittye, ten Bishopps, wth their pontificall adornments revested, and many Abbotts mytored, and other men of the Church in greate number, with a right great multitude of Cittizens of the same Cittie, went out thereof to meet the Corps, and receaued it with due honnour. And all ye saide Spiritualls singinge, the officers accustomed in like case, conveyed the same Corps by London Bridge, and by Lumbart Streete, thoroughe the Cheape vnto ye Cathedrall Churche of Saint Paule.' This life of King Henry is partly a translation from the Latin of Titus Livius, an Historian of his reign, who called himself by that name, and the French Chronicles of Enguerrant. The other particulars you will find set down in Stow, as I have already cited him, and in two Manuscript volumes of Heraldic ceremonies, in the Harleian Library, No. 2076, folio 6 b, and No. 6079, folio

23 b; and in finishing our imperfect notices of this reign, let me close with almost the very words of the good old London Historian to whom we are so much indebted—'Thus this most victorious and renowned King entred the way decreed for every creature, in the flower and most lusty time of his age, to wit, when he was six and twenty years old, when he had reigned nine years, and five months with glory.'

"You must, doubtless, worthy Mr. Barbican, well remember the discord which Shakspeare represents to have existed between the Protector, Humphrey Plantagenet, Duke of Gloucester; and Cardinal Beaufort, Bishop of Winchester: and the fray which takes place between their serving-men in blue coats and tawny coats, on Tower-hill. This is in his *First Part of Henry the Sixth,* Act I, Scene 3; but we learn from Fabyan's *'Chronicle,'* page 413, that they once disturbed London Bridge with a brawl that wore a much darker aspect. It was customary in the more ancient days of this City, that the Lord Mayor should be elected on the Feast of St. Simon and St. Jude, on the 28th of October; and that on the day following he should be sworn in at Westminster. It was then, during the subsequent banquet of Sir John Coventry, Citizen and Mercer, that the Protector sent for him in great haste, and commanded him to watch the City securely during the night following; and on Tuesday, the 30th of October,—for, in 1425, St. Simon and St. Jude's day happened on a Sunday, and therefore the Lord Mayor was elected the day after,—about nine in the morning, some of the Bishop's servants came from his Palace on the Bankside, to enter at the Bridge Gate, when the warders, as they were commanded, kept them out by force. Upon which repulse, they retired in great discontent, and, gathering together a larger body of Archers and men-at-arms than that which kept the gate, assaulted it as a hostile City. All London was immediately alarmed; the Citizens shut their shops and hastened down to the Bridge in great multitudes; and a conflict would speedily have commenced, had it not been for the prudence and mediation of the Lord Mayor and Aldermen, Henry Chicheley, Archbishop of Canterbury, and the Prince of Portugal; who rode between the Protector and the Bishop, eight several times, ere they could bring them to any agreement; until, at length, they both consented to refer their dispute to the decision of John Plantagenet, Duke of Bedford, and Regent of France. The quarrel was, however, not concluded until the following Easter, which began on the last day of March. In defending London Bridge, the Protector appeared to be only retaliating upon the Bishop; for, in the third article of his charges against him, he stated, that once, when he was quietly riding to attend the King, the Bishop attempted his death at the Bridge foot, by assembling archers and soldiers in Southwark; by setting up engines to stop his way; by drawing the chain, used in ancient fortifications, across the Bridge; and by placing men in windows and turrets to cast down stones upon the heads of him and his followers.

"I have already mentioned to you, that there were several Towers erected on London Bridge, both for defence and ornament; although we have not any authentic historical notice concerning them, until we arrive at the year 1426, when Stow tells us in his *'Survey,'* volume i., pages 61, 65, that the Tower at the North end of the Drawbridge, over which the heads of Traitors were wont to be set, was then began to be newly built, in the Mayoralty of Sir John Raynewell, Citizen and Fishmonger; who bore for his Arms, Parted per pale indented Argent and Sable, a Chevron Gules. He laid one of the first stones of the edifice, and the Bridge-Master, with John Arnold and John Higham, the Sheriffs, laid the others. Upon each of these four stones, the name IHESUS was engraven in fair Roman characters, and at the rebuilding of this Gate and Tower in April 1577, they were laid up as Memorials in the Bridge House. The Drawbridge over which it was erected, was, at this period, readily raised up or lowered, that ships might pass up the River to Queenhithe; which was, during the use of this convenience, a principal strand for their lading and unlading, as being in the centre and heart of the City.

"In the year 1428, we find a short, but certain proof, that the passing beneath London Bridge was not less dangerous, than it is at present. You will see the circumstance mentioned in Stow's *'Annals.'* page 369, but I prefer giving it you in the words of the often-mentioned Harleian Manuscript, No. 565, folio 87 b, which was, very probably, the original authority of the good old Chronicler. 'Also this same yere,'—says the record,—'the viij day of Nouember, the Duke of Norfolk, with many a gentil man, squyer, and yoman, tok his barge at Seynt Marye Ouerye be twen iiij and v of ye belle a yens nyzt, and proposyd to passe thorugh London Bregge. Where of the forseid barge, thorugh mysgouernance of stearyng, fell vp on the pyles and ouerwhelmyd. The whyche was cause of spyllyng many a gentil man and othere; the more ruthe was! But as God wolde, ye Duke him self and too or iij othere gentyl men, seying that myschief, leped vp on ye pyles, and so were saved thorugh helpe of them that weren a bove ye Brigge with castyng downe of ropes.' The Duke of Norfolk, to whom this misfortune happened, was John Mowbray, the second of that title, who had served under King Henry V. in France, and who died October the 19th, 1432.

"We next come down to the April of 1431, when an association was formed at Abingdon, in Berkshire, headed by one William Mandeville, a weaver, and Bailiff of the Town, who entitled himself Jack Sharp, of Wigmore's land, in Wales. The Protector took instant order for his apprehension, and when examined, he confessed that it was intended 'to have made Priests' heads as plenty as Sheeps' heads, ten for a penny.' His own, however, did not remain on his shoulders long after, for he was executed as a traitor, at Abingdon, and his head erected on London Bridge, whilst his companions were also hanged and quartered in other places. You find this fact related by Fabyan in his '*Chronicle*,' page 422.

"From these scanty notices of misery, infatuation, and crime, it is with much delight that we turn to a spectacle of the greatest magnificence, and the most distinguished character, which London Bridge ever witnessed: the entrance of King Henry VI. to the City, after his Coronation as King of France, in the Church of Nôtre Dame, at Paris, on Friday, the 7th of December, 1431. On the 9th of the February following, he landed at Dover, and upon Thursday, the 21st of the same month, he was met by the Mayor and Corporation of London at Blackheath. Of their ceremony in conducting him towards the City, and the numerous Pageants which they had prepared to meet him at London Bridge, I shall now proceed to give you an account, extracted from Alderman Fabyan's '*Chronicle*,' volume ii., pages 423-425, and from Lydgate's Poem on the '*Comynge of ye Kynge out of Fraunce to London*;' of which a very fair copy is preserved in that Harleian Manuscript which I have already quoted, No. 565, folio 114 b. The verses by Lydgate are not very common in any form, and they have, as I think, been but once printed in connection with the history of London Bridge, which is in Malcolm's '*Londinum Redivivum*,' already cited, volume ii., page 397; and, although you may conceive that I quote too much of them, I cannot deny myself the pleasure of beginning at the very commencement, since it is but little less beautiful than Chaucer's immortal Tales. Listen, then, Mr. Barbican, I pray you listen; if you have ears for either Poesy or Romance.

'Towarde the ende of wyndy Februarie,
Whanné Phebus was in ye fyssh ronne
Out of the signe whiche callyd is Aquarie;
Newe kalendas were entred, and begonne
Of Marches comyng, and the mery sonne
Vp on a thorsday, shed hys bemys bright
Vp on london, to make them glad and light.

The stormy reynes of all there heuynesse
Were passyd a way, and allé there greuaunce;
For the syxte Henry, rote of there gladnesse,
Ther herty's joye, the worldis suffissaunce,
By trewe assent was crownyd king of Fraunce.
The heven reioysyng the day of his repaire,
Made at his comynge the wether to be so faire.

A tyme J trowe of God for hym prouydyd,
Jn alle the heuenes there was no clowdé sayne;
From other dayes that day was so deuydyd,

And fraunchisyd from mystys and from rayne.
The erthe attempred, the wyndes smothe and playne,
The Citezeines thorughe out the Citté
Hallow'd that day with gret solemnnyte.

And, lyk for Dauid after his victorie,
Reioysyd was al Jerusalem;—
So this Cité with laude, pris, and glorie,
For ioye mustred like the sonné beme,
To geue ensample thorughe out this reem.
Al of assent who can so conceyue,
There noble Kyng were glad to resceyue.

There clothyng was of colour ful couenable,
The noble Mair was clad in red velvet;
The Shireves, the Aldermen ful notable
In furryd clokes, the colour of Scarlet;
In stately wyse whanné they were met
Ech one were wel horsyd and mad no delay,
But with there Maire rood forthe in there way.

The Citezeyns, ech one of the Citté,
(In there entent that they were pure and clene)
Chose them of white a ful faire lyuerye,
In euery crafté as it was wel sene:
To showe the trowthe that they dede mene
Toward the kyng, hadde made them feithfully
Jn sundry deuyses embrowdyd richely.

And for to remembre of other alyens,
First Geneweys,—though thei were strangéres
Florantynys and Venyciéns,
And Esterlyngés clad in there manéres;
Conveyd with serjaunts and othere officéres,
Statly horsyd after the Mair ridyng
Passyd the subbarbes to mete with the Kyng.

To the Blake heth whauné they dyd atteyne
The Mair,—of prudence in especiall,—
Made them hove in renges tweyne
A strete be twen ech party lik a wall;
All clad in whit, and the most principall

A fore in red, with the Mair rydyng
Tyl tymé that he saw the Kyng comyng.

Thanne with his sporys he tok his hors a non—
That to be holde it was a noble sight
How lyk a man he to the Kyng is gon,
Right well cheryd of herté glad and light;
Obeinge to hym as hym ought of right,
And after that be kunnyngly a braid,
And unto the King even thus he sayd.

'Souereigne Lord and noble Kyng ze be wolcome out of youre Rem of Fraunce in to this zoure blessyd Rem of Jngelond, and in especial vn to zoure most notable Citee of London, other wise called youre chambre; we thankynge Almyghty God of the good and gracious acheuyng of zoure crowne of Fraunce: Besechynge of his mercyful grace to sende zow prosperite and many yeris to the comfort of alle zoure lovyng pepille.'

'But for to tellen alle the circumstauncys
Of euery thyng, shewyd in centents,—(*sentence*)
Noble deuyses, diuerse ordinauncys
Conveid by Scripture with ful gret excellence,—
Al to declare y have none eloquence;
Wherfore y pray to alle tho that it schalle rede
For to correcte, where as they se nede,'"

"So came the procession to London Bridge; and I very much suspect that the Corporation of our good City was so economical, as to entertain King Henry with some of the very same pageants which it had displayed to his father seventeen years before: for we find Fabyan stating, that 'when the Kyng was comen to yᵉ Bridge, there was deuised a mightie Gyaunt, standyng with a sweard drawen.' However, Lydgate will tell the story in the more interesting terms, and he continues thus:—

'First, when they passyd, was yᵉ Fabour
Entring yᵉ Briggé of this noble Towne,
There was a peler reysyd lik a Tour,
And theron stod a sturdy champyoun;
Of look and cheré stern as a lyoun,
His swerd, vp rered prowdly, 'gan manace
Alle foreyn enemyes from the Kyng to enchace.

And in defens of his estat Rialle
The geaunt wolde abyde ech auenture;
And alle assautés that were marcyall
For his sake he proudly wolde endure;
In token wher of he hadde a long scripture
On either syde, declaryng his entent,
Whyche saydé thus by good avisement.

'Inimicos ejus induam confusione.'—Psalm cxxxii. 18.

'Alle those that ben enemys to the Kyng
J schal them clothé withe confucion:
Make hym myghti by vertuos leuyng,
His mortall fone to oppressen and bere a down;
And hym to encreasen as Criste's champion,
Allé myschevys from him to abrigge
With the grace of God at the entryng of this Brigge.'

Too Antilopis stondyng on either syde,
With the Armes of Jngelond and of Fraunce;
Jn token that God schalle for hym provide
As he hath title by iuste eneritaunce,
To regne in pees, plenté, and alle plesaunce:
Cesyng of werre, that men myzte ryden and gon,
As trewe liegis there hertys mad bethe oon.'

"'And when,' says Fabyan, 'the Kyng was passed the first gate, and was comen to the Draw-bridge, there was ordeined a goodly tower, hanged and apparailed with silke and clothes of arras, in most riche wise.' Of which building thus speaks Lydgate.

'Forthermore, so as the Kyng 'gan ryde,
Myddes of the Brigge ther was a toure on lofte;
The Lord of Lordes beynge ay his gyde
As he hath be, and yit wil be full ofte:
The toure araied with velwetty softe,
Clothys of gold, silk, and tapicerie,
As apperteynyth to his Regalye.

And at his comyng, of excellent beauté
Benygne of port, most womanly of chere,
There issued out Emperesses thre,
Ther hair displaied as Phebus in his sphere;

- 130 -

With crownettys of gold, and stonés clere,
At whos out comyng thei gaf swyche a light
That the beholders were stonyed in there sight.

Nature.
The first of them was callyd Nature,
As sche that hathé vndyr here demayne
Man, beest, and foul, and euery creature,
With jnne the bondys of here goldyn cheyne:
Eke heuene, and erthe, and euery creature,
This Emperesse of custum dothe embrace;
Grace.
And next her com her Suster callyd Grace.

Passyng famous and of gret reuerence,
Most desyryd in allé regiouns;
For where that euere shewith here presence
She bryngith gladnes to Citees and to townys;
Of all well fare she halt the possessionys:
For, y dar sey, prosperite in no place
No while abidith, but if there be Grace.

Jn tokene that Grace shal longe continue,
Vn to the Kyng she shewyd here ful benygne;
Fortune.
And next here com the Emperesse Fortune,
To hym aperyng with many a noble signe
And Rialle tokenys, to shewe that he was digne
Of God disposyd, as lust ordeygne
Vp on his hed to weré crownés tweyne.

Natura, Gracia, et Fortuna.
These thre Ladies, al of on entent,
Thre goostly gyftés, heuynly and deuyne,
Vn to the Kyng a non they dyd present,
And to his hignesse they dyd a non enclyne:
And what they weren pleynly to determyne,
Grace gaf hym first at his comynge
Two ryché gyftés, Sciens and Cunnynge.

Nature gaf hym eke Strengthe and Fayrnesse,
For to be louyd and dred of euery wight;
Fortune gaf hym eke Prosperite and Richesse,

With this scripture aperyng in ther sight,
To hym applied of verey due right:—
'*First vndirstonde, and wilfully procede,*
And longe to regne,' the Scripture seide in dede.

'*Intende prosperitate procede et regna.*'

'This is to mene, who so vndirstondith a right,
Thou schalt by Fortune haue long prosperité;
And by Nature thou shalt have strenghthe and might,
Forth to procede in long felicité;
And Grace also hath grauntyd vn to the,
Vertuosly long in thi Roialle Citeé
With Sceptre and crowne to regne in equyté.'

On the right hand of these Emperesses
Stode vij madenys, very celestiall;
Like Phebus bemys shone there golden tresses,
Vp on there hedes ech hauyng a crownall:
Of port and cheré semyng immortall,
In sight transsendyng alle erthély creatures,
So angelik they weren of there figures.

All clad in white, in token of clennesse,
Liche pure Virgynés as in there ententys,
Schewynge outward an heuenly fresh brightnesse;
Stremyd with sonnys weren alle there garmentys.
A forum prouydyd for pure jnnocentys,
Most columbyne of chere and of lokyng,
Mekly roos vp at the comyng of the Kyng.

They hadde on bawdrikes al on saphir hewe
Goynge outward, 'gan the kyng salúe;
Hym presentyng with ther gyftés newe,
Lik as thei thought it was to hym duwe:
Whiche gostly giftés here in ordre 'suwe
Down descendyng as siluer dewe from heuene,
Al grace includyd with jnne the giftés sewene.

These riall giftés ben of vertu most,
Goostly corages most soueraygnely delite;
The giftés callyd of the Holy Goost
Outward figuryd by seven dowys (*doves*) white;

Seyenge to hym, lik as clerkés write,
'*God the fulfille with intelligence,*
And with a spirit of goostly sapience.
Impleat te Deus Spiritu sapientiæ, et intellectus,
Spiritu consilii, et fortitudinis, scientiæ, et pietatis,et spiritu timoris Domini.'

'*God sendé also, to thi moost availe,*
The to preserué from all heuynesse,
A spirit of strenghthé, and of good counsaile,
Of cunnyng, drede, pite, and of lownesse.'

Thus thise ladies 'gan there gyftés dresse,
Graciously at there out comyng,
By influence light vp on the kyng.

These Emperesses hadde on there left syde
Othere vij Virgines pure and clene;
By accordaunce continually to a byde,   (*shining stars*)
Al clad in white samete, (*satin*) ful of sterres shene;
And to declaré what they woldé mene
Vn to the Kyng with ful gret reuerence,
These wreten there gyftes shortly in sentence:

'*Induat te Dominus Coronâ Gloriæ, Sceptro Clementiæ,*
Gladio Justitiæ, Pallio Prudentiæ, Scuto Fidei,
Galiâ Salutis, et Vinculo Pacis.'

'*God the endue with a crowne of glorie,*
And with a Sceptre of clennesse and pité;
And with a sheld of right and victorie,
And with a mantel of prudence clad thou be:
A shelde of feith for to defendé thee,
An helme of helthé wrought to thine encres,
Girt with a girdell of loue and perfect pees.'

These vij Virgynes of sight most heuenly
With herte, body, and handys reioysyng,
And of there cheres aperid murely,
For the Kynge's gracious hom comyng:
And for gladnesse they be gan to synge
Most angelik, with heuenly armonye,
This same roundell which y shall now specifie.

'Souerayne lord wolcome to zoure Citee,
Wolcome oure Joye, and our hertys plesaunce;
Wolcome, wolcome, right wolcome mote ye be,
Wolcome oure gladnes, wolcome oure suffisaunce:
Syngyng to fore thi Rialle mageste
We saye of herte with oughten variaunce
Souereign lord wolcome, wolcome oure Joye,
Wolcome you be, vnto your owne newe Troye.'
'Mayr, Citezines, and al the commonté,
At zoure hom comyng newé out of Fraunce,
By grace releuyd of there olde greuaunce,
Synge this day with gret solempnyté.'

Thus resceyuyd, an esy paas rydyng
The King is entred in to yis Citee.'

"The King next passed on to the Conduit in Cornhill, where he was awaited by other Pageants equally sumptuous and interesting; but as these are out of our province, we shall mention them no farther.

"There seems to have gone abroad a singular conception, that the Chapel of St. Thomas on London Bridge did not exist beyond the time of King Henry the Sixth; in the 23rd year of whose reign,—1458,—there were four Chaplains serving in it; though it was originally founded but for two Priests, four Clerks, and their officers, independently of the several chantries, or revenues, left to the establishment, for the singing of daily mass for the souls of its benefactors. The income of the Chapel, however, more than ten years before that period, was considered as worthy of some inquiry on the part of a neighbouring ecclesiastic; for we find, in Newcourt's '*Repertorium*,' which I have already cited, volume i., page 396, the following particulars concerning it. 'In the year 1433,' says this Author, 'Sir John Brockle, then Mayor of London, upon a controversie that was then like to arise, between the said Mayor and Commonalty of London, and the Bridge-Masters on the one part, and Richard Morysby, Archdeacon of London, and Rector of St. Magnus Church, on the other, about the oblations and other spiritual profits, which were made in a certain Chapel, called the Chapel of St. Thomas on the Bridge, within the precincts of this parish; there was a composition, or agreement, then made, and confirmed by Robert Fitzhugh, then Bishop of London, whereby (inter alia) it was agreed, that the Chaplains of the Chapel, and their successors, should receive all the profits of the Chapel to the use of the same, and the Bridge, and should pay yearly at Michaelmas the sum of xx*d.* to the said Church of St. Magnus, and to the Rector of the same, and to his successors for ever.'

"And now that we are speaking of the property appertaining to London Bridge, it will be a fit place to give you some idea whence it was in general derived; I say, in general, because the inquiry into all its sources would be not only difficult, but almost impossible. Stow tells you in his '*Survey*,' volume i., page 59, that after the erection of buildings upon London Bridge, 'many charitable men gave lands, tenements, or sums of money, towards the maintenance thereof: all which was sometimes noted, and in a table fair written for posterity remaining in the Chapel, till the same Chapel was turned to a dwelling-house, and then removed to the Bridge-House.' The honest old Antiquary states, however, that he would willingly have given a copy of this table of benefactors, but that he could not procure a sight of it; for, as he was known to be a notable restorer of decayed and dormant charities, he was occasionally refused admission to such records as would have enabled him to compile a lasting register of all the pious gifts and benefactions in London. He never hesitated to reprove unfaithful Executors, whether Corporations, or private persons, some of which he caused to perform the testaments which they proved; whilst the dishonesty of others he left on record to futurity. It is then not to be wondered at, if he often-times met with a repulse instead of information; ignorance opposed him in one quarter, and interest in another; and he might very well have taken up the significant, though homely complaint of Ames, when he was composing his History of Printing, 'Some of those persons *treats* folks, as if they came as spies into their affairs.' We have, however, some particulars of the Bridge property, as well collected by Stow, as gathered since his time; and, firstly, I must notice to you, that at page 60 of his '*Survey*,' he states that 'John Feckenham, *Civis et Bracciator*,'—Citizen and Brewer, or perhaps, Corn-Meter, 'by his will, dated May 11th, 1436, bequeathed to the Mayor and Commonalty of the City of London, a Tenement with a Shop and Garden, in the Parish of St. Augustine Pappey,'—that is to say in St. Mary at Axe,—'between the tenement and lands of the Bridge of the City of London on the East, &c. To have to the Mayor and Commonalty of London, *ad usum et sustentationem operis Pontis prædictis in perpetuum*,'—for the use and support of the work of the aforesaid Bridge for ever,—'on condition that the Chaplains of the Chapel of St. Thomas the Martyr, on the Bridge, celebrating, have his soul, and also the souls of the late Lord Richard II., King of England, Edward Boteler, knight, and the Lady Anne his wife, Richard Storme, and Alice his wife, and the soul of Joan, his'—the said Feckenham's—'wife, perpetually recommended in their prayers.' You may see both the original and an authentic copy of this Will, and that which I shall hereafter mention, in the Bishop of London's Registry in St. Paul's Cathedral. The Chamber in which they are kept, is entered through the Vestry on the Northern side of the nave; whence a flight of dark winding stairs, lighted only by loop-holes, leads you to a small square room, surrounded by oaken presses containing the original Wills tied up in bundles.

The Calendar, or Index to the Register Books, extends from 1418 to 1599; all after that year being kept at the Bishop's Consistory Court in Great Knight-Ryder Street. It is a small folio volume, having a parchment cover, anciently tied with strings, and is written in a small neat black text upon parchment, though now much soiled by time and the continual dust of the chamber. If ever you visit this Registry, however, I would not have you trust too much to this Calendar; for in referring to the Will which I have now quoted, its volume and page are called '*Moore, prima pars, folio* iiij.;' though the true reference is '*3 Moore, folio* cccclxij a.' This volume, *Moore*, is so called from the first Will entered in it, and it contains registers of Wills from the year 1418 to 1438, beautifully written in a small black text upon parchment, in a very thick square folio.

"Another benefactor to London Bridge mentioned by Stow, was one John Edwards, Citizen and Butcher, who 'gave by his Will, dated the 8th of November, 1442, to John Hatherle, Mayor of the City of London, and to John Herst and Thomas Cook, Masters of the work of the Bridge of London, for ever, his tenement, with a garden, in the Parish of St. Botolph, Aldgate, situate between the tenement lately John Cornwallys's on the South, &c., and extending from the King's Street leading from Aldgate towards the Tower on the West, &c. towards the sustaining and reparation of the said Bridge.' You will find this Will in the Register called 4 *Stacy*, now *Prowet*, folio ciiij b, which extends from 1438 to 1449; though the Calendar marks it as entered at folio xxv. Both of these Wills are in Latin.

"Without, at present, referring to the multitudes of books and records of Bridge property, which must exist in the office of the Comptroller of its Estates, I will give you an abstract of one of these volumes, of which a Manuscript copy is to be found in the Harleian Collection in the British Museum, No. 6016, folio 152. This book is entitled '*A Repertory by way of Survey, of all the forren landes belonging to London Bridge, to geather with all the quitt rents due to, and other rents due from the same:*' and the industrious mortal who copied it out has added, 'Borrowed the booke 21°. ffebr. 1653 of Captaine Richard Lee, Clarke of the Bridge-house.' The Survey is written in corrupt and abbreviated Latin, which, from the expressions which are made use of, would appear like the language of the fifteenth century; and it contains many curious particulars of the names of persons and places, not elsewhere to be found. I purpose, however, giving you only a general statement of the amount of Bridge property in different places, with a few notices and extracts from the more interesting parts; reminding you, that these abstracts have never yet been printed.—In the Parish of St. Andrew the Bishop, London Bridge possessed 20 huts or cabins, occupied by the Brotherhood of Friars Minors, which were valued at £12. 3*s*. 4*d*. Then follows an entry of 'Lands and Meadows belonging to the Bridge of London without the bar of

Southwark, at Le Loke, in Hattesham, Camerwelle, Lewesham, and Stratford.' In Lambeth field without Southwark, or St. George's bar, 19 acres of land, lying towards Newington and Lambeth, held of the Prior of Bermondsey, for the yearly rent of 14*s.* 10*d.* At Le Loke,—that is to say, partly on the site of the New Kent Road, and on part of which was, doubtless, built that row of houses in Blackman Street, now called Bridge-house-Place,—4 acres of arable land, called Longland, and 2½ acres and 1 rood of meadow land, held by the yearly rent of 5*s.* 10*d.*, payable at the Feast of St. Michael. Also, on the South part of King Street, 2 acres of arable, and 2 acres of meadow land, called Carpenterishawe, held of the Archbishop of Canterbury, at the yearly rent of 6*d.*, payable at the Feast of St. Michael the Archangel. Also near St. Thomas Wateringgs, on the South part of King's Street, 7 acres of arable, and 2 acres of meadow land, called Fourecrofts, by the yearly rent of 4*s.* 8*d.*, payable at the Feast of St. Michael, and at Easter; another piece of land lying towards Hattesham,—perhaps Hatcham Manor,—containing 10 acres of arable, and 2½ acres and 1 rood of meadow land, called Tevatree, was held for the same sum. At Le Steerte, near the wall of Bermondsey, one acre of meadow ground, for the rent of 2*d.* per annum; and at Hattesham, at the entrance of the Marsh, 6 acres of arable land enclosed by a ditch, were held of the heirs of Simon de Kyme, for the rent of one penny per annum. In Lewisham, London Bridge seems to have had large possessions, since they were let out to farm at the immense rent of £3. 4*s.*; and to the property of the Manor was attached the ancient feudal rights of heriot,—taking of the best beast, when a new tenant came on the estate; wardship,—the holding and enjoying the profits of a tenant's land, who was a minor; marriage,—claiming assistance from all the tenants once, to furnish a dowry for the Lord's eldest daughter; Reliefs and Escheats,—the payment of a certain sum on the entry of a new tenant, and the return of forfeited estates. The land itself was divided, and the original rents were as follow.

"'24 and 11 acres of arable land, called the Greggehouse, 5 acres of wood, in two groves, 42 acres of arable land, and 2 acres of meadow land, held of the Abbot of Gaunt, at the yearly rent of 14*s.* 9½*d.*; 22 acres held of the heirs of Lord John de Backwell, Knight, at the yearly rent of 3*s.*; 10 acres, and 10 acres in the field called Edwinesfelde, held of the Abbot of Stratford, at the yearly rent of 10*d.*; 2 acres held of the heirs of Lord William Bonquer, Knight, at the yearly rent of 8*d.*; 1½ acre lying in the road near Depeford Bregge, held of the heirs of William Clekots, at the yearly rent of 1½*d.*; 3 acres in a croft near Leuesham Street, held of the heirs of Henry Boyding, and William Atteford, at the yearly rent of 2*d.*; 1½ acre at Rombeigh, for which nothing is paid; 10 acres in the field called Brodefelde, held of the heirs of William de Hinntingfeld, Knight, at the yearly rent of 1*s.* 8*d. Item.* There is owing for the said Manor to the heirs of Nicholas de Farndon, the yearly rent of 1*d.* At Leuesham, a water-mill, with 2 acres of pasture belonging to it, held of divers persons for the rent of 1*s.* 5*d.* and half a quarter of corn out of the tolls yearly, and the value of the tenths, from this time forth for ever.'

"The possessions of London Bridge, at Stratford, have been already referred to, but for the sake of perspicuity, I repeat them, and they were as follow:— One water-mill, called 'Saynesmelle,' and four acres of meadow land belonging to the same; 'whereof one acre lies within the close of the said mill, and four roods opposite to it on the East; and they are every where planted round with willows.' One acre and one rood of meadow land lie near 'Wyldemersh-bregge,' and are called 'Horslese.' They are held of the heirs of the Lord Richard de Playz, Knight, for the yearly rent of £1. 17*s.*—Also at Stratford are ten acres of meadow-land held of the same, and for the same rent: whereof four acres are adjoining to the mill-pond called 'Spileman's Melle,' and four acres are lying near to the meadow called 'Gryggewyche's Mead,' and adjoin, in like manner, to the same mill-stream. And one acre lies near the Bridge called 'Wildenmersshbregge,' and is enclosed by willows; and three roods of the same meadow lie near 'Golynant,' and one acre and one rood of the same meadow are lying in one piece, adjoining to the mill-stream of 'Saynesmelle.' At Royeshope, is one acre of meadow land, formerly held by John Breggewrythe, at the yearly rent of 2*s.* which is held, &c. as aforesaid. Also there are of the same, 1½ rood near Horslese, originally bought by Roger Atte-vyne, and John Sterre, then Keepers of the Bridge, which are held of the heirs of Thomas le Belevere, for the annual rent of 1*d.* The Vicar of West-Ham also held one acre of meadow, assigned to him for his tythe for the whole meadow; and 13*s.* 4*d.* were paid to him yearly, as tythe for the two mills. At Stratford, also, was another water-mill belonging to London Bridge, called 'Spylemanne's Melle,' which was held of the heirs of Lawrance Stede, for the payment of 1*d.* yearly; which mill being of Sutler's estate, tythes were paid for it by that estate, and it was therefore free for ever. There were also four acres of meadow and pasture belonging to it. All the foregoing were, at the time of this survey, let out to farm by London Bridge.

"Such were some of its possessions out of the metropolis; and I now proceed to notice that more interesting part of the volume, entitled '*Quit-rents of London Bridge, issuing from divers tenements of London and Southwark, according as they lie in different Parishes; and, firstly, of its property in the Parish of St. Magnus the Martyr.*'

"'Three shops, with galleries built upon them, now held by Robert Kots and Lawrence Schrouesbury, Glovers, standing at the Bridge stairs towards London, with the houses belonging to London Bridge on the South side. They were formerly belonging to the Fraternity called '*Le Salue,*' in the Church aforesaid. Two shops with galleries built thereupon, held by Peter Wydynton, Spicer, belonging to the same Fraternity, which are situated by the same stairs, between the way leading down to the common sewer on the

South; the tenements belonging to the same Fraternity on the North, the tenements of John Zakesle on the East, and the King's road on the North; and they owe yearly to the Bridge of London, 3*s.*' Another Tenement, held by Henry Ziuele, Mason, paid 5*s.*: and it was situate between the King's Road on the East, and the Oyster Gate on the West. Another Tenement paid 5 marks,—£3. 6*s.* 8*d.*;—it stood 'at the corner opposite to St. Magnus' Church,' between the King's Road towards 'Byllyngesgate' on the South, and the King's Road, called 'Brigge-streete,' on the West. It belonged to a certain perpetual Chantry in St. Magnus' Church, for the soul of Thomas le Bener; also belonging to the same Chantry, and standing about the same spot, was a tavern, which paid to the Bridge 2*s.* 6*d.* yearly, and the shop of the same paid 1*s.* 3*d.* Certain other shops and tenements belonging to Richard, the son of John Horne,—perhaps the eminent Town-Clerk of that name, whom I have already mentioned,—paid £2. of yearly rent; and they were lying near the narrow way called Rederes lane on the East, in the Parishes of St. Magnus and St. Roth'i. A house belonging to the Priory and Convent of St. Mary, in Southwark, paid 1*s.*: it stood between Oystergate on the East; and the houses belonging to St. Magnus' Church on the West; and extended from the King's Road called 'Stokfissmongeres Rewe,' on the North, down to the River Thames on the South. Another house in the Bridge Street, standing by that of John Somervyle, the Goldsmith, paid 8*s.* 9*d.* to the Bridge; as did also an adjoining shop and house; thus making the whole Bridge Rents in St. Magnus' Parish amount to £7. 8*s.* 11*d.* per annum. I have been the more particular in detailing the property of London Bridge in this part of City, because it in some measure illustrates the ancient state of it; but I shall be much more brief,—and, I dare say, much more to your content,—in speaking of its possessions in the other parishes mentioned in this Manuscript.

"'In the Parish of St. Botolph, near Byllyngesgate,' the Bridge owned the following:

"'One Tenement in the King's Street leading to 'Byllyngesgate,' 16*s.* One Tenement, a Granary, or Brewery, with two Shops in the same, 12*d.* Total 17*s.*

"'In the Parish of St. Mary atte Hulle.' One Messuage on 'Byllyngesgate' Quay, called the 'Boleheued,' 11*s.* 8*d.* The Priory and Convent of the Holy Trinity on the Quay called 'Treyerswarfe,' 6*s.* 8*d.* The house of William Walworth in the narrow way leading to 'Treyerswarfe,' 3*s.* 4*d.* Total £1. 1*s.* 8*d.*

"'In the Parish of St. Dunstan the Bishop, towards the Tower of London.' A Tenement called 'Cokeden-halle,' standing 'at the corner of the narrow way called Martelane,' on the East, and the Tenements belonging to St. Dunstan's

Church on the West, and the King's Road called 'le Tourstreete' on the South, 8s. A Tenement adjoining the same, 7s. A Tenement belonging to John Atte Vyne, son and heir of William Atte Vyne, standing near 'the narrow way called Mengehouslane,' 3s. A Tenement belonging to 'Gyhalle,' standing between the corner of the narrow way called 'le Chirchelane,' Eastward, and the foregoing, 4s. 8d. The House of Andrew the Canon, standing West of the foregoing, 4s. 8d. Tenements of John Pyebaker, belonging to the same Canon, 2s. 6d.; of Alie. Bemehoo, belonging to the same Canon, 2s. 6d.; of John Morton, Clerk, in the corner of the Church-yard of St. Dunstan's, near the narrow passage leading to the Tower, 4s. 8d.; of Isabella Rotheryng and her sister, standing by the Thames, 2s. Total £1. 19s.

"'In the Parish of All Saints de Berkyngcherch.' A Tenement of John Longe, the Fishmonger, standing between the Tenements of London Bridge, on the East, the Tenements of Walter Denny, the Fishmonger, on the West, and 'le Tourstreete' on the North, 3s.

"'In the Parish of St. Andrew Hubert in Estchepe.' A corner Tenement held by Richard Croydon, standing by the said Church on the North, between the narrow way adjoining, and the King's way called 'Seyntandrewys-lane' on the West, 12s.

"'In the Parish of St. Margaret in Brigge Streete.' A Tenement of John Littele, the Fishmonger, standing in 'le Crokedelane,' 4s.

"'In the Parish of St. Leonard, the Abbot, in Estchepe.' One Tenement in 'Candelwykstreete,' held by William Yuory, £1. 6s. 8d. A Shop held by the same, between the Tenements of the Prior and Convent of 'Cristecherche,' on the North, and the King's road, called 'Grascherchestrete,' on the East, 8s. Another Tenement, 1s. Another Tenement standing by the corner Tenement of the Hospital of the Blessed Mary without 'Busshopisgate,' on the North, and the King's road, called 'Estchepe,' on the East, 2s. A Tenement of the Prioress of St. Helen's, having 'Grascherchestrete' on the West, 13s. 4d. There was also another Tenement of 1s. rent, having Eastcheap on the East. Total £2. 12s.

"'In the Parish of St. Benedict de Grascherche.' One Tenement, a Granary, or Brewery, with two Shops, of Benedict de Cornewayle, having the King's road, called 'Fancherchestreete' to the South, 9s. 4d.

"'In the Parish of All Saints de Grascherche.' One Tenement with a forge and 4 Shops, standing between the corner Tenement of the Prior and Convent of Ely on the South, and the Tenement belonging to the Brethren of the Cross, called 'le Cardinaleshat' on the North, and the King's road, called 'Grascherchstrete' on the West, 40s. A Granary, 5s. Total £2. 5s.

"'In the Parish of St. Katherine de Cricherch.' A Granary standing in a corner between the narrow way called Bellezeterslane on the East, and the Tenement of Philip Page on the West, 8*s*.

"'In the Parish of St. Mary Attenaxe.' Ten Shops, with Galleries built upon them, standing in a corner, between the King's way, which is between London Wall and the aforesaid Shops, and the way that leads from the Church of St. Mary Attenaxe, to the Church of 'St. Augustine Papheye,' on the West, 1*s*.

"'In the Parish of St. Augustine Papheye.' The Tenement of Richard Schet, Fuller, standing by the Tenements of London Bridge on the East, and the King's road under London Wall on the North, and the Garden of the Prior of Cricherch on the South, 12*d*.

"'In the Parish of St. Martin Otiswych.' A Tenement with a large door, and a Shop on both sides of it, standing between the Church-yard on the North, and the King's road, called 'Bisshopisgatestreete,' on the East, 3*s*.

"In the Parish of St. Michael upon Cornhulle.' A Tenement with two Shops, having Cornhill upon the South, 8*s*.

"'In the Parish of St. Edmund in Lumbardstrete.' Certain Tenements with Shops, standing between the Tenements of St. Thomas's Hospital in 'Sothewarke,' on the North, and the King's way, called 'Berchers-lane,' on the West. They owe yearly to London Bridge, by the Will of Henry of Gloucester, Goldsmith, 5*s*.

"'In the Parish of St. Clement, near Candelwyk-stret.' A tenement of the Abbot and Convent of Stratford, standing between the Tenement of Thomas Clench, Fishmonger, on the South, the Tenement of the perpetual Chantry of the said Church, which was formerly John de Charteneys, on the North, and the narrow way called 'Seyntclementslane' on the West. It owes yearly to London Bridge, by the legacy of Henry of Gloucester, 2*s*. A Tenement with four Shops, 2*s*. Three Shops with galleries erected upon them, and a certain place called 'Wodehagh,' bounded on the South by Candlewick-street, 4*s*. Total 8*s*.

"'In the Parish of St. Michael in le Crokedelane.' A Tenement in 'Stokfisschmongeresrewe,' belonging to the Chaplain of 'Kyngeston,' 5*s*. An ancient Tenement, having the Tenement of the perpetual Chantry of the said Church, which was formerly John Abel's, on the West, and the narrow way called 'Crokedelane' on the North, 5*s*. Total 10*s*.

"'In the Parish of All Saints the Less.' A Tenement having the Tenements of St. Bartholomew's Hospital on the West, and the King's way called 'Tamystrete' on the South, 4*s*. Certain Tenements standing in the short narrow way of St. Lawrence, between the Tenement of the Master of St. Lawrence's College on the North, and Thames-street on the South, 10*s*. The Tenement of the said Master, 6*s*. Total 20*s*.

"'In the Parish of St. Lawrence, near Candelwyk-stret.' A Tenement belonging to 'Gyldhalde' of London, having the College of the said Church on the East; the narrow way which goes from the Church-yard of the same Church to Candlewyck-street, on the West; the said Church-yard on the South; and a Tenement belonging to a perpetual Chantry in the Church of St. Swythin on the North, 19*s*. 8*d*.

"'In the Parish of the Blessed Mary of Abbecherch.' A Tenement, having the Tenement of the Hospital of St. Katherine, near the Tower, on the North, and the Burial-place of the aforesaid Church on the East, 10*s*.

"'In the Parish of St. Swythin the Bishop. A Tenement held by Solomon Faunt, standing between the Church aforesaid on the South; the Tenement of Henry Fyuyan, Draper, on the North, and the King's way called 'Swythynislane' on the East, 2*s*. 6*d*. The Tenement of the said Henry Fyuyan, standing by that of John Hende, Draper, 2*s*. Total 4*s*. 6*d*.

"'In the Parish of St. Mary de Bothhaghe.' A Tenement held by Lord Thomas de Salesbury, Knight, standing between the Tenement with the Great Gate also belonging to the same, on the East, and Candlewick-street on the South, 12*d*.

"'In the Parish of St. Stephen de Walbrok.' Two Tenements under one edifice, standing by the Tenement of John Norwich, the Goldsmith, on the South, and the King's way, called Walbrook, on the West, 2*s*.

"'In the Parish of St. Mary Woolnoth.' A corner Tenement, which formerly was Hamon Lumbard's, having the narrow street, called 'Seyntswythinislane,' to the East, and that called 'Berebyndereslane,' to the South, 13*s*. 4*d*. Another Tenement standing in a corner in 'Schytelboanelane,' 2*s*. Total 15*s*. 4*d*.

"'In the Parish of St. Bartholomew the Less. A Tenement, a Granary, or Brewery,' having the King's way called 'Braddestrete' on the North, 2*s*. 6*d*.

"'In the Parish of St. Pancras.' One Cell, called 'le Brodecelde,' of which one entrance is by the large open place towards 'Soperslane' on the East, and another is toward 'Chepe,' at the sign of the Key, on the North, 6*s*. 8*d*.

"'In the Parish of St. Michael at Queen's bank,'—or Wharf.—'A Tenement, with its offices, which belongs to the Abbot and Convent of the Monastery of the Blessed Mary of Grace, near the Tower of London: it stands in a corner between the narrow way that leads to the Saltewarf on the East, and the Tenement of the Abbot of Jesus on the West, and it extends from the narrow way, called 'Ratonneslane,' on the North, down to the Thames Southward,' 2s.

"'In the Parish of St. Martin at Ludgate.' A Tenement with a forge standing in a corner without Ludgate, having the narrow street, called 'Little-bayly,' on the West, and the King's way, called 'Fletestrete,' on the North, 9s.

"'In the Parish of St. Bridget, the Virgin, in Flet-strete.' A Tenement, a Granary called 'le Horsothehop,' with two Shops, having Fleet-street on the North, and belonging to a certain Chantry in St. Paul's Church, for celebrating Mass for the Soul of Walter Thorpe, 8s.

"'In the Parish of St. Alban de Wodestret.' A Tenement, called 'le Horsscho,' 4s. Another Tenement, having the Tenement of the Hospital of the Blessed Mary without 'Busschopesgate,' on the South, and the King's way, called 'Wodestret,' on the West, 2s. Total 6s.

"'In the Parish of the Blessed Mary of Athelmanbery.' A Tenement standing in a corner between the narrow way called 'Phylippeslane,' on the West; that called 'Paddelane' on the South, and the Tenements of St. Paul's Church on the North, 2s.

"'In the Parish of St. Michael de Bassyngeshawe.' A Tenement with eight Shops, standing in a corner, towards London Wall, having the King's way, called 'Bassyngeshawe,' on the West, 2s. Two other Tenements, 6s. 6d. Total 8s. 6d.

"'In the Parish of St. Olave at the Wall.' A Tenement, formerly belonging to the Prior of the Hospital of the Blessed Mary without Bishopsgate, having the King's way, called 'Mugwelle stret,' to the East, 3s. 6d.

"'In the Parish of St. Stephen in Colmanstret.' Certain vacant places, by the legacy of Henry of Gloucester, 2s.

"'In the Parishes of St. Faith and St. Gregory.' Certain Shops standing in 'Paternostrerewe,' under the Palace of the Bishop of London, newly erected by the venerable Lord Michael de Northborough, formerly Bishop of London, 40s.

"A Tenement in 'Redecrouchstrete,' which cannot be found, 4d. Also in 'Est Smethfeld' was formerly a Tenement, which is now the common Church-yard, 4d. Another in 'Blachynglegh,' 12d. Also in Stratford, a piece of meadow land, formerly held to farm of the Bridge keepers, being the sixth part of a meadow called 'Ruschope,' 2s. Also at 'Sabryschesworth,' a Tenement, 3d. Total 3s. 11d.

"'In the Parish of St. Olave of Sothewerk.' Two Shops of the Hospital of St. Thomas of Sothewark, standing in a corner at the stairs of London Bridge towards Southwark, between the Tenements belonging to the said Bridge on the North, the King's way of Southwark on the South, and the stairs aforesaid on the East, 8*s*. A corner Tenement, now belonging to the Church of St. Michael in 'le Reole, which is called Paternostercherche,' and standing at the aforesaid stairs, having the King's way leading to 'Bermundeseye,' on the South; the Tenements of the Bridge aforesaid on the North, and the aforesaid stairs on the West, 13*s*. 4*d*. Total 21*s*. 4*d*.

"'In the Parish of St. Margaret in Sothewerk.' One Tenement of the Hospital of St. Thomas of 'Sothewark,' having the King's way of 'Sothewerk' on the East, 4*s*.

"'In the Parish of St. George in Sothewerk.' A certain Tenement and Garden called 'Exuuiwe,' which the Prior and Convent of the Blessed Mary of Southwark now hold; standing in a corner at the Cross in 'Kentestreete,' between the King's way which leads to Bermondsey on the North, the King's way called Kent-street on the West, and a garden on the South, 13*s*. 4*d*. A Tenement called 'le Mote,' having the Tenement of the Hospital of St. Thomas of Southwark on the North, a garden on the South, and Kent-street on the West, 8*s*. A Tenement standing at 'Le Loke,' near the Bridge Tenements, 2*s*. Total 23*s*. 4*d*.'

"Such, Mr. Barbican, were the gifts to London Bridge of Quit-rents, or small sums reserved by various landlords out of their charters and leases, for the support and improvement of this noble edifice. Their whole amount was £30. 0*s*. 2*d*. *per annum*, a splendid revenue, if, as I imagine from several circumstances, this very curious survey was made about the middle of the thirteenth century. Several of these gifts are authenticated by references to the original grants, read and enrolled in the Court of Hustings at Guildhall, at various meetings held during the reign of King Edward I.: whilst another authority, often cited, is called 'the Red Rental,' which also makes mention of Godardus, a Chaplain, and his brethren of London Bridge. The light these very brief but curious notices shed upon Parochial history and antiquities, has made me give you a more particular account of them, than might be perfectly agreeable to you; though, as I have not quite finished the volume, I must request you patiently to hear me a little longer speak of the ancient landed property of London Bridge."

"Oh! go on, Sir, pray go on!" said I, in a tone of mock resignation, "take your own time, Mr. Barnaby; though, to be sure, there seems but little reason why I should say so. I had, indeed, fondly hoped, that when you could no longer plague me with a Patent Roll, I might rest secure from any thing more provoking; but I must certainly own I was a most short-sighted mortal for thinking so, since your genius can never want a weapon to be drowsy with: but, I suppose that you rarely meet with a hearer so quiet, so mild, so undoubting, and so easily satisfied as I have proved: and therefore, suffer I must."

"I have truly," said he, in a short dry voice, "seldom met with a companion like you: but, I am sure, you will not think these extracts wearisome, when you remember that so little is known about the possessions of London Bridge; and that the fragments which I have repeated to you are all of the most undoubted authority, as yet unprinted, and almost locked up in a barbarous mixture of abbreviated and corrupt French, Saxon, and Latin. To return then to the Survey,—which, I assure you, I have very nearly concluded,—it next records the Bridge property at 'Les Stocks,' somewhat of which, you may remember, I have already spoken: and contains one of the most curious and ancient descriptions of that once-famous market now extant:—thus commences the entry.

"'Near the Church of the Blessed Mary of Wolcherchehawe, is a certaine Cattle-Fold called *les Stocks*, ordained for Butchers and Fishmongers, where the same may sell flesh and fish; the rent of which is uncertain, because any greater or smaller value arises from the way in which places in it may be occupied by the Butchers upon Flesh-days, and by the Fishmongers on Fish-days. Upon this Cattle-stall are three mansions, and one slaughter-house, built above it, the principal of which mansions is towards Cornhill, being now held by William Vale, Fishmonger, and it yields to London Bridge, yearly, 30*s*. Also, on the West side, towards the Conduit, is another mansion, held by John Louekyn, Fishmonger, which pays yearly 20*s*. Also there is another little mansion in the middle of the house upon the Stocks on the North side, paying 10*s*. Also on the South part of the Stocks is a slaughter-house, for which rent is not paid. Total 60*s*. And in the stalls aforesaid, called the Stocks, are places measured for the Fishmongers' tables, namely four feet and a half and two thumbs breadth in length, and called *Poulisset*, having legs, the which places are occupied by the Butchers on Flesh-days at the price of 4*d*. the week. And the same places are occupied by the Fishmongers on Fish-days, at the price of 3*d*. by the week. Of these places there are 19 on the South part next the Church; 18 on the North; 15, in one row, in the middle of the house on the South; and at the Eastern front of the said house are four places for Fishmongers, three of which are occupied by Butchers on the Flesh-days. In the West front of the said house are two places, occupied as well by Butchers as by Fishmongers; but the certain amount of the rents of these cannot be ascertained, because any of the aforesaid places may be occupied or not, and thus a larger or a smaller sum may appear upon the account-rolls of the gate-keepers of the place aforesaid, in different weeks and years. Without the Stocks, at the West front, are five places for Fishmongers, where, on Fish-days, they sell their fish; and, on Flesh-days, three of them are occupied by the Butchers. There are also 22 places and a half under the walls of the house, appointed for Butchers to sell flesh on Flesh-days; whereof 18 places are under the North wall, and 4 places and a half are under the wall of the Eastern front, of which places the value, when they are occupied, is 4$d.$ per week: but now they are not fully engaged, and therefore no certain sum can be stated.'

"'Also, it is to be known that the gifts, legacies, and oblations of the Corbell-Chapel, standing on the Bridge, with'—the Pontage from—'the carts carrying bread for sale crossing over it, and the passage of vessels under it, are uncertain in amount, because they may be greater or less in value, as they appear in the account-rolls of the Keepers of the said Bridge for different years.'

"The Survey concludes with an abstracted list of rents paid by London Bridge for lands and tenements held in various places, both in, and out of, the City; but as I have already given you several particulars of these, and as they do not contain any great additional information, I shall but observe from them that their total amount appears to be £20. 0. 9¼$d.$; and as we are occasionally informed that the lands were let out to farm, we may conclude that the Bridge-keepers were amply recompensed for the payment of a sum even so great as this. The disbursements of London Bridge were, indeed, always considerable, for Stow observes in his '*Survey*,' page 59, that the account of William Mariner and Christopher Elliott, Wardens of that edifice, from Michaelmas, in the 22nd year of Henry VII.—1506,—to the Michaelmas ensuing, amounted to £815. 17$s.$ 2½$d.$, all payments and allowances included.

"We must now set sail again on the ocean of English History, as it is connected with London Bridge; and you are to remember that we are yet in the reign of King Henry VI., though we have mentioned a multitude of dates since the commencement of our digression: and the next event in its Chronicles, relates to the destruction of a considerable portion of it in the year 1437. I have already cited to you some of the writings of William of Worcester, and in another work of which he was also the author, entitled '*Annales Rerum Anglicarum*,' he gives a slight notice of this event, which you will find in the edition printed in Hearne's '*Liber Niger*,' volume ii. page 458, taken from an autograph manuscript in the Library of the College of Arms. The best accounts, however, are furnished by Fabyan, on page 433, of his Chronicle, and by Stow in his '*Annals*,' page 376. From these we learn that on Monday, January the 14th, the Great Stone Gate, and Tower standing upon it, next Southwark, fell suddenly down into the River, with two of the fairest arches of the same Bridge: 'and yet,' adds the habitually pious Stow, 'no man perished in body, which was a great worke of God.'

"In the year 1440, the Annals of London Bridge became again interwoven with the great historical events of the kingdom, which impart such dignity to its own records, inasmuch as the Bridge-Street, by which is meant as well the passage over the Thames as the main street beyond it on each side, was one scene of the public penance of Eleanor Cobham, Duchess of Gloucester, for Witchcraft. The inflexible honesty of the Duke, who was Protector of England during the minority of Henry VI., and presumptive heir to the crown, had created a violent party against him, the heads of which were Cardinal Henry Beaufort, Bishop of Winchester, and William de la Pole, first Duke of Suffolk. With regard to his Sovereign, however, not all the spies, which were placed about Humphrey Plantagenet, Duke of Gloucester, by these powerful and inveterate enemies, could find even a pretence for the slightest charge; though that which they were unable to discover in him, they found in his Duchess, who was then accused of Witchcraft and High Treason: it being asserted that she had frequent conferences with one Sir Roger Bolinbroke, a Priest, who was supposed to be a necromancer, and Margaret Jourdain, a witch, of Eye, near Westminster; assisted and advised by John Hum, a Priest, and Thomas Southwell, Priest, and Canon of St. Stephen's, Westminster. Shakspeare, in his *'Second Part of Henry the Sixth,'* Act i. Scenes 2 and 4, and Act ii. Scenes 1 and 4, has recorded several particulars of this circumstance; and makes the Duchess ask some questions concerning the King's fate; though she was, in reality, charged with having his image made of wax, which, being placed before a slow fire, should cause his strength to decay as the wax melted. The result of the enquiry was, that Jourdain was burned in Smithfield; Southwell died before his execution, in the Tower; Bolingbroke was hanged, drawn, and quartered, at Tyburn; and, on November the 9th, the Duchess was sentenced to perform public penance at three open places in London. On Monday the 13th, therefore, she came by water from Westminster, and, landing at the Temple-bridge, walked, at noon-day, through Fleet-street, bearing a waxen taper of two pounds weight to St. Paul's, where she offered it at the High Altar. On the Wednesday following she landed at the Old Swan, and passed through Bridge-street and Grace-Church-street to Leadenhall, and at Cree-Church, near Aldgate, made her second offering: and on the ensuing Friday, she was put on shore at Queen-Hythe, whence she proceeded to St. Michael's Church, Cornhill, and so completed her penance. In each of these processions her head was covered only by a kerchief, her feet were bare; scrolls, containing a narrative of her crime, were affixed to her white dress, and she was received and attended by the Mayor, Sheriffs, and Companies of London.

"The leading features of these events are of course in all the numerous volumes of English History, but for the more particular circumstances I must refer you to Stow's *'Annals,'* pages 381, 382; to folio lxiiii. a, of the Chronicle of Edward Hall, an eminent Lawyer who died in 1547, and whose work is entitled '*The Vnion of the two Noble Houses of Lancastre and Yorke*,' London, 1550, folio; and, finally, to the Harleian Manuscript No. 565, page 96 a. Of which latter most curious work we now take leave, for soon after recording this event it terminates imperfectly; though I may observe, that when speaking of the fate of Roger Bolingbroke, on page 96 b, it adds, concerning him, that the same day on which he was condemned at Guildhall, he 'was drawe fro ye Tower of London to Tiborn and there hanged, hedyd, and quartered, and his heed set up on London Bridge.' His quarters were disposed of at Hereford, Oxford, York, and Cambridge.

"In 1444, William de la Pole, whom I have just mentioned, was one of the King's Ambassadors in France, when, with his usual lofty and impetuous spirit, he suddenly proposed a marriage between Henry VI., and Margaret, daughter of Réné, Duke of Anjou, and titular King of Jerusalem, Sicily, Arragon, Valence, &c. without any instructions from his Sovereign, or even acquainting his fellow-commissioners with his design. Notwithstanding the Duke of Gloucester opposed this union at the Council Board in England, yet the Earl managed his proposal so skilfully, that he procured himself to be created a Duke, and despatched into France to bring over the Queen: and on Thursday, the 22nd of April, 1445, she was consequently married to Henry at Tichfield Abbey, Southwick, in the County of Southampton. It was, probably, in her way from Eltham Palace to Westminster, before her Coronation, that she was greeted by the famous pageants prepared for her on London Bridge, on Friday, the 28th of May; for you will remember that she was crowned at Westminster Abbey, on Sunday, the 30th of the month, by John Stafford, Archbishop of Canterbury. However it might be, she was met at several places by many persons of rank, with numerous attendants having their sleeves embroidered, or decorated in the most costly manner, with badges of beaten goldsmith's work; and especially by the Duke of Gloucester, who received her with 500 men habited in one livery. At Blackheath, according to custom, the Mayor, Sheriffs, and Aldermen, clothed in scarlet, attended her with the several City companies, all mounted and dressed in blue gowns, having embroidered sleeves and red hoods: and in this manner Queen Margaret and her followers were conducted through Southwark and the City, 'then beautified,'—says Stow in his '*Annals*,' page 384, where he relates all these particulars,—'with pageants of diuers histories, and other showes of welcome, maruellous costly and sumptuous.' He gives, however, but a very brief statement of them in his printed book; though in his Manuscripts, several of which are extant in the Harleian Collection in the British Museum, there are the very verses spoken to the Queen on the Bridge, composed, as he says, by John Lydgate. The Manuscript I allude to, is one to which I have already made a reference, being No. 542, a small quarto volume written on antique paper, in Stow's own plain, but minute hand-writing. In this volume, therefore, article 16, on page 101 a, is entitled, '*The speches in the pagiaunts at ye cominge of Qwene Margaret wyfe to Henry the syxt of that name Kynge of England, the 28th of Maye, 1445, ye 23rd of his reigne.*' The first pageant, which was an allegorical representation of Peace and Plenty, was erected at the foot of London Bridge, and the motto attached to it was '*Ingredimini et replete Terram,*'—Enter ye and replenish the earth,—taken from Genesis ix. according to the Vulgate Latin. The verses addressed to Queen Margaret were as follow:—

'Most Christian Princesse, by influence of grace,
Doughter of Jherusalem, owr plesáunce
And joie, welcome as ever Princess was,
With hert entier, and hoole affiáunce:
Cawser of welthe, ioye, and abundáunce,
Youre Citee, yowr people, your subgets all,
With hert, with worde, with dede, your highnesse to aváunce,
Welcome! Welcome! Welcome! vnto you call.'

"Upon the Bridge itself appeared a pageant representing Noah's Ark, bearing the words '*Jam non ultra irascar super terram,*'—Henceforth there shall no more be a curse upon the earth,—Genesis viii. 21. and the following verses were delivered before it:—

'So trustethe your people, with assuráunce
Throwghe yowr grace, and highe benignitie.—'
Twixt the Realmes two, England and Fraunce,
Pees shall approche, rest and vnité:
Mars set asyde with all his crueltyé,
Whiche too longe hathe trowbled the Realmes twayne;
Bydynge yowr comforte, in this adversité,
Most Christian Princesse owr Lady Soverayne.

Right as whilom, by God's myght and grace,
Noé this arké dyd forge and ordayne;
Wherein he and his might escape and passe
The flood of vengeaunce cawsed by trespasse:
Conveyed aboute as god list him to gye.
By meane of mercy found a restinge place
Aftar the flud, vpon this Armonie.

Vnto the Dove that browght the braunche of peas,—
Resemblinge yowr symplenesse columbyne,—
Token and signé that the flood shuld cesse,

Conducte by grace and power devyne;
Sonne of comfort 'gynneth faire to shine
By yowr presence whereto we synge and seyne
Welcome of ioye right extendet lyne
Moste Christian Princesse, owr Lady Sovereyne.'

"We shall here take our leave of the poet Lydgate, by whose descriptive verses we have illustrated three splendid scenes in the history of London Bridge; and I pray you, if it be but in gratitude for this single circumstance, reject, as malignant and untrue, the character given of him by Ritson, when he calls him a 'voluminous, prosaick, and drivelling Monk.' Warton is not only more liberal, but more just, in his estimate, when he says that 'no poet had greater versatility of talents, and that he moves with equal ease in every mode of composition.' He admits that he was naturally verbose and diffuse, tedious and languid: but he asserts, also, that he had great excellence in flowery description; that he increased the power of the English language; and that he was the first of our writers whose style is clothed with modern perspicuity. 'His Muse was of universal access,' he continues, 'and he was not only the poet of his monastery, but of the world.' Alike happy in composing a Masque, a Disguising, a May-game, a Pageant, a Mummery, or a Carol, for Ritson's list of his poems, amounting to 251, embraces all these, and numerous other subjects.

"The year 1450 was made memorable by the daring insurrection of Jack Cade and the commons of Kent, which arose, partly, out of the popular belief that the Duke of Suffolk had caused the loss of a great portion of France to the English Crown; and, partly, from the pretensions of Richard, Duke of York, to the throne; in consequence of the haughtiness, despotism, and usurpation of Queen Margaret, and William De la Pole, her favourite. After some vain attempts to satisfy the commons concerning the Duke of Suffolk, King Henry banished him from the realm for five years; when after his embarkation his vessel was chased by an English ship called the Nicholas, belonging to the Constable of the Tower, by which it was captured, the Duke seized, and his head struck off on the side of a boat in Dover-roads; after which, it was carelessly cast with the body upon the sands. This murder, however, did not restore quietness to England, for the Duke of York being thus relieved from a powerful enemy, immediately proceeded in his own designs upon the Crown. By his instigation, therefore, one John Cade assumed the name of Sir John Mortimer, of the house of March, who, in reality, had been beheaded in 1425, on a charge of treason. Cade was a native of Ireland, and formerly a servant to Sir Thomas Dacre, Knight, of Sussex; but having cruelly murdered a pregnant woman, he took sanctuary, and forsware the kingdom. With such a character, he began his work of reformation in Kent, in May, 1450; assuming also, as some tell us, the title of

John Amendall, and easily drew so many malcontents together, that, in a few days, he was enabled to approach London, and to encamp with his rebel forces upon Blackheath. When Henry marched against him, he retired into a wood near Sevenoaks; where he remained, until the King, supposing his followers dispersed, returned to London, and contented himself with despatching after them a detachment of his army commanded by Sir Humphrey Stafford; which division falling into the ambush, was cut in pieces, and its leader slain. Elated by this success, Cade again marched towards London, whilst Henry and his Court retreated to Kenilworth Castle in Warwickshire; leaving a garrison in the Tower, under command of the Lord Scales. The rebels, however, now became increased by multitudes, which joined them from all parts; and on Wednesday, the 1st of July, Cade arrived in Southwark, where he lodged at the Hart, for, says Alderman Fabyan, in his '*Chronicle*,' from whom Stow almost verbally copies this story, 'he might not be suffered to enter the Citie.' Jack Cade, however, had but too many friends within the gates of London. The Commons of Essex were already in arms, and were mustered in a field at Mile-end; and upon a discussion in the Court of Common-Council on the propriety of admitting the rebels over the Bridge, the loyal-hearted Alderman Robert Horne so incensed the populace, by speaking warmly against the motion, that they were not reduced to order until he was committed to Newgate. About five o'clock then, on the afternoon of Thursday, July 2nd, London stained her Annals by opening the Bridge-gates to Cade, and his rabble rout. As he crossed the Draw-bridge, he cut with his sword the ropes which supported it; and on entering into the City, so beguiled the inhabitants, and even Nicholas Wilford, or Wyfold, the Lord Mayor, that he procured a free communication between his followers and London, though he himself again withdrew to his lodging in Southwark.

"In Shakspeare's vivid scenes of this rebellion, in his '*Second Part of King Henry the Sixth*,' Act iv., Scene 4th, a messenger tells King Henry,—

'Jack Cade hath gotten London Bridge; the Citizens
Fly and forsake their houses:'—

and in the next scene a Citizen says, 'they have won the Bridge, killing all that withstand them.' In Scene 6th, Cade cries, 'Go and set London-Bridge on fire;' and Edmund Malone, in his note upon this passage, tells us, what we certainly cannot find by any other history, that 'at that time London Bridge was built of *wood*;' adding, from Hall, that 'the houses on London Bridge were, in this rebellion, burnt, and many of the inhabitants perished.' This note you may see in the Variorum edition of '*Shakspeare's Plays*,' by Isaac

Reed, London, 1803, 8vo., volume xiii., page 341. London Bridge, however, was not even yet entirely captured, and two robberies which Cade had committed in the City, speedily roused the wealthier inhabitants to a sense of his outrage, and their own danger. Whereupon, 'what do they,' as honest John Bunyan says of the Captains in Mansoul, 'but like so many Samsons shake themselves?' and send unto the Lord Scales, and the valiant Matthew Gough, at the Tower, for assistance. The latter of these commanders was appointed to aid the City, whilst the former supported him with a frequent discharge of ordnance; and on the night of Sunday, July 5th, Cade being then in Southwark, the City Captains, the Mayor, Aldermen, and Commonalty of London mounted guard upon the Bridge. 'The rebelles,' says Hall in his '*Chronicle*,' folio lxxviii. a, which contains the best version of the story,—'the rebelles, which neuer soundly slepte, for feare of sodayne chaunces, hearing the Bridge to be kept and manned, ran with greate haste to open the passage, where betwene bothe partes was a ferce and cruell encounter. Matthew Gough, more experte in marciall feates than the other Cheuetaynes of the Citie, perceiuing the Kentishmen better to stand to their tacklyng than his ymagination expected, adused his company no farther to procede toward Southwarke, till the day appered; to the entent, that the Citizens hearing where the place of the ieopardye rested, might occurre their enemies and releue their frendes and companions. But this counsail came to smal effect: for the multitude of the rebelles drave the Citizens from the stoulpes,'—wooden piles,—'at the Bridge foote, to the Drawe-bridge, and began to set fyre in diuers houses. Alas! what sorow it was to beholde that miserable chaunce: for some desyringe to eschew the fyre lept on hys enemies weapon, and so died: fearfull women, with chyldren in their armes, amased and appalled lept into the riuer; other, doubtinge how to saue them self betwene fyre, water, and swourd, were in their houses suffocate and smoldered, yet the Captayns nothyng regarding these chaunces, fought on this Draw-Bridg all the nyghte valeauntly, but in conclusion the rebelles gat the Draw-Bridge and drowned many, and slew John Sutton, Alderman, and Robert Heysande, a hardy Citizen, with many other, besyde Matthew Gough, a man of greate wit, much experience in feates of chiualrie, the which in continuall warres had valeauntly serued the King, and his father, in the partes beyond the sea. But it is often sene, that he which many tymes hath vanquyshed his enemies in straunge countreys, and returned agayn as a conqueror, hath of his owne nation afterward been shamfully murdered and brought to confusion. This hard and sore conflict endured on the Bridge till ix. of the clocke in the mornynge in doubtfull chaunce and Fortune's balaunce: for some tyme the Londoners were bet back to the stulpes at Sainct Magnes Corner; and sodaynly agayne the rebelles were repulsed and dryuen back to the stulpes in Southwarke, so that both partes beynge faynte, wery, and fatygate, agreed to desist from fight, and to leue battayll till the next day, vpon condition that neyther Londoners shoulde passe into Southwarke, nor the Kentish men into London.' William Rastall, who produced his curious Chronicle, called *'The Pastimes of People,'* in the year 1529, adds to this account, that 'the Kentysshemen brent the Brydge;' see page 265 of the excellent edition of that work, by the Rev. T. F. Dibdin, D. D. &c. London, 1811, quarto.

"During the truce that followed this most valiant defence of London Bridge, and which nearly effaced the deep stain of the Citizens opening their gates to a rebel, a general pardon was procured for Cade and his followers, by John Stafford, Archbishop of Canterbury, Lord High Chancellor. Upon which, some accepted of the King's grace, and all began, by degrees, to withdraw from Southwark with their spoil, whilst Cade himself was soon after slain by Alexander Iden, Esquire, of Kent, in consequence of a reward being offered for his apprehension. His dead body was brought to London, and his head erected on the Bridge-gate, where he had so recently placed that of one of his greatest victims, Sir James Fynes, Lord Say, Treasurer of England. Concerning these events see also Shakspeare's *'Second Part of King Henry the Sixth,'* Act iv., Scenes 7th and 10th; Fabyan's *'Chronicle,'* pages 451-453; and Stow's *'Annals,'* pages 391, 392.

"I have but little more to subjoin to close the history of this rebellion; but I may add, that in January 1451, twenty-six of the Kentish rebels were tried before the King and his Justices Itinerant, and executed at Dover, and other places in the County; and that on Tuesday, February 23rd, as Henry returned to London, great numbers more met him on Blackheath, dressed in their shirts only, and imploring his clemency on their knees, were all pardoned. Against his entering the City, nine heads of those who had been executed were erected on London Bridge, that of their leader standing in the centre. 'This,' says Hall, in closing his account of Cade's insurrection, 'is the successe of all rebelles, and this fortune chaunceth ever to traytors: for where men striue against the streame, their bote neuer cometh to his pretensed porte.'

"In June 1461, previously to his Coronation, King Edward IV. crossed London Bridge with some ceremony, on the way from his Palace of Sheen to the Tower; whence it was anciently customary for the English Sovereigns to ride to Westminster in solemn procession the day before they were crowned. We have this information in an article printed by Hearne, and attached to his *'Thomæ Sprotti Chronica.'* Oxford, 1719, 8vo. It is entitled *'A remarkable Fragment of an old English Chronicle, or History of the Affairs of King Edward the Fourth, Transcrib'd from an old MS.;'* and on page 288, we find the following particulars. 'The same xxvi[th] of Juny, the King Edward movid from Sheene towardis London, then being Thursday;'—in reality though it was Friday, as this very extract subsequently shews—'and upon the way receyvid him the Maire and his brethirn all in scarle, with iiii c commoners well horsid and cladde in grene, and so avauncing theime self passid the Bridge, and thurgh the Cite they rode streigte unto the Toure of London, and restid there all nigt.' The day following, King Edward made 32 Companions of the Bath. He then proceeded to Westminster, attended by the new Knights habited in the white silk dress of the Order; and on the morrow,—which was St. Peter's day, and Sunday,—he was crowned at Westminster by Thomas Bourchier, Archbishop of Canterbury.

"The revenues of London Bridge seem greatly to have flourished under the reign of this Sovereign, for in his 5th year, 1465, the Wardens of the same, Peter Alford and Peter Caldecot, paid, on account thereof, the immense sum of £731. 10s. 1½; as you may see in Maitland's *History,* volume i., page 48, which information he has quoted from Stow's *Survey.* You, doubtless, remember, that although Edward IV. was, at this period of our history, seated on the English throne, yet that King Henry VI. was only deposed by the partizans of Edward Plantagenet, Earl of March, and son to the late Duke of York, and the Earl of Warwick, in March, 1461. In October 1470, therefore, Henry was again restored to his crown, which he retained with a disturbed sway for seven months only, and in April, 1471, was again imprisoned in the Tower, whence he had been taken to remount the throne. There were, however, not even then wanting some zealous adherents to the declining House of Lancaster, who made several brave, though unavailing efforts on the behalf of King Henry, Margaret of Anjou, and the young Edward, Prince of Wales. Under the sanction of their cause an impudent attack was made upon London in 1471, which forms an important feature in the history of this Bridge; which being mentioned by Stow in his *Survey,* volume i., page 61, is thence copied by all who have written its Annals. The Earl of Warwick had appointed to be Vice-Admiral of the Channel, one Thomas Neville, an illegitimate son to William, Lord Falconbridge, and thence called 'the Bastard of Falconbridge.' When he lost this employment, as he was a man alike devoid of morals and of money, he saw, says Rapin, with a very singular expression, 'no other way to subsist than turning Pirate;' for which, however, he probably required very little transmutation. As Edward was, at this time, engaged in pursuit of Elizabeth, his Queen, Falconbridge collected some ships, and a number of persons of desperate fortunes, and landing on the coast of Kent, intended no less than to surprise London, and enrich himself with the plunder of the City. He arrived in Southwark in May, giving out that he came to free King Henry from his captivity, and soon becoming possessed of that place, on Tuesday, the 14th, he ordered 3000 of his followers to cross the river in boats, and assault Ald-Gate and Bishops-Gate, whilst he himself attempted to force the Bridge. This he endeavoured to effect by firing it, by which he destroyed sixty houses standing upon it; though the Citizens were so well provided with ordnance, that even if the passage had been entirely open, says an ancient Chronicler, 'they should have had hard entering that way.' It is singular, however, that in this account of the number of the houses burned on London Bridge, Stow should be so greatly at variance with the earlier Historians; since they state it to be sixty, whilst, in his '*Survey*,' he says only that Falconbridge 'burned the Gate and all the houses to the Draw-Bridge, being at that time *thirteen* in number.' It is, perhaps, possible that the old Citizen is in the right; and that the other Annalists include some of those buildings which were destroyed in the suburbs of Southwark.

"One of the bravest defenders of London Bridge was Ralph Joceline, Alderman and Draper, afterwards made a Knight of the Bath, and Lord Mayor, in 1464 and 1476; since he not only manfully resisted Falconbridge and his party, when they attacked the Draw-Bridge, but upon their retiring, as they were at last forced to do, as well from the City as from the Bridge, he sallied forth upon them, and following them along the water-side beyond Ratcliffe, slew and captured very many of them. The Arms of this worthy were Azure, a mullet within a circular wreath Argent and Sable, having four hawk's bells joined thereto in quadrature, Or. I have given you these particulars from Stow's '*Annals*,' page 424; from Holinshed's '*Chronicle*,' volume ii., page 690; and from Fabyan's '*Chronicle*,' page 590; in which last authority it is added that 'the Bastarde, with his shipmen, wer chased vnto their shippes lying at Blackewall, and there in the chase many slaine. And the saied Bastarde, the night followyng, stale out his shippes out of the riuer and so departed, and escaped for that tyme.'

"Another record of the destruction of part of London Bridge, marks the year 1481, for page 61 of volume i. of Stow's '*Survey*,' informs us, that a house called '*the Common Stage*,' then fell down into the Thames, and by its fall five men were drowned. What this building really was, you may see in Holinshed's '*Chronicle*,' volume ii., page 705, where this fact is quoted from the volume entitled '*Scala Temporum*,' or, the Ladder of the Times, a contemporary record of remarkable occurrences.

"We are indebted to that singularly curious work, known by the name of '*Arnold's Chronicle*,' for an account of the expenses of London Bridge in several of the latter years of the fifteenth century, beginning with 1482, and terminating with 1494. The best edition of this volume is that edited by Francis Douce, Esq., London, 1811, quarto, for the series of modern reprints of ancient English Chronicles, which appeared about that time. The modern title of the book is '*The Customs of London, otherwise called Arnold's Chronicle*;' but in its original state it was devoid of a Title-page, the Table of Contents being headed thus: 'In this booke is conteyned the names of ye Bayliffs, Custos, Mairs, and Sherefs of the Cite of London, from the tyme of King Richard the Furst; and also th' Artycles of the Chartur and Libarties of the same Cyte; and of the Chartur and Libarties off England, wyth odur dyuers matters good for euery Citezen to vndirstond and knowe; whiche ben shewid in Chaptirs after the fourme of this kalendir following.' The first edition of '*Arnold's Chronicle*' is usually supposed to have been printed by John Doesborowe, at Antwerp, about the year 1502, in small folio; though it is without either date, or name of place, or Printer. It seems that Richard Arnold himself was a Citizen and Haberdasher, who resided in the Parish of St. Magnus, London Bridge, where he flourished in the year 1519. His work is a most singular compilation, for it not only contains all the subjects which I have already named to you, but numerous others which seem to have no sort of connection with it: such, for instance, as forms for legal instruments, 'the crafte to make a water to haue spottys out of clothe;'—'the vij ægesse of the worlde fro Adam forewarde;'—'the crafte of graffyng and plantyng of tryes;'—'to make a pickell too kepe fresh sturgeon in;' and the ancient original of Prior's beautiful ballad of the Nut-brown Maid! But now to shew you its references to London Bridge in particular, I must observe that one of its articles is entitled 'The lerning for to make a count by ye yerly rentis of London Brygge, Fo. 270;' nearly all of Arnold's examples being given from real and public documents: indeed, he was, as Mr. Douce observes of him, 'a very active, and even a meddling character.' To that activity and meddling, however, we owe too much extremely valuable information, to visit his sins of officious curiosity with any very severe censure; or to blame him too violently for having compiled his volume of such very singular materials. The first extract from these Account-rolls is for 1482, and is as follows:—

"'The Yerely stint of the Lyuelod belonging to London Brydge. Fyrst, for all maner ressaitis in ye yere vii. C. *li.* or therabout;' namely £700. 'The Chargis goyng out.

	Li.	*s.*	*d.*
'For wagis and fees of the Officers	lxix.	vj.	viij.
Item, for rewardis of the Officers	xxiij.	vj.	viij.
Item, paid out for quyt rentis	xxx.	xiiij.	vj.
Item, for quyt rentis dekayed	ix.	iij.	viij.

Item, for vacacions	xxx.	—	—			
Item, for costis of the Chapell	xxxiiij.	v.	iij.			
Item, the expencis vpon the Auditors	—	xl.	—			
Somme of this parte	C.lxxxxviij.	xvj.	ix.	£198.	16s.	9d.
Rest cler	v.C.i.	iij.	iij.	£501.	3s.	3d.'

"As there is not in this account any mention of the particular salaries actually received by the Bridge Keepers, I must refer you for information to a modern copy of some ancient documents, entitled '*An Account of the Fees or Salaries and Rewards of the Wardens or Keepers of London Bridge, from the 20th year of the reign of King Edward IV. Ann. Dom. 1482, to the present year, 1786, stating the times when their salaries were augmented, and also the Rental, or yearly income of the Bridge-House estate at each particular period.*' Single folio sheet.—'A. D. 1482. William Galle and Henry Bumsted, Wardens, to the said Wardens because of their office, to either of them, £10. Also for their Clothing, or Livery, to each, £1. Also allowed to the said Wardens, in reward for their attendance and good provision done in their office this year, to either of them as hath been allowed in years past, £10. Total to each of them, £21. Total Income, or Rental of the Bridge-House Estate this Year, £650. 13s. 7½d.'

"I regret, Mr. Barbican, and I am very sure that *you* do, that our Bridge Annals must, for some few years, be carried on principally by these documents; for I do not, in my limited reading, find any more interesting matter to record in them. Thus much, however, may be said in their defence, that we may certainly learn from them the increasing prosperity of the Bridge, and discover, in the items of their charges, many a curious fragment of the ancient value of money, and the articles contained in them. Having thus then, Mr. Geoffrey, deprecated your wrath against these matters, which certainly are somewhat dull in the recital, I proceed to the accounts of London Bridge for the years 1483-85, as they are given in '*Arnold's Chronicle.*'

'The Acompte of Willyam Galle and Hery Bumpsted, Wardeyns of London Bredge, from Mychelmasse Anno xxij. Edw. iiij. into Mychelmasse after, and ij yeres folowynge. The Charge. First the areragis of the last acompte, ij. C.

lxvij. *li.* xiiij. *s. ob.*'—£267. 14*s.* 0½. 'Item, all maner resaytis the same yere, vij. C. xlvi. *li.* xvi. *s. ob.* Somma, M. xiiij. *li.* x. *s.* i. *d.*'—£1014. 10*s.* 1*d.* 'Allowans and paymentis the same yere, vij. C. xliiij. *li.* x. *s.* ij. *d. ob.* Rest that is owyng ij. C. lxx. *li.* xix. *s.* x. *d. ob.*—Wherof is dew by Edward Stone and odur, of ther arrearagis in ther tyme, liij. *li.* vj. *s.* vj. *d. ob.* Item, ther is diew by the sayd Wyllyam Galle and Hery Bumpstede, Somma, ij. C. xvij. *li.* xiij. *s.* iiij. *d.*'

'The acompte the next yere suyng, from Mychelmasse in the first yere of the reign of King Rycharde the iij. vnto Mychelmasse next folowyng, the space of an hole yere. The Charge.

	Li.	*s.*	*d.*	
'First the Areragis of the last acompte	ij.C.xvij.	xiij.	iiij.	
Item, proper rentis	v.C.lxviij.	xij.	iiij.	
Item, foreine rente	lix.	xi.	v.	ob.
Item, ferme of the Stockis	lix.	ix.	xi.	
Item, quite rente	xxxi.	xij.	vj.	
Item, passage of cartis	xx.	xij.	vij.	
Item, incrementis of rentis	—	vj.	vj.	
Item, casuell ressaitis	vi.	—	—	

'"Somma of all their charge, ix.C.lxiij. *li.* vii. *s.* ix. *d. ob.*

"Allouaunce and Dischargis the same yere. Fyrst, in quyt rentis, xxx. *li.* xiiij. *s.* vj. *d.* To Saint Mary Spytell, w^t annuities, l. *s.* viij. *d.* Item, decay of quyt rente, ix. *li.* iij. *s.* viij. *d. ob.* Item, allowaunce for store-houses, xxxv. *s.* iiij. *d.* Item, in vacacions, xxxiiij. *li.* xvij. *s.* iij. *d.* Item, in decrements, iij. *li.* vij. *s.* i. *d.* Item, allowaunce for money delyuerd to the Mayre, xl. *li.* Item, for buying of stone, xvij. *li.* xiij. *s.* iiij. *d.* Item, for buying of tymbre, lath, and bord, li. *li.* xi. *s.* v. *d.* Item, for buying of tyle and brik, xiij. *li.* ix. *s.* iij. *d.* Item, for buying of chalke, lime, and sond, xxiiij. *li.* xi. *s.* xi. *d.* Item, for yren werke, xxxij. *li.* viij. *s.* iij. *d. q.* Item, requisites bought, xviij. *li.* viij. *s.* iiij. *d.* Item, in expencis, viij. *li.* xviij. *s.* xi. *d.* Item, costis of cariage, xij. *li.* xix. *s.* vj. *d.* Item, led and sowder, xiij. *li.* viij. *s.* Item, for glasyng, xxxvij. *s.* i. *d.* Item, costis of the rame, xxxiij. *li.* vj. *s.* ix. *d.* Item, masons wagis, xlviij. *li.* xviij. *s.* iiij. *d. ob.* Item, Carpenters wages, C. xiiij. *li.* v. *s.* Item, laborers wages, xxij. *li.* x. *s.* ix. *d. ob.* Item, Costis of the Chapel, xxxiij. *li.* v. *s.* iij. *d.* Item, the wagis of the tylers, xij. *li.* xij. *s.* vi. *d.* Item, for wagis of the dawbir, xij. *li.* vi. *s.* Item, for sawiars, xij. *li.* xv. *s.* vi.

d. Item, for wagis of paviours, xviij. *s.* viij. *d.* Item, to the Baker at the Cok, l. *s.* Item, for fees and wagis of Officers, lxix. *li.* vi. *s.* viij. *d.* Rewardis of Officers, xxiij. *li.* vi. *s.* viij. *d.* Item, expencis vpon the auditours, xlij. *s.* viij. *d.* Somme of all the paymentis and allowaunce, vij. C. xx. *li.* ix. *s.* iiij. *d. qu.*:' or £720. 9*s.* 4¼*d.* 'Reste, CC. xlij. *li.* xviij. *s.* vi. *d. qu.* Wherof is owynge and dieu by Edward Stone, for arereage in his tyme, Somma liiij. *li.* vi. *s.* vi. *d.* Item, by W. Galle and H. Bumpsted, C. lxxxix. *li.* xi. *s.* xi. *d. ob. qu.*'

"The last document of this nature recorded in '*Arnold's Chronicle*,' is for the year 1484, and it contains the following particulars.—'Ther Acompte, Anno ij. Ric. Tercij. The Charge. First, the arreragis of ther last acompte, C. lxxxix. *li.* xi. *s.* xi. *d. ob. qu.* Item, all maner ressaitis, vii. C. xliiij. *li.* x. *s.* v. *d. qu.* Somma of the Charge, ix. C. xxxiiij. *li.* ij. *s.* iiij. *d.* Discharge. Fyrst, allowaunce of paymentis the same yere, vi. C. xxiij. *li.* iiij. *s.* x. *d.* Soo there remayneth the somme CCC. x. *li.* xvij. *s.* v. *d. ob.* Wherof is dieu by Edward Stone and other of their arrerage in their tyme, liij. *li.* vi. *s.* vi. *d. ob.* And soo remayneth clerly dieu by William Gale and Herry Bounsted CC. lvij. *li.* x. *s.* xi. *d.*' I must not omit to notice, before quitting these particulars of the ancient expenses of London Bridge, that they are to be found also printed in Maitland's '*History*,' volume i., pages 48, 49.

"We have frequently, in the course of these fragmenta, mentioned various officers set over the affairs of London Bridge, and some of the instruments which I have quoted, have shewn that several of them were anciently appointed by the King's Writ or Patent. The principal of these Officers are two Bridge-Masters, having certain fees and profits, yearly elected, or continued, by the Livery at the Common Hall, held upon Midsummer day, after the Sheriffs and Chamberlain. Strype, the continuator of Stow's '*Survey*,' whose signature is J. S., states, in volume ii., page 25, that the Bridge-Master is some freeman elected by the City and set over the Bridge-House, 'to look after the reparations of the Bridge;' he adds, too, that 'he hath a liberal salary allowed him; and that the place hath sometimes been a good relief for some honest citizens fallen to decay.' We are also farther told by the same author, on page 472 of the same work and volume, that at a Court of Common Council, held on Friday, April 15th, 1491, in the 6th year of King Henry VII., it was enacted that at the election of Bridge-Master, the Lord Mayor and Aldermen should annually present four men to the Commonalty, from whom they were to elect two to be Bridge-Masters. This act appears to have been in force until Thursday, April the 15th, 1643, when it was repealed, and the whole election has since remained in the Livery. Of the names and ancient fees of these Bridge-Masters I have already given you some specimens, and shall cite you several others in the future years of our history.

"We must again be indebted to '*Arnold's Chronicle*' for a fragment illustrative of the property, persons, and houses, in the Parish of St. Magnus, and on

London Bridge, in the year 1494; for on page 224 of that mass of singular information, we find an article entitled *'The Valew and stynt of the Benefyce of St. Magnus at London Brydge yerly to the Person. The Rekenyng of the same the fyrst day of Decembre, Anno Domini* M. CCCC. lxxxxiiij.' I am not going to give you the long bead-roll of names, rents, and rates which follow; but I shall observe that, at this period, the rents amounted to £434. 12s. 8d., and the offerings paid to the Parson came to £75. 8s. 8½d. The rent of 'the Shoppis in Brigstrett,' amounted to £70. 3s. 4d., and their offerings to £12. 3s. 3d.; but the only building that is mentioned as immediately connected with our present subject is 'the Ymage of our Lady on the Brydge, valet iiij marke,' or £2. 13s. 4d. You may, perhaps, remember that this very article from *'Arnold's Chronicle,'* was afterwards printed in a small volume commonly supposed to have been compiled by the learned Dr. Brian Walton, Bishop of Chester, and Editor of the famous London Polyglot Bible, in 1657. This tract is entitled *'A Treatise concerning the payment of Tythes and Oblations in London. By B. W., D. D.;'* 1641, 4to., and the original manuscript, written in an ancient hand on folio paper, is, to our delight, yet remaining in the Archiepiscopal Library at Lambeth Palace, No. 273. Whilst I am speaking of this collection, I may observe that it contains another manuscript in which are some few curious particulars concerning the buildings on London Bridge. This is marked No. 272; was written in 1638, on folio paper; and is entitled *'A Catalogue of inhabitants of the several Parishes in London, with the rent of houses and tythes paid out of them; in order to a new settlement of Tythes.'* The contents of this manuscript set forth not only the names of the dwellers in the various houses, but also 'a moderate valuacion' of them, 'and other things tithable;' wherein, however, it is added, of St. Magnus, that 'the Parish would not ioyne.' This district forms article 48 of the volume, and we find mentioned in it the following buildings 'on London Bridge.' 'One great house, shop, warehouse, cellars, &c. clear value £50., Tithes, £1. 16s.; it hath bin letten for above £8.'—'One faire house and shop, part of the Little Nonesuch,' value £40., Tythes, £1. 7s. 6d.; and the same for the other part. 'One Ale-cellar, Tythes, 3s.' On the South side of Great Thames Street, the following buildings are mentioned connected with the Bridge: 'One house, wharf, and Engines to carry water, valued at £500. cleere profitt.'—'One great house divided into divers tenements, Bridge-House Rents, over them, value £20.'

"In giving you these particulars, I must own that I have considerably anticipated the period to which they belong, but as it is my wish to say something of the history of St. Magnus' Parish, it could scarcely be more properly introduced than when we were noticing the ancient amount of its tythes, &c. The earliest mention of the Church of St. Magnus is said by Pennant to be in 1433, though Stow speaks of several monuments considerably older; and if you will turn to Newcourt's *'Repertorium Ecclesiasticum,'* volume i., page 396, you will find that Hugh Pourt, one of the

Sheriffs of London, in 1302, and Margaret his wife, founded a perpetual Chantry in this edifice: and further, that the list of Rectors commences with Robert de Sancto Albano, who resigned his office on the 31st of August, 1323. There was also a Guild, or Fraternity, called 'Le Salve Regina,' held in this Church, as Stow shows you in his '*Survey*,' volume i., page 495, which was flourishing in the 17th year of Edward III.,—1343.—The intent of that convention will best be shewn by an extract from Stow's translation of the certificate of this species of religious Benefit Society, which is as follows:— 'Be it remembered that Rauf Capeleyn, du Bailiff; William Double, Fishmonger; Roger Lowher, Chancellor; Henry Boseworth, Vintener; Stephen Lucas, Stock-Fishmonger; and other of the better sort of the Parish of St. Magnus, near the Bridge of London, of their great devotion, and to the honour of God and his glorious Mother, our Lady Mary the Virgin, began, and caused to be made a Chantry, to sing an Anthem of our Lady called '*Salve Regina*,' every evening: and thereupon ordained five burning wax lights at the time of the said anthem, in the honour and reverence of the five principal joys of our Lady aforesaid, and for exciting the people to devotion at such an hour, the more to merit to their souls. And thereupon many other good people of the same Parish, seeing the great honesty of the said service and devotion, proferred to be aiders and parteners to support the said lights and the said anthem to be continually sung; paying to every person every week an halfpenny. And so that hereafter, with the gift that the people shall give to the sustentation of the said light and anthem, there shall be to find a Chaplain singing in the said Church for all the benefactors of the said light and anthem.'

"I do not find that the Patron Saint of this edifice is at all mentioned by Alban Butler; nor are all writers perfectly agreed as to who he actually was; seeing that there were two Saints named Magnus, whose festival day was kept on the 19th of August. One of these was Bishop of Anagnia in Italy, and was martyred in the persecution raised by the Emperors Decius and Valerian, about the middle of the third century after the Birth of Christ. The other St. Magnus; was the person to whom Newcourt supposes this Church was dedicated, though he erroneously calls his feast August the 18th. He is named, by way of distinction, St. Magnus the Martyr of Cæsarea, in Cappadocia, because he suffered at that City, under Alexander the Governor, in the time of the Emperor Aurelian, A. D. 276. Having vainly endeavoured to make him do sacrifice, he caused him to be twice exposed to the flames of a furnace, and thrice to be thrown to wild beasts; but none of these things moving him, he was at length stoned, and when all imagined that he was dead, he suddenly prayed that his soul might have a peaceful exit, and presently gave up the ghost. An extended history of these famous men, you will find in that wonderful work the '*Acta Sanctorum*,' which I have before quoted, in the third volume for August, pages 701-719: though there is a much longer account of the Swedish St. Magnus, the Abbot, whose festival is September the 6th, and whom I pray you never to mistake for the Martyr of London Bridge. The Rectory of St. Magnus, says the tract which I last quoted from the Lambeth Library, is rated higher in his Majesty's books than any living in, or about, London, being valued at £69. and 40*s*. more in pensions, but is without any glebe attached to it. Before I close these *spicilegia* of the rents, &c. of St. Magnus and London Bridge, I must observe to you that when Arnold is speaking in his '*Chronicle*' of the fifteenths raised by every Ward in London, he states, at page 48, that the quarter of the Bridge itself, at a fifteenth, amounted to £14. 3*s*. 4*d.*; and that the Bridge-street quarter produced £11. 5*s*. 8*d.* So much then for a few particulars of the history of this Church and Parish, the North-East boundary of London Bridge, to the Chronicles of which we shall now return, taking them up again with the year 1497.

"It was in this year, you may remember, that the forces of Henry VII., which were proceeding to Scotland, were suddenly recalled to subdue a commotion raised in Cornwall, in consequence of a subsidy voted by Parliament, in 1496. The rebels were headed by one Thomas Flamoke, a Lawyer and a gentleman; and a Blacksmith, or Farrier, of Bodmin, called Michael Joseph; both of them, says Stow, in his '*Annals*,' page 479, 'men of stout stomackes.' Under these leaders, then, they penetrated even to Blackheath, but on their march were so valiantly opposed in Kent, that numbers of the insurgents fled from their company. On Blackheath the Royal troops were already encamped under several valiant commanders, by whom the rebels' retreat was immediately cut off; and in a short engagement which ensued on June the 22nd, Flamoke and Joseph were both taken prisoners. On the 28th following they were executed at Tyburn; and their quarters were to have been erected in various places in Cornwall, but Hall states, in his '*Chronicle*,' folio 43 b, that, as it was supposed it would incite the Cornishmen to new insurrections, they were set up in London: and their heads greeted Henry VII. on London Bridge, as he triumphantly returned over it from Blackheath.

"During this same year, London Bridge appears to have been repaired to some extent, although it is probable that the only notice of it may exist in the manuscript records of the Bridge Comptroller. In the '*Gentleman's Magazine*,' however, for October 1758, volume xxviii., page 469, is a Letter from Joseph Ames, Secretary to the Society of Antiquaries, and Author of the '*Typographical Antiquities*,' containing three inscriptions engraven on stone, found in pulling down a part of the edifice. These, it is supposed, were laid in the building at the different times of its repair, specified by their several dates; but though so very ancient, yet the descriptive account states that, 'they are all as fresh as if new cut;' they being then in the possession of Mr.

Hudson, the Bridge-Master. The oldest inscription is sculptured upon a stone 9¾ inches in height, by 16¾ inches long;

the letters being raised and blacked, and the words, within a border, being '*Anno Domini,*' with the date of 1497, in small black-letters, and ancient Arabic figures. I shall introduce the other stones to your notice in the years to which they refer; and only now remark, that they are engraven in Plate 1, Numbers I. II. III. page 470, of the work to which I have already referred you, whence they were copied into Gough's '*Sepulchral Monuments,*' volume ii., part i., page cclxvi., plate xxv.

"Hitherto, Mr. Geoffrey Barbican, I have quoted you an abundance of authorities which make mention of the history, or appearance, of London Bridge, but notwithstanding my researches I find only a very few ancient representations of it. If, however, you would see an interesting and sweetly-touched portraiture of it about the year 1500, look into that stout roan-coated folio, marked 16 F. ii. xv. in the Royal Library of Manuscripts in the British Museum, and you will be enraptured. The volume professes to treat of '*Grace entiére sur le gouvernement du Prince,*' and it is written in prose and verse, in the common large black script of the fifteenth century, on vellum, with most noble illuminations, executed in the best style of the best period of the art in England, and by one of the most gifted of the Brethren of St. Luke. The Author of the poems was Charles, Duke of Orleans, father of Louis XII.; and this particular copy of his works seems to have been illuminated for Henry the Eighth, when Prince of Wales; for it not only contains numerous initial letters and borders richly coloured and embossed with gold; but in the frontispiece, on the first page, are his father's well known badges of the red and white roses; the former of which are supported by the white hound, and red dragon: with glorified white roses in the margin. The poems are divided into several books of various amatory subjects, as '*Venus et Cupidon,*'—'*Epitres d'Abelard et Eloise,*'—'*Les Demandes d'Amours;*' and the second division of the volume is adorned with a large and beautiful illumination representing the

Duke of Orleans in the Tower, sending despatches to his friends abroad. The Tower, wharf, and river before them, occupy the whole foreground of the painting; and in the back appears the East side of London Bridge, with numerous houses standing upon it, the Chapel of St. Thomas reaching down to the sterlings, and the violent fall of the river through the different arches; whilst, beyond it, rise the spires of several Churches, especially the very high one of old St. Paul's, and the other buildings of London erected along the banks of the Thames. It is, indeed, hardly possible to give you an adequate idea of the spirit and beauty of this view of LONDON BRIDGE IN THE YEAR 1500,

the colouring is so vivid and harmonious: a sky of ultra-marine blue is spread over the whole of the back-ground, against which the distant buildings appear in white, the nearer ones being touched with different shades of brown. You will, however, find a fair copy of this noble painting, engraved by Basire, in Gough's *'History of Pleshy,'* which I have already cited, page 193; and the *same plate* has also been published as an additional illustration to the Rev. T. D. Fosbrooke's *'Encyclopædia of Antiquities,'* London, 1825, volume ii., page 923.

"You must, doubtless, recollect that in November 1501, Arthur, Prince of Wales, and son to King Henry VII., was married to Katherine, daughter of Ferdinand V., King of Spain, and that on Friday, the 12th of that month, the young Princess was conveyed from Lambeth, through London, to witness the pageants which had been prepared by the Citizens to do honour to her nuptials. The whole City was full of triumph and splendour; and Stow, in his *'Annals,'* page 482, says that on London Bridge there was ordained a costly pageant of St. Katherine and St. Ursula, with many virgins. 'I passe ouer,' says Hall, in a very brilliant paragraph, folio, liii a, and using that most powerful oratorical figure called Paralepsis, or Omission, which declares that of which it denies saying any thing:—'I passe ouer,' says the old Chronicler,—'the wyse deuises, the prudent speches, the costly woorkes, the conninge portratures practised and set foorth in vij goodly beautifull pageauntes erected and set vp in diuers places of the Cite. I leaue also the goodly ballades, the swete armony, the musicall instrumentes, which sounded with heavenly noyes on every side of the strete. I omit farther the costly apparel both of goldsmythes woorke and embraudery, the riche jewelles, the massy cheynes, the styrrynge horsses, the beautifull bardes and the glytteryng trappers bothe with belles and spangles of golde. I pretermyt also the ryche apparell of the Pryncesse, the straunge fasshion of the Spanishe nacion, the beauty of the Englishe ladyes, the goodly demeanoure of the young damoselles, the amourous countenaunce of the lusty bachelers. I passe ouer also the fyne engrayned clothes, the costly furres of the Citizens standing on skaffoldes, rayled from Gracechurche to Paules. What should I speake of the oderiferous skarlettes, the fyne veluet, the plesaunt furres, the massye chaynes, which the Mayre of London with the Senate, sitting on horseback, at the Litle Condyte in Chepe, ware on their bodyes, and about their neckes. I will not molest you with rehersyng the ryche arras, the costly tapestry, the fyne clothes bothe of golde and syluer, the curious veluettes, the beautiful sattens, nor the plesaunt sylkes, which did hang in every strete wher she passed, the wyne that ranne continually out of the condytes, the graueling and rayling of the stretes nedeth not to be remembered.' I have given you the whole of this fine, but certainly extended, extract, that you may derive from it some general idea of the pageantry of this festival, concerning which our Bridge historians are, in general, altogether silent.

"The night of Thursday, November 21st, 1504, was rendered memorable by a dreadful Fire, which commenced at the sign of the Pannier, at the Northern end of London Bridge, where six tenements were consumed, 'that could not be quenched.' Fabyan and Holinshed tell us this in their *'Chronicles,'* page 534 and volume II., page 791; adding, that on the 7th of the following month certain other houses were also destroyed, near St. Botolph's Church, in Thames Street. It was, probably, when the repairs occasioned by these conflagrations were completed, that another of those sculptured stones which I lately mentioned, was placed at the Bridge. It measures 10 inches in height, by 13¾ inches broad; and, carved in the same characters, and figures, as the former, are the words *'Anno Domini* 1509.' At the end of the date is an arbitrary mark of a cross charged with a small saltire, which is supposed to have been the old device for Southwark, or the estate of London Bridge: and you know that the Arms used for those places are still Azure, an Annulet, ensigned with a Cross pateé, Or interlaced with a saltire conjoined in base, of the second. I have yet to mention a third sculptured stone, which, it is supposed, records the public benefits conferred by Sir Roger Achiley, Draper, upon the City during his Mayoralty in 1511. This tablet is 11½ inches wide, by 9½ high; and the inscription is '*Anno*'—the City sword—'*Domini*. R. 1514 A;' these letters being the initials of that very eminent Citizen, who was then senior Alderman, representing the Ward of Bridge Within. Such were the other two ANCIENT STONES FOUND AT LONDON BRIDGE IN 1758.

"I have already mentioned to you the situation, and general intent, of the Bridge-House and Yard, and I have now to remark, that they seem, at a very early period, to have been used for the erection of Granaries for the City to preserve Corn, &c. in, during the times of famine and scarcity of provisions. This information we derive from Stow's '*Survey*,' volume ii., page 24; where he adds, that there were also certain public ovens built in the same places, for the baking of such bread-corn as was there laid up, for the relief of the poor Citizens at such seasons. These ovens were ten in number, six of them being very large, and the remainder only half the size; and for their erection, Stow observes, that John Throstone, or Thurston, Citizen and Goldsmith, one of the Sheriffs in 1516, gave, by his testament, the sum of £200.

"We have now arrived at the days of King Henry the Eighth, about the period when Pope Alexander the Sixth sent over the celebrated Polydore Vergil to receive the tribute called Peter-pence, of which he was the last Collector in England. As he was already celebrated for his Poems and his books, '*On the Invention of Things*,' and '*on Prodigies*,' he met with great encouragement in this country; where he not only received several ecclesiastical preferments, being made Archdeacon of Wells, and Prebendary of St. Paul's, but in 1521 he was employed by the King to write a History of England, which he performed in most elegant Latin, and which was first printed at Basil, bearing the date of 1533 for 1534. He left England in 1550, and died at his birth-place, Urbino, in Italy, in 1555. The best edition of this work, entitled '*Polydori Vergilii Urbinatis Historiæ Angliæ*,' which contains a descriptive eulogy on London Bridge, is that of Leyden, 1651, octavo;—though I quote from the Basil folio of 1570,—and if you turn to page 4 of that volume, you will find the passage commencing '*Is fluvius amœnissimus*,' &c. of which I shall attempt to give you a translation. 'This most delightful river'—the Thames,—'rises a little above the road to Winchcomb, whence flowing several ways, it is first increased at Oxford; and the beautiful wonder, having washed the City of London, pours itself into the Gallic Ocean, who welcomes it into the impetuous waves of his seas; from which, twice in the space of twenty-four hours, it flows and returns more than the distance of sixty miles, and is of the greatest national advantage, for, by it, merchandise may easily be returned to the City. In this River there is a stone Bridge, certainly a most wonderful work! for it is erected upon twenty square piers of stone, 60 feet in height, 30 feet in breadth, and distant from each other about 20 feet, united by arches. Upon both sides of the Bridge there are houses erected, so that it might appear not to be a Bridge, but one substantial and uninterrupted street.' The same author, at page 25 of the same '*History,*' says farther of London Bridge:—'This part of the City, which looks Southward, is washed by the River Thames, in which stands the Bridge, as we have said before, leading towards Kent, erected upon 19 arches, and having a series of extensive magnificent houses standing upon both sides of it.'—But I fear you are drowsy, Mr. Barbican; take another draught of the sack, good Master Geoffrey, and then we'll to it again."

"Eh!—What!"—said I, starting up and shaking myself, "drowsy, did you say? Oh no! Heaven defend that I should be drowsy, when a gentleman of your inveterate learning and lungs condescends to give me a lecture! I was, indeed, for a moment thinking of the Chinese devotee who vowed never to sleep at all, and so cut off his eyelids: but I never slept, my ancient; I never winked over your homily, though I would fain have you come to your nineteenthly, lastly, and to conclude. However, whilst we live we must drink, and so here's to your reformation, friend Postern. Now, by St. Thomas of the Bridge!" ejaculated I, as I took up the tankard, "you're either a wizard, Master Barnaby, or else this tankard hath no bottom; and, truly, it's the first time I ever saw wine keep hot on a mahogany table."

"Fancy, Mr. Geoffrey, mere fancy," replied the placid old man with a shrewd smile; "but even as it is, it will serve as a good prelude to some of the more amusing scenes with which the fragments of Bridge history furnish us in the sixteenth century. Indeed, all I have been able to lay before you are but fragments: cyphers which derive their value by connection, and look considerable only by their number.

"It was then in the year 1526, when Cardinal Wolsey was meditating a marriage between King Henry VIII., and the Duchess of Alençon, that his adversaries had anxiously contrived for him to be despatched on an embassy to France, in order to remove him from about the throne, or, at the least, to weaken his power. On July the 26th, the Cardinal left England, and in that extraordinary and entertaining piece of biography, called '*Cavendish's Life of Cardinal Wolsey,*' we have a particular account of the grand procession in which he rode through the City to cross London Bridge, on his road to

Dover. The best edition of this work is, past question, that by Samuel Weller Singer, Esq., 1825, octavo, 2 volumes; in the first of which, at page 86, you may see an engraving of the Cardinal's progress, from a Manuscript in the possession of Francis Douce, Esq., and read the passage I have alluded to in the following words. 'Then marched he forward out of his own house at Westminster, passing all through London, over London Bridge, having before him of gentlemen a great number, three in a rank, in black velvet livery coats, and the most part of them with great chains of gold about their necks. And all his yeomen, with noblemen's and gentlemen's servants following him in French tawny livery coats; having embroidered upon the backs and breasts of the said coats these letters: T. and C., under the Cardinal's hat. His sumpter mules, which were twenty in number and more, with his carts and other carriages of his train, were passed on before, conducted and guarded with a great number of bows and spears. He rode like a Cardinal, very sumptuously, on a mule trapped with crimson velvet upon velvet, and his stirrups of copper and gilt; and his spare mule following him with like apparel. And before him he had his two great crosses of silver, two great pillars of silver, the Great Seal of England, the Cardinal's Hat, and a gentleman that carried his valaunce, otherwise called a cloak-bag; which was made altogether of fine scarlet cloth, embroidered over and over with cloth of gold very richly, having in it a cloak of fine scarlet. Thus passed he through London, and all the way of his journey, having his harbingers passing before to provide lodging for his train.'

"As the Account Rolls of the Bridge estates, in 1533, furnish us with a very good conception of its prosperity and revenues at that period, I shall request you to listen to only a very short abstract of the charges as they appear upon a printed document which I have already quoted. '1533, Thomas Crull and Robert Draper, Wardens of London Bridge, Salary to each of them, £16. 8s. 4d.—£32. 16s. 8d. Winter's Livery to each, £1.—£2. Reward to each, £10.—£20. For horse-keeping to each, £2.—£4. Total to each of them, £29. 8s. 4d. Sum of the whole, £58. 16s. 8d. Rental this year, £840. 9s. 3¼d.'

"I have next to speak of an event occurring on London Bridge, in 1536, which is probably better known, and more often related, than most other portions of its history; I allude, as you will guess, to the anecdote of Edward Osborne leaping into the Thames from the window of one of the Bridge Houses, to rescue his master's daughter. The particulars of this circumstance are given by Stow in his '*Survey*,' volume ii., page 226, in the list of Lords Mayors of London; when having arrived at the year 1559, and the Mayoralty of Sir William Hewet, a Cloth-worker, he farther speaks of him as follows:—'This Mayor was a Merchant, possessed of a great estate, of £6000 per Annum; and was said to have had three sons and one daughter,'—Anne,—'to which daughter this mischance happened, the father then living upon

London Bridge. The maid playing with her out of a window over the River Thames, by chance dropped her in, almost beyond expectation of her being saved. A young gentleman, named Osborne, then Apprentice to Sir William, the father, which Osborne was one of the ancestors of the Duke of Leeds, in a direct line, at this calamitous accident leaped in, and saved the child. In memory of which deliverance, and in gratitude, her father afterwards bestowed her on the said Mr. Osborne, with a very great dowry, whereof the late estate of Sir Thomas Fanshaw, in the Parish of Barking, in Essex, was a part, as the late Duke of Leeds told the Reverend Mr. John Hewyt, from whom I have this relation; and together with that estate in Essex, several other lands in the Parishes of Hartehill, and Wales, in Yorkshire; now in the possession of the said most noble family. All this from the old Duke's mouth to the said Mr. Hewyt. Also that several persons of quality courted the said young lady, and particularly the Earl of Shewsbury; but Sir William was pleased to say '*Osborne saved her, and Osborne should enjoy her.*' The late Duke of Leeds, and the present family, preserve the picture of the said Sir William, in his habit as Lord Mayor, at Kiveton House in Yorkshire, to this day, valuing it at £300.' Pennant, in his collection of anecdotes, called '*Some Account of London,*' which I have already cited, page 322, says, after relating this story, 'I have seen the picture of Osborne's master at Kiveton, the seat of the Duke of Leeds, a half-length on board; his dress is a black gown furred, and red vest and sleeves, a gold chain, and a bonnet.' There is also an engraved portrait of Osborne himself, said to be unique, in a series of wood-cuts in the possession of Sir John St. Aubyn, Bart. They consist of the portraits of forty-three Lord Mayors in the time of Queen Elizabeth, reduced copies of six of which, exclusive, however, of Osborne, one of the most interesting, were, between the years 1794 and 1797, published by Richardson, the print-seller, of Castle-street, and the Strand.

"This gallant action of Osborne has, likewise, been the subject of a graphical record; for there is a small, but rather uncommon, engraving of him leaping from the window, executed for some ephemeral publication, from a drawing by Samuel Wale. As this artist died in 1786, it is of course but little authority as being a representation of the fact, but it is, nevertheless, interesting as giving a portraiture of the dwellings on London Bridge in his time; and with this print I may also mention one designed by the same hand, and engraved by Charles Grignion, of the first Duke of Leeds pointing to a portrait of Hewet's daughter, and relating to King Charles II. the foregoing anecdote of his ancestor. You will find it in William Guthrie's '*Complete History of the Peerage of England,*' having '*vignettes at the conclusion of the history of each family,*' London, 1742, quarto, volume i., page 246."

"Before you pass on to any other event, Mr. Postern," said I, as the old gentleman came to a period, "let *me* say a word or two of the fortunate hero of this anecdote. Sir Edward Osborne was the son of Richard Osborne, of Ashford, in Kent, a person certainly in a most respectable situation in life, if not immediately of gentilitial dignity. He became Sheriff of London in 1575, and Lord Mayor in 1583-84, the 25th of Queen Elizabeth, when he received the honour of Knighthood at Westminster. 'He dwelled,'—says a manuscript in the Heralds' College, to which I have already referred, Pb. No. 22, folio 18 a,—'in Philpot Lane, in Sir William Hewet's house, whose da: and heire he married, and was buried'—in 1591,—'at St. Dennis in fanchurch Streete.' His Armorial Ensigns, according to the same authority, were Quarterly, 1st and 4th. Quarterly, Ermine and Azure, a Cross Or; for Osborne: 2nd. Argent, 2 bars Gules, on a Canton of the second, a Cross of the first; 3rd. Argent, a Chevron Vert, between three annulets Gules. To these we may add the coat of Hewet on an Escutcheon of Pretence, it being Parted per pale, Argent and Sable, a chevron engrailed between three rams' heads erased, horned Or; all counterchanged, within a bordure engrailed Gules, bezantée. On the 15th of August, 1675, Sir Thomas Osborne, the great-grandson of Sir Edward, was raised to the Peerage by the titles of Viscount Latimer, and Baron Kiveton, in the County of York, by Patent from King Charles the Second; on the 27th of June, in the year following, he was created Earl of Danby; on April the 20th 1680, he was advanced to the dignity of Marquess of Caermarthen; and he became First Duke of Leeds on May the 4th, 1694. So much then, Mr. Postern, for an historical and genealogical illustration of the anecdote of the gallant apprentice of London Bridge."

"I regret, Mr. Geoffrey Barbican," recommenced my visitor, after thanking me for having added the above information to his narrative, "I regret that I have so little to lay before you, touching the state and revenues of the Chapel of St. Thomas on London Bridge, at the time of the Dissolution of Monasteries, &c. by the famous act of the 31st year of King Henry VIII.,—1539,—Chapter the 13th. It does not appear that its revenues yielded any considerable profit to the King's Augmentation Office; but yet it certainly must have existed even in the form of a religious establishment so late as that King's reign, because we find it mentioned in several lists of those institutions in London made about that period; though it does not appear in the '*Valor Ecclesiasticus*,' also made by order of the same Monarch. This celebrated and most authentic historical record, was an ecclesiastical survey of England, made in pursuance of an Act of Parliament passed in the 26th of Henry VIII.,—1534,—chapter iii., section x., for the payment of First Fruits, Pensions, &c. to the King. The survey was, of course, executed by Commissioners, and many of the original returns to their enquiries are yet preserved in the First-Fruits and Tenths' Office, in the Court of Exchequer: whilst the '*Valor Ecclesiasticus*' itself has been printed under the direction of the Commissioners of Records, in five volumes folio, London, 1810-1821. The survey for the City of London is contained in the first volume, in which we find London Bridge frequently mentioned as receiving certain reserved rents from the property of other establishments. Thus, on page 388, column ii., in the rents paid to divers persons by St. Bartholomew's Hospital in West Smithfield, 9*s*. are set down as being paid 'to the Master or Keeper of the Bridge of London, out of the corner tenement at the Litill Bayly without Ludgate.' On page 390, column i., Elsyng Spital is stated to pay 33*s*. 4*d*. to the Master of London Bridge, out of the tenements in the Parish of St. Benedict, Grace-Church: and on page 431, column ii., it is recorded that the House of the Carthusians was to pay 9*s*. 4*d*. to the House of London Bridge: though the Chapel of St. Thomas is never mentioned in the valuation of St. Magnus' Rectory, which amounted to £71. 7*s*. 3½*d*.

"I have hardly less regret in stating our absolute want of information relating to the Bridge Chapel at the Dissolution, than I have to speak of that concerning the Common Seal belonging to the officers of London Bridge. Stow tells us, as you may remember, in volume ii., page 25, of his '*Survey*,' that 'at a Common Council, July 14th, Anno 33, Henry VIII.—1540,—it was ordered, that the Seal of the Bridge-House should be changed; because the image of Thomas Becket, sometime Archbishop of Canterbury, was graven therein; and a new Seal to be made, devised by Mr. Hall, to whom the old Seal was delivered. *Note*, this was occasioned by a Proclamation, which commanded the names of the Pope, and Thomas of Becket, to be put out of all books and monuments; which is the reason you shall see them so blotted out in all old Chronicles, Legends, Primers, and Service-books, printed before these times.' Of these erasures, the best account is in Bishop Burnet's '*History of the Reformation of the Church of England*,' London, 1681, folio, volume i., book iii., page 294; where it is asserted that such alterations were but slight, and that the old Mass-books were still in use, until the time of Queen Mary, when the castrated volumes were every where brought in, and destroyed; all Parishes being compelled to furnish themselves with new copies of the Church Offices: and Stow, on page 191 of the second volume of his '*Survey*,' states that in the book marked D of the City Records, the name of St. Thomas was omitted, in pursuance of the King's edict.

"We have thus come down to the times of that most eminent and laborious Antiquary, John Leland, to whose works I have already made some slight illustrative references; and the volume to which I am now about to request your attention, is one of the most rare, and curious, though not the greatest, of his productions. Let me remind you, however, before I mention the work itself, that Leland was, very probably, born in the Parish of St. Michael le Quern, London, in September, about the year 1506; that he was educated at St. Paul's School, in both the Universities, and in France; that he made a literary and an antiquarian tour, of amazing minuteness and research, by virtue of a commission from King Henry VIII., in 1533; and that he died in a state of mental derangement, April the 18th, 1552, having lived about five years under its heaviest pressure. The particular volume of his writings to which I would refer you, as containing much original and curious matter concerning London Bridge, is a Latin poem, written in verses of five feet, yet not strictly in pentameters, entitled '*Kykneion Asma, Cygnea Cantio: A Swan's Song: the Author, John Leland, the Antiquary.*' Of this book there are two editions; a quarto, printed at London in 1545; and a duodecimo, also published here in 1658: though the poem and commentary were again inserted in the 9th volume of Hearne's edition of '*Leland's Itinerary;*' since, as he states in his Preface thereto, they 'ought to be looked upon as part of the Itinerary;' and that they were grown so very rare, that though twice reprinted, they had sold, even so far back as 1712, for forty shillings in auctions. Bishop Nicolson, in his '*English Historical Library,*' page 3, characterises this work as 'a poetical piece of flattery, or a panegyric on King Henry; wherein the author brings his Swan down the River of Thames, from Oxford to Greenwich, describing, as she passes along, all the towns, castles, and other places of note within her view. And the ancient names of these, being sometimes different from what the common herd of writers had usually given, therefore, in his commentary on this Poem, he alphabetically explains his terms, and, by the bye, brings in a great deal of the ancient geography of this island.' The first passage that I shall cite you from this curious volume, is from page 8, verse 213, edition 1658; which commences '*Mox et nobilium domos virorum;*' but as I have, for the first time, done it into English verse, I will repeat you only my paraphrase, rather than the original Latin, observing that I have strictly adhered to all the actual facts.

'More plainly now, as o'er the tide
With swift, but gentle course we glide;
The sight embraces in its ken
Those dwellings of illustrious men,
Where Thames upon his banks descries
The brave, the courteous, and the wise.
But, Oh! that sight too well recalls
The name of one, whose love was shrined
Within his river-seated halls,
Less richly furnish'd than his mind!
For Wisdom had endow'd his heart
With all that gilds mortality;
But he *was* man, and Death's keen dart
Changed so much of him as *could* die,
Into his body's native earth,
To give his soul an heavenly birth.
Yet, whilst we muse on Time's career,

And hail his care-worn kindred here,
The streaming river bears us on
To London's mighty Babylon:
And that vast Bridge, which proudly soars,
Where Thames through nineteen arches roars,
And many a lofty dome on high
It raises towering to the sky.

'There are, whose truth is void of stain,
Who write, in Lion Richard's reign,
That o'er these waves extended stood
A ruder fabric framed of wood:
But when the swift-consuming flames
Destroy'd that bulwark of the Thames,
Rebuilt of stone it rose to view,
Beneath King John its splendours grew,
Whilst London pour'd her wealth around,
The mighty edifice to found;
The lasting monument to raise
To his, to her eternal praise,
Till, rearing up its form sublime,
It stands the glory of all time!

'Yet here we may not longer stay
But shoot the Bridge and dart away,
Though, with resistless fall, the tide
Is dashing on the bulwark's side;
And roaring torrents drown my song
As o'er the surge I drift along.'

"Such then, Mr. Barbican, is my rapid version of those interesting verses contained in the '*Cygnea Cantio;*' and we shall next refer to the famous passage in the Commentary upon it, though, in order to be perfectly explicit, I must previously mention some of the circumstances which caused it to be written.

"John Bale, an intimate friend, and most fervent admirer of Leland, admits, in the Preface attached to his '*New Year's Gift*,' that he was not quite free from the weakness of boasting and vain-glory. An instance of this is to be found in the Commentary on that part of the '*Cygnea Cantio*,' where he is speaking of London Bridge; and you will find the passage referred to in a work to which I have been greatly indebted for these notices of Leland and his writings:—'*The Lives of those eminent Antiquaries John Leland, Thomas Hearne, and Anthony à Wood*,' Oxford, 1772, 8vo., volume i., page 47, where it is also stated, that London Bridge was then the subject of much public attention.

By far the most curious reference to Leland's invective, however, is to be seen in an original Letter written from Hearne to Bagford, and preserved in the Harleian Collection of Manuscripts, No. 5910, Part iv. at the end; whence I shall give it you in all its original simplicity.

'*Oxf. 11th July, 1714.*

"'SIR,

'Tis a pretty while since I received another part of your observations about London, together with some fragments and books, and a copy of Leland's '*Encomia illustrorum virorum.*' The gentleman who lent this copy is a person for whom I have a great honour, and I desire you would return him my service and thanks, altho' I have already done this myself in a letter I writ to him. I should be glad to know whether he be Esq., or what other title I may call him by, if I should have occasion to make public mention of his name. I am extremely obliged to you for your care and trouble, and for your readiness to assist me. As for what Leland says about London Bridge, 'tis in the word *Pontifices* in his Com. upon the '*Cygnea Cantio.*' Some ignorant persons, and particularly one, had found fault with his making only *nineteen arches*, in London Bridge, when, as they alleged, there were *twenty*. Mr. Leland acknowledges there were *twenty cataracts*, or *passages*, but observes that one of them was only a sluice, or Draw-Bridge, and that there were only *nineteen stone arches*. Upon this he takes occasion to animadvert in short upon the aforesaid person, who had been so pert, and promises to take more notice of him afterwards, and at the same time to expose him according to his deserts. He tells us he had survey'd the whole City, and took notes of every thing of consequence in it, and insinuates that he would publish a most full and exact account of its History and Antiquities. 'Twas in this work the remarks of the aforesaid Observator were to be fully considered; but Mr. Leland dying before he could finish either this, or divers other undertakings, his papers came into other hands, and those about London (which were considerable) coming to Mr. Stowe, many of them are published in the Survey of London as Mr. Stowe's own, and others are entirely lost, or, at least, 'tis not at present known who has the possession of them.'

****

'*For Mr. John Bagford, at the
Charter House, London.*'

"After this flourish of trumpets, concerning Leland and London Bridge, I proceed to translate for you the very amusing passage itself, premising only that you will find it on page 133, in that edition of the work which I have already cited.—'*Pontifices: Bridge Masters*, officers who derive their name from the nature of their employment, namely, the constructing of Bridges, or the keeping of them in order; of whom also are the two Governors charged with the care of London Bridge. These officers have an excellent house in the suburb of Southwark, as well as a storehouse containing every thing belonging to their occupation. Rodolphus à Diceto relates in his History, that Peter of Colechurch, a Priest, laid the foundations of a new Bridge: but though it was at first very inconsiderable, Royal and Civic munificence afterwards brought it to be the edifice which it now appears. Upon this subject, Courteous Reader, I am assailed by a whole herd of blustering smatterers, of whom there is one more insignificant than even the rest; a fellow more notorious for loquacity than eloquence, and prodigiously self-conceited; he, truly, shamelessly asserts me to have mistaken in my enumeration of the Arches of London Bridge. And he being, I warrant you, a critic of rare sagacity, plucks up by the roots, rends, and mangles, all by his own mighty authority, an't please you, the pretended oversight on my part. But no more at present; for upon another opportunity I am about to overwhelm his intolerable stupidity, and trample down his arrogance: I merely then reply to him, that one eye-witness is of more value than ten hearsays. I am a Citizen of London, nor do I repent me of my country; and I hope also that she may never have any reason to repent her of her son. To thee then, thou vile companion, Geta,'—the name, you may remember, of a very knavish servant in Terence's *'Phormio,'*—'to thee I say

To none the City better known *can* be,
All London is a monument to me!

Suppose thou wert to try thy skill at searching into that antiquity which involves this wonder of our City? Perchance thou mayest learn something, unless thou art half-ashamed to learn under my tuition. But why should we not now return to the matter of the Bridge? London Bridge then, as it extends itself from North to South, has *twenty cataracts*; but of *arches*, incurvated passages formed of solid stone, there are no more than *nineteen*. That platform, having the figure of a Bridge, made of level wooden planks, capable of being raised or lowered by machines, that an enemy may not find an open passage, I neither can, nor will, nor ought reasonably to call an arch. And yet thou wert greatly in hope of a mighty triumph over me in this matter; but by these words thus easily do I snatch away from thee thine air-built castles.

For though Antæus thou should'st be, or Polyphemus vast,
Or Atlas, on whose shoulders broad the world itself was cast,
To hope to triumph o'er me were but labour spent in vain,
And thou, I deem, wilt wiser be if e'er we meet again.

'And now, get thee hence, thou Geta, and fail not to proclaim to all your pot-companions, your notable discovery of *twenty arches in London Bridge!*'

"I have next, Mr. Barbican, to commend to your notice the account of London Bridge and the Thames, given to us by that most learned man and voluminous writer, Paulus Jovius, Bishop of Nocera, an historian who was born at Como, in Italy, in 1483, and died in 1552. The passage to which I allude, is in his *'Descriptio Britanniæ, Scotiæ, Hyberniæ, et Orchadum,'* Venice, 1548, small quarto, or octavo, page 12 a, beginning *'Sed harum et denique omnium et famam Londinum penitus obscurat;'* but I shall here again take the freedom to anticipate time a little, and give you under one year a translation of Paulus Jovius, and Sir Paul Hentzner's description of the same object; since the former is cited by the latter, and both are excellently well rendered into English in that very curious and rare production of the Strawberry-Hill press, entitled *'A Journey into England, by Paul Hentzner, in the Year M.D.XC.VIII.,'* printed in 1757, octavo; on page 4 of which the passage thus commences. 'On the South is a Bridge of stone, 800 feet in length, of wonderful work; it is supported upon 20 piers of square stone, 60 feet high, and 30 broad, joined by arches of about 20 feet diameter. The whole is covered on each side with houses, so disposed as to have the appearance of a continued street, not at all of a Bridge. Upon this is built a tower, on whose top the heads of such as have been executed for high treason are placed upon iron spikes: we counted above thirty. Paulus Jovius, in his description of the most remarkable towns of England, says, 'All are obscured by London; which, in the estimation of many, is Cæsar's City of the Trinobantes, the capital of all Britain, famous for the commerce of many nations; its houses are elegantly built, its churches fine, its towers strong, and its riches and abundance surprising. The wealth of the world is wafted to it by the Thames, swelled by the tide, and navigable to merchant ships, through a safe and deep channel for 60 miles, from its mouth to the City. Its banks are every where beautified with fine country seats, woods, and farms; below, is the Royal Palace of Greenwich; above, that of Richmond; and between both, on the West of London, rise the noble buildings of Westminster, most remarkable for the Courts of Justice, the Parliament, and St. Peter's Church, enriched with the Royal tombs. At the distance of 20 miles from London, is the Castle of Windsor, a most delightful retreat of the Kings of England, as well as famous for several of their tombs, and for the most renowned ceremonial of the Order of the Garter. This river abounds in swans, swimming in flocks; the sight of them, and their noise, are vastly agreeable to the fleets that meet them in their course. It is joined to the City by a Bridge of stone wonderfully built; is never encreased by any rains, rising only with the tide, and is every where spread with nets, for the taking of salmon and shad.' Thus far Paulus Jovius.'

"I have given you the whole of this passage, because it is curious in itself, most elegantly translated by Lord Orford, and because, in the accounts of ancient London which we derive from the foreigners who have visited it, there is most commonly a delineation of some feature which others have neglected; as I shall have several opportunities of shewing you hereafter. I have only to add at present, that Paul Hentzner was an eminent German Counsellor and traveller, who died in 1623; and whose work, whence I have extracted the foregoing description, is entitled *'Itinerarium Germaniæ, Galliæ, Angliæ, et Italiæ,'* &c. best edition, Nuremberg, 1629, 4to. It was written during a journey which he made through those countries with the young Count Rhediger, with whom he had been at the University of Strasburg; its elegance of language is particularly remarkable, and the part relating to England is generally considered as the best.

"In the fourth year of the reign of King Edward the Sixth,—1550,—those extensive Letters Patent were granted to Southwark, by which the famous Fair was instituted in that Borough, to be held on the 7th, 8th, and 9th of September. The Patent was dated the 20th of April, and the sum of £647. 2s. 1d. was paid for it to the King, by the Mayor and Corporation of London. At the time of this Fair, anciently called 'Our Lady Fair in Southwark,' the Lord Mayor, and Sheriffs, used to ride to St. Magnus' Church after dinner, at two o'clock in the afternoon; the former being vested with his collar of SS., without his hood, and all dressed in their scarlet gowns, lined, without their cloaks. They were attended by the Sword-Bearer wearing his embroidered cap, and carrying 'the Pearl Sword;' and, at the Church, were met by the Aldermen, all of whom, after Evening Prayer, rode over the Bridge in procession, passed through the Fair, and continued either to St. George's Church, Newington Bridge, or to the stones pointing out the City liberties at St. Thomas of Waterings. They then returned over the Bridge, or to the Bridge-House, where a banquet was provided, when the Aldermen took leave of the Lord Mayor, and, all parties being returned home, the Bridge-Masters gave a supper to the Lord Mayor's officers. Stow and his continuators are my authorities for these particulars; see volume ii. of his *'Survey,'* pages 5, 249.

"Our voyage down the stream of history, and of time, has at length conducted us to the reign of Queen Mary, and the year 1554; when her proposed marriage with Philip II., of Spain, alarmed all the nation, lest the Inquisition should be established in England, and the people become the vassals of the Spanish crown. But although the Protestants were the most alarmed at this marriage, when the treaty was made public the complaints and murmurs against it became almost universal; and, finally, produced a conspiracy against Mary, of which it was certainly either the cause, or the pretence. One of the principal leaders of this plot was Sir Thomas Wyat, a gentleman of Kent, who had frequently been Ambassador to Spain, where the cruelty and subtilty of the people had alarmed him for the future fate of his own country. As the insurrection was intended to be general, *his* sphere of action was to be Kent; whilst Sir Peter Carew excited a rising in Cornwall, and the Duke of Suffolk in Warwickshire, as being the centre of the kingdom. From too hasty preparations, however, and too rapidly assembling his forces, the designs of Carew were discovered before they were entirely perfected; one of his accomplices was arrested; and he saved himself only by deserting the enterprise and escaping to France. This unexpected discovery accelerated all the other measures; for, though it was intended to await the arrival of King Philip, to give a colour to the rebellion, Wyat, notwithstanding he was unprepared, marched his few followers to Maidstone, and gave out that he took up arms to preserve England from being invaded. He had little success on his way to London, but the City Trained-bands being, by a manœuvre, induced to desert to him, he arrived with about 4000 men in Southwark, on Saturday, February the 3rd, 1553-54. The prudence of that excellent man, Sir Thomas White, then Lord Mayor, had, however, already prepared for his coming; added to which, the Queen, who remained in Guildhall, appointed Lord William Howard Lieutenant of the City. The Draw-Bridge at London Bridge was then cut down and thrown into the River; the Bridge gates were shut; ramparts and fortifications were raised around them; ordnance was planted to defend them; and the Mayor and Sheriffs, well armed for the conflict, commanded all persons to shut their shops and windows, and to stand ready harnessed at their doors for any event which might occur. As Wyat found there was no opposition made to him in Southwark, some of his soldiers completely sacked the Bishop of Winchester's Palace, and destroyed his extensive library; whilst at the Bridge foot he laid two pieces of ordnance, and dug an extensive trench between the Bridge and his forces. In order to gain an entrance to the Bridge, Sir Thomas brake down the wall of a house adjoining the gate, by which he ascended the leads over the gate, and then coming down into the Porter's lodge, about eleven at night, he found the Porter sleeping, but his wife, with several others, watching over a coal fire. On beholding Wyat, they suddenly started, when he commanded them to be silent, as they loved their lives, and they should have no hurt; and, they timidly yielding to him, he and some others went upon the Bridge to reconnoitre. On the other side of the Draw-Bridge he saw the Lord Admiral, the Lord Mayor, Sir Andrew Judd, and one or two more in consultation, for defence of the Bridge, as we may suppose, by fire or torch light; and after, for some time, carefully observing their deliberations, he returned to his party, unseen and in safety. Having stated to his followers the active measures of the Citizens, they began to consult what course they had better adopt to secure their own success and safety. The advice of some was to return to Greenwich, and crossing the water into Essex, enter London at Aldgate;

others, though they were suspected of treachery, were for going back into Kent to meet some friends and supplies; when, at length, it was concluded that they should march along the Thames towards Kingston, and, crossing the Bridge of that place, enter the City on the West.

"On the night previously to their departure, Monday, the 5th of February, as 'Thomas Menschen, one of the Lieutenant's men of the Tower,'—says Stow, in his '*Annals*,' page 619,—'rowed with a sculler over against the Bishop of Winchester's Palace, there was a water-man of the Tower stayres, desired the sayd Lieutenant to take him in, who did so, which being espied of Wyatt's men, seauen of them with harquebusses called to them to land againe, but they would not, whereupon each man discharged their piece, and killed the sayd Waterman, which foorthwith falling downe dead, the sculler with much paine rowed through the Bridge to the Tower wharfe, with the Lieutenant's man and the dead man in his boat; which thing was no sooner knowne to the Lieutenant, but even the same night, and the next morning, hee bent seauen great pieces of ordnance, cvluerings and demi-canons, full against the foote of the Bridge, and against Southwarke, and the two steeples of Saint Olaues and Saint Mary Oueries, besides all the pieces on the White Tower, one culuering on the Diueling Tower, and three fauconets ouer the Water-gate: which so soone as the inhabitants of Southwarke vnderstood, certaine both men and women came to Wyat in most lamentable wise, saying, 'Sir, wee are all like to bee vtterly vndone, and destroyed for your sake, our houses shall by and by bee throwne downe vpon our heads, to the vtter spoyle of this borrough, with the shot of the Tower, all ready bent and charged towards vs, for the loue of God therefore take pittie vpon vs:' at which wordes hee being partly abashed, stayed a while, and then sayd: 'I pray you my friends bee content a while, and I will soone ease you of this mischiefe, for God forbid that you, or the least here, should be killed, or hurt, in my behalfe.' And so, in most speedie manner, hee marched away.'

"He next proceeded to Kingston, where he devised the means of crossing the river, though the bridge was destroyed; and on the 7th of February he entered London. His unhappy story is no farther connected with that of London Bridge; and it will therefore be sufficient to observe that he was executed on the 11th of April, on Tower-hill, his quarters being set up in several places, and his head on the gibbet at Hay-hill, near Hyde Park; whence, however, it was soon after stolen and carried away. In addition to Stow's '*Annals*,' let me observe that I have also quoted from Holinshed's '*Chronicle*,' volume iii., page 1097.

"Although, as I have fully shewn you, London Bridge was, in general, most intimately connected with the principal executions of the times, yet I do not read that it was rendered remarkable, in the days of Queen Mary, by being made the scene of any of the numerous Protestant martyrdoms, which have eternally blotted her short, but sanguinary reign. There is, however, in Fox, a short anecdote connected with our present subject, which I quote the more readily, as it also bears a reference to the Church of St. Magnus. Upon the death of Pope Julius III., in 1555, Stephen Gardiner, Bishop of Winchester and Lord Chancellor, wrote to Bonner, Bishop of London, to command him, in Queen Mary's name, to order those prayers to be used throughout his diocese, which the Roman Church has appointed during a vacancy in the Papal See. 'Vpon this commandment,'—says John Fox, in his immortal '*Acts and Monuments of Martyrs*;' London, 1610, volume iii., page 1417, column 2,— 'on Wednesday in Easter weeke,'—which, in 1555, was the 17th of April,— 'there were hearses set vp, and diriges sung for the said Julius, in diuers places. At which time it chanced a woman to come into Saint Magnus Church, at the Bridge-foot in London, and there seeing an hearse and other preparation, asked what it meant: and other that stood by, said that it was for the Pope, and that she must pray for him. 'Nay,' quoth she, 'that I will not, for he needeth not my prayer: and seeing he could forgiue vs all our sins, I am sure he is cleane himselfe: therefore I neede not to pray for him.' She was heard speake these words of certaine that stood by: which by and by carried her vnto the cage at London Bridge, and bade her coole her selfe there.' In some of the editions of Fox there is an engraving representing this circumstance, which shews that the Stocks and Cage stood by one of the archways on the Bridge, and in one of the vacant spaces which looked on to the water.

I will but add, that Cages and Stocks were ordered to be set up in every Ward of the City by Sir William Capell, Draper, and Lord Mayor, in 1503.

"I cannot illustrate the year 1556 farther than by an extract from the Account-Rolls of the Bridge-Keepers, taken from the printed document already mentioned; and the general particulars are as follow. '1556. Andrew Woodcock and William Maynard, Bridge-Masters, received for this year's fee, each, £26. 13s. 4d.—£53. 6s. 8d. Horse-keeping, to each, £2.—£4. Livery, each £1.—£2. Total, to each of them, £29. 13s. 4d. Sum of the whole £59. 6s. 8d. Rental, £1069. 11s. 6¼d.'

"The next view which we find representing London Bridge, is supposed to have been taken about this time, or at least *before* the year 1561, since it shews the Cathedral of St. Paul surmounted by its famous spire, which was then destroyed. The picture, itself, is a prospect of London, taken from St. Catherine's, below the Tower, over the gate of which are two turrets, since gone, and behind the Tower is a view of Grace Dieu Abbey in the Minories, with the spires and tops of several other Churches and buildings. Mr. Gough, in his *British Topography*,' volume i., page 748, esteems this to be the oldest view of London extant; and states that it was a painting in the possession of Mr. John Grove, of Richmond, who had it engraven in Nov. 1754, by J. Wood, and dedicated to the Right Honourable Philip, Lord Hardwicke, Lord Chancellor, &c. This view consists of a whole-sheet folio plate, executed in the line-manner; the Bridge is shewn in the distance, having fifteen arches only, with three separate piles of buildings and towers above: and in the front are several ancient vessels and boats. Though Mr. Gough states that the plate has been mislaid, impressions from it are by no means exceedingly rare, excepting when they are in fine preservation, as to colour and margin; and, it should be remarked, that there is also a quarto copy of it in the second number of a singular, but unfinished work, published by Messrs. Boydell and Co. in 1818, entitled '*London before the Great Fire*.' This view of London Bridge is, however, much too distant for *our* purpose; even if its authority were less apocryphal, than it is generally supposed to be.

"The year 1564 was remarkable, inasmuch as it concerned London Bridge, for a severe frost upon the Thames, which began on Thursday, December the 21st, and of which Stow, in his '*Annals*,' page 658, and Holinshed in his '*Chronicle*,' volume iii., page 1208, give you some particulars. It is there stated, that the frost continued to such an extremity, that on New-Year's Eve 'people went ouer and alongst the Thames on the ise from London Bridge to Westminster. Some plaied at the football as boldlie there, as if it had beene on the drie land: diuerse of the Court being then at Westminster, shot dailie at prickes set vpon the Thames; and the people, both men and women, went on the Thames in greater numbers, than in anie street of the Citie of London. On the third daie of January at night, it began to thaw, and on the fift there was no ise to be seene betweene London Bridge and Lambeth, which sudden thaw caused great floods and high waters, that bare downe bridges and houses, and drowned manie people in England: especiallie in Yorkshire, Owes Bridge was borne awaie with others.'

"Stow relates in his '*Survey*,' volume i., page 64, that in April, 1577, the Tower which stood at the Northern end of the Draw-Bridge on London Bridge, was become so decayed as to require taking down and removing. A new building was consequently then commenced, and the heads of the traitors which had formerly stood upon it were re-erected on the Tower over the Gate at the Bridge foot, Southwark; which was subsequently known by the name of TRAITORS' GATE.

"Whilst I am speaking to you of the removal of these heads to the South end of London Bridge,—though it comes a little out of the order of time,—I must not forget to notice the increase of their number, by those of several persons who were executed for not acknowledging King Henry VIII. as Supreme Head of the Church of England. The Act, by which he was so constituted, was passed in the 27th year of his reign,—1535,—and it ordained that all who refused to take the Oath of the King's Ecclesiastical Supremacy, and renounce that of the Pope, whether Clergyman or layman, should be considered as guilty of High Treason. The first who suffered under this Act were several of the Carthusian Monks of the Charter-house,— preceded by their Prior, John Houghton, on Tuesday, May the 4th,—whose heads were then set up on the Bridge: but two of the most eminent and remarkable instances, were those of Bishop Fisher, and Sir Thomas More, to which I shall request your attention whilst I give you a few particulars.

"John Fisher, Bishop of Rochester, was executed on St. Alban's day, Tuesday, the 22nd of June, 1535, about ten in the morning; and his head was to have been erected upon Traitors' Gate the same night, but that it was delayed to be exhibited to Queen Anne Boleyn. We gather these particulars from that most curious little duodecimo, written by Hall, but attributed to Dr. Thomas Baily, entitled '*The Life and Death of that renowned John Fisher, Bishop of Rochester,*' London, 1655; in which also, at page 211, there is the following interesting passage concerning London Bridge. 'The next day after his burying, the head, being parboyled, was pricked upon a pole, and set on high upon London Bridge, among the rest of the holy Carthusians' heads that suffered death lately before him. And here I cannot omit to declare unto you the miraculous sight of this head, which, after it had stood up the space of fourteen dayes upon the Bridge, could not be perceived to wast nor consume: neither for the weather, which then was very hot, neither for the parboyling in hot water, but grew daily fresher and fresher, so that in his life-time he never looked so well; for his cheeks being beautified with a comely red, the face looked as though it had beholden the people passing by, and would have spoken to them, which many took for a miracle, that Almighty God was pleased to shew above the course of Nature, in this preserving the fresh and lively colour in his face, surpassing the colour he had being alive, whereby was noted to the world the innocence and holinesse of this blessed father, that thus innocently was content to lose his head in defence of his Mother, the Holy Catholique Church of Christ. Wherefore the people coming daily to see this strange sight, the passage over the Bridge was so stopped with their going and coming, that almost neither cart nor horse could passe: and, therefore, at the end of fourteen daies, the executioner was commanded to throw downe the head, in the night time, into the River of Thames, and, in the place thereof, was set the head of the most blessed and constant martyr, Sir Thomas More, his companion, and fellow in all his troubles, who suffered his passion'—on Tuesday,—'the 6th of July next following,' about nine o'clock in the morning.

"The circumstances attendant upon the relique of this most eminent man, were but little less singular than the preceding; and Thomas More, his great-grandson, in his very interesting Life of him, printed at London, in octavo, 1726, pages 276, 277, says, 'his head was putt vpon London Bridge, where as trayters' heads are sett vpon poles:—and hauing remained some moneths there, being to be cast into the Thames, because roome should be made for diuerse others, who, in plentiful sorte, suffered martyrdome for the same Supremacie, shortly after it was bought by his daughter Margarett, least,—as she stoutly affirmed before the Councell, being called before them for the same matter—it should be foode for fishes; which she buried where she thought fittest. It was very well to be knowen, as well by the liuelie fauour of him, which was not all this while in anie thing almost diminished; as also by reason of one tooth which he wanted whilst he liued: herein it was to be admired, that the hayres of his head being almost gray, before his martyrdome, they seemed now, as it were, readish or yellow.' The pious daughter of this most celebrated Chancellor, is said to have preserved this relique in a leaden case, and to have ordered its interment, with her own body, in the Roper vault, under a chapel adjoining St. Dunstan's, Canterbury, where it was seen in the year 1715; and again very recently.

"About the time of removing the black and decaying fragments of these heads, there seem to have been several other alterations and improvements effected upon London Bridge; for Stow tells us that, to replace the Tower which was taken down, 'a new foundation was drawn, and Sir John Langley, the Lord Mayor, laid the first stone of another building, in presence of the Sheriffs, and Bridge Masters, on Wednesday, the 28th of August, 1577. In September, 1579, the Tower was finished, being a beautiful and chargeable piece of work, and having all its fabric above the Bridge formed of timber.' This erection, then, formed a second SOUTHWARK GATE AND TOWER.

The structure consisted of four circular turrets, connected by curtains, and surmounted by battlements, containing a great number of transom casements; within which, having their roofs and chimneys rising above the Tower, were several small habitations, whilst beneath, was a broad covered passage; the building itself projecting considerably over each side of the Bridge, the width of the carriage-way, at this part, being about 40 feet. Perhaps, however, the most splendid and curious building which adorned London Bridge at this time, was the famous NONESUCH HOUSE;

so called, because it was constructed in Holland, entirely of wood, and, being brought over in pieces, was erected in this place with wooden pegs only, not a single nail being used in the whole fabric. It stood at some distance beyond the edifice which I last described to you, nearer the City, at the Northern entrance of the Drawbridge; and its situation is even yet pointed out to you, by the 7th and 8th Arches of London Bridge, from the Southwark end, being still called the Draw Lock, and the Nonesuch Lock. On the London side of the Bridge, the Nonesuch House was partly joined to numerous small wooden dwellings, of about 27 feet in depth, which hung over the parapet on each side, leaving, however, a clear space of 20 feet in the centre; though, over all these, its carved gables, cupolas, and gilded vanes, majestically towered. Two Sun-dials, declining East and West, also crowned the top on the South side; on the former of which was painted the old and appropriate admonition of *'Time and Tide stay for no man;*' though these ornaments do not appear to have been erected until the year 1681, in the Mayoralty of Sir Patience Ward. This we learn from Edward Hatton's *'New View of London,'* volume ii., page 791.

"Like most of those other buildings, this celebrated edifice also overhung the East and West sides of the Bridge; and there presented to the Thames two fronts, of scarcely less magnificence than it exhibited to Southwark and the City; the columns, windows, and carving, being similarly splendid; and, thus, equally curious and interesting, was the NONESUCH HOUSE ON LONDON BRIDGE, SEEN FROM THE WATER.

Its Southern front only, however, stood perfectly unconnected with other erections, that being entirely free for about fifty feet before it, and presenting the appearance of a large building projecting beyond the Bridge on either side; having a square tower at each extremity, crowned by short domes, or Kremlin spires, whilst an antiquely-carved gable arose in each centre. The whole of the front, too, was ornamented with a profusion of transom casement windows, with carved wooden galleries before them; and richly sculptured wooden panels and gilded columns were to be found in every part of it. In the centre was an arch, of the width of the Drawbridge, leading over the Bridge; and above it, on the South side, were carved the Arms of St. George, of the City of London, and those of Elizabeth, France and England quarterly, supported by the Lion and Dragon; from which circumstance, only, can we estimate the time when the Nonesuch House was erected."

"Allow me, however, to observe at this place," said I, as Mr. Postern pronounced these last words, "that we have another, and a very curious piece of evidence too, for believing that the Nonesuch House on London Bridge was placed there about this very period: inasmuch as that excellent and indefatigable antiquary, Mr. Sharp, of the most ancient City of Coventry, has discovered, in the manuscript accounts of that place, a memorandum which certainly has reference to this very building; and which, as he has favoured me with a copy, I shall repeat to you.—'1585. Paid to Durram, the paynter, to bye Coulors to paynt the *Vawte* at the Maior's palace, in parte of payment of xxx *s.*, to ley the vawte in oyle Colers substancially, the greate posts in jasper Collur, as *the newe house on London Bridge ys*: all the rayles in stone Coulo^r, the smale pillors in white leade Coulors, the great pillars in perfect greene Coullo^r xiij.*s.* iiij.*d.*'—'The *Vawte*,'—he adds,—'was a balcony, or colonnade, in front of the Mayor's Parlour, supported by large pillars, and having a ballustrade of smaller pillars round the flat-leaded roof of it.' This, Mr. Barnaby, it must be confessed, is very like the features of the Nonesuch House on London Bridge: and it is not at all improbable but what we have here almost the very year of its erection."

"You are right, worthy Mr. Barbican, you are right," said the old Historian of the Bridge; "and I would to Heaven, that no Antiquarian discussion ever demanded a heavier concession. But now let us return for a while from the buildings on London Bridge, to the scattered events which illustrate its history; for I purpose again speaking of its appearance when we arrive at the close of this century, and of then mentioning all the ancient prospects of it, whence I have drawn my descriptions of its edifices.

"It was in 1582 that the idea was first formed of erecting Water-works against the Arches of London Bridge; and of adapting the violence of the torrent, as it rushed through its narrow locks, to some purpose of general utility. As a good account of these original works is given in Stow's '*Annals*,' page 696, and in Holinshed's '*Chronicle*,' volume iii., page 1348, I shall give you the very words, as conveying the best illustration of them. 'This year,'—says Abraham Fleming, Holinshed's continuator,—'Peter Moris, a Dutchman, but a Free-Denizen, having made an engine for that purpose, conueied Thames water in pipes of lead ouer the steeple of St. Magnus Church, at the North end of

London Bridge, and so into diuerse men's houses in Thames Street, New Fish Street, and Grasse-street, vp vnto the North-west corner of Leadenhall,—the highest ground of the Citie of London,—where the waste of the first maine pipe ran first this yeare, one thousand five hundred eightie and two, on Christmasse eeuen; which maine pipe, being since at the charges of the Citie brought vp into a standard there made for that purpose, and diuided there into foure seuerall spouts, ranne foure waies, plentifullie seruing to the vse of the inhabitants neere adioining, that will fetch the same into their houses, and also clensed the chanels of the streets, North towards Bishopsgate, East towards Aldgate, South towards the Bridge, and West towards the Stocks Market. No doubt a great commoditie to that part of the Citie, and would be farre greater, if the said water were mainteined to run continuallie, or at the least at euerie tide some reasonable quantitie, as at the first it did; but since is much aslaked, thorough whose default I know not, sith the engine is sufficient to conueie water plentifullie: which, being well considered by Bernard Randolph, Esquier, Common Sergeant of the Citie of London, he, being aliue, gaue and deliuered to the Company of Fishmongers, in London, a round sum to be imploied towards conducting the Thames water, for the good seruice of the Commonwealth, in conuenient order.' It was probably the success of this engine which occasioned another of four pumps, worked by horses, to be erected at Broken-Wharf, near Queenhithe; invented, as Stow observes in his '*Annals*,' page 769, by Bevis Bulmar, 'a most ingenious gentleman.' It was at first intended to convey the Thames water, by leaden pipes, to the whole Western part of London; but after working it for a short time, it was laid aside, on account of its great charge both to the tenants and the proprietors.

"After this I meet with but little to notice in our Bridge Annals, for several years, excepting, that in 1583, Sir Edward Osborne, being then Lord Mayor, is said to have introduced the custom of drinking to the new Sheriffs, although there is a ludicrous instance of such a ceremony in 1487; and that Stow's '*Annals*' inform us, at page 698, that on the conclusion of the Irish rebellion, James, Earl of Desmond, a principal leader, 'secretly wandering without any succour, being taken in his cabine by one of the Irish, his head was cut off and sent into England, where the same,—as the head of an arch-rebell,—was set on London-Bridge on the thirteene of December.'

"It was on December the 4th, 1586, that the Commissioners appointed to try the unfortunate Mary, Queen of Scots, issued their sentence against her from Richmond; which, on the 6th, was openly read in London, by William Sebright, the Town-Clerk. This proclamation, as Stow relates in his '*Annals*,' page 741, was made with the Serjeants at Arms, and by sound of trumpets, about ten o'clock in the morning, at four places in the City; namely, at the end of Chancery lane; at the Cross in Cheapside; at the corner of Leadenhall;

and also at St. Magnus, London Bridge. It was witnessed by several of the Nobility; the Lord Mayor, and Aldermen, in their scarlet dresses; the City Officers; the principal part of the gentry of London, and the most eminent Citizens habited in velvet with gold chains; all mounted on horseback. The tidings which were thus made known, were received by the people with every kind of rejoicing; 'as manifestly appeared,'—says Stow,—'by ringing of bells, making of bonfires, and singing of psalmes in euery of the streetes and lanes of the Citie.'

"I do not find, in the preparations for defending London against the Spaniards, in 1588, any orders concerning the guarding of the Bridge; though in the scheme for marshalling the City, then drawn up by Edmund York, and printed in volume ii. of Stow's '*Survey*,' page 569, it is observed that the Bridge is to be one of the places watched as a gate of London. This, however, was not the first time that the Citizens had been under military discipline, for Stow relates, in the same volume, page 567, that in September, 1586, when so much danger was anticipated from the conspiracies of the Papists, a series of orders was drawn up for their instruction. In these regulations it was stated, that the gates should be shut every night, and the Portcullises put in order; and that one of the stations of the watch by the water-side, should be by the engine which supplied the City with water, which was at the North-West corner of London Bridge, and almost adjoining to the present site of Fishmongers' Hall. Both these anticipated dangers, however, passed away without any other effect upon London, than that of evincing the courage of the Citizens; and, after the notable defeat of the Armada, eleven of the captured standards were hung upon London-Bridge, towards Southwark, on Monday, September the 9th, the day of the Fair in that place, to the great rejoicing of all who saw them.

"Besides the before-mentioned engines for supplying the City with water, there were, however, also Corn Mills erected near London Bridge, at a very early period in the sixteenth century: for Stow, in volume i. of his '*Survey*,' page 42, observes that they were built on the Thames, about the year 1508. These were, however, not the most ancient machines of that nature erected about this place; for in the year 1197, in an exchange of the Manor of Lambethe for the Manor of Darent, made between Hubert Walter, Archbishop of Canterbury, and the Monks of Rochester, there is a notice of a Mill which 'the aforesaid Monks have without Southwark on the Thames, towards the East, against the Tower of London.' You may see the original instrument in the third volume of Dugdale's '*Monasticon Anglicanum*,' London, 'In the Savoy,' 1673, folio, page 4. It was therefore, upon these precedents, for the better supply of the City, in consequence of the dearth and scarcity of corn which had extended for several miles round London, and also on account of the difficulty of grinding meal for the poor, that in March 1588, the Mayor, Aldermen, and Commonalty, petitioned Queen Elizabeth that they might erect four Corn Mills under two roofs on the Thames, near the Bridge, in parts where they could not occasion any injury. On the 1st of April, therefore, a commission was addressed from the Court, at Greenwich, to Mr. Rokesby, Master of St. Katherine's, Mr. Fanshaw, Master of the Requests, and Mr. Peter Osborn, Remembrancer of the Exchequer, to call before them such persons as should be appointed by the City to manage their cause; some of the principal Officers of the Navy, and certain Masters of the Trinity-House, to consult with them whether the erection of such Mills would be beneficial, or inconvenient; and to consider in what places they should be set up, in order that the Queen might be moved to grant the City's petition. After this consultation, a certificate, dated May the 16th, was returned by all the parties summoned, and the eight Masters and Overseers of the River, and others of the Assistants of the Company of Watermen, that the erecting of such Mills could not in any way be hurtful to the Thames. But as Stow has left on record the Trinity-House Certificate, I shall give it you in the original form and words.

"'Whereas it hath pleased the Lords of Her Majesty's most Honourable Privy Council to direct their letter to the Worshipful Mr. Rookesby, Master of St. Katherine's, Mr. Fanshaw, Mr. Osborn, Commissioners for the building of certain Mills on the South side of Thames upon the starlings above the Bridge: and the Commissioners above-named, have sent for us, the Master and Assistants of the Trinity-House of Deptford-Strand in Kent, that we should make the survey, whether the erecting of those Mills might be prejudicial, or hurtful, to the said River; We whose names are hereunder written, with others, have taken a view of the said place, and do find, as far as we can judge and foresee, it will not be hurtful, nor prejudicial, to the said River in any way. April 4th, 1588.

John Hawkins.	William Holstock.
Richard Gibs, *Master.*	*By me*, Edw. Wilkinson.
By me, Will. Harris.	*By me*, Peter Hills.'
By me, Tho. Andros.	

"In Stow's same work and volume, page 62, he states, that as soon as these Mills were set up, complaint was made to the Court, which produced the foregoing enquiry; and that it was then ordered, that the water should have free course through the arches of the Bridge, and that the parts of the Mills which stood nearest to the stone-work of the edifice, should still be twelve feet distant from any part of it. The intent of these Mills was to provide a remedy for times of dearth, when the common people paid from 4*d.* to 6*d.*

the bushel for grinding their corn, and often, for a considerable time, could not get it ground at all; to supply which they were constrained to buy meal at the meal-sellers' own prices, which they increased at their pleasure.

"We have no very perfect idea left us of the appearance of either the Mills, or the ancient Waterworks erected against London Bridge. Gough, in his *British Topography*,' volume i., page 735, states on the authority of Bagford, that in the Pepysian Library, at Cambridge, there is 'a draught of London Bridge, expressing the Mill at the end;—as also a very old drawing of this Bridge on Fire, on vellum.'"

"Yes, Master Postern," said I, "he does so; and that same 'very old drawing,' is nothing less than a most fair and interesting view of the Western side, as it appeared about the time of Elizabeth, or James I., delicately drawn with a pen, slightly shaded, coloured, and gilded, but all faded by time, and nearly worn out by having been folded in two, from the continual friction of the surfaces. It measures about 24¼ inches, by 4⅜ inches; and is now contained in the portfolio marked '*London and Westminster*, 1. 246, 247. C.' As the Bridge is represented with the Northern end in a perfectly entire state, it must have been drawn anterior to the great conflagration which destroyed it in 1632-33; though it was probably to commemorate that event, that some rude and barbarous hand has disfigured it with those numerous streaks of red, which Bagford and Gough supposed to represent flames. From the minute and careful manner in which it is drawn, it may certainly be esteemed as peculiarly authentic; and, therefore, I proceed to notice to you, that it, very probably, contains a representation of the four Mills, which you have already mentioned as being set up near this place. At the Southern end, below the Traitors' Gate, is a kind of long shed, formed of shingles, or thin boards, erected on three of the sterlings, and covering, as the Citizens proposed, four water wheels, which edifice is, doubtless, intended to represent the ANCIENT CORN MILLS AT LONDON BRIDGE.

"Now, Mr. Barnaby, as this building stands out so far from the Bridge itself as to leave a considerable space between them, though enclosed on all sides, a sort of water-square open at the top, it appears to me an evident proof that it represents those very Mills. In the roof of the building are three sets of windows; and an open stage, or floor, appears a short distance below it. At the North end, also, of this most interesting prospect, against the first sterling, is a high square building, like a tower, having a low wooden gallery in front of it; and a single water-wheel turning beneath it; which are, most probably, intended for the WATERWORKS AND TOWER AT LONDON BRIDGE.

"With regard to the other principal features of the Pepysian view, I shall remark to you only, that the Western side of the Nonesuch House is delineated in the richest and most delicate manner, all its carvings and columns being minutely drawn and touched with gold; whilst a whole grove of heads and quarters raised upon staves stands upon the top of the Traitors' Gate beyond it; and so much then for a brief description of this ancient prospect of London Bridge."

"I am much your debtor, most worthy Master Geoffrey," said Mr. Postern, as I concluded, "I, truly, am greatly your debtor, for these curious notices of a view, at once so rare, so interesting, and so antique: and, touching the Water-house, or Tower, to which you have alluded, although we have not any certain information of the time when it was erected, yet from the circumstance of its appearing with a name in John Norden's very scarce view of London Bridge, which I shall presently mention, it may be supposed to have been set up in the time of Elizabeth, and was, perhaps, as old as the Water-works themselves. In the first edition of Stow's *'Survey,'* by Strype, London, 1720, volume i., book ii., page 174, there is a passage relating to the Water-house, which does not appear either in the original edition of 1598, nor in the last ancient one of 1633; and therefore may be very justly supposed to refer to the wooden building erected *after* the Great Fire; when it will most properly be noticed.

"I must here again refer to the Account-rolls of the Bridge Keepers, for the memoranda of some past years' revenues and expenditure, to inform you that in the year 1562 the rental was £1071. 6s. The salaries, and allowance for horsekeeping, to William Draper and Robert Essington, the Wardens, were the same as those paid in 1556; but the liveries were increased to £3. 6s. 8d. each. The whole amount for the year being £64. In 1565,—says the same authority,—the allowance to each Bridge-Master for fees, livery, &c. was £33.: and the rental of the estates amounted to £1168. 8s. 5½d.: while in 1590, the Bridge rental was £1369. 7s. 2d.; and Robert Aske and James Conneld, the Wardens, paid the two Bridge-Masters for their Year's fee, £50. each, with £3. each for their horses and liveries; making the whole charge £106.

"In the year 1591, a most singular instance of drought occurred in the vicinity of our history, as you may read in Stow's *'Annals,'* page 765, where he states, that on 'Wednesday, the sixth of September, the wind West-and-by-South, as it had beene for the space of two days before, very boysterous, the riuer of Thamis was so voyd of water, by forcing out the fresh and keeping backe the sault, that men in diuers places might goe 200 paces ouer, and then fling a stone to the land. A Collier, on a mare, rode from the North side to the South, and backe againe, on either side of London Bridge, but not without danger of drowning both wayes.'

"The year 1594 was particularly remarkable for a dearth of corn, occasioned, as Stow tells us, it was supposed,—see his *'Annals,'* page 769,—by the English Merchants having exported it too largely. The summer had been extremely wet; for not only much rain fell in May; but, in the following two months, it commonly rained every day, or night, until the 25th of July, the Feast of St. James, and two days after, without intermission. Notwithstanding these floods a fair harvest followed in August, but the price of grain rose to 5s. for a bushel of Rye, whilst Wheat was sold from 6s. to 8s. the bushel, and increased even still higher. In consequence of this, Sir John Spencer, the Lord Mayor, procured it to be ordered, that the several Companies of the City should presently provide themselves with certain proportions of wheat and rye, to be laid up in the public granaries at the Bridge House. In December, however, the greatest part of their stores was yet wanting, and the Lord Mayor, therefore, issued a new order on the 13th of that month, directing that the whole quantity should be laid up in the Bridge-House before the 8th of the ensuing January; since corn was then being imported into England. At this period, Elizabeth was, most probably, preparing those twenty-six vessels, which she despatched, the following year, to Spanish America, under Sir John Hawkins; since, in his capacity of Treasurer of the Navy, he demanded of the Lord Mayor the Bridge-House, granaries, ovens, &c. for the use of the Queen's Navy, and baking biscuits for the fleet. Cecil, Lord Burleigh, who was then Lord Treasurer, being a great patron and protector of the City; to him the Lord Mayor addressed a remonstrance against Sir John Hawkins, stating all the foregoing circumstances, that the City would be deprived of its provision, if he lent the granaries; that the Companies would neglect to lay up the corn they were enjoined to do, and that grain must either be bought from the Badgers, or Meal-sellers, or else the Merchants be discouraged from importing any more. He added also, that the ovens in the Bridge-House were required for baking bread for the City poor, at reduced rates; and he concluded by representing that the Queen had not only granaries about Tower Hill, Whitehall, and Westminster, but that Winchester House was also in her possession, in which large quantities of corn might be deposited. This honest and spirited conduct of the Lord Mayor produced, on the part of Admiral Hawkins, the reply 'that he should hear more to his further dislike,' as well as some letters from the Privy Council in censure of his proceedings. Upon which he again addressed the Lord Treasurer, entreated his favour and protection, and petitioned that the granaries might still be employed for the use of the City, lest the dearth of corn should yet increase, or the poor of London should be distressed for provision: adding that, as the City was then unprovided, his Lordship would hold him excused from resigning the Bridge House, and submitting himself to his good pleasure. With these answers, Hawkins was probably forced to be content, as we meet with no farther correspondence upon this subject.

"With these particulars, then, terminate our annals of London Bridge for the sixteenth century; but before we pass on to the opening of the following one, let me mention to you the views of this edifice which we possess, illustrative of the period we have now arrived at, and give you a general idea of its appearance, whilst it yet remained in its greatest state of splendour.

"One of the most ancient representations of London Bridge is contained in that painting of the procession of King Edward VI. from the Tower, to his Coronation at Westminster, February the 19th, 1547; the original of which was executed to decorate a part of the Great Dining Room of Cowdray Hall, Sussex, the seat of Viscount Montague, where it was destroyed by fire in 1793. An engraving of this interesting picture was, however, published by the Society of Antiquaries in May, 1797; and the Bridge is there represented at the left hand of the engraving, containing four or five buildings erected on the side, in the centre of which rises a spire, perhaps meant for the Chapel of St. Thomas; and at the Southern end appears the gate. This, however, is but an oblique view, and by no means to be depended upon for its accuracy; though, at the same time, the plate contains numerous other interesting features of antiquity, which render it invaluable to all the admirers of London in the olden times. The next most ancient prints of this edifice are those maps and plans of London which include the Bridge; such as that contained in the *'Civitates Orbis Terrarum,'* by George Braun and Francis Hohenberg, volume i., Cologne, 1523, folio, signature A:—the famous map of Radulphus Aggas, published about 1588; and some others of less note, of which you have a tolerably accurate account in Richard Gough's *'British Topography,'* volume i., pages 743-760. These plans, however, although exceedingly interesting, are, from their great extent, less pleasing than a view, as it regards particulars; for the buildings are sometimes so rudely and minutely sketched, as to convey no perfect idea to the minds of such as desire to contemplate old London in all its original quaintness and antique beauty.

"But, perhaps, the rarest and most curious prospect of London Bridge in the reign of Elizabeth, is that engraven by John Norden, of which an impression rests in Mrs. Sutherland's sumptuously-illustrated copy of Lord Clarendon's History of the Rebellion, in 31 volumes imperial folio, comprising 5800 prints and original drawings. Norden, you will recollect, was Surveyor to Henry, Prince of Wales, and died about 1626; and his view of London Bridge was, most probably, published two years before, for, though it is without date, it bears the arms of, and is dedicated to, Sir John Gore, Lord Mayor in 1624. The dedication states, however, that Norden had 'described it in the time of Queene Elizabeth, but that the plate had bene neare these 20 yeares imbezeled and detained by a person till of late vnknowne.' The view of the Bridge is taken from the Eastern side, and the edifice is represented horizontally, from South to North; though it is singularly enough stated to be from East to West: it measures 20½ inches by 10⅝, and is engraved in a border surmounted by the arms and supporters of James I., having its name written upon a scroll. At each end of the print is a naked boy flying; the one bearing a shield with the City Arms, and the other those of the person to whom it is dedicated. With respect to the Bridge itself, it is filled with buildings, in which the Traitors' Gate with the heads, the Nonesuch House, and the Chapel of St. Thomas, are particularly visible; whilst above the houses, at the North end, is seen the top of *'The Water Worke.'* From the windows of several of the houses, buckets are being let down by long ropes into the water, which is seen rushing through the arches with great impetuosity, although there is no fall. On the right appears a boat overturned, its oars floating about, one man drowning, and two others being saved by another boat; whilst two or three more vessels, &c. are seen in different parts of the picture. Along the lower part of the water are engraven the words

'*Tame Isis Flvvius vulgo Temms;*' and below the print are the Dedication, and '*The description of London Bridge,*' in letter-press in three columns, surrounded by a border of metal flowers, and signed John Norden. As this account is, of course, very short, and is chiefly taken from Stow, it gives us but little information; though, perhaps, the concluding paragraphs may not be unworthy of your attention.—'It were superfluous to relate vnto such as well know, and duely do consider the forme and beauty of this famous Bridge: but to intimate it to the apprehension of strangers, I haue deliniated the same to the eye, how it is adorned with sumptuous buildings, and statelie and beautifull houses on either side, inhabited by wealthy Citizens, and furnished with all manner of trades, comparable in it selfe to a little Citie, whose buildings are so artificially contriued, and so firmly combined, as it seemeth more than an ordinary streete, for it is as one continuall vaute or roofe, except certaine voyde places, reserued from buildings, for the retire of passengers from the danger of carres, carts, and droues of cattell, vsually passing that way. This description representeth vnto the eye the true forme of this famous pyle, as neare as arte—in this kinde of deliniation,—can be demonstrated: the number and forme of euery arch, and all the buildings; their true height, breadth, and distance of euery particular, from the East towards the West: as for the other side it like wise appeareth in my prospectiue description of the Citie; the vaults, sellers, and places in the bowels as it were of the same Bridge,—which are many and admirable,—excepted, which arte cannot discouer to the outward view. The situation, arte, and workmanship, in and about the Bridge, are affirmed by obseruing trauailers in all respects to exceede all the Bridges of the world. And, therefore, I thought it fit to represent it to the view of the world, that it may know, that if one part of this Citie be so famous, how much more the whole: which, for state and Christian gouernment, may well challenge place before any Citie in Christendome. And therefore I present vnto you this simple modell of one of the wonders of the world.' So concludes the descriptive eulogy of Master Norden. And now, Sir, having mentioned to you the great rarity of this print of London Bridge, and that if another impression of it were to appear, it would probably produce the respectable price of ten, or fifteen guineas; I must add that there has been an excellent fac-simile of it published by Mr. William Scott, of Great May's Buildings, St. Martin's Lane, for the more moderate sum of 10*s.* 6*d.*, which no genuine lover of London, or London Bridge, should hesitate to procure.

"The last view of this edifice which I shall at present notice to you, is one copied by Thomas Wood, Engraved by J. Pye, and dedicated to Brass Crosby, Esq., Lord Mayor, the Aldermen, and Common Council of the City of London; and it represents the '*South View of the said City and part of Southwarke, as it appeared about the year 1599.*' I am half inclined to believe, however, that this prospect is made up from Hollar's View, published in 1657; as it is certainly taken from the same point. The Bridge rises obliquely on the right hand: at the South end of it appears the Southwark Gate, and beyond it is placed the rich tower which I have already described to you; whilst a series of buildings, forming two distinct groups, with spaces between them, finish the picture, which has the old Church of St. Magnus for its Northern boundary. Even at this period, probably, some of the Arches of London Bridge had received those names by which they were so long afterwards known, though they were first inserted in Stow's '*Survey*,' by Richard Bloome, one of the last of his Continuators before Strype; but his account of these locks I shall speak of in the next century, and I will now only observe that such were the features of LONDON BRIDGE IN THE YEAR 1599.

"'Thanks be praised!' Master Barnaby," said I, as my indefatigable historian arrived at this period, "'thanks be praised!' as the Countryman says in the Play, 'I thought we would never ha' got hither, for we've had a power of crosses upo' the road.' If you do not make the better speed through the next two centuries, mine honest friend, you will scarcely allow me time to conclude your narrative by a brief account of the New Bridge, and the grand ceremonial of its foundation: here's your health, however, and if contributing to one's repose, be a praiseworthy action, why, truly, I'm much your debtor, good Mr. Postern."

"Rest you merry, Sir," replied he of the sack tankard; "I see that you're one of the humourists of Old London; and, methinks, you ought to be somewhat grateful to me for furnishing you with occasion to be witty; but, to speak more seriously, I pray you to recollect that I have conducted you through a period of more than six hundred years, and that too in a history of which the materials are to be sought for, and extracted, from a vast multitude of very opposite sources. And even when we have found them, you know, my good Mr. Barbican, that they resemble those grains of gold which the wandering

Bohemians recover from the sand; of little or no value till collected into a mass, and even then surprising by their insignificance. Surely, he is to be pitied, who becomes the historian of a subject equally ancient, interesting, hopeless, and unknown."

"A very good reason," answered I, "for not becoming one at all, Master Barnaby; Odzooks! do men write your thick folios, only because they know nothing of the matter? But you have no such excuse, for you quote me a dozen authors to tell of one event; and then there's such 'fending and proving' about a handful of years, that where subjects are lacking, 'fore George! you seem to me to create them."

"Well, Sir, well," resumed the mild old man, "your wit becomes you; but as we may never meet again, I would fain pour into your bosom all the little knowledge which I possess upon this point; and so we will pass on to the Chronicles of London Bridge in the seventeenth century.

"The inhuman cruelties which Queen Mary, Bishop Bonner, and others of their faith, practised upon the Protestants, may reasonably be supposed to have so embittered their minds, as to have excited in them no slight feelings of revenge, when, in their turn, they came into power. Indeed, it is difficult to imagine any other cause for the severities which they practised, or for the laws which were enacted to authorise them. The principal of these Statutes, you may remember, were five: one in the 27th of Elizabeth, 1585, chapter ii., entitled *'An Act against Jesuits, Seminary Priests, and other such like disobedient persons;'* and a second passed in her 35th year, 1593, chapter ii., and called *'An Act for restraining Popish Recusants to some certain place of abode.'* Under King James I., were introduced three others strengthening and confirming the former, the first of which was made in the 1st year of his reign, 1604, chapter iv., being *'An Act for the due execution of the Statutes against Jesuits, Seminary Priests, Recusants, &c.'*: and in his third year, 1606, were passed two others, see chapters iv. and v., namely, *'An Act for the better discovering and repressing of Popish Recusants;'* and *'An Act to prevent and avoid dangers which grow by Popish Recusants.'* History, Master Barbican, blushes to record what cruelties were perpetrated under the sanction of those laws; and I should have omitted all notice of them, but that they are so interwoven with several anecdotes of London Bridge. My authority is a work, entitled *'The Catholic Book of Martyrs, or a true British Martyrology commencing with the Reformation;'* by the Right Rev. Richard Challoner, Bishop of Debora; of which the new edition of 1825 is a singularly curious book. He states from Stow, in volume ii., page 9, that in 1578, February 3rd, John Nelson, a Priest, was executed at Tyburn, for denying the Queen's supremacy, and that his head was erected on London Bridge; whilst, on page 74, is a similar relation of another Priest named James Fenn; but I proceed to notice a much more remarkable instance. In the year 1605, Father Henry Garnet, the Principal of the English Jesuits, was taken up and imprisoned in the Tower, for being a party concerned in the famous Gunpowder Plot: after many examinations, he acknowledged that Father Greenway, a Jesuit, had communicated it to him under the seal of confession from Catesby, the Chief of the conspirators. Both the Priests were struck with horror at the design, and vainly endeavoured to prevent its execution. Greenway fled beyond the seas, but Father Garnet was taken, condemned, and executed in St. Paul's Church Yard, on the 3rd of May, the Anniversary of the Invention, or Finding of the Holy Cross by the Empress Helena, the Mother of Constantine. 'His head,' says Bishop Challoner, in his *'Catholic Book of Martyrs,'* volume iii., page ii., 'was fixed on London Bridge, and it was much remarked, that his countenance, which was always venerable, retained, for above twenty days, the same lively colour which it had during life, which drew all London to the spectacle, and was interpreted as a testimony of his innocence; as was also an image of him wonderfully formed on an ear of straw, on which a drop of his blood had fallen.' Dr. Challoner gives his authorities for this narrative at its commencement.

"But to pass from these unhappy subjects to the story of London Bridge, and the River Thames, let me next observe that the year 1608 was remarkable for a great frost near this edifice, of which we have a very curious account in Edmond Howe's *'Continuation of the Abridgement of Stow's English Chronicle,'* London, 1611, duodecimo, page 481; from which take the following extract. 'The 8th of December began a hard frost, and continued vntill the 15th of the same, and then thawed: and the 22nd of December it began againe to freeze violently, so as diuers persons went halfe way ouer the Thames vpon the ice: and the 30th of December, at euery ebbe, many people went quite ouer the Thames in diuers places, and so continued from that day vntill the third of January: the people passed daily betweene London and the Bankside at euery halfe ebbe, for the floud remoued the ice and forced the people daily to tread new paths, except onely betweene Lambeth and the ferry at Westminster, the which, by incessant treading, became very firm and free passage, vntill the great thaw: and from Sunday, the tenth of January, vntill the fifteenth of the same, the frost grew so extreme, as the ice became firme, and remoued not, and then all sorts of men, women, and children, went boldly upon the ice in most parts; some shot at prickes, others bowled and danced, with other variable pastimes; by reason of which concourse of people, there were many that set vp boothes and standings vpon the ice, as fruit-sellers, victuallers, that sold beere and wine, shoomakers, and a barber's tent, &c.' He adds, that all these had fires; that the frost killed all the artichokes in the gardens about London; and that the ice lasted until the afternoon of the 2nd of February, when 'it was quite dissolued and clean gon.' There is a very rare tract, containing an account of this frost, mentioned by Gough in his *'British Topography,'* volume i., page 731, which has a wood-cut representation of it, with London Bridge in the distance: and is entitled

'*Cold doings in London, except it be at the Lottery: with newes out of the Country. A familier talk, between a Countryman and a Citizen, touching this terrible Frost, and the Great Lottery, and the effect of them.*' London, 1608, quarto. I may observe that the Lottery was then drawn at St. Paul's, the prizes were all of plate, the highest being £150, and the price of each ticket was one shilling only. The same year of 1608 was also memorable for two tides flowing at London Bridge, on Sunday, the 19th of February. Edmond Howes records it in his Continuation of Stow's '*Annals,*' page 893, and states that 'when it should haue beene dead low water at London Bridge, quite contrary to course it was then high water; and, presently, it ebbed almost halfe an houre, the quantitie of a foote, and then sodainly it flowed againe almost two foote higher than it did before, and then ebbed againe vntill it came neere the right course, so as the next floud began, in a manner, as it should, and kept his due course in all respects as if there had beene no shifting, nor alteration of tydes. All this happened before twelue of the clocke in the forenoone, the weather being indifferent calme; and the sixt of February, the next yeere following, the Thames againe shifted tydes very strangely.'

"We know not, Mr. Barbican, at what exact period London Bridge was first occupied by shops, but in the Survey of Bridge-lands which I have already repeated to you, it appears very probable that some of the shops in the Bridge Street were actually erected on the Bridge. Houses with distinguishing signs, however, must have been built upon this edifice at a very early period; for the first notice of one, which I can now recollect, is in the fire which brake out at the Pannier, at the North end of the Bridge in 1504; whilst the next is not older than 1619, and occurs in a letter written October the 6th, by George Herbert, the pious author of the '*Temple,*' and printed at the end of Izaak Walton's '*Lives,*' fourth edition, London, 1675, 8vo., page 340. 'I pray, Sir, therefore,'—says this epistle,—'cause this inclosed to be carried to his brother's house,'—Sir Francis Nethersole,—'of his own name, as I think, at the sign of the Pedlar and his Pack on London Bridge, for there he assigns me.' Norden, as I have already shewn you, says that this place was 'furnished with all manner of trades;' and as this is rather a curious, though an unexplored portion of Bridge story, I shall at once lay before you all the information which I have collected upon it, under the present period of time, since it is infinitely too small to be divided into different years. The principal ancient residences of the London Booksellers were, St. Paul's Church Yard, Little Britain, Paternoster Row, and London Bridge; and of books published at the latter place let me first exhibit to you some titles, taken from that vast collection, which John Bagford made for a General History of Printing, preserved with the Harleian Manuscripts in the British Museum. The ensuing are from No. 5921, pages 5 b, 6 a, 7 a, and 9 b,

"'The Merchandises of Popish Priests; or, a Discouery of the Jesuites Trumpery, newly packed in England. Laying open to the world how cunningly they cheate and abuse people with their false, deceitfull, and counterfeit wares. Written in French, by John Chassanion, and truly translated into English. Printed at London, for Henry Gosson, and are to be sold at his Shop on London Bridge. 1629.' Small quarto. Above the imprint is a rude wood-cut of a corded bale, labelled with the words 'A Packe of Popish Trinkets,' and exhibiting a crucifix, rosary, bell, book, taper, a chalice signed with the cross, and an Aspergillum for scattering holy-water.—'The Wise Merchant, or the Peerless Pearl; set forth in some meditations, delivered in two Sermons upon Matth. xiii. 45, 46. By Thomas Calvert. London. Printed by H. Bell, for Charles Tyns, dwelling at the Three Bibles on London Bridge. 1660.' octavo.—'The Seaman's Kalender: By Henry Phillippes, Philo-Nauticus. London. Printed by W. G., for Benjamin Hurlock, and are to be sold at his shop over-against St. Magnus Church, on London Bridge, near Thames Street. 1672.' small quarto.—'England's Grievances, in times of Popery. London. Printed for Joseph Collyer, and Stephen Foster, and are to be sold at the Angel on London Bridge, a little below the Gate, 1679.' small quarto.—'The Saints' Triumph; or, the Glory of Saints with Jesus Christ. Discoursed in a Divine Ejaculation; by J(ohn) B(unyan). Printed by J. Millet for J. Blare, at the looking Glass on London Bridge. 1688.' small quarto. A rude, but characteristical wood-cut portrait of Bunyan is indented in the margin of this title-page. We also find one Hugh Astley living 'at St. Magnus corner,' in 1607; and, in 1677, R. Northcott kept 'the Marriner and Anchor upon Fish-street Hill, near London Bridge.'"

"Whilst you are speaking of the Booksellers and Tradesmen who lived on old London Bridge, Mr. Postern," observed I, as he came to a period, "let me add to your account some other circumstances which, at various times, and from different sources, I have collected illustrative of that subject. The sign of *'the Three Bibles'* seems to have been a very favourite device upon that edifice, and, most probably, continued so until the houses were removed; for we trace it into the eighteenth century, at which time there were two shops so denominated; and one of them also appears to have been famous for the sale of a Patent Medicine, as you will find from the following particulars communicated to me by Mr. John Thomas Smith, Keeper of the Prints and Drawings in the British Museum. 'The Mariner's Jewel; or, a Pocket Companion for the Ingenious. By James Love, Mathematician. The sixth edition, corrected and enlarged. London. Printed for H. and J. Tracy, at the Three Bibles on London Bridge. 1724.' duodecimo. At the end of the volume bearing this title, is an advertisement of a medicine, called *'The Balsam of Chili,'* which is succeeded by the following curious note. 'All persons are desired to beware of a pretended Balsam of Chili, which, for about these seven years last past, hath been sold, and continues to be sold, by Mr. John Stuart, at the *Old Three Bibles*, as he calls his sign, although mine was the sign of the Three Bibles twenty years before his. This pretended Balsam sold by Mr. Stuart, resembles the true Balsam in colour, and is put up in the same bottles; but has been found to differ exceedingly from the true sort by several persons, who, through the carelessness of the buyers intrusted, have gone to the wrong place. Therefore all persons who send, should give strict order to enquire for the name Tracy; for Mr. Stuart's being the very same sign, it is an easy matter to mistake. All other pretended Balsams of Chili, sold elsewhere, are shams and impositions; which may not only be ineffectual, but prove of worse consequence. The right sort is to be had of H. Tracy, at the Three Bibles on London Bridge, at 1*s.* 6*d.* a bottle, where it hath been sold these forty years.' There also appear to have been two Booksellers' shops known by the sign of '*the Looking Glass* on London Bridge;' for you have already mentioned that '*the Life and Death of John Overs*' was printed for T. Harris at such a sign, in 1744; and at the very same time, as well as earlier, one T. Hodges was an extensive publisher of popular books, '*at the Looking Glass on London Bridge over against St. Magnus Church,*' as you will find in the title-pages to a multitude of small volumes of that period. One of the little tracts to which his name appears, is '*The whole Life and merry exploits of bold Robin Hood, Earl of Huntingdon,*' 1737. duodecimo; and we also read the name of S. Crowder and Company, London Bridge, attached to '*The Delightful, Princely, and Entertaining History of the Gentle Craft; adorn'd with Pictures suitable to each story.*' 1760. duodecimo. I could easily, Mr. Postern, increase this list of books published on London Bridge, from the advertisements which continually appeared in the columns of '*The Daily Post,*'—'*The Daily Courant,*' and other Newspapers of the early part of the last century, but I rather wish to point out to you the names and signs of some other persons dwelling in the same place; for it seems to have been occupied by a variety of trades. Thus, in 1722, we have John Body, Silversmith, at the White Horse on London Bridge;—Hotham, Bookseller, at the Black Boy; and E. Herne, Milliner, at the Dolphin and Comb. The shop-bills of these tradesmen, however, from whence we generally derive this kind of information, are so exceedingly rare, that after a very careful search through that extensive collection belonging to the late Miss Banks, now preserved in the Print Room of the British Museum, I have found only *one*! although the Portfolios contain many thousands. But what I there sought for in vain, has been supplied to me from two private sources; for Henry Smedley, Esq., of Whitehall, and Mr. William Upcott, of the London Institution, are in possession of impressions of several, of which they have kindly permitted me to take the following copies.

"1. A copper-plate shop-bill, card size, having the figure of a Roebuck enclosed in a rich architectural square frame, surmounted by a shield of arms, 3 roebucks statant regardant, probably a copy from the sign of the house. On the lower parts of the frame are the date '1714,' and the initials '*W. O.*;'

beneath which is '*William Osborne, Leather seller, at the Roe-buck upon London Bridge.*'

"2. A copper-plate shop-bill, 5 inches by 3½, having, within a rich cartouche frame, a pair of embroidered small-clothes and a glove; beneath is written '*Walter Watkins, Breeches Maker, Leather Seller, and Glover, at the Sign of the Breeches and Glove, on London Bridge, Facing Tooley Street, Sells all sorts Leather Breeches, Leather, and Gloves, Wholesale and Retail, at reasonable rates.*'

"3. The copper-plate head of a bill, '*London 17.., Bought of Churcher and Christie, Leather Sellers and Breeches Makers, at the Lamb and Breeches, London Bridge.*'

"4. Copper-plate shop-bill, 5⅜ inches by 3¾, with the device of a Crown and Anchor, in a square cartouche frame; below which appears '*James Brooke, Stationer, at ye Anchor and Crown, near the Square, on London Bridge, sells all sorts of Books for Accounts, Stampt Paper, and Parchm.^{nts}, variety of Paper Hangings for Rooms, and all sorts of Stationary Wares, Wholesale and Retail, at reasonable rates.*'

"5. A small copper-plate Tobacco-paper, with a coarse and rude engraving of a Negro smoking, and holding a roll of tobacco; above his head a crown, two ships in full sail behind, and the sun issuing from the right hand corner above. In the fore-ground are four smaller Negroes planting and packing tobacco, and beneath is written '*Iohn Winkley, Tobacconist, near ye Bridge, In the Burrough Southwark, London.*'

"6. An elegant ornamental copper-plate shop-bill, 5⅝ inches by 4⅖, with an allegorical design of two figures representing Genius and Prudence, with books and articles of stationery below; and between them, a circle, with the words, '*John Benskin, Stationer, at ye Bible and Star on ye Bridge, London.*'

"7. A copper-plate shop-bill, 6 inches by 3½, with a rich cartouche shield, enclosing three tufts of hair curled and tied; beneath is written '*John Allan, at the Locks of Hair on London Bridge. Sells all sorts of Hair Curled or Uncurled, Bags, Roses, Cauls, Ribbons, Weaving, Sewing Silk, Cards and Blocks. With all goods made use of by Peruke Makers at the Lowest Prices.*'

"One of the most eminent and well-known tradesmen on London Bridge, however, was William Herbert, the Print-seller, and Editor of Joseph Ames's '*Typographical Antiquities*;' who, upon his return from India, having probably acquired a considerable knowledge of the relative situations of the coasts, countries, and rivers, which he had seen and surveyed abroad, thought himself qualified to undertake the occupation of an Engraver, and Publisher, of Maps and Charts. With this view he took a house upon London Bridge, and continued in it, until the houses were taken down in 1757-58; when he removed to Leadenhall Street, and thence to Goulston Square, White-Chapel. The very first night which Mr. Herbert spent in his house on London Bridge, there was a dreadful fire in some part of the metropolis, on the banks of the Thames; which, with several succeeding ones, suggested to him the plan of a floating fire-engine. He proposed it to Captain Hill, of the Royal Exchange Assurance, who told him that 'there must be a fire every now and then for the benefit of the insurance:' Herbert, however, published his proposal in the Gazetteer, and it was soon after adopted. You will find these anecdotes originally printed in the *'Gentleman's Magazine,'* for 1795, volume lxv., part i., page 262; supposed to have been written by Mr. Gough; whence they were incorporated into the Memoirs of Herbert, attached to the Rev. Dr. Dibdin's edition of the *'Typographical Antiquities,'* volume i., London, 1810, quarto, page 76. The pretty copper-plate shop-bill of Master Herbert is yet preserved in a most beautiful state, in the vast collection of the late Miss Banks, to which I have already alluded, volume iii., class, *Print-sellers*. It bears the date of 1749, and represents a country view, surrounded by columns, vases, temples, statues, &c. On the left are two figures, one in the full dress of the time, and the other in a morning dress, exhibiting a portrait to him. Round the whole print is a rich ancient frame, ornamented with flowers, laurel branches, busts, books, instruments, scrolls, and a globe standing in the centre beneath. At the top is an eagle supporting a large robe, or piece of drapery, which hangs half way down, and on which the following words are inscribed in ornamental writing. *'Great variety of English Maps and Prints, plain and colour'd. Also French, and other Foreign Prints, chiefly collected from the works of the most celebrated artists. Sold by William Herbert, at the Golden Globe, under the Piazzas on London Bridge. N. B. Prints neatly framed and glazed for Exportation, Rooms and Staircases fitted up in the modern or Indian taste.'*

"Another source whence we derive much of our information concerning the old shopkeepers of London, and, of course, those of London Bridge, is to be found in that species of unauthorised coin commonly known by the name of Tradesmen's Tokens. For many centuries, you remember, gold and silver money only was regularly current in this kingdom; for, though the earliest inhabitants of Britain probably used copper, there was none coined of an authorised mintage, until the time of Charles II. The silver pence, and even halfpence, which were previously current, were of so minute a size, that, as an eminent author on this subject observes, 'a dozen of them might be in a man's pocket, and yet not be discovered without a good magnifying glass;' and, consequently, they were not adapted to any very extensive circulation. To remedy this, and to provide change for the increase of retail trade, these Tokens were originally issued; being pieces of coin of a low value, to pass between Grocers, Bakers, Vintners, &c., by which the lower classes might have smaller quantities of goods, than they would otherwise be obliged to procure. These Tokens were first issued about the latter end of the reign of Henry VII., or the beginning of the following one, when they were made of lead, tin, latten, and even of leather. In the time of Elizabeth their numbers increased; and, though the silver farthings, coined by James I., and Charles

I., for a while supplied the want of small coins, yet, in the Civil Wars, the private Tokens multiplied to a great excess, and every petty tradesman had his pledges for a halfpenny payable in silver, or its value in goods, to bearer upon demand, at his shop: upon the credit of which it therefore depended, whether they should circulate through one or two streets, a whole town, or to some little distance in the country round. The London Gazettes for July the 25th, 1672, and February the 23rd, 1673, contained advertisements against these Tokens, and of the issuing of the first national copper coinage, referring to 'the Farthing Office in Fen-Church Street,' as the place of exchange. Previously, however, to the issue of a lawful coinage in 1797, the debased state of the copper money gave rise to another general striking of Provincial and Tradesmen's Tokens, which was commenced by the famous Anglesey Penny in 1784. Such, then, is a general view of the nature and history of these coins, and we now proceed to notice those which record for us some particulars of London Bridge.

"The general impresses of these Tokens consisted of the names, residences, initials, and signs of their owners, by whom they were issued and paid; and the quantity used in London was so great, that Sir Robert Cotton supposed, about 1612, that there were 3000 persons who cast leaden Tokens to the amount of £5. annually, upon the average; of which they had not one tenth remaining at the year's end. Notwithstanding this immense quantity, we meet with but few relating to London Bridge; and yet, by the experience and kindness of Edward Hawkins, Esq., Assistant Keeper of the Coins and Medals of the British Museum, and of Mr. M. Young, the well-known Dealer in those articles, I am furnished with a list, and drawings, of most of those which are known to be extant, and of which I shall now give you a description.

"1. *A Brass Token*,—Farthing size: *Obverse*, a Lion rampant, *Legend*,—'JOH. WELDAY. AT. Y^E LYON,'—*Reverse*,—'ON LONDON BRIDGE. I.W. 1657.'

"2. *A Brass, or base copper Token,*—Farthing size: *Obverse*, a Sugar Loaf, *Legend,*—'EDW. MUNS AT THE SUGAR'—*Reverse,*—'LOAF ON LONDON BRIDGE. 1668. HIS HALFEPENNY.'

"3. *A Copper Token,*—Farthing size: *Obverse*, a Bear passant, chained, *Legend,*—'ABRAHAM BROWNE. AT. Y^E'—*Reverse,*—'BRIDG FOOT. SOVTHWARK. HIS HALF PENY.'

"4. *A Brass, or base Copper Token,*—Farthing size: *Obverse*, a Dog, *Legend,*—'JOSEPH BROCKET,'—*Reverse,*—'BRIDGFOOT SOUTHWARK. B.IM.'

"5. *A Copper Token,*—Farthing size: *Obverse*, a Bear passant, chained, *Legend,*—'CORNELIVS. COOK. AT. THE'—*Reverse,*—'BEARE. AT. THE. BRIDG. FOT. C.CA.'

"6. *A Brass Token,*—Farthing size: *Obverse*, a Lion rampant, *Legend,*—'AT. THE. WHIT. LYON,'—*Reverse,*—'NEIR LONDON BRIDGE. C.T.A.'

"7. *A Copper Token,*—Farthing size: *Obverse*, a Sugar loaf, *Legend,*—'HENRY. PHILLIPS, AT.'—*Reverse,*—'BRIDG. FOOT. SOVTHWARK. P.H.S.'

"Such, then, are some specimens of the Tradesmen's Tokens current on London Bridge; and though they are sufficiently rude in their workmanship, and base in their metal, yet with some collectors, they are of a far greater degree of rarity, and of value too, than the handsomest modern silver coin you could present them with. You will observe, however, that I have noticed those Tokens only, on which the Bridge is actually mentioned; but an extensive list of such as were issued in Southwark, will be found in Messrs. Manning's and Bray's '*History of Surrey*,' already referred to, volume iii., Appendix, pages cxi-cxv. Let me add too, that my authorities for these historical notices of coins, have been '*An Essay on Medals*,' by John Pinkerton, London, 1789, octavo, volume i.; and '*Annals of the Coinage of Britain*,' by the Rev. Rogers Ruding, London, 1819, octavo, volume iii., pages 127, 319, 324, volume iv., page 61. I must not, however, conclude these particulars of the numismatic reliques of London Bridge, without observing to you that there are some Medalets also extant, commemorative of its buildings. Of these coins we find a list in James Conder's elegant volumes, entitled '*An Arrangement of Provincial Coins, Tokens, and Medalets, issued in Great Britain, Ireland, and the Colonies, within the last twenty years, from the farthing to the penny size.*' Ipswich, 1798, octavo. Medalets, you know, Mr. Postern, are of that description of coins which were struck by the Romans, and used for scattering to the people upon solemn occasions: and those of which I am now speaking are of the class distinguished by bearing the representation of public buildings. In volume i., pages 72 and 73, of Mr. Conder's work, are mentioned the following Medalets of London Bridge, of the penny size, executed by P. Kempson.

No. 40. A Bronzed or Copper Medalet: *Obverse*, a view of a Bridge, *Legend*,— 'LONDON BRIDGE THE FIRST OF STONE, COMPLEATED 1209.' *Legend on the Exergue*,—'THE HOUSES ON THE BRIDGE TAKEN DOWN, AND THE BRIDGE REPAIR'D, 1758.'—*Reverse*, a figure of Britannia with spear and shield, seated on a rock, holding an olive-branch;—*Legend*, indented on a raised circle round the field, 'BRITISH PENNY TOKEN.' On the Exergue a cypher 'P.K.— MDCCXCVII.' *Legend on the edge*,—'I PROMISE TO PAY ON DEMAND THE BEARER ONE PENNY.'

No. 47. A Bronzed or Copper Medalet: *Obverse*, an ancient gateway,— *Legend*,—'BRIDGE GATE AS REBUILT 1728.'—*Legend on the Exergue*, 'TAKEN DOWN, 1766.' *Reverse*, an upright figure of Justice. Legend and date on the rim as before.

There were also two Medalets of the halfpenny size, executed by P. Skidmore, of Coppice Row, Clerkenwell, which are likewise mentioned by Conder, in volume i., pages 103, 106.

No. 267. A Bronzed or Copper Medalet: *Obverse*, a view of a church,—*Legend*,—'ST. MAGNUS LONDON BRIDGE. 1676.'—*Reverse*, a cypher, 'P.S.Cº.,' in a circle, *Legend*,—'DEDICATED TO COLLECTORS OF MEDALS AND COINS.'

No. 300. A Bronzed or Copper Medalet: *Obverse*, an ancient gateway,—*Legend*,—'BRIDGE GATE, BT. 1728:' within the Archway the name of 'Jacobs.'—*Reverse*, as before.

"I am inclined to think, Mr. Barnaby Postern, that there have been several traditional mistakes perpetuated, as to persons supposed to have dwelt upon London Bridge; for, upon investigating the subject, I can find no authority to support my recording them as inhabitants of that part of London. The author of an exceedingly amusing work, entitled '*Wine and Walnuts*,' London, 1823, octavo, in which are contained many witty scenes and curious conversations of eminent characters in the last century, has entitled the seventh chapter of his second volume '*Old London Bridge; with portraits of some of its inhabitants.*' In this article, on page 81, we are told that 'Master John Bunyan, one of your heaven-born geniuses, resided, for some time, upon London Bridge;' though I cannot discover any such circumstance in either of the lives of that good man now extant, though he certainly preached, for some time, at a Chapel in Southwark. Perhaps, however, this assertion may be explained by the following passage from the Preface affixed to the Index attached to the first volume of '*The Labours of that eminent servant of Christ Mr. John Bunyan*,' London, 1692, folio. It is there stated, that in 1688 'he published six books, being the time of K. James 2d's. liberty of conscience, and was seized with a sweating distemper, of which, after his some weeks going about, proved his death, at his very loving friend's Mr. Strudwick's, a Grocer,'—at the sign of the Star,—'at *Holborn Bridge*, London, on August 31st.' It is also recorded on the same page of '*Wine and Walnuts*,' that 'Master Abel, the great importer of wines, was another of the marvels of old London Bridge; he set up a sign, Thank God I am *Abel*, quoth the wag, and had, in front of his house, the sign of a bell.' As I have also heard the same particulars repeated elsewhere, it is possible that there may be some traditionary authority for them; but upon carefully reading over the very rare tracts relating to Mr. Alderman Abel, preserved in the British Museum, I find nothing concerning his residence on London Bridge, and I should rather imagine, from their statements, that he lived at his Ticket, or Patent Office, situate in Aldermary Church-Yard. The same chapter, however, contains some authentic notices of Artists who really did live upon this venerable edifice. Of these, one of the most eminent was Hans Holbein, the great painter of the Court of Henry VIII.; but though we can hardly suppose that he inhabited the Nonesuch House, yet his actual residence here is certified by Lord Orford, in his '*Anecdotes of Painting*,' vide his '*Works*,' edit. London, 1798-1822, quarto, volume iii., page 72, note. 'The father of the Lord Treasurer Oxford'—says the noble author in that place,—'passing over London Bridge, was caught in a shower; and stepping into a goldsmith's shop for shelter, he found there a picture of Holbein,—who had lived in that house,—and his family. He offered the goldsmith £100. for it, who consented to let him have it, but desired first to shew it to some persons. Immediately after, happened the fire of London, and the picture was destroyed.' Another famous Artist of London Bridge, who is mentioned in both the works which I last cited, was Peter Monamy; so excellent a painter of marine subjects, as to be considered but little inferior to Vandevelde himself. Lord Orford says of him, at page 421, that he 'received his first rudiments of drawing from a sign and house-painter on London Bridge;'—and that 'the shallow waves, that rolled under his window, taught young Monamy what his master could not teach him, and fitted him to paint the turbulence of the ocean.' This artist died at Westminster in 1749. We are also informed, by Edward Edwards, in his *'Continuation of Walpole's Anecdotes of Painting,'* London, 1808, quarto, page 214, that Dominic Serres, the Marine Painter, who died in 1793, also once kept a shop upon London Bridge. To these celebrated men, the author of *'Wine and Walnuts'* adds Jack Laguerre, the Engraver, 'a great humourist, wit, singer, player, caricaturist, mimic, and a good scene-painter,' son to that Louis, who painted stair-cases and saloons, where, as Pope says, 'sprawl the saints of Verrio and Laguerre.' His residence, according to our lively author, who states that he received his information from 'old Dr. Monsey and others,' was on the first floor of the dwelling of a waggish bookseller, and author of all-work, named Crispin Tucker; the owner of half-a-shop on the East side, under the Southern gate. The artist's *studio* was, chiefly, in a bow-windowed back room, which projected over the Thames, and trembled at every half-ebb tide; in which Hogarth had resided in his early life, when he engraved for old John Bowles, of the Black Horse in Cornhill. It resembled, we are told, on page 135 of the work and volume which I have already quoted, one of the alchemist's laboratories from the pencil of the elder Teniers. It was 'a complete smoke-stained confusionary, with a German-stove, crucibles, pipkins, nests of drawers, with rings of twine to pull them out; here a box of asphaltum, there glass-stoppered bottles, varnishes, dabbers, gravers, etching-tools, walls of wax, obsolete copper-plates, many engraved on both sides, caricatures, and poetry scribbled over the walls; a pallet hung up as an heir-loom, the colours dry upon it, hard as stone; an easel; all the multifarious *arcanalia* of engraving, and, lastly, a Printing-press!' This curious picture is also from the information of Dr. Monsey, but I cannot produce you any other authority for its truth; and I shall likewise, therefore, leave you to read, and judge for yourself, the amusing account of Dean Swift's and Pope's visits and conversations with Crispin Tucker, of London Bridge, in chapters viii. and ix. of the work I have referred to.

"It was, however, not only the ordinary buildings in the Bridge-street, which were formerly occupied as shops and warehouses, but even the Chapel of St. Thomas, which, in its later years, was called Chapel-House, and the Nonesuch-House, were used for similar purposes before they were taken down. Mr. John Nichols, in his '*Literary Anecdotes*,' tells us, volume vi., part i., page 402, note, on the authority of Dr. Ducarel, that 'the house over the Chapel belonged to Mr. Baldwin, Haberdasher, who was born there; and when, at seventy-one, he was ordered to go to Chislehurst for a change of air, he could not sleep in the country, for want of the noise,'—the roaring and rushing of the tide beneath the Bridge,—'he had been always used to hear.' My good friend, Mr. J. T. Smith, too, in his very interesting volume of the '*Ancient Topography of London*,' which you have already quoted, page 26, has also the following observations concerning the modern use of this Chapel. 'By the *Morning Advertiser*,' says he, 'for April 26th, 1798, it appears that Aldermen Gill and Wright had been in partnership upwards of fifty years; and that their shop stood on the centre of London Bridge, and their warehouse for paper was directly under it, which was a Chapel for divine service, in one of the old arches; and, long within legal memory, the service was performed every sabbath and Saint's day. Although the floor was always, at high-water mark, from ten to twelve feet under the surface; yet such was the excellency of the materials and the masonry, that not the least damp, or leak, ever happened, and the paper was kept as safe and dry as it would have been in a garret.' In that '*Survey of the Cities of London and Westminster*,' printed in 1734, and purporting to have been compiled by Robert Seymour, Esq., but which was in reality the production of the Rev. John Motley, the famous collector of Joe Miller's Jests, it is stated in volume i., book i., page 48, that at that time one side of the Nonesuch House was inhabited by Mr. Bray, a Stationer, and the other by Mr. West, a Dry-Salter. So much then, Mr. Barnaby, for the few anecdotes which I have been able to collect of the dwellings and inhabitants of old London Bridge."

"And a very fair Memorial too, Master Geoffrey," answered the Antiquary, "especially when we consider the extreme difficulty of procuring such information as this is: but, to carry on our history, I must now enter upon a less amusing subject; the summary of the Bridge Accounts for the years 1624 and 1625, taken from the printed sheet which I have so often cited. '1624. To John Langley, and Richard Foxe, Bridge-Masters, half a year's fee at our Lady-day, £50: and for the other half year augmented by order of the Court of Aldermen, £66. 8*s*. 4*d*., and for their Liveries, &c. £6. Total £122. 8*s*. 4*d*. Rental £2054. 4*s*. 2*d*.—1625. To the said Bridge-Masters, £133. 6*s*. 8*d*. Liveries, &c. £6. Total to each of them, £69. 3*s*. 4*d*. Rental, £2054. 4*s*. 2*d*.' These notices of the prosperity of this edifice, conduct us down to the time when so much of its glory was lost in devastating flames and mouldering ruins.

"The year 1632-33 must be ever memorable in the history of London Bridge: for scarcely in the awful conflagration which consumed almost the whole City, did our brave old edifice suffer so severely. And now, Mr. Barbican, you must forgive me if I be a little prolix in describing that desolating fire, since it not only destroyed more than a third part of the Bridge Houses, but, at one time, its ravages were feared even in the City itself. I shall commence my account then by reminding you that Richard Bloome, one of Stow's continuators, on page 61 of his '*Survey*,' thus speaks of the calamity. 'On the 13th day of February, between eleven and twelve at night, there happened in the house of one Briggs, a Needle-maker near St. Magnus Church, at the North end of the Bridge, by the carelessness of a Maid-Servant setting a tub of hot sea-coal ashes under a pair of stairs, a sad and lamentable fire, which consumed all the buildings before eight of the clock the next morning, from the North end of the Bridge to the first vacancy on both sides, containing forty-two houses; water then being very scarce, the Thames being almost frozen over. Beneath, in the vaults and cellars, the fire remained glowing and burning a whole week after.'

"There are not wanting several general views of London taken before this fire, by which we are made acquainted with those extensive piles of dwellings it destroyed; several of which I have already mentioned to you. Another also, which is most excellent and rare, is that entitled in Latin, '*London the most flourishing City of Britain, and the most celebrated emporium of the whole world.*' It was engraven by John Visscher in 1616, and published in Holland, 'by Jud. Hondius at the sign of the Watchful Dog;' a four sheet print measuring 7 feet 1½ inch by 1 foot 4¾ inches, with an English description beneath it. 'A Capital View,' adds Gough, in his '*British Topography*,' already cited, volume i., page 749, 'the plates destroyed in Holland about twenty years ago. T. Davies sold the only impression of it to the King for ten guineas.' There is, likewise, a variation of this view, without a date, having eight Latin verses at either corner, with the name of 'Ludovicus Hondius Lusitt.' It is, says Mr. J. T. Smith, in his '*Ancient Topography of London*,' page 25, 'extremely well executed, and exhibits a wind-mill standing in the Strand, very near where the New Church is now erected; and another above the Water-works at Queenhithe.' He considers it as earlier than the productions of Hollar, from the circumstance that the Palace of Whitehall appears in its original state, before the Banquetting House and York and Somerset Water-gates were erected by Inigo Jones. It is also shewn to be a view of the time of King James I., by a royal procession being introduced on the water, in which the royal barge is surmounted by the thistle. London Bridge forms a very large and important feature in this engraving, and I have been informed, that the edifice alone was copied in quarto, for the work entitled '*London before the Great Fire;*' but as that publication stopped with the second number, it was never exhibited for sale.

Of the very curious print by Visscher, however,—and I must not forget to observe that a fine impression of it is in the possession of John Dent, Esq.— there was also an imitation of the same size, but somewhat inferior, called, from the place where it was engraven, 'the Venetian copy of Visscher's View.' It is, like its prototype, entitled in Latin, *London the most flourishing City in Britain*,' &c. to which is added, *'Printed in Venice, by Nicolo Misserini, 1629, Franco Valegio fecit:'* it also contains a Latin dedication, and a description in Italian. There is an impression, probably, of this latter print, preserved in volume xiii. of the famous illustrated Pennant's London, bequeathed by the late Charles Crowle, Esq. to the British Museum; but all the inscriptions have been cruelly cut away, and the print itself doubled in numerous folds to make it fit to the size of the volume! This engraving, however, bears the name of Rombout Vanden Hoege, and shews us, with great minuteness, on rather a large scale, the GROUP OF BUILDINGS ON LONDON BRIDGE, BURNED DOWN IN 1632-33,

which extended to the first opening, and which, from the very appearance which they present, must have contained a considerable number of inhabitants; but of the fire itself, and of all the distressing events attending it,

I am about to give you a very particular and interesting account, from the pen of an eye-witness of the conflagration. This narrative is contained in a coarse paper Manuscript volume, of a small quarto size, written in the print-hand of the 17th century, with some lines of faded red ink and chalk interspersed. The volume contains 517 pages in all, and is entitled '*A Record of the Mercies of God; or, a Thankefull Remembrance;*' it being a collection, or journal, of remarkable providences and reflections, made by one Nehemiah Wallington, a Puritan Citizen and Turner, who lived in Little East-cheap, and who was evidently a friend of Burton and Bastwick, he having been several times examined concerning them before the Court of Star-Chamber. In this most singular record then, at pages 479-488, is an article entitled '*Of the great fire vpon the Bridge;*' preceded by Mottoes from Psalms lxvi. 5; lxxi. 17; cxi. 2; Isaiah xlv. 7; and Amos iii. 6; which runs in the following terms.

"'1633. It is the bounden dutie of vs all that haue beene the beholders of the wonderfull workes of the Lord our God, his mercyes and iudgements shewed heretofore; and now of late of a fearefull fire, wee should not forgett itt ourselues, and we should declare it to all others, euen to ye generations to come.—On the xi. day of February, (being Monday, 1633) began, by God's iust hand, a fearefull fire in the house of one Mr. Iohn Brigges, neere tenn of the clocke att night, it burnt down his house and the next house, with all the goods that were in them; and, as I heere, that Briggs, his wife, and childe, escaped with their liues very hardly, hauing nothing on their bodies but their shurt and smoke: and the fire burnt so fearcely, that itt could not be quenched till it had burnt downe all the houses on both sides of the way, from S. Magnes Church to the first open place. And allthough there was water enough very neere, yet they could not safely come at it, but all the conduittes neere were opened, and the pipes that carried watter through the streets were cutt open, and the watter swept down with broomes with helpe enough; but it was the will of God it should not preuaile. And the hand of God was the more seene in this, in as much as no meanes would prosper. For the 3 Engines, which are such excellent things, that nothing that euer was deuised could do so much good, yet none of these did prosper, for they were all broken, and the tide was verie low that they could get no watter; and the pipes that were cutt yeilded but littel watter. Some ladders were broke to the hurt of many, for some had their legges broke, some had their armes, and some their ribbes broken, and many lost their liues. This fire burnt fiercely all night, and part of the next day (for my man was there about twelue a cloke, and he said he did see the fardest house on fire) till all was burnt and pulled downe to the ground. Yet the timber, and wood, and coales in the sellers, could not be quenched all that weeke, till the Tuesday following, in the afternoone, the xix of February, for I was there then my selfe, and had a liue cole of fire in my hand, and burnt my finger with it. Notwithstanding there were as many night and day as could labour one by another to carry away timber, and brickes, and tiles, and rubbish cast downe into the liters. So that on Wensday the Bridge was cleared that passengers might goe ouer.'

"'At the begining of this fire, as I lay in my bed and heard ye sweeping of the channels and crying for water, water, I arose about one of the cloke, and looked downe Fish-street-hill, and did behold such a fearfull and dreadfull fire vaunting it selfe ouer the tops of houses, like a Captaine florishing and displaying his banner; and seeing so much meanes and so little good, it did make me thinke of that fire which the Lord threateneth against Ierusalem, for the breach of his Sabbath day. He saith thus: 'But if ye will not here me to sanctifie the Sabbath day, and to beare no burden, nor to goe through ye gates of Ierusalem in the Sabbath day, then will I kindle a fire in ye gates there, and it shall deuoure the palaces of Ierusalem, and it shall not be quenched.' Iere. xvii. 27.

"'I did heere that on the other side of ye Bridge, the Bruers brought abundance of watter in vessells on their draies, which did, with the blissing of God, much good; and this mircie of God I thought on, that there was but littel wind; for had ye wind bin as high as it was a weeke before, I thinke it would have indangered ye most part of the Citie; for in Thames Street there is much pitch, tarre, rosen, and oyle, in their houses: Therefore, as God remembers mercy in iustice, let us remember thankefullnes in sorrow. 'Therefore will I praise the Lord with my whole heart, and I will speake of all thy marvellous workes;' 'for it is of the Lord's mercy that wee are not consumed,' Lament. iii., 22. The Names, and Trades, and number of the Houses burnt vpon the Bridg, heere you may see vnder nethe.—

"'1. Mr. William Vyner,—*Haberdasher of smal Wares*. 2. Mr. Iohn Broome,—*Hosier.* 3. Mr. Arther Lee,—*Haberdasher of smal Wares.* 4. M^ris. Iohane Broome,—*Hosier.* 5. Mr. Ralph Panne,—*Shewmaker.* 6. Mr. Abraham Marten,—*Haberdasher of Hattes.* 7. Mr. Ieremiah Champney,—*Hosier.* 8. Mr. John Terrill,—*Silke man.* 9. Mr. Ellis Midmore,—*Milliner.* 10. Mr. Francis Finch,—*Hosier.* 11. Mr. Andrewe Bouth,—*Haberdasher of small Wares.* 12. Mr. Samuel Petty,—*Glouer.* 13. Mr. Valentin Beale,—*Mercer.* 14. M^ris. ——— Chambers, *Senior.* 15. Mr. Ieremiah Chamley,—*Silke man.* 16. The Blew Bore,—*empti.* 17. Mr. Iohn Gouer,—*Stiller of Strong Waters.* 18. Mr. Iohn Wilding, *Iunior,*—*Girdler.* 19. Mr. Daniel Conney,—*Silke man.* 20. Mr. Stephen Beale,—*Lyning Draper.* 21. M^ris. Iane Langham,—*Mercer.* 22. Mr. Iames Dunkin, *Wolling Draper.* 23. Mr. Matthew Harding,—*Salter.* 24. Mr. Abraham Chambers,—*Haberdasher of smal Wares.* 25. and 26.—Mr. Lyne Daniel,—*Haberdasher of Hattes, a double house.* 27. M^ris. ——— Brookes,—*Glouer.* 28. Mr. ——— Couerley,—*Hosier.* 29. Mr. Iohn Dransfielde,—*Grocer.* 30. Mr. Newman, *emptie.* 31. Mr. Edward Warnett, and 32. Mr. Samuel Wood, *partoners,*—*Haberdashers of Small Wares.* 33. Mr. Iohn Greene,—*Haberdasher of Hattes.* 34. Mr. Heugh Powel,—*Haberdasher of Hattes.* 35. Mr. Samuel

Armitage,—*Haberdasher of Small Wares.* 36. Mr. Iohn Sherley,—*Haberdasher of Small Wares.* 37. Mr. John Lawrymore,—*Grocer.* 38. Mr. Timothy Drake,—*Woolling Draper.* 39. Mr. Iohn Brigges,—*Needle-maker.*'—at whose house the fire commenced,—'40. Mr. Richard Shelbuery,—*Scriuener.* 41. Mr. Edward Greene,—*Hosier.* 42. Mr. —— Hazard,—*the Curate,* and 43. Mr. —— Hewlett,—*the Clarke,—at S. Magnus Cloyster.*'

"This narrative has, however, already appeared in print in the *'Gentleman's Magazine'* for November, 1824, pages 387, 388; the extract having been furnished by the possessor of the volume, Mr. William Upcott, of the London Institution.

"Of the ground-plot of London Bridge, after the damage done by this fire, there is yet extant a very curious survey, preserved under the care of Mr. Smith, in the British Museum. It consists of an unpublished drawing on parchment, measuring four feet five inches in length, by ten inches in breadth: and it, perhaps, belonged to Sir Hans Sloane, as it is kept with some other fragmenta of his property. In this drawing, the piers are represented in a tint of yellow, placed upon sterlings of Indian ink; and it was executed, as I suppose, soon after this fatal conflagration, since there is a note written in an ancient hand attached to the seventh pier from the City end, stating that *'the Fire burnt to the prickt line,'* which is drawn from it; and which accords with all the subsequent views taken of the platform, and houses on the Bridge.

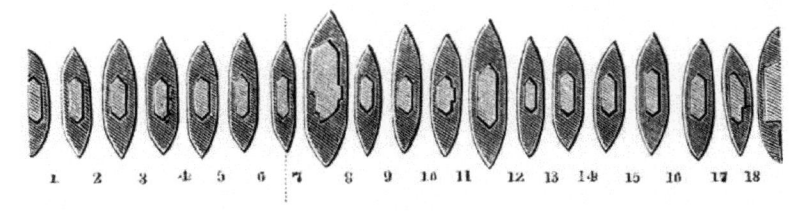

"I am next to speak," continued my unwearied Historian, "of the manner in which this terrible destruction of London Bridge was repaired: and concerning this we are informed by Richard Bloome, a Continuator of Stow, who tells us in his *'Survey,'* volume i., page 61, that after the fire, 'this North end of the Bridge lay unbuilt for many years, only deal boards were set up on both sides, to prevent people's falling into the Thames, many of which deals were, by high winds, oft blown down, which made it very dangerous in the nights, although there were lanthorns and candles hung upon all the cross beams that held the pales together.' We have two views of London Bridge, in which the Northern end of it appears in this state, but in each of them the temporary erection is quite of a different nature; and it is somewhat singular that the writer whom I last cited, should positively speak as follows, concerning the early restoration of the destroyed houses, when there seems no real authority to support his assertions. 'For about the year 1645,'—says he,—'the North end of this part last burned, began to be rebuilt; and in the year 1646 was finished: the building was of timber, very substantial and beautiful, for the houses were three stories high, besides the cellars, which were within and between the piers. And over the houses were stately platforms leaded, with rails and ballusters about them, very commodious and pleasant for walking, and enjoying so fine a prospect up and down the River; and some had pretty little gardens with arbours. This half being finished, the other half was intended to be rebuilt answerable to this, which would have been a great glory to the Bridge and honour to the City, the street, or passage, being twenty feet broad; whereas the other part, at the South end, was not above fourteen, and, in some places, but twelve.'

"Now, notwithstanding this particular description of these new buildings, neither of the engravings which I have alluded to have any indications of them; although one of them was published in 1647, and the other in 1666. The first of these represents the North end of London Bridge, from St. Magnus' Church to the houses beyond the first opening, as occupied by a *covered* passage formed of planks, leaving recesses standing out from the main erection, which was supported by buttresses of wood fastened to platforms on the outside of the Bridge.

"We derive this view of the dilapidations of London Bridge from a very rare and magnificent print, well known to collectors and antiquaries, by the name of the '*Long Antwerp view of London;*' for which, Mr. Geoffrey Barbican, if you ever meet with it, you may consider twenty guineas as a very moderate price.

This famous engraving is an etching by the matchless Wenceslaus Hollar; it is in seven sheets, measuring two yards and an half in length, by 17½ inches in height: it bears a dedication to Queen Henrietta Maria, and William Prince of Orange, with a copy of Latin verses written by Edward Benlowes, Esq.; and, though it was sold in London, the following publication line appears on one side written in Latin:—'*Sold at Amsterdam by Cornelius Danckers, in Calf Street, at the sign of the Image of Gratitude, in the year 1647.*' The e is, by the way, a pretty fair, but smaller copy of this view of London and Westminster in two sheets, in a series of prints commonly called '*Boydell's Perspectives*,' measuring 37½ inches, by 10¼ inches, signed '*R. Benning, del. et sculp.*,' and entitled '*A View of London as it was in the year 1647.*' The publication line is, '*Sold by J. Boydell, Engraver, at the Unicorn in Cheapside, London, 1756.*' You will find both the original, and the copy, in the xiii.th and xiv.th volumes of Mr. Crowle's Illustrated Pennant, which I have already cited to you, and the view takes in from above the Parliament House at Westminster to beyond St. Catherine's; but the Bridge is the *keimelion* of the plate, for that noble edifice is represented with all its buildings, from St. Magnus' Church, down to the Southwark Tower, the size of 10 inches in length, with the principal buildings about two inches square. The other view to which I have alluded, was also etched by Hollar, upon two sheets measuring 27 inches by 4¼: and it consists of two prospects, one over the other, on the same plate, the upper one representing, '*London from St. Mary Overies Steeple in Southwark, in its flourishing condition before the Fire;*' and the lower one entitled, '*Another prospect of the said City, taken from the same place, as it appeareth now after the said calamity and destruction by Fire.*' Copies of these interesting etchings are, however, neither dear nor uncommon; though, if you would have so fine an impression as that in the Print Room of the British Museum, you will scarcely procure it under three Guineas. In the upper of these prospects, the Northern end of London Bridge is shewn to be a passage fenced by wooden palings without any houses, excepting one building, which occupies the whole width of the Bridge; having a gate in it surmounted by the King's Arms, and standing immediately before the old Church of St. Magnus.

"Independently of these views, we have another very strong evidence that this part was not built upon even in the year 1665, contained in that most interesting and curious work, the *'Memoirs and Diary of Samuel Pepys, Esq., F.R.S. and Secretary to the Admiralty in the reigns of Charles II. and James II.'* Edited by Richard, Lord Braybrooke, London, 1825, 4to. volume 1., page 388: where, under the date of January 24th, 1665-66, that observant journalist has the following entry. 'My Lord,'—Edward Montague, Earl of Sandwich,—'and I, the weather being a little fairer, went by water to Deptford; and the wind being again very furious, so as we durst not go by water, walked to London round the Bridge, no boat being able to stirre; and, Lord! what a dirty walk we had, and so strong the wind, that in the fields we many times could not carry our bodies against it, but were driven backwards. It was dangerous to walk the streets, the bricks and tiles falling from the houses, that the whole streets were covered with them; and whole chimneys, nay, whole houses, in two or three places, blowed down. But above all, *the pales on London Bridge, on both sides, were blown away;*'—almost the very words, you observe, which I have quoted you from Richard Bloome,—'so that we were forced to stoop very low, for fear of blowing off the Bridge. We could see no boats in the Thames afloat, but what were broke loose, and carried through the Bridge, it being ebbing water. And the greatest sight of all was, among other parcels of ships driven here and there in clusters together, one was quite overset, and lay with her masts all along in the water, and her keel above water.' The desolation, and wintry chillness of this picture, is enough to make one shiver even in the Dog-days."

When the worthy old Chronicler had arrived at the conclusion of this narrative, as usual I took up the story, and began thus:—"This, Mr. Barnaby

Postern, was indeed a fatal destruction, and one would imagine that it was no such happy event as to cause a jesting ballad to be made to commemorate it; but yet, though in the following verses there are some discordant circumstances, and even the date is at variance with that which you have already given, there can be little doubt but that they relate to the Fire of which you have now spoken. You will find them printed at the end of a very rare, but, at the same time, a very worthless publication, entitled *'The Loves of Hero and Leander, a mock Poem: Together with choice Poems and rare pieces of drollery, got by heart, and often repeated by divers witty Gentlemen and Ladies that use to walke in the New Exchange, and at their recreations in Hide Park.'* London, 1653, 12mo., pages 44-48. There is also another edition of 1682; but I pray you to remember, that many of the fescennine rhymes, some of which would have done honour to Hudibras, and many of the witty points of this song, are, in that latter copy, most vilely perverted; I shall give it you, therefore, as it stands in the former impression.

'*Some* Christian people *all* give ear
Unto the grief of us:
Caused by the death of three children dear.
The which it happen'd thus.

And eke there befel an accident,
By fault of a Carpenter's son,
Who to saw chips his sharp ax-e-lent
Woe worth the time may Lon——

May London say: Woe worth the Carpenter!
And all such *block-head* fools;
Would he were hanged up like a *sarpent* here
For meddling with edge tools.

For into the chips there fell a spark,
Which put out in such flames,
That it was known into South-wark
Which lies beyond the Thames.

For *Loe*! the Bridge was wondrous *high*
With water underneath:
O'er which as many fishes fly
As birds therein do breathe.

And yet the fire consumed the Brigg,
Not far from place of landing;
And though the building was full big,
It fell down,—*not with standing*.

And eke into the water fell
So many pewter dishes,
That a man might have taken up very well
Both boil'd and roasted fishes!

And thus the Bridge of London Town,
For building that was sumptuous,
Was *all* by fire *half* burnt down,
For being too *contumptious*!

Thus you have *all* but *half* my song,
Pray list to what comes *ater*;
For now I have *cool'd* you with the *fire*,—
I'll *warm* you with the *water*!

I'll tell you what the River's name's
Where these children did slide—a,
It was fair London's swiftest Thames
Which keeps both Time and Tide—a.

All on the tenth of January,
To the wonder of much people;'
Twas frozen o'er that well 'twould bear
Almost a country steeple!

Three children sliding thereabout,
Upon a place too thin;
That so at last it did *fall out*,
That they did all *fall in*.

A great Lord there was that laid with the King,
And with the King great wager makes;
But when he saw that he could not win
He sigh'd,—and would have drawn stakes.

He said it would bear a man for to slide,
And laid a hundred pound;

The King said it would break, and so it did,
For three children there were drown'd.

Of which, one's head was from his should—
ers stricken,—whose name was John;
Who then cried out as loud as he could
'Oh Lon-a! Lon-a! Lon-don!'

'Oh! tut—tut—turn from thy sinful race!'
Thus did his speech decay;
I wonder that in such a case
He had no more to say.

And thus being drown'd, Alack! Alack!
The water ran down their throats,
And stopp'd their breath three hours by the clock,
Before they could get any boats!

Ye parents all that children have,
And ye that have none yet,
Preserve your children from the grave,
And teach them at home to sit.

For had these at a sermon been,
Or else upon dry ground,
Why then I never would have been seen,
If that they had been drown'd!

Even as a huntsman ties his dogs,
For fear they should go fro him;
So tye your children with severity's clogs,
Untie 'em—and you'll *undo 'em*.

God bless our noble Parliament,
And rid them from all fears;
God bless *all* the Commons of this land,
And God bless—*some* of the Peers!'

"And now, Sir, I shall, by your favour, say a few words with respect to the tune to which these verses were formerly sung; which I am the better enabled to do by the researches of a gentleman, to whom, in several other particulars of our history, I have been considerably indebted. By his information, I shall first inform you, that the foregoing Song exists in its original state, in the

Pepysian Collection of Ballads preserved in Magdalen College, Cambridge, volume ii., page 146; where it is called *'The Lamentation of a bad market, or the drowning of three children on the Thames. To the tune of the Ladies' Fall. Printed for F. Coles, T. Vere, J. Wright, and J. Clarke.'* Now the old verses, entitled *'A Lamentable Ballad of the Lady's Fall,'* you will find, with some account of it prefixed, in Bishop Percy's *'Reliques of Ancient English Poetry,'* volume iii., book ii., article x., page 137, fourth edition, London, 1794, octavo; or, indeed, you may consult any edition but the last. From the Editor's notice of this latter poem, we learn that it was sung to the tune of the verses called *'The Shepherd's Slumber,'* better known by the first three words of the commencing stanza.

'In pescod time, when hound to horne
Gives eare till buck be kill'd;
And little lads with pipes of corne,
Sate keeping beasts a-field.'

"I have not, Mr. Barnaby, found the musical notation of *this* song, though I am almost inclined to think it was sung to the very common tune of *'Flying Fame,'* so familiar to every body under the name of *'Chevy Chace;'* for in volume iv., page 1, of Tom D'Urfey's collection of Songs called *'Wit and Mirth,'* London, 1719, 12mo., you may see this very ballad on London Bridge, entitled *'Three children sliding on the Thames. Tune, Chevy chace.'* Listen then, my good Sir, whilst, with my very unmelodious voice, I attempt to give you some idea of it;—the music I have alluded to, runs thus:—

'Some Chris-tian peo-ple all give ear,
Un-to the grief of us:
Caused by the death of three Chil-dren dear.
The which it hap-pened thus.'"

"Thank ye, thank ye, honest Master Geoffrey Barbican," said my visitor, as I concluded; "my thanks to you, both for your music and poetry; for I verily think as you do, that the verses which you have repeated relate to this conflagration of 1633, although there was the difference of a month between the actual fact, and your rhyming record of it. It appears to me, too, as if I recognized in the 16th stanza,—where the last words of the drowning victim are uttered by his head in broken accents,—the original of Gay's description of the death of Doll, the Pippin-woman, contained in the 2nd book of his 'Trivia,' since she died in much the same place and manner.

"The rental of the Bridge House was, doubtless considerably lessened by this destructive fire; but in the printed document of the Bridge-Masters' Accounts, there is not any notice of the amount of rents for some years after it. In 1636, however, we are informed that the salaries, horsekeeping, and liveries, of John Potter, and David Bourne, the Wardens, amounted to £71. 3s. 4d. each; and in the following year the rental is stated to have been only £1836. 7s. 6d., whilst the fees, &c. of John Hawes and Noadiah Rawlins amounted to £72. In that Manuscript treatise on the payment of Tythes, which I have mentioned to you as being in the Archiepiscopal Library at Lambeth, Cornelius Burgess, the then Rector of St. Magnus, observes that 'the best third part of the Parish was consumed by the late fire on London Bridge: yet no part of the annual charges lying on the Parsonage is abated. And it is yet capable of a large improvement, by reason that a good part of it being Citty land, provisions have been accordingly made to keepe downe the tithes generally throughout the Parish to vnreasonable low proportions, some very few houses excepted.' According to Newcourt, in his 'Repertorium Ecclesiasticum,' volume i., page 396, these tythes before this conflagration amounted to £109. for 90 houses, of which about 40 houses were destroyed; though, in the Manuscript valuation of 1638, they are reduced to £81. 12s. 8d.

"The destruction of London Bridge, however, was not allowed to pass without a more appropriate memorial than the song which you have repeated; for in the parochial records of the Church adjoining, it is stated, that Susanna Chambers by her will, dated the 28th day of December, 1640, left 'unto the Parson of the Parish Church of St. Magnus, on, or near, London Bridge, or unto such other Preacher of God's word as my said son Richard Chambers, his heirs, administrators, and assignees shall yearly appoint, the yearly sum of twenty shillings of lawful English money, for a Sermon to be preached on the 12th day of February, in every year, within the said Parish Church of St. Magnus, London Bridge, or any other near thereunto, in commemoration of God's merciful preservation of the said Church of St. Magnus from ruin in the late and terrible fire of London Bridge; and also the sum of seventeen shillings and sixpence to the poor of that Parish of St. Magnus; and two shillings and sixpence to the clerk and sexton.' This gift is mentioned by most of the London Historians; and I would observe to you that I am informed, with regard to the present state of this bequest, that the money for the Sermon, the Clerk, and the Sexton, has not been claimed within the memory of the oldest inhabitant of the Parish: but that the poor have, ever since, duly received their legacy. Whilst I am speaking of St. Magnus' Church, I may also remark, that in consequence of the dissolution of the Fraternity belonging to it, which I have before mentioned, there has been a perpetuity of £21. 6s. 8d. paid by the Exchequer ever since the time of Queen Mary.

"In the 43rd volume of that most extraordinary collection of Tracts, which the late excellent King George III. presented to the British Museum, there is a pamphlet of four leaves commemorating a remarkable flow of the Thames at London Bridge, the title to which is given by Gough in his 'British Topography,' volume i., page 731: and it bears the same proportion to its contents, as the show-cloth of a travelling menagerie does to the actual exhibition. *'A Strange Wonder, or the Citie's Amazement. Being a Relation occasioned by a wonderfull and vnusuall accident, that happened in the River of Thames, Friday, Feb. 4, 1641. There flowing Two Tydes at London Bridge, within the space of an houre and a halfe, the last comming with such violence and hideous noyse, that it not onely affrighted, but even astonished above 500 watermen that stood beholding it on both sides the Thames. Which latter Tyde rose sixe foote higher then the former Tyde had done, to the great admiration of all men.'* London, 1641. Small quarto. This tract is subsequently named *'True Newes from Heaven,'* and the author takes occasion, from the event which he records, to lament the vices and confusion of his time. The fact itself occupies but a small portion of his text; and he relates it thus.—'Fryday, Februarie 4, 1641, it was high water at one of the clocke at noone, a time—by reason so accommodated for all imployments by water or land,—very fit to afford witnesse of a strange and notorious accident. After it was full high water, and that it flowed its full due time as all Almanacks set downe; and water-men, the vnquestionable prognosticators in that affaire, with confidence mainetaine it stood a quiet still dead water, a full houre and halfe, without moving or returning any way never so litle: Yea, the water-men flung in stickes to the streame, as near as they could guesse, which lay in the water as vpon the earth, without moving this way or that. Dishes likewise, and wodden buckets, they set a swimming, but it proved a stilling, for move they would not any way by force of stream or water; so that it seemed the water was indeed asleepe or dead, or had changed or borrowed the stability of the earth. The water-men not content with this evidence, would needs make the vtmost of the tryall, that they might report with the more boldnesse the truth of the matter: and with more credible confidence they tooke their boates and lanched into the streame or very channell: but the boates that lay hailed up on the shore moved as much, except when they used their oares; nay,—a thing worthy the admiration of all men,—they rowed under the very arches, tooke up their oares and slept there, or, at least, lay still an houre very neare, their boates not so much as moved through any way, either upward or downeward: the water seeming as plaine, quiet, even, and stable as a pavement under the arch, where, if any where in the Thames, there must be moving by reason of the narrownesse of the place. In this posture stood the water a whole houre and halfe, or rather above, by the testimony of above five hundred water-men, on either side the Thames, whom not to believe in this case were stupiditie, not discretion. At last, when all men expected its ebb, being filled with amazement that it stood so long as hath been delivered, behold a greater wonder, a new Tyde comes in! A new Tyde with a witnesse, you might easily take notice of him; so lowde he roared, that the noise was guessed to be about Greenwich when it was heard so, not onely clearly, but fearfully to the Bridge; and up he comes tumbling, roaring, and foaming in that furious manner, that it was horror unto all that beheld it. And as it gave sufficient notice to the eare of its comming, so it left sufficient satisfaction to the eye that it was now come; having raised the water foure foote higher then the first Tyde had done, foure foote by rule! as by evident measure did appear, and presently ebbed in as hasty, confused, unaccustomed manner. See here, Reader! a wonder, that—all things considered,—the oldest man never saw or heard of the like.'

"Lord Clarendon, in his *'History of the Rebellion,'* volume i., part ii., book iv. page 521, Oxford, 1819, 8vo., states that when John Hampden and the four other members of Parliament were accused of High Treason, and were, by their own party, brought back in triumph from the City, January the 11th, 1641-42, 'from London-Bridge to Westminster, the Thames was guarded with above a hundred lighters and longboats, laden with small pieces of ordnance, and dressed up with waistclothes and streamers, as ready for fight,' These forces, together with the City Trained-bands under Major General Skippon, were not less to honour, than to defend, the return of the accused Members. The same noble Historian tells us farther, in the same volume and part, book v. page 661, that about the end of March in the same year, the Justices, and principal gentlemen of the County of Kent, prepared a Petition to the two Houses of Parliament, that the Militia might not be otherwise exercised in that County than according to Law, and that the Common Prayer Book might still be observed. This was construed by the Parliament into a commotion in Kent; the Earl of Bristol and Judge Mallet were committed to the Tower only for having seen it; and strong guards were placed at London Bridge, where the petitioners approaching the City were disarmed, and forced to return, and only a very few permitted to proceed with the petition to Westminster.

"That it was the unhappy custom, even late in the seventeenth century, to erect heads over the South Gate on London Bridge, we have, Alas! too many proofs; though, indeed, it seems to have been only the case with such as were considered traitors, as were those unfortunate Romish Priests executed under the Statutes of Elizabeth and James I. When Bishop Challoner is speaking, in his work already cited, volume iii., page 112, of the death of Bartholomew Roe, a Priest of the Order of St. Benedict, in January, 1642, he states that, on the morning of his execution, he exhorted the Catholics who were present at his Mass in the prison, and desired them 'that as often as in passing through the City, they should see that hand of his fixed on one of the Gates, or in crossing the water, should see his head on London Bridge, they would remember those lessons which he had preached to them, of the importance of holding fast the Catholic faith, and of leading a Christian and holy life.' In October, 1642, the head of Thomas Bullaker, a Priest of the Order of St. Francis, was also set up on London Bridge. See Bishop Challoner, page 132, in the same volume: and another unhappy instance of a similar execution is to be found in Dr. Challoner's life of Henry Heath, a Father of the Order of St. Francis, contained on pages 141, 143, of the same volume of his work. Having left Douay and landed in England, this Priest travelled to the metropolis in the greatest poverty. 'At London he arrives wearied, as well he might, having travelled barefoot forty miles that day, and it being the Winter season. It is now time to take up his quarters, and give some little rest and refreshment to the body. But how shall this be done, for money he has none, nor acquaintance? however, he ventures to call at the Star Inn, near London Bridge, but the people of the house finding that he had no money, turned him out of doors at eight o'clock in a cold winter night.' In this distress, he laid down to rest at a Citizen's door, where the owner of the house had him seized for a shoplifter, and, when examined by the watch, some writings in defence of the Romish faith being found in his cap, he owned himself to be a Priest. He was then tried and convicted upon the Statute of Elizabeth, and was executed on April the 17th, 1643, at Tyburn, and his head erected upon London Bridge.

"On the 7th of March, 1642, the two Houses of Parliament ordered that the City of London should be fortified, for its better security and safety; and on the day following the order was printed, in small quarto, a copy of which is in the King's Collection of Tracts in the British Museum, volume 97; and of which, if I repeat you a portion of the title, you will receive all the information contained in the pamphlet itself. '*An Ordinance and Declaration of the Lords and Commons assembled in Parliament, that the Lord Mayor and Citizens of the City of London, for the better securing and safetie thereof, shall have full power and authority, according to their discretion, to trench, stop, and fortifie all high-waies leading into the said City, as well within the Liberties, as without, as they shall see cause. And for the better effecting thereof, shall impose upon all the inhabitants within the same, upon every house worth £5. a year, six pence, and every house of greater rent, after the rate of two pence in the pound.*' Another copy of this ordinance was printed in April, 1643, and is to be found in volume 104 of the same collection. Maitland, in his '*History*,' volume i., pages 368, 369, also mentions an act of Common Council passed for the same purpose, February the 23rd, 1642-43: and gives a plan of the fortifications erected round the City. It was enacted, says he, that 'all the passages and ways leading to the City should be shut up, excepting those entering at Charing Cross, St. Giles's in the Fields, St. John's Street, Shoreditch, and Whitechapel; and that the exterior ends of the said streets should be fortified with breast-works and turnpikes, musket-proof; and all the sheds and buildings contiguous to London-Wall without, be taken down; and that the City Wall, with its bulwarks, be not only repaired and mounted with artillery, but, likewise, that divers new works be added to the same at places most exposed.' When this act had been confirmed by the above ordinances of Parliament, the fortifications were commenced and carried on with considerable rapidity; men, women, and children, were employed upon the works; and, in a short time, an earthern rampart, with redoubts, horn-works, batteries, forts, and bulwarks, was erected round the Cities of London and Westminster, and the Borough of Southwark. We have no particular account, however, of the manner in which London Bridge was fortified at this period; and the great events which took place in the history of the Civil Wars seem to have swallowed up every circumstance connected with this edifice. We learn, indeed, that in the year 1647, the Parliamentary Army entered the City, whilst the Corporation was engaged in an irresolute debate as to the measures to be adopted for its defence: when frequent conciliatory messages passed between the chief Officers and London; and, the less to alarm the Metropolis, the soldiers were quartered at some distance from it. 'However, in this calm,'—says Lord Clarendon, who relates these circumstances in his *'History,'* volume iii., part i., book x., page 104,—'they sent over Colonel Rainsborough with a brigade of horse, and foot, and cannon, at Hampton Court, to possess Southwark, and those works which secured that end of London Bridge; which he did with so little noise, that in one night's march he found himself master, without any opposition, not only of the Borough of Southwark, but of all the works and forts which were to defend it; the soldiers within shaking hands with those without, and refusing to obey their officers which were to command them: so that the City, without knowing that any such thing was in agitation, found in the morning that all that avenue to the Town was possessed by the enemy; whom they were providing to resist on the other side, being as confident of this that they had lost, as of any gate in the City.'

"Bulstrode Whitelock, in his *'Memorials of the English Affairs,'* London, 1732, folio, page 263, enables us to add to this account, that on Colonel Rainsborough's advance to Southwark, he found the Bridge gates shut, the Portcullis lowered, and a guard within; but upon placing a counter-guard with two pieces of ordnance, against the gate, in a short time the great fort was surrendered; about two in the morning of Monday, the 2nd of August, 1647.

"A curious invention, which, very probably, was never carried into execution, was, in the year 1643, connected with the history of London Bridge; being the scheme of an unsuccessful engineer named Captain John Bulmer. You may see an original copy of his *'Propositions in the Office of Assurance, London, for the Blowing up of a Boat and a man over London Bridge,'* in the King's Collection of Tracts in the British Museum, Miscellaneous Pieces, volume 3*, folio, article 88. In this statement, which consists of a broadside of one page, he thus commences. 'In the name of God, Amen, John Bulmer, of London, Esquire: Master and Surveiour Generall of the King's Maiestie's Mines Royall, and Engines for Water-workes, propoundeth—by God's assistance,—that he, the said John Bulmer, shall and will, at and in a flowing water, set out a Boat or Vessell with an Engine, floating with a man or a boy in and aboard the said Boat, in the River of Thames, over against the Tower-wharfe, or lower. Which said Boat, with the said man or boy in or aboard her, shall the same tide, before low-water againe, by art of the said John Bulmer, and helpe of the said engine, be advanced and elevated so high, as that the same shall passe and be delivered over London Bridge, together with the said man or boy in and aboard her, and floate againe in the said River of Thames, on the other side of the said Bridge, in safety.' He then proceeds to covenant for himself, his heirs, &c., to perform this within the space of one month, after he shall have intimated at the Assurance Office that he is about to put it in practice. This announcement was to be made 'so soone as the undertakers wagering against him six for one,' should have deposited in the Office such a sum as he should consider sufficient to 'countervaile his charges of contriving the said Boat and Engine.' Captain Bulmer was also to deposit his proportion of the money, and the whole, being subscribed and signed, was to remain in the office, until he had either performed his contract, when he was to receive it; or till his failure, when it was to be re-delivered to the subscribers. This curious paper is dated November the 6th, and concludes with the following promise: 'And all those that will bring in their monies into the Office, shall be there assured of their losse or gaine, according to the conditions above mentioned.' I imagine, however, that this scheme met with but little or no encouragement, because I find a new edition of it, dated March the 20th, 1647, printed in small folio, and inserted in the King's Tracts marked *'Single Sheets,'* volume 5, article 130. It varies, however, somewhat from the foregoing, and states that 'the blowing up of a Gun from under the water by the breath of a man's mouth, shall occasion the raising of such Boate or vessell; which said gun shall then forthwith after be discharged by fire given thereunto, and presently sinke againe: after the sinking whereof, another gunne shall be raised by such meanes as aforesaid, which shall be discharged also, forthwith upon the floating of the said Boate or Vessell on the other side of the sayd Bridge.' He no longer mentions his terms to be 'six for one,' but states that his performance shall take place within a month after the amount of his expenses shall be subscribed by 'persons pleasing to afford assistance and furtherance to arts and mysteries of this nature.' He adds too, that security will be given at the office, and that his reason for desiring these deposits is, 'for that losse of time in collection of the same after performance, would hinder him from prosecution of businesse of greater consequence, and tending to the publique good. He was, however, I doubt not, still unsuccessful; for his time was not only one of national poverty, arising from the Civil Wars, but it was also one of projectors as forward and as promising as himself: whilst the people, in general, seemed but little disposed to encourage any new scheme, however wonderful, and to be of the mind of Goldsmith's Scrivener, when he said, 'For my part, I believe all the money is gone to the Devil, or beyond the seas, and he who has a little is a fool if he don't keep it to himself.' The Captain, notwithstanding, seems to have made another effort in November, 1649, in the form of a small folio sheet, entitled *'A note of such Arts and Mysteries as an English Gentleman, a Souldier, and a Traveller, is able, by God's assistance, to perform; he having means to perfect the same;'* of which there is also a copy in the King's Tracts, marked *'Single Sheets,'* volume 8, Article 90. It consists of five propositions concerning Mines, Warlike Engines, Draining and raising water, and Machines for recovering goods from the sea: which secrets he states himself to have discovered 'with much study, travell, and expenses of many thousands of pounds;' and that now 'being old and out of employment, he is willing to shew his art in these things to any which are desirous to learn, upon assurance of such reward as they shall agree upon.' To this is added a certificate of his ability to perform several of his projects, from Emanuel College, Cambridge, dated 1646; and the paper concludes by a copy of most lamentable verses vindicating himself from his detractors.

"In February, 1644-45, the head of Henry Morse, a Priest of the Society of Jesus, was set up on London Bridge. See Bishop Challoner's *'Martyrology,'* volume iii., page 164.

"The manuscript Survey of Bridge Lands which I have already mentioned, bears a memorandum that it was lent in 1653; and it commences with a regulation, which, from its language and orthography, appears to have been made much before that period, relating to an officer called the *Sheuteman*, who was, probably, an overseer of the Bridge works, and watched the cataracts or falls in the arches. The article is entitled *'An Order taken and made for the Sheuteman, by us Symond Ryse, and William Campion, Wardens of London Bridge;'* and in substance it is nearly as follows. 'For as much as diuerse and sundry nights the Sheuteman hath occasyon to ryse in the night-seison to come to his boots, (boats) to see the tydes as they fall erly or late for the occupations of the Bridgehouse, so that the Porter muste open him the gate at vn due tymes of the night, contrary to the ordinances made for the same;

whiche is not onely to his greate payne and daunger, but also to the great perell and daunger that myght fall to the house; for, when the gates be opened at ded tymes of the night, it is to be doutyd that some lewed persons myght entre in after them, and not onely robbe thys house, but also putt in daungre of their liues so many as be within. For Remedye whereof, we, the said Wardene, have ordeyned and appoynted a lodging to be made att the ende of the Crane Howse, within the Bridge-howse Yarde, with a chemnye in the same lodging, and sufficient for two or three persons to lye in yt; to the entente that the Sheuteman, with such persons as of consequence he moste have with him for causes requysyte for the tydes, may lye there drye, and tarye theyre tydes when theye fall in the nyght, very erly or late, hauing business to do for the howse; and also when they come from theyre labour weete, or att vn due tymes of the nyght, to goo home to theire houses, may tarye there, and make them fyre to drye them and keepe them warme, of such chyppes as ys hughed of the timber in the yerd, and none other, and nott to keepe any hospitalitie, or dwelling there at ony tyme, but att such tyme and tymes afore rehersed. And according to the old vse and custome, that when the Sheuteman by daye tyme be not occupyed with the boats about the affairs of the Bridge workes, that then he is to doe all such workes within the Bridge-house yerde and in all other places as other laborers doeth, and so he is to receyue his wages, or els not. And this ordinance to be alwayes kept.'

"In the year 1657, James Howel published his volume entitled '*Londinopolis; an Historicall Discourse, or Perlustration of the City of London,*' to which he attached some Latin verses in praise of London Bridge, on the leaf immediately following the title-page. They are entitled in Latin, '*Concerning London Bridge, and the stupendous site and structure thereof, in imitation of those celebrated six verses of the Poet Sannazarius, on the City of Venice, commencing 'Viderat Hadriacis.*' This beautiful hexastichon is to be found in that old and fair edition of his Latin Poems printed at the Aldine Press, Venice, 1535, 8vo., in the first book of Epigrams, page 38 b, and it is entitled '*On the Wonders of the City of Venice.*' Now, that you may have some slight idea of the original of Howel's rhymes, before I recite them, perhaps you will permit me to repeat to you an English paraphrase of Sannazario's *own* verses, fairly composed in the Sonnet stanza, but not possessing the elegant conciseness of the Latin?"

"Pray, go on, Sir," answered I, with a good deal of satirical ceremony in my voice; "Pray go on, Mr. Barnaby; it's long since I have had any choice as to what you shall put in, or what you shall leave out, of your discourse; and, therefore, let's have the Sonnet, such as it is: you know the proverb,—in for a penny, in for a pound."

"A facetious gentleman, truly," was the Antiquary's reply; "but let me observe for your consolation, Master Geoffrey, that we are now rapidly passing through the history of the Bridge, and that on later events I shall frequently have but little information to impart. However, to return to the matter in hand,—this is the Sonnet.

"As Neptune saw, reclined upon his waves,
In the fair Adriatic Venice stand
A City, o'er its waters to command,
And placed in rule o'er all its billowy caves!
He cried, in wonder at the pile it laves,—
Thy Tarpeian arches Jove himself hath plann'd,
And thy vast walls were wrought by Mars's hand.
Hail, City! which the main in triumph braves!
Though some esteem the Tiber's royal pile
The glory of the deep Pelagian sea;
Venice, look round on mainland and on isle,
There is not one so mighty and so free!
'They are of men,' thou say'st with lofty smile,
But God alone hath rear'd and planted thee!

"This is truly somewhat 'in Ercles' vein,'" continued the old gentleman, as he finished the Sonnet; "but I think you will agree with me that it is completely 'out-heroded' by Howel's imitation of it; as, indeed, his Latinity is vastly inferior to Sannazario's. I really cannot imagine, how some have supposed that Howel's Latin verses were written by the Italian; but this grievous mistake has been made, in consequence, perhaps, of the words '*ad instar*,'—after the manner of,—being overlooked. The original poem you may read and criticise at your leisure, but his well-known English translation runs thus.

"'When Neptune from his billows London spyde,
Brought proudly hither by a high spring-tyde;
As through a floating wood he steer'd along,
And dancing castles cluster'd in a throng;—
When he beheld a mighty Bridge give law
Unto his surges, and their fury awe;—
When such a shelf of cataracts did roar,
As if the Thames with Nile had changed her shore;—
When he such massy walls, such tow'rs did eye,
Such posts, such irons, upon his back to lye;—
When such vast arches he observed, that might
Nineteen Rialtos make, for depth and height;—
When the Cerulean God these things survay'd,
He shook his trident, and astonished said,

Let the whole Earth now all her wonders count,
This Bridge of wonders is the paramount!'

"I cannot imagine, Mr. Barbican, why the '*Londinopolis,*' in which these verses are printed, should ever be quoted in preference to Stow's '*Survey,*' from which it is little more than a transcript, as Howel himself acknowledges in his Advertisement. I should mention, however, that it contains two fine prints, for which it is, perhaps, chiefly desirable: one consisting of a very spirited whole-length portrait of the author, resting against a tree, and executed in that singular style for which Claude Mellan was so famous; and the other an interesting half-sheet etching by Hollar, of London, before the Great Fire. With these embellishments, and its own popularity, the volume sells for about £1. 11s. 6d.; but a fine impression of the latter engraving alone will produce the sum of 10s. 6d. From this work, then, at page 22, we learn that the destruction occasioned by the 'most raging dismal fire' of 1633, was not wholly repaired at the time of its publication; for, after stating that it consumed a third part of the buildings on the Bridge, it is added, 'by the commendable care of the City, there are other goodly structures rais'd up in some of their rooms, of a stronger, and more stately way of building; and pity it is, that the work were not compleated, there being no object,—after the Church of St. Paul,—that can conduce more to the glory and ornament of this renowned City.' Yet, notwithstanding this Author's praises of 'the Bridge of the World,' as he calls it, on page 20, he makes us acquainted with what may be considered as an ancient satire upon it; since he says, '*If London Bridge had fewer eyes, it would see far better.*' The arches of this edifice, and the dangerous passage through them, have also given rise to another quaint saying, which is recorded in the Rev. J. Ray's '*Compleat Collection of English Proverbs,*' London, 1737, octavo, pages 13 and 251, and which is, 'London Bridge was made for wise men to go over, and fools to go under.'

"On Tuesday, the 29th of May, 1660, King Charles the Second entered London in triumph, after having been magnificently entertained in St. George's Fields. About three in the afternoon he arrived in Southwark, and thence proceeded over the Bridge into the City, attended by all the glory of London, and the military forces of the kingdom. Lord Clarendon, who makes this 'fair return of banished Majesty' the concluding scene of his noble History, gives us but little information as to the King's reception at London Bridge, though we learn from him that 'the crowd was so great, that the King rode in a crowd from the Bridge to Whitehall; all the Companies of the City standing in order on both sides, and giving loud thanks to God for his Majesty's presence. 'All the streets'—says White Kennet, Bishop of Peterborough, in his '*Historical Register of English Affairs,*' London, 1744, folio, page 163,—'were richly adorned with tapestry, from London Bridge to Whitehall;' and beyond Temple-bar, were lined with the Trained bands, and a troop of the late King's Officers, headed by the loyal Sir John Stawell. The procession, which was chiefly an equestrian one, was begun by Major-General Brown, and 300 Citizens in cloth of silver doublets; who were followed by 1200 more all in velvet, with footmen and liveries in purple. Alderman Robinson then led other parties habited in buff coats with sleeves of silver tissue, and green silk scarfs; some in blue liveries with silver lace; and footmen and trumpeters in sea-green, grey, and silver liveries. Eighty of the Sheriffs' followers attended in red cloaks lined with silver, holding half-pikes; and 600 of the City Companies rode in black velvet coats and gold chains, with their respective servitors in cassocks and ribbands. Drums, trumpets, streamers, and the Life-guards, in satin, scarlet, and silver, followed; then came the City Marshal, with 8 footmen in French green, trimmed with crimson and white; whilst the City Waits and Officers, the Sheriffs, the Aldermen, and their attendants, blazed in red, and cloths of gold and silver in the next rank. Heralds and Maces, in their splendid habits, preceded Sir Thomas Allen, the Lord Mayor; who, to gratify the City, was permitted to carry the Sword of London immediately before the King, which had not been done in any former public entry, excepting when Charles I. returned from Scotland in 1641, and even then the Sword of State had the precedence.

"I have next to mention a very rare and curious pamphlet, never yet cited in the history of London Bridge, of a Vision seen upon that edifice in March, 1661. It is contained in Article 6, No. 867, of that invaluable collection of Tracts which the late King presented to the British Museum. Like most of the wonderful pamphlets of the seventeenth century, its title is truly astounding, but the book itself is only a small quarto of four leaves; of which, as all that now concerns us is contained in three pages, I shall give you the whole, and first for the magnificent Title-page.

"*'Strange News from the West, being a true and perfect account of several Miraculous Sights seen in the Air Westward, on Thursday last, being the 21 day of this present March, by divers persons of credit standing on London Bridge between 7 and 8 of the clock at night. Two great Armies marching forth of two clouds, and encountring each other; but, after a sharp dispute, they suddenly vanished. Also, some remarkable Sights that were seen to issue forth of a cloud that seemed like a mountain, in the shapes of a Bull, a Bear, a Lyon, and an Elephant with a Castle on his back, and the manner how they all vanished. London, Printed for J. Jones, 1661.*' Such is the entry into this exhibition of wonders; the tract itself commences thus.

"'An exact relation of severall strange wonders, that were seen on Thursday last, by several persons then on London Bridge, appearing in the West of England.—Apparent hath been many signs and wonders made to us here in England, whereby the incredulous have been convinc'd of their obstinacy. It being a great question, and doubtfull now with the generality of people, whether those things lately published which appeared in foreign parts were feasible or no, they have since been verified by other credible persons from those parts, to the great satisfaction of some hundreds: therefore I shall forbear mentioning them, and give you an exact account of what hath lately been visible to divers persons now resident in the City of London, which was as followeth, *viz.*

"'Upon the 21 day of March, about, or between 7 and 8 of the clock at night, divers persons living in the City—as they came over London Bridge,—discovered several clouds in strange shapes, at which they suddenly made a stand, to see what might be the event of so miraculous a change in the motion of the Heavens. The first cloud seemed to turn into the form or shape of a Cathedral, with a Tower advancing from the middle of it upwards, which continued for a small space and then vanished away. Another turned into a tree, spreading itself like an oak,—as near as could be judged,—which, in a short space, vanished. Between these two was, as it were, standing, a great mountain, which continued in the same form near a quarter of an hour; after which, the mountain still remaining, there appeared several strange shapes one after another, issuing out of the said mountain, about the middle of the right side thereof: the first seemed to be formed like a Crokedile, with his mouth wide open; this continued a very short space, and, by degrees, was transformed into the form of a furious Bull; and, not long after, it was changed into the form of a Lyon; but it continued so a short time, and was altered into a Bear, and, soon after, into a Hog, or Boar, as near as those could guess who were spectators. After all these shapes had appeared, the mountain seemed to be divided and altered into the form of two monstrous beasts, fastened together by the hinder parts, drawing one apart from the other: that which appeared on the left hand, resembled an Elephant with a castle upon his back; that upon the right hand, we could not so well determine, but it seemed to us like a Lyon or some such like beast.

"'The Castle on the back of the Elephant vanished, the Elephant himself loosing his shape; and, where the Castle stood, there rose up a small number of men, as we judged, about some four or six: these were in continual motion. The other beast, which was beheld on the right hand, seemed to be altered into the form of an Horse, with a rider on his back, and, after a small proportion of time, the whole vanished, falling downward. Then arose another great cloud, and in small time it formed it selfe into the likenesse of the head of a great Whale, the mouth of which stood wide open. After this, at some distance on the right hand, appeared a cloud, which became like unto a head, or cap, with a horn, or ear, on each side thereof, which was of very considerable length. Between these two rose a few men, who moved up and down with a swift motion; and immediately after they all vanished except one man, who still continued moving up and down with much state and majesty.

In the mean time arose near adjacent unto this head, or cap, another cloud, out of which cloud issued forth an Army, or great body of men; and upon the left hand, arose another Army, each of which marched one towards the other; about this time the single man vanished away,—and the two Armies seemed to approach very near each other, and encounter, maintaining a combat one against the other, and, after a short contest, all vanished. During all this time there seemed, to our best apprehension, a flame of fire along the Strand, towards the City of London.' Such is the notice of these 'strange sights,' as they are truly called; but, though I do not cite them, the remaining two pages of the pamphlet are filled with an account of some much stranger seen in Hamburgh, in the preceding February: and now that I have finished, Mr. Barbican, pray what do you think of it?"

"What do I think of it?" returned I: "Why, as *Captain Ironside* says in the Play, 'that it's a lie, to be sure!' You very well know, Mr. Postern, that a great part of the seventeenth century was quite an age for seeing wonders in the air: for they were continually being exhibited to all sorts and conditions of men; whilst, ever and anon, came forth a pamphlet full of marvel and trumpery, detailing the last revelation, occasionally ornamented 'with a type of the vision curiously engraven on copper.' You may remember how the Author of *'The History of the Great Plague,'* tells you that he was in some danger from a crowd in St. Giles's, because he could not discern an Angel in the air holding a drawn sword in his hand. Believe me, good Mr. Barnaby, such visions are extremely rare; and, when they *do* appear, they come not in the uncertain forms of that which you have now referred to. Minds of more weakness than piety gave a ready faith to them, and in convulsed or sorrowful times, were often hearing voices which spake not, and seeing signs which were never visible: willing to deceive, or be deceived, they saw, like *Polonius*, clouds 'backed like an ousel,' or, 'very like a whale;'

'So hypochondriac fancies represent
Ships, Armies, Battles, in the firmament;
Till steadier eyes the exhalations solve,
And all to its first matter, clouds, resolve!'"

"Truly, Mr. Barbican," answered the Antiquary, as I concluded, "truly, Sir, I should never have divined that you had any dislike to dull reflections, had you not yourself assured me so; but now if you will pledge me in another draught of sack, I'll furnish you with a new scene of London Bridge, from the pencil of an eminent foreigner, as it appeared in May, 1663. This is selected from the very amusing *'Voyages de Mons. de Monconys,'* and the best edition of his book is that bearing the imprint of Paris, though it was in reality published at Lyons, in 1695, duodecimo. In the second volume of this work, and on page 14 of the part relating to England, he thus speaks of London

Bridge. 'After having passed this place,'—that is Greenwich, which the Author calls *Grenuche*,—'we soon came to London, of which the length is truly incredible; but more than two thirds of the River sides are occupied by warehouses and very small buildings of wood, even upon the Bridge, at the foot of which, on the City side, is a large edifice erected wholly of wood, without any iron, which seems to be of hewn stone it is so regularly built. At the other extremity of the Bridge, above the towers of a castle, are many of the heads of the murderers of King Charles.' On page 21, M. Monconys is speaking of the '*bots*'—boats,—which formerly plied on the Thames to carry persons to the City, or Westminster, by way of avoiding the rude English coaches, and the ruder paved streets of London: 'They never,' says he, 'go below the Bridge; although there is not any place to which they cannot be had, but it is considered dangerous for these small boats to go under the Bridge when the tide is running up, for the water has then an extreme rapidity, even greater than when it is returning, and the two currents are united.' On page 121, in mentioning his visit to the Tower, he states that neither in going nor returning did his boat pass under the Bridge; for the tide being running up, there was a fall of more than two feet. The passengers left the boat, crossed to the other side of the Bridge, and then re-entered it: whilst the watermen, he adds, had no difficulty in descending the fall, but a great deal in mounting up it again.

"It has been reported, that during the awful time when London was being devastated by the terrible Plague of 1665, the inhabitants of the Bridge were free from its ravages; which is attributed to the ceaseless rushing of the river beneath it. I have not yet discovered, however, the least foundation for such a tradition in any of the numerous publications which appeared concerning the pestilence; and, indeed, the only place in which I find this edifice at all mentioned, is in that terrible volume attributed to Daniel Defoe, and called '*A Journal of the Plague Year, by a Citizen who continued all the while in London;*' London, 1722, octavo, where, on page 255, when speaking of the fires made in the streets for clearing the air after the pestilence, he says, 'I do not remember whether any was at the City gates, but one at the Bridge foot there was, just by St. Magnus' Church.'

"I cannot imagine, Mr. Geoffrey Barbican, that in the fearful conflagration of London, which occurred between the night of Saturday and the morning of Sunday, the 2nd of September, 1666, the Bridge suffered in any proportion to the rest of the City; for I have already shewn you, from Strype's Stow's '*Survey*,' that some of the original houses of King John's time, were subsequently standing at the Southwark end. I attribute this preservation to the vacancy opposed to the flames at the North end of the Bridge; but as the fire forms so memorable an epoch in the history of London, I shall bring before you some evidence concerning its actual effect upon this building.

"'Twas at still midnight,' says one of the most particular accounts of it extant, 'when all was wrapt in a peaceful silence, and every eye shut up in quiet slumber, that this dreadfull fire brake forth, whose hidden flames at first obscurely crept within close limits; but quickly scorning to be so confined, in a bright blaze brake openly upon us. And now the voice of fire in every street—with horrid emphasis,—is echoed forth: these dreadfull screems disturb our midnight quiet, and raise affrighted people from their beds, who, scarce awake, all seems to be a dream. Each one appears but as a moving statue, as once Lot's wife, viewing her flaming Sodom, transformed into a pillar: a powerfull wind aided these raging flames, which, like a growing foe, increaseth still.' Such is the commencement of a broadside, entitled '*A Short Description of the fatal and dreadfull Burning of London; divided into every day and night's progression. Composed by Samuel Wiseman*;' but yet this most particular sheet relates nothing concerning the Bridge. We have, however, some little information in a narrative written by Thomas Vincent,—a non-conformist Minister, who was ejected from the living of St. Mary Magdalen, in Milk-street;—and called '*God's terrible Judgements in the City, by Plague and Fire.*' Now, says the Author, it 'rusheth down the hill towards the Bridge; crosseth Thames-street, invadeth St. Magnus' Church at the Bridge-foot; and, though that Church were so great, yet it was not a sufficient barricado against this Conqueror; but, having scaled and taken this fort, it shooteth flames with so much the greater advantage into all places round about; and a great building of houses upon the Bridge is quickly thrown to the ground: then the conqueror, *being stayed in his course at the Bridge*, marcheth back to the City again, and runs along with great noise and violence through Thames-street, Westward.' The minute and pathetic narrative of the accomplished John Evelyn, adds nothing to these particulars; for he says only in his '*Diary*,' edit. 1818, volume i., page 375, on September the 7th, upon the destruction of certain houses erected about the Tower, if they had 'taken fire and attacked the White Tower, where the magazine of powder lay, they would undoubtedly not only have beaten and destroyed all ye Bridge, but sunke and torne the vessells in ye River.' The report of Samuel Pepys, in his '*Diary*,' already quoted, does not give us much additional information; though he tells us in volume i., page 445, that on the morning of the 2nd, he went on the Tower battlements, whence he saw 'the houses at that end of the Bridge all on fire; and an infinite great fire on this and the other side the end of the Bridge, which, with other people, did trouble me for poor little Michell and our Sarah on the Bridge.' He subsequently adds that the fire increased on both sides the North end of London Bridge, but there is nothing said farther concerning its attack upon the edifice itself.

"There are several prospects of this dreadful conflagration, though few of them are worthy of any credit, most having been executed in Holland; and it is probable, indeed, that the best was a small and spirited etching by

Wenceslaus Hollar, measuring 7 inches by 2¾, and inserted on the right hand side of '*A New and Exact Map of Great Britaine. Published by John Overton, at the White Horse, without Newgate*. 1667.' Single sheet. This view is taken from Hollar's old observatory, the tower of St. Mary Overies Church; and represents the fire spreading furiously Westward, whilst the Bridge appears untouched. This fine little print you will find to be the first illustration in volume ii. of Mr. Crowle's Pennant in the Print Room of the British Museum; and it is entitled '*Prospect of the City of London, as it appeared in the time of its flames*.' it has frequently sold for 10*s*. 6*d*., and sometimes for 15*s*., even without the plate it belongs to. Hollar's long view of the City immediately after the conflagration, I have already mentioned; and in that we see with much more certainty the actual damage sustained by our unhappy old edifice, in the RUINS OF THE RIVERSIDE AND BRIDGE AFTER THE FIRE.

"The alteration appears chiefly to consist in the destruction of that large square building, which terminated the Northern end of the Bridge; and, of course, the entire demolition of the wooden pales and passage, which had been erected after the fire of 1633; but beyond this the flames do not seem to have penetrated. The banks of the River, indeed, presented a more entire picture of ruin. Of the grand Church of St. Magnus nothing remained but some of the walls, and the buildings in front of it were destroyed even to the water's edge; whilst on the Western side of the Bridge, the Water-works and Tower, numerous houses lining the River, and the ancient edifice of Fishmongers' Hall, were reduced either to smouldering fragments, scarcely bearing even the forms of what they once had been, or else had not one stone left upon another. '*The Long Antwerp View of London*,' which has been already so minutely described, furnishes us with a good representation of FISHMONGERS' HALL BEFORE THE FIRE OF 1666;

and it appears to have been a plain narrow edifice, castellated and covered with lead on the top, having two principal stories, the lower one of which had a kind of gallery or balcony, an ornament which was very common to buildings in this part of London. The Companies of the Salt-fish and Stock-fish mongers were anciently possessed of so many as six Halls; of which two stood in New Fish-street, now called Fish-street Hill; two more were in Old Fish-street, and two others were erected in Thames-street; in each place one for each Company. These, however, were all united in the year 1536, the 28th of Henry the Eighth; after which they were to have but one Hall, namely, the house given to them by Sir John Cornwall, afterwards created Baron Fanhope, in 1427, the 6th year of Henry VI., which I take to have been the building represented in the print; since Stow, in his '*Survey*,' volume i., page 499, from whom we derive these few particulars, says that it was in the Parish of St. Michael, Crooked Lane: and adds on the preceding page, that 'Fishmongers' Hall, with other fair houses for merchants, standeth about midway between the Bridge foot and Ebgate, or Old Swan-lane.' Still more brief, however, are the notices, which he furnishes us concerning the Company's other Halls, which once stood about the same spot. 'On the West side of this Ward,'—says the old Citizen,—'at the North end of London Bridge, is a part of Thames-street, which is also of this Ward, to wit, so much as of old time was called Stock-Fishmonger Row,'—a place, you will remember, referred to in that manuscript Survey of Bridge lands which I some time since recited to you—'of the Stock-fishmongers dwelling there, down West to a Water-gate, of old time called Ebgate, since Ebgate Lane, and now the Old Swan.' I will not enter into the history of the Fishmongers' Company, Mr. Barbican, because it does not belong to our present subject, and you may read the chief particulars for yourself, in Stow's '*Survey*,' volume i., page 498, and volume ii., page 268; and shall therefore only add a very few particulars concerning the present Hall. According to the splendid plan of Sir Christopher Wren, for adorning the banks of the Thames, it presents to the river, a handsome, though somewhat old-fashioned front of red brick, having the windows ornamented with stone cases. From the wharf on which the Shades' Tavern is situate, a grand double flight of stone steps leads to the chief apartments; and the door is decorated with Ionic columns supporting an open pediment, containing a shield with the Company's Arms, all of stone. I shall say nothing, however, of the handsome North front of this building, its spacious court-yard, and its beautiful carved gateway in Thames-street; nor yet of the rich state chambers, their fine paintings of fish, their massive and richly-chased silver branches, their large brazen chandeliers, the interesting relique of Sir William Walworth, nor of the interior of the spacious Hall. I will tell you nothing of either of these, Mr. Geoffrey, since they cannot be observed from London Bridge; but before I entirely quit the Fishmongers, let me observe that Strype, in his Fifth Book of Stow's '*Survey*,' has two very singular notices concerning them, which I do not remember to have seen mentioned in any historical account of yonder passage across the Thames. They consist of certain ancient statutes peculiar to this Company, taken from the record called '*Horn*,' in the Chamber of London; and they state that it should be prohibited that any Fishmonger should 'buy a fresh fish before Mass at the Chapel upon the Bridge be celebrated:' which Chapel, it is elsewhere stated, is one of the bounds, beyond which no Fishmonger ought to go to buy fish.

"I have already observed that Hollar's View of London after the Fire, shews the fine old Church of St. Magnus, which we may consider the North-East boundary of London Bridge, reduced to a pile of ruined walls; having all those costly repairs and beautifyings, which Stow, in his '*Survey*,' volume i., page 494, records as having taken place from 1623 to 1629, destroyed in the flames. Before I speak, however, of the re-edification of this fane, I shall notice the means employed for that of the Bridge itself, as they are related by the continuators of Stow in his '*Survey*,' volume i., page 62. Most of the buildings erected upon it, were, as they tell us, totally consumed; excepting the Chapel, and a few edifices standing on the South end, of the time of King John: though this, as I have shewn you, must be erroneous. We may believe, however, from all the circumstances attendant upon the fire, that the stone-work of the Bridge was so battered and weakened, 'that it cost the Bridge-House £1500. to make good the damage in the piers and arches, before the leaseholders could attempt to rebuild the premises destroyed by the fire.' Though 'the stone work,' continues this passage, 'was no sooner secured, than a sufficient number of tenants offered; who conditioned with the Bridge-House for building-leases of 61 years, at the rate of 10*s.* per foot, running, yearly, and to build after such a form and substantial manner as was prescribed.' This was so rapidly carried into effect, that in five years the North end was all completely finished, with houses four stories high, and a street of 20 feet in breadth between them, measuring from side to side. To make the South end equally perfect, however, and, at the same time, to equalize the rent of the whole, required the invention of some expedient; since the older buildings were already leased to several tenants, with longer and shorter portions of their time yet to elapse, whilst the leases of others were entirely expired. To arrange all these with propriety, the Lord Mayor, Aldermen, and Commonalty, who were appointed for the letting of the Bridge-House lands, with the assistance of Mr. Philip Odde, then Clerk Comptroller of those estates, took the following method. For the first class of tenants, they measured the number of feet in the front of each house; and ascertained the amount of rent, and the time of the lease yet unexpired: whilst a second and third classes were formed of those whose leases were nearly out, or entirely finished. To such as had the longest term to run, a moderate time was added, with an abatement of rent answerable to the cost of re-erecting their buildings, in uniformity with those at the North end. Of the tenants whose leases were nearly expired, and who were unable to build, they were redeemed for valuable considerations; the dilapidated stone-work for the new buildings was then repaired by the City, at an expense of nearly £1000; and in about four or five years the whole edifice was completed.

"We are not, however, now informed of any repair of the Draw-Bridge, although it certainly existed until the great alteration of 1758; but, probably, even long before *this* time, had ceased to be of any great utility. You may see, in Stow's historical notices of Queenhithe, (vide his '*Survey*,' volume i., pages 697-700,) that in the reign of King Henry III. ships and boats laden with corn and fish for sale, were compelled to pass *beyond* the Bridge to that most ancient wharf and market. In 1463, however, the third year of King Edward IV., the same authority informs us that the market at Queenhithe was 'hindered by reason of the slackness of drawing up of London Bridge,' which seems to infer some difficulty in raising it even at that period; fresh ordinances being then made to cause vessels with provisions to proceed up the river. I cannot, however, tell you at what time the Draw-Bridge was made wholly stationary; though it seems not to have been till *after* the publication of the last ancient edition of Stow's '*Survey*,' in 1633, folio, as, in Strype's excellent new one, of 1720, volume i., book i., page 58, he adds some notices of the arches, in which occurs the following passage. 'Two of these arches are much larger than the rest, *viz.* that over which is the Draw-bridge; and the other called *the Simile Lock*. These were for the use of greater vessels that went through Bridge Westward. The Draw-Bridge formerly was, upon such occasions, taken up; but now-a-days never, but when it wants repairing.' The additions of Richard Bloome also, on page 56 in the same volume, furnish us with several particulars of these arches, which I shall introduce to you in this place, because they apply, almost equally, both to the Bridge before the Fire, and to the ancient appearance of the present one. 'There were,' says he, 'three vacancies, with stone walls, and iron grates,'—rather rails,—'over them, on either side, opposite to each other; through which grates, people, as they pass over the Bridge, may take a view of the river both East and West; and also may go aside, more to each side, out of the way of carts and coaches, the passage being but narrow, and not only troublesome but dangerous. These three vacancies are over three of the middle arches, for all the piers are not of a like thickness, nor stand at equal distance one from the other; for under those three vacancies are much wider than the rest, and are called the navigable locks, because vessels of considerable burthen may pass through them. One of these is near unto the second gate, and is called the Rock Lock. The second is under the second vacancy, and is called the *Draw-Bridge Lock*. And the third is near the Chapel, and is called *St. Mary's Lock*. There is a fourth between St. Magnus' Church and the first vacancy, and is called the *King's Lock*, for that the King in his passage through Bridge, in his barge, goes through this lock.' In Strype's additions to these particulars, which I have already referred to, he says, 'The two Arches next London are now stopped up for the use of the Water-mills, but without any prejudice to the current of the Thames. The third arch on the Southwark side is seldom, and very rarely, passed through, because of a rock grown there a little to the East, which is visible at low water. This rock hath been observed this many a year, and is called the *Rock Lock*. The reparation of these arches, and the striking down piles for securing them, is continual, and men are kept on purpose to take care of it, and to do it. Whereof they have two Master-workmen, *viz.* a Head-Carpenter,'—whose name in Strype's time was Wise,—'and a Head-Mason, whose office it is to look after the Bridge under the Bridge-Masters.' The common report of the rock growing beneath the water, under one of the Arches of London Bridge, is, however, one of those popular traditions which are generally to be found connected with almost every edifice, engendered partly by ignorance, and partly by the desire mentioned by the Indian in Robinson Crusoe, 'To make the great wonder look!' 'We have been assured,' says the Rev. John Motley, in '*Seymour's Survey of London*,' volume i. page 48, 'by a person of great veracity as well as curiosity, that a friend of his in the year 1715, when the tide was so kept back that many people walked over the river, went near enough to examine this, and found it to be stones joined together with cement, and iron in some places; and therefore supposed it was part of an arch that had formerly been broken down, and never since removed,' It has been generally believed, that these ruins were the fragments of the two arches, and the Bridge-gate, which, as I have related to you, fell down in the year 1437: and which, having now lain nearly four centuries, and been increased by the deposits which millions of tides have cast upon them, have become almost as impenetrable as a solid rock, and the arch, therefore, retains its ancient name. Such was London Bridge after it was rebuilt, 'peopled'—as Evelyn says of the City, but a very few days after the fire,—'with new shops, noise, and business, not to say vanity.'—'A Bridge,' exclaims Richard Bloome, in his continuations to Stow, volume i. page 499, 'not inferior to any in Europe for its length, breadth, and buildings thereon, being sustained by nineteen great stone arches, secured by piles of timber drove to the bottom of the river, having a Draw-Bridge towards Southwark, as also strong gates; and, by its houses built thereon on both sides, it seemeth rather a street than a Bridge, being now garnished with good timber buildings, which are very well inhabited by sufficient tradesmen, who have very considerable dealings, as being so great a thoroughfare from Southwark into London.'

"Whilst I am mentioning this praise of London Bridge, I may express my wonder that Michael Drayton, in his '*Poly-Olbion*,' London, 1613, folio, says so little concerning it, whilst John Selden, in his very learned notes to that poem, wholly omits it. As I purpose next to say a few words touching the rebuilding of St. Magnus' Church, I will close this part of our Bridge history by repeating Drayton's verses from Song xvii., page 259: where, speaking of the Thames, he says,—

'Then goes he on along by that more beauteous strand,
Expressing both the wealth and brauery of the land;——
So many sumptuous bow'rs, within so little space,
The all-beholding sun scarce sees in all his race:—
And on by London leads, which like a crescent lies,
Whose windowes seem to mock the star-befreckled skies:
Besides her rising spyres, so thick themselues that show,
As doe the bristling reedes within his banks that growe:
There sees his crowded wharfes, and people-pester'd shores,

His bosome overspread with shoales of labouring oares;
With that most costly Bridge, that doth him most renowne,
By which he clearly puts all other Riuers downe.'

"Bloome, the continuator of Stow, to whose labours we are in general little less indebted than we are to those of the old historian himself, gives us but few particulars concerning the rebuilding of St. Magnus' Church; stating only that it was erected of free-stone, with 'a tower and steeple of curious workmanship; to which Church,' he adds, 'is united the Parish of St. Margaret, New Fish-street, that Church not being rebuilt.' Newcourt, in his account of the Rectory of St. Magnus, says likewise very little as to its history; though he tells us, that when the Parishes were united, the yearly value of them was made £170, whereas, in 1632, that of St. Magnus amounted only to £83, and that of St. Margaret to £70: and he states also, that part of their Church, before it was rebuilt, was laid into the street, for enlarging the passage. We have, however, a very fair though brief description of the new Church of St. Magnus, in the *Memoirs of the Life and Works of Sir Christopher Wren*,' by James Elmes; London, 1823, quarto, pages 357, 490; wherein he states that it was begun in 1676, and that the lofty tower, lanthorn, cupola, and spire, were added in 1705. It is then, as all may see for themselves, an elegant and substantial Church, built of stone and oak timber, covered with lead, and crowned with a handsome lofty steeple, consisting of a tower, a lanthorn containing ten bells, and a cupola surmounted by a well-proportioned spire. The interior, measuring 90 feet in length, 59 in breadth, and 41 in height, is divided into a nave and two aisles, by columns, and an entablature of the Ionic Order; whilst the roof, over the nave, is camerated, and enriched with arches of fret work, executed in stucco. For the monuments, epitaphs, and benefactors of this Church, both ancient and modern, I must refer you to Strype's Stow, volume i., page 494; and will mention only the gift of the clock by Sir Charles Duncomb, in the year 1700, at the cost of £485. 5*s*. 4*d*. The dial of this clock was formerly ornamented with several richly gilded figures, which have since been removed, but a view of the Church, before the archway was opened,—of which we shall speak hereafter,—having also the clock in its original state, will be found in Stow's '*Survey*,' at my last reference, and in Maitland's '*History of London*,' volume ii., page 1124. Tradition says, that it was erected in consequence of a vow made by the donor, who, in the earlier part of his life, had once to wait a considerable time in a cart upon London Bridge, without being able to learn the hour, when he made a promise, that if he ever became successful in the world, he would give to that Church a public clock, and an hour-glass, that all passengers might see the time of day. There is in '*The Protestant Mercury*,' of September the 11th, 1700, the following rather curious mention of this clock: 'On Monday last, the Right Honourable the Lord Mayor, accompanied by the worshipful Aldermen and Sheriffs, went, with the usual formalities, to proclaim Southwark fair; after which they were nobly entertained at the Bridge House, according to an ancient annual custom. In their passing by St. Magnus' Church, they were presented with the view of that noble and magnificent Dial erected at the West end, at the charge of the generous Sir Charles Duncomb, which equalizing, if not exceeding, all others of that kind, seems to answer the design of the donor.' This donation is also recorded upon the clock itself; for upon a small metal plate, shaped like a shield, and silvered, screwed to the interior, are engraven the giver's arms,—a chevron between three talbot's heads erased,—with the following inscription: 'The Gift of Sir Charles Duncomb, Knight, Lord Major, and Alderman of this Ward. Langley Bradley fecit, 1709.' The same liberal Citizen also presented the modern fane of St. Magnus with an organ, of which the *'Spectator'* of February the 8th, 1712, thus speaks: 'Whereas Mr. Abraham Jordan, senior and junior, have, with their own hands, joynery excepted, made and erected a very large organ in St. Magnus' Church, at the foot of London Bridge, consisting of four sets of keys, one of which is adapted to the art of emitting sounds by swelling notes, which never was in any organ before; this instrument will be publicly opened on Sunday next, the performance by Mr. John Robinson. The above-said Abraham Jordan gives notice to all masters and performers, that he will attend every day next week at the said Church, to accommodate all those gentlemen who shall have a curiosity to hear it.' I will conclude these notices by referring you to Malcolm's *'Londinum Redivivum,'* volume iv., pages 30-35, where you will find several other particulars concerning St. Magnus.

"Upon the rebuilding of London, after the Great Fire, it was the proposal of Sir Christopher Wren to form a grand quay, or esplanade, from the foot of London Bridge to the Temple; of which scheme there is the fullest information, from an original manuscript, in Mr. Elmes's *'Memoirs,'* pages 270 to 284, *Notes*. It was proposed that the Quay should be 40 feet in width, between the Thames and the houses on its banks; and, in the year 1670, a petition from the inhabitants of this part of London was presented to the Privy Council, stating that it would be of great detriment to them if such way or wharf should not be carried into effect, from London Bridge to Bridewell Dock, the petitioners having commenced their several houses near the Bridge, as well as the pipes and engines of the Water-House. Of the ancient Water-House at this place, I have already given you some idea; but I may observe, from the authority last cited, that its supplies were constantly defiled by the public drains, and other offensive buildings erected upon this spot. Notwithstanding that the Commissioners of Sewers had ordered their removal, and the King's Surveyor General had directed that no such contagious places should be constructed here, even so late as 1670 they had been again renewed, polluting both the water and the passage across the

Thames. In consequence of the petition, Sir Christopher Wren, assisted by the City Surveyors, inspected the whole line of the intended wharf; and his report was:—That the houses then begun to be built fronting the Thames, which were not a third in number of what the range would contain, were, in general, conformable to the act, as to their being 40 feet distant from the River, and that some of them towards the Bridge were not ungraceful; but that others were unequally low, and, as well as the warehouses, irregularly built; whilst some habitations were constructed only of board. The Quay between the row of houses and the River, which should have been left open for passage, was every where enclosed either with pales or brick walls; and covered with stacks of timber, faggots, and coals. The cranes erected West of the Bridge, he states to be unhandsome, and larger than were required, boarded down to the ground, and having warehouses beneath them. The old towers of Baynard's Castle, he observes, were also still standing upon the wharf; the walls, wharfings, and landing-stairs, were, for the most part, unrepaired; and, in some places, the Quay was likely to be broken by bridges and docks. Sir Christopher's report also mentions numerous other obstacles, in consequence of which, their immediate removal was ordered, and the construction of the Quay directed, by an Act of Parliament, in the 22nd of Charles II., 1670, chapter 11, Sections xliv.-xlix.; as well as by a Patent passed in the year following.

"The impediments to this design, however, were never entirely removed; and, in modern times, their number has considerably increased. Of these, Calvert's Brewery is one of the most prominent, which is supposed to occupy the exact site of the mansion anciently called Cold Harbour; where it now forms the two sides of Champion-lane, formerly called Quay-Wharf-lane, which, with All-hallows and Red-bull lanes, was once open to the river. The last important remains of Sir Christopher's grand Civic esplanade was shewn in a line of wharf 40 feet in width, and extending from London Bridge to the Steelyard, entitled New Quay; and it may be seen in the plans in Strype's '*Stow's Survey*,' volume i., pages 486, 510; and in Maitland's '*History*,' volume ii., pages 790, 1046.

"The Act of Parliament which I have recently cited, also contains a very considerable portion of information relative to the new buildings of London; and from section liii. we learn, that the Water-House at London Bridge was not renewed at the time of its being passed, though in the Act for rebuilding London, passed in 1667, the 19th of Charles II., chapter 3, section xli., it is ordained: 'that it shall and may be lawful for the Water-House, called Mr. Thomas Morris his Water-House, formerly adjoining to London Bridge, to be rebuilt upon the place it formerly stood, with timber, for the supplying the South side of the City with water, as it for almost an hundred years hath done.' Most of the ancient engravings of London Bridge, after the Fire, present us with a view of this Water-House, by which it appears that it was a lofty narrow wooden building, standing close to the North West corner of the Bridge. On its Western side, a flight of stairs led down to the river; and its front looked on to the wooden stage which supported the Water-works. Strype, in his '*Stow's Survey*,' volume i., page 500, says, that 'by wheels, iron chains, &c., it drinketh, or rather forceth up water through leaden pipes to the top, where there is a cistern, and from thence descendeth in other leaden pipes to the bottom, and thence, received by other pipes, is conveyed under the pavements of the streets, and so serveth many families in this part of the City with water; who have branches, or small pipes, laid from the main ones unto their houses, to their great convenience, and no small profit to the City.' In the very amusing '*Voyages*' of Mons. Aubri De la Motraye, Hague, 1727-32, folio, volume iii., pages 360-362, and plate iv., we have an engraving of the interior mechanism of a public fire-engine erected near this building, with an account of the means employed in it for raising of the water. One of the most picturesque and interesting representations of this modern WATER-HOUSE at LONDON BRIDGE,

is contained in a series of five views by S. and N. Buck, which forms a sort of panoramic prospect of London, from Westminster to below the Tower; each being taken from a different point of observation. They are dated September the 11th, 1749, and the Bridge as it then appeared, covered with buildings, forms a very prominent feature. I have to add only, that you will find a set of these prints in volume xiii. of Mr. Crowle's Illustrated Pennant in the British Museum."

"Well, Master Barnaby," said I, as well as I was able for yawning, "though *you* can find no more to say about this Water-House, I must add a few fragments which would otherwise be lost; even as the song says,

'Mister Speaker, though 'tis late,
I must lengthen the debate.'

I have been informed, upon the evidence of a very ancient servant of the present London Bridge, that the water rose in this Tower to the height of 128 feet, through a pipe 12 inches in calibre, often bringing very fine fish up with it; and that from beneath the cistern at the top, issued nine main pipes which supplied all London. As the particular direction of each of these pipes was, of course, entirely different, in the event of a fire, all of them were stopped excepting the one which led immediately through that district; and thus the whole weight of water was thrown towards any place desired. From the same source, I have also received a curious and very particular drawing upon vellum, in colours, representing the North end of London Bridge, the Water-House and works, and the directions of the pipes issuing therefrom, taken from actual measurement, and executed, as I should suppose, before the fire by which they were destroyed, on Sunday, October the 31st, 1779; but this view shall be referred to hereafter. The fire to which I have alluded, brake out in the warehouse of Messrs. Judd and Sanderson, Hop Merchants, at the foot of London Bridge, and having speedily communicated to the Water-works, in less than an hour they were reduced nearly to a level with the river. The wooden Water-Tower having been pitched but a few days before, all the efforts of its engines were, therefore, ineffectual. But enough of water, Mr. Postern: what say you to another draught of sack, and then another spell at the history of London Bridge itself?"

"I like your motion mightily," replied my companion, "and, once more, here's your health. In speaking of the Great Fire of London, its consequences, and the new buildings to which it gave birth, I have brought forwards many fragments of our Bridge annals, and anticipated several events, because I wished to draw my information, as much as possible, into one focus. We next pass to the year 1669, though I should not mention to you the short notice of London Bridge by Lorenzo Magalotti, which occurs in '*The Travels of Cosmo III., Grand Duke of Tuscany, through England, during the reign of King Charles II. 1669,*' London, 1821, quarto; but that it affords something like a proof that the destruction occasioned by the Fire of London was not extensive, so far as it regarded this building, which by that time seems to have been repaired. You will find the passage at page 317, and it runs thus. 'On the morning of the 27th'—of May,—'after hearing Mass, his Highness went through the City as far as London Bridge, on which are erected many large buildings, almost half of which escaped the fire there; and those which were consumed have been rebuilt of smaller size, the upper part being used as dwellings, and the lower part as Mercers' shops, all of which are abundantly filled with goods of various sorts. We crossed the Bridge with some difficulty, owing to the number of carts which are constantly passing and repassing.' He then proceeds to speak of the Marshalsea, the prisoners of which, he adds, have liberty to take a walk over the Bridge, their promise being first taken that they will not pass the limits, which they very rarely infringe.

"Having mentioned to you, Mr. Geoffrey, several famous Frosts which occurred in the earlier periods of our history, I must not omit to notice that which overspread the Thames from the beginning of December, 1683, until the 5th of February, 1684. 'It congealed the River Thames,'—says Maitland, in his '*History*,' volume i., page 484,—'to that degree, that another City, as it were, was erected thereon; where, by the great number of streets, and shops, with their rich furniture, it represented a great fair, with a variety of carriages, and diversions of all sorts; and, near Whitehall, a whole ox was roasted on the ice.' Evelyn, however, who was an eye-witness of this scene, furnishes the most extraordinary account of it in his '*Diary*,' volume i., page 568; where, on January the 24th, 1684, he observes that 'the frost continuing more and more severe, the Thames before London was still planted with boothes in formal streetes, all sorts of trades and shops furnish'd, and full of commodities, even to a printing-presse, where the people and ladyes tooke a fancy to have their names printed, and the day and yeare set down when printed on the Thames: this humour tooke so universally, that 'twas estimated the printer gain'd £5. a day, for printing a line onely, at sixpence a name, besides what he got by ballads, &c. Coaches plied from Westminster to the Temple, and from several other staires to and fro, as in the streetes; sleds, sliding with skeetes, a bull-baiting, horse and coach races, puppet-plays, and interludes, cookes, tipling, and other lewd places, so that it seem'd to be a bacchanalian triumph, or carnival on the water.'"

"It is singular, Master Postern," said I, as he finished this extract, "that the author whom you have now quoted, never once mentions that King Charles the Second visited these diversions, and even had his name printed on the ice, with those of several other personages of the Royal Family. The author of some curious verses, entitled, '*Thamasis's Advice to the Painter, from her Frigid Zone: or Wonders upon the Water. London: Printed by G. Croom, on the River of Thames*,' 74 lines, small folio half sheet, says,

"'Then draw the *King*, who on his *Leads* doth stay,
To see the *Throng* as on a *Lord Mayor's day*,
And thus unto his *Nobles* pleas'd to say;

With these *Men* on this *Ice*, I'de undertake
To cause the *Turk* all *Europe* to forsake:
An Army of these *Men*, arm'd and compleat,
Would soon the *Turk* in *Christendom* defeat.'

"The original of this poem is in the possession of my friend, Mr. William Upcott, of the London Institution, whose invaluable collection of rarities can also boast one of the very papers on which the King and his Royal companions had their names printed! This truly interesting document consists of a quarter sheet of coarse Dutch paper, on which, within a type border, measuring 3¼ inches by 4, are the magnificent names of

        CHARLES, KING.
        JAMES, DUKE.
        KATHERINE, QUEEN.
        MARY, DUTCHESS.
        ANN, PRINCESSE.
        GEORGE, PRINCE.
        HANS IN KELDER.

London: Printed by *G. Croom*, on
the ICE, on the River of *Thames, January 31, 1684.*

"Here, then, we have King Charles the Second; his brother James, Duke of York, afterwards James the Second; Queen Catherine, Infanta of Portugal; Mary D'Este, sister of Francis, Duke of Modena, James's Second Duchess; the Princess Anne, second daughter of the Duke of York, afterwards Queen Anne; and her husband, Prince George of Denmark: and the last name, which I think was doubtless a touch of the King's humour, signifies 'Jack in the Cellar,' alluding to the pregnant situation of Anne of Denmark. This most remarkable paper may, with great probability, be considered *unique*; and not to mention several of a similar nature containing common names, I may notice to you that there is in the same collection another bearing the noble titles of 'Henry, Earl of Clarendon,' son of the Chancellor; 'Flora, Countess of Clarendon,' and 'Edward, Lord Cornbury.' The date of this is February the 2nd, and I will conclude these notices of printing on the ice, by some lines from the poem I have already quoted, which tell its readers

'—————————— to the *Print-house* go,
Where *Men* the *Art of Printing* soon do know:
Where, for a *Teaster*, you may have your *Name*
Printed, hereafter for to shew the same;
And sure, in *former Ages*, ne'er was found,
A *Press* to *print*, where men so oft were dround!'"

"I am very much bounden to you, honest Mr. Geoffrey," recommenced the Antiquary, as I concluded, "for these most appropriate and interesting illustrations: for although the sports of this frost can hardly be said to form an immediate portion of the history of London Bridge, yet so memorable an event on the Thames well deserves some pains to be bestowed in recording it.

"The principal scene of this Blanket-Fair, indeed,—for so the tents and sports on the Thames were denominated,—was opposite to the Temple stairs, for few, or none, of the festivities approached very near to London Bridge; as we are informed by the many rude, but curious memorials of it, which are yet in existence. One of the most interesting of these is an original and spirited, though unfinished, sketch in pencil, slightly shaded with Indian ink; supposed to have been the production of Thomas Wyck, an artist particularly eminent for his views at this period. In the right hand corner, at the top, the drawing is dated in an ancient hand, '*Munday, February the 4*: 1683-4;' and it consists of a view down the River from the Temple-stairs to London Bridge, the buildings of which are faintly seen in the back ground. In front appear various groups of figures, and a side prospect of that line of tents which stretched all across the Thames, known during the frost by the name of Temple-street. You will find this drawing in volume viii. of Mr. Crowle's Illustrated Pennant, in the British Museum, after page 262; and it measures 28 inches by 9$\frac{3}{8}$. Gough, in his '*British Topography*,' volume i., pages 731, 784,* mentions several other publications 'illustrative of this frost, some of which are also in the same volume of Mr. Crowle's Pennant, and the principal particulars of them I shall give you briefly in the following list.

"A large copper-plate, 20$\frac{1}{2}$ inches by 16$\frac{5}{8}$, entitled '*A Map of the River Thames, merrily call'd Blanket Fair, as it was frozen in the memorable year 1683-4, describing the booths, footpaths, coaches, sledges, bull-baiting, and other remarks upon that famous* river.' Dedicated to Sir Henry Hulse, Knt. and Lord Mayor, by James Moxon, the Engraver.

"A large and coarse engraving on wood, representing the sports, tents, and buildings on the ice, taken from opposite the Temple buildings, which are shewn in the back ground; beneath are 106 lines of very inferior verse, and the title:—'*A true description of Blanket-Fair, upon the River Thames, in the time of the great Frost. In the year of our Lord 1683.*' Broadside sheet, 12¾ inches by 16½.

"'*Wonders on the deep, or the most exact description of the frozen river of Thames; also what was remarkably observed thereon in the last great frost, which began about the middle of December, 1683, and ended the 8th of February following: together with a brief Chronology of all the memorable strong frosts for almost 60 years, and what happened in the Northern kingdoms.*' A wood-cut.

"'*A wonderfull fair, or a fair of wonders; being a new and true illustration and description of the several things acted and done on the river of Thames in the time of the terrible frost, which began about the beginning of Dec. 1683, and continued till Feb. 4, and held on with such violence that men and beasts, coaches and sledges, went common thereon. There was also a street of booths from the Temple to Southwark, where was sold all sorts of goods: likewise bull-baiting, and an ox roasted whole, and many other things, as the map and description do plainly shew.*' Engraved and printed on a sheet, 1684.

"A volume of coarse and worthless narratives, entitled '*An historical account of the Late Great Frost, in which are discovered, in several Comical Relations, the various Humours, Loves, Cheats, and Intreagues of the Town, as the same were mannaged upon the River of Thames during that season.*' London. 1684. 12mo.

"'*Freezland-Fair, or the Icey Bear Garden. 1682.*'

"'*News from the Thames; or the frozen Thames in tears. January 1683-4.*' Half sheet, folio.

"'*A winter wonder, or the Thames frozen over; with remarks on the resort there. 1684.*'

"'*A strange and wonderfull relation of many remarkable damages sustained, both at sea and land, by the present unparaleled Frost.*' London. 1684. Half sheet small folio, 2 pages.

"Notwithstanding the admiration with which London Bridge had long been regarded, on account of its appearance as an actual street over the Thames; in 1685 its very confined limits seem to have attracted attention, and to have produced at least somewhat of reformation. There is a tradition extant, though I have not as yet been able to trace it to any printed authority, that the cross over the dome of St. Paul's having been cast in Southwark, the street of London Bridge was too narrow, and its numerous arches too low, to allow of it being that way brought into the City: and Hatton, in his '*New

View of London,' volume ii., page 791, shews us that in his time the enlarging of the Bridge was recorded upon the North side of the Nonesuch House, in the following inscription:—

"'ANNO MDCLXXXV., ET PRIMO JACOBI II. REGIS,

This Street was opened and enlarged from 12, to the width of 20 foot:

SIR JAMES SMITH, KNIGHT, LORD MAYOR.'

"Even until the time, however, when London Bridge was entirely cleared of its houses, the street over it has always been described as dark, narrow, and dangerous. 'The houses on each side,'—says Pennant, page 320,—'overhung, and leaned in a most terrific manner. In most places they hid the arches, and nothing appeared but the rude piers.—I well remember the street on London Bridge, narrow, darksome, and dangerous to passengers, from the multitude of carriages: frequent arches of strong timber crossing the street, from the tops of the houses to keep them together, and from falling into the river. Nothing but use could preserve the repose of the inmates, who soon grew deaf to the noise of falling waters, the clamors of watermen, or the frequent shrieks of drowning wretches. Most of the houses were tenanted by pin or needle-makers, and economical ladies were wont to drive from the St. James's end of the town, to make cheap purchases.'

"The '*New and Universal History, Description, and Survey of the Cities of London and Westminster, the Borough of Southwark, and their adjacent parts,*' by Walter Harrison, London, 1776, folio, furnishes some few additional features to this scene: although the work itself is, perhaps, anything but reputable; being chiefly a compilation from Stow and Strype, without much acknowledgment of the originals. Some particulars of London Bridge, however, the compiler himself actually knew, and on page 24, he says,—'Across the middle of the street there were several lofty arches, extending from one side to the other, the bottom part of each arch terminating at the first story, and the upper part reaching near the top of the buildings. These arches were designed to support the houses on each side the street, and were therefore formed of strong timbers bolted into the houses, which, being covered with lath and plaister, appeared as if built with stone.' The Rev. J. Motley, in his '*Seymour's Survey of London,*' volume i., page 48, also says,—'On each side, between the houses, are left three vacancies, opposite to each other, two with stone walls, upon which are iron rails, that people passing along may take a view of the river East and West, and may also step out of the way of carts and coaches, the passage being formerly very narrow, and the floors of the houses that lay cross the streets being low, they not only rendered those places dark, but likewise obstructed the free passage of carts, if they were loaded any way high, and coaches, so that they could not pass by one another, which oftentimes occasioned great stops upon the Bridge, and was a great hindrance to passengers.' As there was no regular foot-way over the Bridge, it was therefore the most usual and safest custom to follow a carriage which might be passing across it. The brief notice of London Bridge in Hoffmann's '*Lexicon Universale*' is not worth repeating, but you will find it in volume iii., page 833, column i., character ξ: and though a much better account of it in 1697 appears in Motraye's '*Voyages*,' volume i., page 150, it contains nothing new. He calls it 'one of the strongest buildings which he had seen in this nation.'

"A very melancholy instance of suicide which took place in April, 1689, bears testimony to the power of the torrent at London Bridge at that period; and you will find it recorded in that very interesting work, entitled '*The Travels and Memoirs of Sir John Reresby, Baronet,*' best edition, with a Preface by Edmund Lodge, Esq., London, 1813, 8vo. page 406.—'About this time,'—says the Author of this volume,—'a very sad accident happened, which, for a while, was the discourse of the whole town: Mr. Temple, son to Sir William Temple, who had married a French lady with 20,000 pistoles; a sedate and accomplished young gentleman, who had lately by King William been made Secretary of War; took a pair of oars, and drawing near the Bridge, leapt into the Thames and drowned himself, leaving a note behind him in the boat, to this effect: 'My folly in undertaking what I could not perform, whereby some misfortunes have befallen the King's service, is the cause of my putting myself to this sudden end; I wish him success in all his undertakings, and a better servant.' Pennant, in repeating this anecdote in his '*Account of London*,' page 323, adds that it took place on the 14th of April; that the unhappy suicide loaded his pockets with stones to destroy all chance of safety; and that his father's false and profane reflection on the occasion was, 'that a wise man might dispose of himself, and make his life as short as he pleased!'

"From a very remote period, the City of London has protected the persons and property of its Orphans; and so early as the year 1391 the Orphans' Fund was possessed of very considerable wealth, since the sum of 2000 marks, or £1333. 6s. 8d., was then borrowed from it to procure corn during a dearth. In the year 1693, the City stood indebted to the same source, as well as to other creditors, in the amount of £747,500, and an Act of Parliament was at length procured, establishing a fund for their re-payment; by which all the City estates, excepting those belonging to the Hospitals, London Bridge, and such places as were liable to its repairs, were charged with raising the annual sum of £8000, clear of all deductions, as a perpetual deposit for paying an interest of 4 per cent. to the said creditors. The act itself is in volume iii. of Owen Ruffhead's '*Statutes at Large*,' London, 1770, 4to., the 5th of William and Mary, 1694, chapter x., section 2. In which year also, during the

Mayoralty of Sir William Ashurst, the Common Council passed an Act, on Wednesday the 15th of June, that as the ensuing Midsummer day, the time for delivering the Bridge-House accounts, would fall on a Sunday, for ever after, in such a case, they were to be delivered the next day following. An original copy of which Act is in the xxv.th volume of London Tracts in the British Museum, folio.

"I have already mentioned several particulars of the Bridge-House revenues, and the salaries of the Wardens at various periods; and I shall now shew you the ancient estimation of several other offices of the same establishment. In the xxviii.th volume of London Tracts last cited, is a folio sheet, entitled '*A List of the Rooms and Offices bought and sold in the City of London;*' the total amount of which is £145,586; and there occur in it the following valuations of places belonging to the Bridge. '1 Clerk of the Bridge House, £1250.—2 Carpenters of the Bridge-House, £200 each.—1 Mason of the Bridge-House, £200.—1 Plasterer to the Bridge-House, £200.—1 Pavier to the Bridge House, £250.—1 Plummer to the Bridge-House, £250.—2 Porters of the Bridge-House, £100 each.—1 Purveyor of the Bridge House, £200.—1 Shotsman of the Bridge-House, £200.' The whole of this list is also printed in Motley's '*Seymour's Survey of London,*' volume i., page 261: and at the end of the original is the following note, more particularly fixing the time when these offices were held in such estimation. 'Whereas, James Whiston, in a late book, intituled '*England's Calamities Discovered,*' &c.—London, 1696, quarto,—'set forth the mischievous consequences of buying and selling places in Cities, States, and Kingdoms: and the discovery of the disease being the first step towards the cure; for that end some persons, well-affected to the government of this City and Kingdom, have taken great pains to find out the number and value of ye places bought and sold within this City; which are to ye best information that can at present be got, as followeth.'—And now, pledge me once more, Mr. Geoffrey Barbican, in a farewell libation to the seventeenth century, for this notice brings us down to the year 1701."

"Marry, Sir, and I'm heartily glad on't," said I, "for I began to be like honest Bunyan's Pilgrims on 'the Enchanted Ground,' and to have much ado to keep my eyes open: but as I now really think there is some *little* prospect that your tale will have an end, I shall do mine endeavour to be wakeful during the next century and a quarter, which you have yet to lecture upon. And, in the meanwhile, like Peter the Ziegenhirt, in Otmar's German story, which gave Geoffrey Crayon the idea of Rip Van Winkle, I shall take another draught of the wine-pitcher; and so once again, Mr. Barnaby, here's to you."

"My most hearty thanks are your's," replied he, "and let me add, for your consolation, that I really have comparatively but little to say in the next century; for a great portion of it was occupied in doubting whether the Bridge would stand, in surveying its buildings, in repairing it, in disputing concerning the erection of a new one, in receiving the reports of architects, and in adopting schemes for its alteration.

"The year 1701 may be considered as the important period, when the Waterworks at London Bridge began to advance towards that extent and power at which they afterwards arrived. Peter Moris, the original inventor, had a lease from the City for 500 years, paying 10*s.* of yearly rent for the use of the Thames water, one arch of the Bridge, and a place on which he might erect his mill. The Citizens soon experiencing the benefit of his invention, granted him, two years after, a similar lease for a second arch, by which his wealth considerably increased; and, with various improvements, the property continued in his family until this time, when the proprietor finding his profits lessened by the works at the New River, it was sold to one Richard Soams, Citizen and Goldsmith, for £36,000. That it might be the more secure, Soams procured from the City, in confirmation of his bargain, another grant for the fourth arch,—the third belonging to a wharfinger,—and a new lease of the unexpired term, at the yearly rent of 20*s.*, and a fine of £300. He then divided the whole property into 300 shares of £500 each, and formed it into a company; all which information you will find in Strype's 'Stow's *Survey*,' volume i., page 29; and in Maitland's '*History*,' volume i., pages 51, 52. Subsequently, however, a fifth arch was granted by the Court of Common Council, after a long debate, on June the 23rd, 1767; under an express condition that if, at any time, it should be found injurious to the navigation of the river, the City might revoke their grant, upon re-payment of the expenses. A particular description of these works, which I shall speak of hereafter, will be found in the '*Philosophical Transactions, volume xxxvii. for the years 1731, 1732*,' London, 1733, 4to. No. 417, pages 5-12, written by Henry Beighton, with a plate, of which I possess the original drawing, executed very carefully in pen-and-ink.

"The earliest view of London Bridge in this century, I take to be that very barbarous print by Sutton Nicholls, an Engraver who resided in London, about the year 1710, was much employed by the booksellers, and who executed several of the plates in Strype's edition of 'Stow's *Survey*.' His prospect of the Bridge is a large and coarse engraving in two sheets, measuring 35 inches, by 22½, and is divided lengthways into two parts; the upper one entitled '*The West side of London Bridge*,' on a ribbon, and the lower one the Eastern side, in the same manner. Both of these views are horizontal, and of most execrable drawing, especially with respect to the water and vessels; and the Print seldom produces more than a few shillings, though I should observe that there are two editions of it. One bearing the imprint of '*Printed for and Sold by I. Smith, in Exeter Exchange in the Strand*,' which is the earliest and best; and another marked '*Printed for, and Sold by, Tho. Millward and Bis. Dickinson, at Inigo Jones Head, next the Globe Tavern, in Fleet Street*;' which latter is probably still in existence, as impressions of it are by no means rare. Below the views are engraven '*An Historical Description of the great and admirable Bridge in the City of London over the River of Thames,*' and Howell's verses, which I have already cited to you. But although its present value is so trifling, it is yet far beyond the original price of it, for in the Harleian MSS., No. 5956, is an impression of the following curious original copper-plate Prospectus for its publication:—

'"Proposals for Printing a Prospect of London Bridge, Thirty-five Inches Long, and Twenty-three Inches Broad.

'1st. Every Subscriber paying half a Crown at the time of subscription, shall have a Prospect pasted on Cloath in a Black Frame, paying half a Crown more at the receipt thereof.

'2dly. Every Subscriber paying one shilling at the time of subscription, shall have one of the Prospects on Paper only, paying one shilling more at the receipt thereof.

'3dly. He that subscribes, or procures subscriptions, for six framed ones, shall have a seventh in a Frame, Gratis; and he that subscribes, or procures subscriptions, for six in sheets, shall have a seventh in sheets, Gratis.

'4thly. Any person that desires it, may see a Drawing of the same in the hands of Sutton Nicholls, Ingraver, against the George Inn, in Aldersgate Street, London, where subscriptions are taken in. At the same place is taught the Art of Drawing, by Sight, Measure, or Instrument; also the Art of Writing: Prints and Mapps, Surveys, Ground Plotts, Uprights, and Perspectives, are there Drawn and Coloured at reasonable rates.' This view of London Bridge is mentioned by Gough, in his '*British Topography,*' volume i., page 734.

"Although the Thames was again frozen over at intervals in the year 1709, and some persons crossed it on the ice, yet the frost was neither so intense nor so permanent as to cause another fair; though, in the illustrated Pennant in the British Museum, there is an impression of a coarse bill, within a wood-cut border of rural subjects, containing the words '*Mr. John Heaton, Printed on the Thames at Westminster, Jan. the 7th, 1709. The Art and Mystery of Printing first invented by John Guttemberg, in Harlem, in 1440, and brought into England by John Islip.*' 7 inches by 5¾.

"About the end of November 1715, however, a very severe frost commenced, which continued until the 9th of the following February, when the sports of 1683 were all renewed; but of this I shall mention only the few curious memorials of it to be found in Mr. Crowle's London collections in the British Museum.

"A copper-plate, 6 inches by 7¼, representing a view of London from the opposite shore, with London Bridge on the right hand, and a line of tents on the left, leading from *'Temple Stairs.'* In front, another line of tents marked *'Thames Street,'* and the various sports, &c. before them: below the print are alphabetical references, with the words *'Printed on the Thames 17$^{16}/_{15}$;'* and above it, *'Frost Fair on the River Thames.'*

"A copper-plate, 16 inches by 20¼, representing London at St. Paul's, with the tents, &c. and with alphabetical references; *'Printed and Sold by John Bowles, at the Black Horse, in Cornhill.'* In the right hand corner above, the arms and supporters of the City; and in the left, a cartouche with the words *'Frost Fayre, being a True Prospect of the Great varietie of Shops and Booths for Tradesmen, with other curiosities and humors, on the Frozen River of Thames, as it appeared before the City of London, in that memorable Frost in ye second year of the Reigne of Our Sovereigne Lord King George, Anno Domini 1716.'*

"'*Frost Fair: or a View of the booths on the frozen Thames, in the 2nd Year of King George, 1716.*' A wood-cut.

"'*An exact and lively view of the booths, and all the variety of shows, &c. on the ice, with an alphabetical explanation of the most remarkable figures, 1716.*' A copper plate.

"In the year 1716, a very remarkable phenomenon occurred at London Bridge, when, in consequence of the long drought, the stream of the River Thames was reduced so low, and from the effects of a violent gale of wind, at West-South-West, was blown so dry, that many thousands of people passed it on foot, both above and below the Bridge, and through most of the arches. Strype, in his edition of Stow's *'Survey,'* volume i., page 58, states, that he was an eye-witness to this event; and observes that, on September 14th, the channel in the middle of the River was scarcely ten yards wide, and very shallow; the violence of the wind having prevented the tide from coming up for the space of four and twenty hours. Whilst the Thames remained in this state, many interesting observations were made on the construction and foundation of London Bridge; and the *'Weekly Packet,'* from September the 15th to September the 22d, states, that a silver tankard, a gold ring, a guinea, and several other things which had been lost there, were then taken up.

"The author of *'Wine and Walnuts,'* in one of his chapters, which relate to this edifice, volume ii., page 112, gives a few notices of a feast held upon it in April, 1722, whilst some repairs were carrying on about the Draw-Bridge: and states, that it being settled that the Bridge should be shut on the Saturday and Sunday, the old street was empty and silent; tables were set out in the highway, where, besides the residents, several of the wealthy tradesmen in the vicinity sat drinking through the afternoon; that they might be enabled to say—adds Malcolm,—who notices the circumstance in his *'Anecdotes of the Manners and Customs of London during the Eighteenth Century,'* London, 1808, quarto, volume ii., page 233,—'however crowded the Bridge is, I have drank punch upon it for great part of a day.' Though I do not find this festivity recorded in any of the public prints, yet in the '*Daily Courant*' for Friday, April the 13th, 1722, is a notice from the Wardens of London Bridge, that the Draw-Bridge Lock, through which hoys, lighters, and other vessels usually passed, would be boomed up on the following Wednesday, the 18th, for repairing; whilst in the same paper for Friday, April the 20th, a second notice appeared, that on Saturday, the 12th of May, between the hours of 9 and 10 in the evening, the Draw-Bridge itself would be taken up in order to lay down a new one, which was completed by the Thursday following. At the same time, the Rulers of the Company of Watermen issued a notice, that the Stairs at Pepper Alley would be dangerous during the repairs; and that persons were requested to take water higher up the River. It is also stated in the '*Daily Post*' of Tuesday, May the 15th, that the new Draw-Bridge was to be considerably stronger than the old one, both in wood and iron; and that the former had been laid down in the Whitsun holidays, exactly fifty years previously, on May the 12th, 1672, the work being completed in five days.

"About the end of the seventeenth century, the improvement of the passage over London Bridge seems to have been actively considered, if not executed: for in 1697, the 8th and 9th year of William III., (chapter xxxvii.,) an Act was passed concerning the Streets in London, Westminster, Southwark, &c. '*and for widening the Street at the South end of London Bridge.*' In section 8 of which, it is stated that 'the Corporation of London have of late years, with great charge and difficulty, pulled down and new built all the houses upon London Bridge, and caused the street or common passage over the same to be opened and enlarged; which good and public intention is not yet perfected, by reason of certain tenements on or near the South end of the Bridge, which yet continue a great hindrance to commerce by occasioning frequent stops, and endangering the lives of many passengers.' Commissioners are then appointed to treat with the owners of such houses, as they shall think fit to be pulled down. See the Act itself in Ruffhead's '*Statutes at Large*,' volume iii., page 687. Again, in the year 1722, during the Mayoralty of Sir Gerard Conyers, an Act was issued by the Corporation of the City, for preserving the passage of the Bridge free, which you may read at length in Motley's '*Seymour's Survey*,' volume i., page 49: it ordains that there shall be three persons, appointed by the Governors of Christ's Hospital, the inhabitants of Bridge Ward Within, and the Bridge-Masters, to give daily attendance at each end of the Bridge. Their duty being, to oblige all carriages coming from Southwark, to keep the West side, and others the contrary; and to prevent any cart from standing across the Bridge to load or unload. It was also ordered, that the Toll Collector—whose station was in the present Watch House, at the North-west corner of the Bridge,—should collect the duties without delay; and, in 1723, they were 'For every cart or waggon with shod wheels, 4*d*.; For a dray with five barrels, 1*d*.; For every pipe or butt, 1*d*.; For a ton of any goods, 2*d*.; for any thing less than a ton, 1*d*.;' which order was directed to be printed and published in the most public places within the City, and upon London Bridge itself. I may merely add, that Maitland tells us in his '*History*,' volume i., page 48, that in 1725, when it was proposed to erect a Bridge at Westminster, Mr. Henry Garbrand, the Deputy Comptroller of London Bridge, and Mr. Bartholomew Sparruck, the Water Carpenter, measured the River at this building, and found it to be 915 feet 1 inch in breadth; the height of the Bridge, 43 feet, 7 inches; the width of the street, 20 feet; and the depth of the houses on each side, 53 feet, or 73 feet in the whole. One of the last fires which happened on London Bridge, took place on the 8th of September in this year, during the Mayoralty of Sir George Mertins, Knight; and, as Motley tells us in his '*Seymour's Survey*,' volume i., page 49, commenced at the house of a brush-maker, near St. Olave's, Tooley Street, through the carelessness of a servant. It burned down all the houses on that side of the way as far as the Bridge-Gate, with several of the buildings on the other; and '*Mist's Weekly Journal*,' of Saturday, September the 11th, describes it in the following words:—'On Wednesday night, between eleven and twelve o'clock, a fire broke out at a Haberdasher's of Hats, on the Bridge foot in Southwark, which burnt on both sides of the way with great violence for four or five hours. We hear that about sixty houses are consumed, some upon the first and second arch of the Bridge; and had it not been for the stone gate which stopp'd the fire very much, the rest of the houses on the Bridge had in all likelyhood been down: the Bridge for some time was, by the fall of the timber and rubbish, render'd impassable for coaches, waggons, and carts, which were oblig'd to cross over at Lambeth Ferry. The damage done amounts to many thousands of pounds, but no just computation can yet be made.' The old Bridge-Gate was so much damaged by this conflagration, that in 1726 it was taken down and re-built, being finished in the year 1728. THE NEW SOUTH GATE ON LONDON BRIDGE,

was furnished with two posterns for foot-passengers, and was decorated with the Royal Arms, under which was inscribed, 'This Gate was widened from eleven to eighteen feet, in the Mayoralty of Sir Edward Becher, Knight, S. P. Q. L.' The medalet, with a representation of this edifice, I have already mentioned to you, and it may now be stated that it was taken down in the year 1760, with all the other buildings on the Bridge, and the materials sold by auction. At which sale, the fine old sculpture of the Royal Arms was bought, with some other articles, by a Mr. Williams, a stone-mason of Tooley Street; who, being soon after employed to take down the gateway at Axe and Bottle Yard, and to form the present King Street, in the Borough, introduced several of the old Bridge materials in erecting it. The ancient Royal Arms, too, are yet to be seen on the front of a small public house, on the right-hand side of the Western end of the same street, between the numbers 4 and 67; with the inscription 'G. III. R. 1760., King Street,' carved around them. Mr. Williams also bought several of the facing stones of the old London Bridge, of which he built a very curious house, the roof being of the same stone, and which, about three years since, was standing in Lock's Fields, near Prospect Row, Newington, usually known by the name of '*Williams's Folly.*' The new Bridge-Gate stood near the corner of Pepper Alley Stairs, and you will find a representation of it in the Frontispiece to the first volume of Maitland's '*History.*' I imagine, that upon the removal of the old gate, the custom of erecting the heads of traitors there was discontinued, as I find no subsequent notice of it; and the last heads which, probably, were placed upon its towers, are said to have been those of the Regicides in 1661, as I have shewn from Monconys, though, in the numerous pamphlets of their Trials, &c., I find no account of their being thus disposed. From *'The Traytors' Perspective Glass,'* London, 1662, 4to., we learn, however, that the heads of Cromwell and Ireton were set over Westminster Hall; and of the others, it is said, 'their heads, *in several places*, are become a spectacle both to angels and men, and a prey to birds of the air.'

In Maitland's *'History,'* volume i., page 49, we are furnished with 'a brief state of the Bridge Account, from Lady-day 1726 to ditto 1727, by the Bridge-Masters, Matthew Snablin and John Web.

'*Charge.*	£.	s.	d.
'By Money in the Bridge-Masters' hands, at the foot of the last Account	576	9	9
By ditto in the Tenants' hands in arrears	4271	13	3
By the General Rental this year	3299	0	5
By Fines this Year	493	4	2
By Casual Receipts	267	6	8
The whole charge.	£8907	14	3

'*Discharge.*	£.	s.	d.
'To Rents and Quit-Rents	49	12	8
To Taxes and Trophy-Money	209	14	3
To Weekly Bills, Expenses, and Emptions	1648	0	7
To Timber and Boards	430	18	9
To Stones, Chalk, Lime, Terrass, and Bricks	197	6	0
To Iron-work	170	0	0
To Plumber, Glazier, Painter, and Paviour	278	8	0
To Shipwrights' Work and Cordage	61	5	0
To Benevolence to the Lord Mayor, &c.	145	6	8

To particular Payments by Order of Court	173	7	0
To Fees and Salaries	270	4	0
To Costs at Audit and Lady Fair	296	2	0
To Money due to balance	4977	9	4
	£8907	14	3'

On Wednesday, the 26th of December, 1739-40, commenced another Frost, the most severe which had occurred since 1716. The Thames, as we are told by the *'Gentleman's Magazine,'* of 1740, volume x., page 35, January 31, floated with rocks and shoals of ice; and when they fixed, represented a snowy field, every where rising in masses and hills of ice and snow. Of this scene, several artists made sketches; whilst tents and printing-presses were erected, and a complete Frost-fair was again held upon the River, over which multitudes walked, though some lost their lives by their rashness. It was in this fair that Doll, the Pippin-woman, whom I before mentioned, lost her life, as Gay relates it in the Second Book of his *'Trivia,'* verses 375-392; the last line of which seems to be an imitation of that song which we formerly considered, and which was extremely popular even in the time of Gay himself. The passage I particularly allude to is this:

'Doll every day had walk'd these treacherous roads;
Her neck grew warp'd beneath Autumnal loads
Of various fruit: she now a basket bore;
That head, alas! shall basket bear no more.
Each booth she frequent past, in quest of gain,
And boys with pleasure heard her thrilling strain.
Ah, Doll! all mortals must resign their breath,
And industry itself submit to death!
The crackling crystal yields; she sinks, she dies,
Her head, chopt off, from her lost shoulders flies;
Pippins she cried, but death her voice confounds,
And pip—pip—pip, along the ice resounds.'

"Mr. J. T. Smith, in his *'Ancient Topography of London,'* page 24, states that another remarkable character, called *'Tiddy Doll,'* died in the same place and manner.

"In the treasures of Mr. Crowle's Illustrated Pennant, are several contemporary memorials of this Fair; which I shall very briefly mention, and give some specimens of the poetry attached to them.

"A coarse copper-plate, entitled *'The View of Frost Fair,'* 10¼ inches by 12, scene taken from York-buildings Water-Works; twelve verses beneath.

"A copper-plate, 7½ inches by 5, representing an altar-piece with the ten commandments, engraven between the figures of Moses and Aaron; and beneath, on a cartouche, *'Printed on the Ice on the River of Thames, Jan$^{y.}$ 15, 1739.'*

"A coarse copper-plate engraving, looking down the River, entitled *'Frost Fair,'* with eight lines of verse beneath; and above *'Printed upon the River Thames when Frozen, Janu. the 28, 17^{39}/$_{40}$.'* 9½ inches by 12¼.

"A copper-plate 5 inches by 8¼, representing an ornamental border with a female head, crowned at the top; and below, two designs of the letter-press and rolling press. In the centre in type, *'Upon the Frost in the year 1739-40;'* six verses, and then *'Mr. John Cross, aged 6. Printed on the Ice upon the Thames, at Queen-Hithe, January the 29th, 1739-40.'*

'Behold the Liquid THAMES now frozen o'er!
That lately SHIPS of mighty Burden bore.
Here You may PRINT your Name, tho' cannot Write,'
Cause numb'd with Cold: 'Tis done with great Delight.
And lay it by; That AGES yet to come
May see what THINGS upon the ICE were done.'

"A copper-plate, representing a view of the Thames at Westminster, with the tents, sports, &c., and alphabetical references, entitled *'Ice Fair.' 'Printed on ye River Thames, now frozen over, Jany 31, 1739-40;'* 7½ inches by 12½.

'Amidst ye arts y^t on ye Thames appear,
To tell ye Wonders of this frozen Year,
Sculpture claims Prior place, since y^t alone
Preserves ye Image when ye Prospect's gone.'

"An altered copy of these verses was printed upon the Thames in the great Frost of 1814; and from an advertisement in the *'London Daily Post'* of Thursday, January the 31st, 1739-40, we learn that this and the following print were originally sold for 6*d.* each.

"A Copper-plate printed in red, 9½ inches by 13¼, the view taken opposite St. Paul's, with tents, sports, &c. in front, sixteen lines of verse beneath, with *'Frost and Ice Fair, shewing the diversions upon the River Thames, began the 26th of Decem^r 1739-40, ended Febru^y the 17th.'*"

"In the beginning of this Frost, the houses on London Bridge appear to have received considerable damage, from the many vessels which broke from their moorings, and lay beating against them; the notice of which, we derive from the two most celebrated newspapers of the time,—the *'Daily Post,'* and Woodfall's *'General Advertiser.'* The latter of these, for Monday, December the 31st, 1739, states that 'all the watermen above the Bridge have hauled their boats on shore, the Thames being very nigh frozen over:' and in the same paper, for Wednesday, January 2nd, 1739-40, it is observed, that 'several vintners in the Strand bought a large Ox in Smithfield on Monday last, which is to be roasted whole on the ice on the River of Thames, if the Frost continues. Mr. Hodgeson, a Butcher in St. James's Market, claims the privilege of selling, or knocking down, the Beast, as a right inherent in his family, his Father having knocked down the Ox roasted on the River in the great Frost, 1684; as himself did that roasted in 1715, near Hungerford Stairs. The Beast is to be fixt to a stake in the open market, and Mr. Hodgeson comes dress'd in a rich lac'd cambric apron, a silver steel, and a Hat and Feathers, to perform the office.' After the mention of numerous accidents near London Bridge, the repetition of which would occupy considerable time with but little gratification, the *'Daily Post,'* of Tuesday, January the 22nd, 1740, thus notices the first breaking-up of this famous frost. 'Yesterday morning, the inhabitants of the West prospect of the Bridge were presented with a very odd scene, for, on the opening of their windows, there appear'd underneath, on the River, a parcel of booths, shops, and huts, of different forms, and without any inhabitants, which, it seems, by the swell of the waters and the ice separating, had been brought down from above. As no lives were lost, it might be view'd without horror. Here stood a booth with trinkets, there a hut with a dram of old gold; in another place a skittle-frame and pins, and in a fourth 'the Noble Art and Mystery of Printing, by a servant to one of the greatest trading companies in Europe.' With much difficulty, last night, they had removed the most valuable effects.' To conclude my information upon this subject, I have to observe only that the *'Daily Post'* of Thursday, February the 14th, states that the Sterlings of London Bridge had received so much damage during the frost from the great weight of ice, that their repairs would amount to several thousand pounds.

"The last extract given us by Maitland, in his *'History'* page 49, from the Bridge-House revenues and accounts, extends from Lady-day 1752 to Lady-day 1753, and consists of the following particulars."

	£	s.	d.
"In the hands of the Bridge-Masters, at the foot of their last account	2669	9	6
In the hands of the Chamberlain of London,	600	0	0

paid to him by Webb's securities							
			—	3269	9	6
In Tenants' hands in arrears at Lady-day, 1752				2413	18	9½
In arrear for fines then				70	6	11
Rental General this year, including Quit Rents				3843	8	7
Fines set this year				662	0	0
		Whole charge		£10259	3	9½
				£	*s.*	*d.*
'Rents and Quit-Rents paid				52	9	3
Taxes and Trophy-money: sums collected for the accoutrements and maintenance of the Militia				194	11	4½
Expenses				351	17	1½
Emptions of Timber	471	7	6			
Stone, Chalk, Terrass	340	4	4			
Iron-work	158	18	0			
				970	9	10
Mason, Painter, Glazier, Carpenter, &c.				1904	13	9
Shipwrights' work and Cordage				104	18	0
Benevolence				232	13	4
Particular Payments by Order				1254	7	3¾

Fees and Salaries	287	4	5
Costs at Audit and Lady Fair	160	11	0
	£5513	15	4¾

	£	s.	d.
'Amount of the preceding Charge	10259	3	9½
Deduct the foregoing expenses	5513	15	4¾
Remainder	4745	8	4¾
Whereof discharged by desperate arrears and remitted	89	0	0
Remaining due to the Bridge-house, at Lady-day, 1753	4656	8	4¾
And thus disposed of.			
Arrears of Fines and Quit-rents	2483	15	1¾
Arrears and Fines	70	6	11
In the hands of the Bridge-Masters	1502	5	5
In the hands of the Chamberlain of London	600	0	0
	£4656	7	5¾'

"There appears to be some little inaccuracy in this statement by Maitland, since the amounts which he sets down are not the products of the sums when added together; but these I have rectified, though the balance of the whole account does not quite accord with the sums remaining in hand.

"We have at length reached that period, when the extensive alteration, or even re-building, of London Bridge, began to form a matter of grave and active consideration; and in relating the proceedings of these times, there will be no little difficulty in condensing into one consecutive account, all the numerous surveys, reports, plans, proposals, and objections, which were then published. In treating of this part of the subject, however, as it will be best and briefest to do it in order, we will first consider the state of old London Bridge, as it was represented by the various Architects employed to survey it;

then give some account of the schemes proposed for its alteration; and lastly, describe that which was adopted, and the means used for carrying it into effect.

"It appears extremely probable, that the contrast presented by the broad and clear road of the new Bridge at Westminster,—which was commenced in September, 1738, and completed in November, 1749,—chiefly contributed to turn the attention of the Corporation of London to the exceeding inconvenience of their own. Though to the building of Westminster Bridge, Maitland, who knew the circumstances, tells us in his *'History,'* volume ii., page 1349, that there was very considerable opposition; and that the City of London, the Borough of Southwark, the Company of Watermen, and the West-Country Bargemen, all petitioned the Parliament against it. On Friday, February the 22d, 1754, as we learn from the *'Public Advertiser'* of the day following, the Court of Common Council took into consideration a motion for the construction of a new Bridge between London and Southwark: when, after a debate of nearly four hours, it was withdrawn, and a Committee appointed, consisting, as usual, of the Aldermen, Deputies, and one Common-Councilman from each Ward, to consider of the best means of rendering the old Bridge safe and convenient; who were empowered to draw upon the Chamberlain to the amount of £100, for plans, surveys, &c. The Report of this Committee stated, that the Bridge foundation was still good, and that, by pulling down the houses, and making such repairs as should then be required, the edifice might be rendered equally serviceable with Westminster Bridge; being capable of receiving four carriages abreast, with a good foot way on each side. By pulling down the houses at the corners of the narrow streets leading to the old Bridge, it was also represented that it would be rendered so convenient as to supersede the erection of any new one. To this it was objected, that most of the houses declined considerably out of the perpendicular; and that those on the Eastern side of the Bridge decayed much faster than the opposite ones. In Harrison's *'History,'* page 24, this account is partly confirmed; since we are there told that 'on the outer part of the Bridge, on the East side, the view from the wharfs and quays was exceedingly disagreeable. Nineteen disproportioned arches, with sterlings increased to an amazing size by frequent repairs, supported the street above. These arches were of very different sizes, and several that were low and narrow were placed between others that were broad and lofty. The back part of the houses next the Thames had neither uniformity nor beauty; the line being broken by a great number of closets that projected from the buildings, and hung over the sterlings. This deformity was greatly increased by the houses extending a considerable distance over the sides of the Bridge, and some of them projecting farther over it than the others; by which means, the tops of almost all the arches, except those that were nearest, were concealed from the view of the passengers on the quays, and made the Bridge appear like a multitude of rude piers, with only an arch or two at the end, and the rest, consisting of beams, extending from the tops of flat piers, without any other arches, quite across the river.'

"The best view of London Bridge in this state, is represented in an engraving by Peter Charles Canot, from a picture painted by Samuel Scott, of whom Walpole says, 'if he were but second to Vandevelde in sea-pieces, he excelled him in variety, and often introduced buildings in his pictures with consummate skill. His views of London Bridge, of the Quay at the Custom-House, &c. were equal to his Marines.' He died October the 12th, 1772; *vide* the '*Anecdotes of Painting*,' page 445. This view is also noticed by Gough in his '*British Topography*,' volume i., page 735: and Mr. J. T. Smith, in his '*Ancient Topography*,' page 25, observes, that it was in the possession of Edward Roberts, Esq., Clerk of the Pells, who probably still retains it. It was exhibited, says the author of '*Wine and Walnuts*,' volume i., page 65, in 1817, at the British Institution; and of the excellent engraving from it there are two editions: the earliest and best is marked, '*Published according to Act of Parliament, Feb*. *25, 1761:*' and the latter may be known by the imprint of '*Printed for Bowles and Carver, R. H. Laurie, and R. Wilkinson.*' This plate has been more than once copied in a reduced form; but the best, engraved by Warren, appeared in that work by Dr. Pugh, known by the name of '*Hughson's History of London*,' London, 1806-9, octavo, volume ii., page 316. Another view of London Bridge with the houses, of considerably less merit, but rather more rarity, was '*Printed and sold for John Bowles, Print and Map-seller, over against Stocks-Market, 1724.*' It consists of a small square plate, and shews the houses on the Western side of the edifice in bad perspective, with a short historical account beneath it; and it forms plate y of a folio volume, entitled, '*Several Prospects of the most noted Buildings in and about the City of London.*' There are also some rather large representations of this Bridge, in most of the old two and three-sheet views of London; as in those published by Bowles '*at the Black Horse in Cornhill*,' about 1732, &c.; and in the series of prints usually called '*Boydell's Perspectives*,' is a folio half-sheet plate very much resembling Scott's, entitled '*A view of London Bridge taken near St. Olave's Stairs. Published according to Act of Parliament by J. Boydell, Engraver, at the Globe, near Durham Yard in the Strand. 1731. Price 1s. J. Boydell, delin. et sculp.*' I could mention several others, as in the Title-page to the old '*London Magazine*;' in Strype's edition of Stow; in Maitland; Motley's 'Seymour's *Survey*;' in Hughson, Lambert, and numerous other works; but for fidelity of feature, and excellence of effect, none of them are in any respect equal to that of Scott, representing LONDON BRIDGE BEFORE THE ALTERATION OF 1758.

"As at this period the public attention was generally directed towards this edifice, the proprietors of Maitland's '*History of London*,' which was then appearing in numbers, issued an Advertisement, in the '*Public Advertiser*' of Saturday, April the 6th, 1754, stating that 'Number xv. will be illustrated with two fine Prospects of London Bridge as it may be altered agreeable to drawings presented to Sir Richard Hoare, by Charles Labelye, Esq.; and humbly inscribed to the Lord Mayor, Aldermen, and Common-Council, who *now* have the state of that Bridge under consideration.—Not one of this Number will be delivered to any but Subscribers, and such as have bought, or shall buy, the former Numbers.' Like Strype's edition of Stow, this work was published at 6*d.* each Number.

"On Thursday, September the 26th, 1754, the Bridge Committee presented their Report to the Court of Common-Council, an original verbatim copy of which is in the xxviiith. volume of '*London Tracts*' in the British Museum, small folio. This Report stated, that the piles, &c. of old London Bridge having been surveyed by Mr. George Dance, then Clerk of the Works to the City, the foundations were declared good, and, with common repairs, likely to last for ages. That the houses on the Bridge being a public inconvenience, it was recommended that they should be removed, from St. Magnus' Church to the City Gate, on the East; and from the corner of Thames Street to the Bear Tavern in the Borough, on the West. That Mr. Dance had produced a plan for an alteration of the Bridge, with estimates amounting to £30,000, in which were a carriage-road of 33 feet, with two foot-paths of 6 feet each; but that such expense might be reduced to £27,000, by leaving the houses standing on the South side of the Gate. That the annual rents of the houses to be taken down amounted to about £828: 6*s.*, which would be lost to the Bridge-House estates; whilst the Parishes of St. Magnus and St. Olave would also lose in taxes, rents, and tythes, about the yearly sum of £484: 19*s.* 10*d.*; and that the estimate of the houses then out upon lease, with others which must be bought, came to £8940: 11*s.* 7*d.*; besides other satisfaction which might be required by the under-tenants.

"The substance of Labelye's plan for altering this edifice, is given in Maitland's '*History*,' volume ii., pages 826-832, together with the result of several other reports made in 1746. His chief objection to old London Bridge was to the sterlings surrounding the piers; which, occupying almost one fourth part in five of the water-way, caused a fall of nearly five feet perpendicular, during the greater part of every tide, thus rendering the passage of vessels through the locks equally difficult and dangerous. He, consequently, proposed casing the piers with four feet of Portland Stone, and to lessen the sterlings so as always to have about 400 feet of water-way, which, being twice as much as the Bridge originally possessed, would reduce the fall to about 15 inches. The expense of this plan, he conceived, would be about £2000 for each pier; two or three of which could be altered in a year, without stopping the passage either over or under the Bridge. He also proposed to adopt the idea of Sir Christopher Wren, in new-modelling the appearance of the building itself, by taking away eleven piers, and forming nine broad-pointed Gothic arches, springing from the lowest low-water mark: these were to be of different dimensions, and the fifth from the South end was to be 90 feet in span. The parapet was to be ornamented with Gothic crocketted recesses surmounting the piers; by a cast-iron ballustrade; or by a dwarf-wall, or even houses; and, according to this plan, there would have been a water-way of 540 feet, and a fall of not more than 9 inches; whilst the amount of time and expense would not be considerably greater than in the former.

"The Reports of Mr. George Dance, Clerk of the City Works, and Bartholomew Sparruck, the Water-Carpenter of London Bridge, in answer to the questions of the Committee, in 1746, also furnish several very curious and interesting particulars concerning the building at that period, and the original is to be found at length in Maitland's '*History*,' already cited; and in Nos. II. and III. of Dr. Charles Hutton's '*Tracts on Mathematical and Philosophical Subjects*,' London, 1812, volume i., pages 115-122. The Report commences with a table of the depth of water, above, immediately under, and below every arch, beginning at the South end of the Bridge, which is to the following effect.

"Name of the Lock.	West Side.		Under the Arch.		East Side.	
	Feet.	Inch.	Feet.	Inch.	Feet.	Inch.
Shore Lock	16	—	5	9	8	10
Second Lock from Surrey Shore	14	6	9	—	10	4
Rock Lock	22	3	3	—	14	—
Fourth Lock from Surrey Shore	14	—	7	—	15	7
Fifth Lock from Surrey Shore	18	9	10	3	18	7
Roger Lock	17	7	8	7	15	11
Draw Lock	18	1	8	10	15	11
Nonesuch Lock	25	1	9	2	18	3
Pedlar's Lock	17	8	5	9	18	6
Gutt Lock	21	2	5	6	17	8
Long Entry Lock	18	11	3	5	12	8
Chapel Lock	17	—	2	4	22	—
St. Mary's Lock	24	6	8	9	20	—
Little Lock	22	3	9	—	17	4
King's Lock	23	9	6	9	20	7
Shore Lock	19	9	6	11	21	10
Mill Lock	20	3	4	6	21	10
Mill Lock	19	4	7	9	14	1
Mill Lock	10	10	4	—	13	10
Mill Lock	6	7	6	1	10	10'

"The Report then proceeds to state, that the height of the under bed of the first course of stones is very unequal; some being 2 feet 4 inches; and others varying from 1 foot 3 inches, to 1 foot 11 inches above low-water mark; and from 4 to 6 feet above the level of the sterlings. The rough and unhewn piles were found to be shod with iron, and but little decayed: in some instances, they were separated from the stone-work by planks of oak and elm, from 4 to 6 inches in thickness, which were probably first inserted at some of the numerous repairs; and each of the piers was protected by a stone base, extending about 7 inches beyond them. It was from these reports, that Mr. Labelye drew up his plans, which, together with his remarks on the old Bridge, were presented to the Committee, on Wednesday, the 17th of September, 1746. As this Architect desired that his designs might be examined by some eminent, scientific, and disinterested individuals, several such persons were called in to assist the deliberations of the Committee; though, after many other inquiries and consultations, the discussions terminated in a proposal for building a new Bridge at Blackfriars.

"At a Court of Common Council holden on Thursday, December 18th, 1755, after a very protracted opposition, the Corporation consequently agreed to petition Parliament for leave to bring in a Bill to erect another Bridge over the Thames at Fleet-Ditch, and on Tuesday, January 13th, 1756, the petition was presented and referred to a Committee; another petition being also presented at the same time, praying leave to bring in a Bill for improving and widening the passage over London Bridge, by removing the houses and other obstructions thereon, and for raising money to enable the Trustees to render the same safer and more commodious. This also was referred to a Committee; on Friday, March 12th, 1756, leave was granted to bring in the Bills; and on Thursday, the 27th of May, they both received the Royal assent, when the King closed the Session of Parliament. These Acts are printed in Maitland's '*History*,' volume ii., page 1387; though the best authority is Ruffhead's '*Statutes at Large*,' volume vii., pages 728-738, 29th of George II., Chapter xl.; and I shall first give a very few particulars of the Act relating to London Bridge, and next shew how the alteration was effected. By this Statute, then, the Corporation was empowered to buy and remove all buildings on, and contiguous to, the Bridge, for enlarging its avenues, improving the passage over, and widening one or more of its arches:—to devise how the same should be executed, and kept in repair:—to erect an uniform ballustrade on each side, with a passage of 31 feet for carriages, &c., and 7 feet for each of the footways:—to have it lighted and watched at the expense of the Bridge-House estates:—to preserve the arches and pipes belonging to the Water-works:—to establish, after the 24th of June, 1756, an additional toll for the payment of the expenses incurred by the alterations:— to keep the Bridge clear of buildings, and of carriages standing upon it for hire, after the houses should be removed; and to make all carriages keep on the Eastern side in going towards Southwark, and on the Western side in coming to London. The Act also provided penalties for destroying the Bridge or any of its works; extensive powers for the Corporation in buying the various property; an equivalent for the tythes, rates, &c., payable to the

Rectors of St. Magnus and St. Margaret, and St. Olave; and particular ordinances concerning the tolls.

"Gates and toll-houses were to be erected on, or near, London Bridge; but to continue only until the principal and interest of the borrowed monies should be discharged. The additional tolls were, 'for every horse drawing any coach, chariot, hearse, berlin, landau, calash, chaise, or chair, over the Bridge, 1*d.*; for every such carriage itself, 1*d.*; and for every horse not drawing, passing across the Bridge, ½*d.*' Loaded vessels also, passing under the Bridge, were to pay 2*d.* for every 5 tons burthen; 3*d.* for ten tons; 6*d.* for 25 tons, and 1*s.* for vessels of greater capacity. In the Act for building a Bridge at Blackfriars, 29th of George II.—1756,—Chapter lxxxvi., it is stated, that the taking away of all tolls from that of London, as soon as possible, would be of general advantage, they being then leased out for 21 years at a fine of £2100, and a yearly rent of £735; the redemption of all which was estimated at £36,000. In 1757, the 31st of George II., Chapter xx., an aid of £15,000 was granted by Parliament towards the rebuilding of London Bridge, because the tolls were not only difficult to collect, but were also a considerable hindrance to commerce and navigation: *vide* the *'Continuation of Maitland's History,'* at the end of volume ii., page 19. The powers of the new Act—which also protected the Bridge and its works, by making it felony to destroy them,—commenced from the 21st of April, and the additional tolls of the former one ceased from the 24th of June, 1758. Whilst I am upon the subject, it will probably be as well to include all our notices of the tolls of London Bridge under one head; and therefore I may remark, that in 1767, the 7th of George III., Chapter xxxvii., an Act was passed for the completing of Blackfriars Bridge, making several improvements in the City, and for treating with Mr. Edward Neale, the Lessee of the tolls of London Bridge, for their redemption; to which latter purpose, the sum of £30,000 was appropriated. About the end of September, 1770, the Corporation proceeded to act upon this power, fifteen years and three quarters being then unexpired of the lease; but the lessee having altered his demand, on account of the tolls having increased upwards of £600 per annum since 1766, it was found, that to reimburse the City, it was essential that they should continue both upon London and Blackfriars Bridges for some years longer. Upon petition of the Corporation, therefore, in the 11th of George III., 1771, Chapter xx., an Act was passed for further continuing the tolls on London Bridge until March the 25th, 1782, when the remainder of the lease was to be bought and the tolls finally to cease. All these particulars will be found in the *'Statutes at Large,'* volumes vii., pages 728-738, 742; viii., page 210; x., pages 306, 307; and xi., pages 154, 155; there is also considerable information upon this subject, to be found in Malcolm's *'Londinum Redivivum,'* volume ii., pages 392-396, derived from authentic documents. From these authorities it appears that the amount of the prescriptive tolls of London Bridge, at Midsummer, 1763, produced £1785:

10*s.* 5*d.*; in 1764, £1946: 4*s.* 1*d.*; in 1765, £1846: 7*s.* 4*d.*; in 1766, £1878: 16*s.* 6*d.*; and in 1770, £2465: 14*s.* 3*d.*; estimating, therefore, the average to be about £1864, and deducting from that sum the Rent, £735; Land Tax, £180: 12*s.* and the expenses of collecting, £150, the lessee's clear annual income would be £798: 15*s.*

"It was upon this calculation that the value of the remainder of his lease was ascertained, and the Act for continuing the tolls first devised; though on Wednesday, April, 24th, 1765, the Committee of City Lands let to Mr. Neale a lease of 21 years of the toll of carts and wheelage over London Bridge, for a fine of 2000 guineas, and the old rent of £735 *per annum*. See the '*Gentleman's Magazine*' for 1765, volume xxxv., page 197.

"Notwithstanding, however, these active proceedings for the improvement of this edifice, the parties in favour of, and against, a new building ran extremely high, as you may see in the '*Continuation of Maitland's History*,' page 4. That several interests were to be consulted in the alteration of London Bridge, is evident, and they are particularly shewn in the counter-petitions presented to Parliament whilst the Bridge Bills were pending; as, one drawn up by the most ardent supporters of the new Bridge at Blackfriars; and another by the Rev. Edmund Gibson, Rector of St. Magnus and St. Margaret, for recompense in loss of tythes, &c. to the amount of £48: 6*s.* 2*d.*, by taking down the houses. *Vide* the '*Journals of the House of Commons*,' volume xxvii., page 574; and the '*Continuation of Maitland's History*,' page 11; on page 7 of which authority it is also stated, that on the 12th of June, 1755, 'the Common-Council allowed the Comptroller of the Bridge-House £410 *per annum*, in lieu of his customary bills, which were so much reduced by the loss that would accrue to the Bridge-House estate, in the repairing and improvement of London Bridge.' But whilst many persons were too much interested even in the worst state of it, with all its inconvenient buildings, not to oppose their alteration, they were found to be almost equally dangerous both on the edifice and on the water. In the proceedings in Parliament concerning the alterations, Mr. Dance, the Architect, stated, that the piers were solid for ten feet above the sterlings, upon which were erected walls of three feet in thickness, forming cellars to the houses; and they having settled, the walls were much injured. In consequence, also, of the contracted passage between the houses upon the Bridge, the inhabitants experienced many inconveniences peculiar to their situation. Mr. Deputy James Hodges declared, that he 'had frequently known it happen, that coals had been thrown through the windows of the houses, out of the barges going under the Bridge; and that, as he is informed, the reason is, that the candle-lights in the houses make it dangerous in the night-time to go through the locks. That people on the river have always a glimmering light by which they can distinguish objects, unless a very thick fog. That light leaves them just when they come to shoot the locks, as far as the shadows of the houses extend; and thereby they lose the possibility of discerning the passage between the sterlings.' See Malcolm's *'Londinum Redivivum,'* volume ii., page 388, and the *'Journals of the House of Commons.'* The improvement of the passage over London Bridge was, however, much accelerated by the passing of an Act in 1755, the 28th of George II., Chapter ix., for taking away the ancient Market then held in High Street, Southwark, after Lady-day, 1756: and in Chapter xxii. of the former year, it was removed to its recent place on the site of Rochester Yard. See Bray's *'History of Surrey,'* volume iii., page 550; and the *'Statutes at Large,'* volume vii., pages 579, 620. Having thus, then, given some idea of the proceedings of the Corporation before the improvement of the old London Bridge, let us now go on to consider the nature and manner of that alteration itself: and so, if you're not asleep, Mr. Barbican, here's your health."

"No, truly," replied I, wakefully endeavouring to appear as brisk as my drowsiness would let me, "Time has a wonderful effect in reconciling us to the most tiresome employments; and I doubt not but to be able to hold out through the remainder of your discourse, with the aid of this Sack-posset, which seems to be little less interminable, and heated beyond the power of cooling again. But go on, Master Barnaby, go on, Sir."

"You are next to be informed then," recommenced the Antiquary, "that we are told by the Rev. John Entick, in his *'Continuation of Maitland's History,'* page 19, that the Committee appointed to repair London Bridge resolved to take down all the buildings and erections which stood upon it, of every kind whatsoever: to remove the great middle pier, and to lay the two adjoining locks into one, by turning an entire new arch, occupying the whole space: to add the depth of the removed houses to the width of the Bridge: and to secure both sides by a stone wall breast-high, surmounted by lofty ballustrades. To effect all this, it was essential to stop up the Bridge, and, at the same time, to provide a convenient passage to Southwark; on which, it was determined to construct a Temporary Bridge of Wood. This edifice consisted of stout unplaned oak timbers, to the amount of £2000; and it was erected on the sterlings in a curved form, on the Western side of the stone one, into which it opened at each end, extending from the water-works to about the fourth arch on the Surrey side of the river. The timber being taken back by the builder, his labour in erecting and removing it being compensated, and one penny per cube foot allowed him for the use of the materials. In Harrison's *'History of London,'* page 409, it is stated, that this temporary Bridge was opened in the month of October, 1757, when it was 'found to be very convenient, not only for foot-passengers, but also for horsemen and carriages;' but there are few notices to be found of it in the public prints of the period. By *'Lloyd's Evening Post and British Chronicle,'* however, a quarto newspaper of several leaves, then published every Monday, Wednesday, and Friday, we are informed, in the paper for Wednesday, September 21st, page 219, that, 'to-morrow they will begin to lay the first coat of gravel on the Temporary Bridge, so that it will be passable by the end of this month:' and the *'Public Advertiser'* of Saturday, October 22nd, thus fixes the time when the Bridge was actually finished. 'Yesterday, the Committee appointed under the late Act of Parliament for the improvement of London Bridge, met and view'd the Temporary Bridge, and gave orders to have it open'd to-morrow morning for foot-passengers.' The houses on the stone edifice, indeed, were already began to be removed; for, in the *'Gentleman's Magazine,'* for 1757, volume xxvii., page 91, it is stated, that on Tuesday, February 22nd, 'three pots of money, silver and gold, of the coin of Queen Elizabeth, were found by the workmen in pulling down the houses on London Bridge.' The whole of these buildings, however, were not entirely taken away until some years after this time; for in the *'London Chronicle'* of Thursday, May 17th, 1759, the name of 'William Herbert on London Bridge,' occurs as one of the publishers of *'The Lives of the Reformers.'* By the same paper, too, for Thursday, August the 14th, 1760, page 161, we are informed, that 'in pulling down the house called the Chapel-House, on London Bridge, there has been found this week a very antique marble font, &c. curiously engraved, and several ancient coins, &c. The stones used in the building of this structure were so strongly cemented with different kinds of mortar, and strong iron clamps, that the workmen found a most difficult task in the demolition of it, which is not yet completed.' The Committee for altering London Bridge had, however, previously advertised for persons to carry their intentions into effect, to meet at Guildhall on the 1st of February, 1757; as may be seen in the *'Public Advertiser'* of Monday, January 24th; and in the same authority for Monday, May the 2nd following, it is further stated, that Messrs. Blackden and Flight, the contractors for taking down and clearing away the houses on London Bridge, completed their engagement on the Saturday evening previously: and that from the commencement of their work, there had not occurred a single accident. The view of old London Bridge and its buildings by Scott, to which I have already referred, furnishes us with large and interesting prospects of several of the principal edifices which, after this period, were removed; and I may add, that in the x.th volume of Mr. Crowle's Illustrated Pennant, there is an enlarged drawing of this picture, executed by John Varley, in colours, measuring 3 feet 9½ inches, by 1 foot 5¾; ruthlessly cut into three parts to fit the size of the book. In these views, one of the most curious objects is a prospect of the EASTERN EXTERIOR OF THE CHAPEL OF ST. THOMAS IN 1757;

a more particular engraving of which you will find in the *'Gentleman's Magazine,'* for 1753, volume xxiii., page 432. But few remains of the original structure were then perceptible on the outside of this building; though its form of a semi-hexagon might be traced, whilst the old pier of the Bridge, the basement standing on the sterling, and some of the pinnacles and buttresses of the Chapel, were discernible in the centre and at the sides. The greater part of it, however, was scarcely to be distinguished from the other houses, being covered with brickwork or boarding; whilst the Upper Chapel was converted into apartments, and the Lower one into the Paper Warehouse of Messrs. Gill and Wright, having a crane attached to it to take in goods from boats. In front of the Bridge pier, a square fish-pond was formed in the sterling, into which the fish were carried by the tide, and then detained there by a wire-grating placed over it: and an ancient servant of London Bridge, now verging upon his hundredth summer, well remembers to have gone down through the Chapel to fish in this pond.

"The Nonesuch House on London Bridge in 1756,

is also represented by Scott in a very dilapidated appearance, especially when contrasted with its splendour in the sixteenth and seventeenth centuries; and, when it was taken down, was probably in the occupation of several persons in trade, or perhaps was shut up and allowed to fall into decay. One of the most picturesque and interesting objects in Scott's View, is that group of buildings formed of the Eastern Side of the Modern Southwark Gate and Towers, with the Second Gate beyond it; beneath which is a very perfect representation of one of the original arches, called the Rock Lock, and one of the old piers, whilst above is shewn the third of those open spaces guarded with iron rails, which alone varied the street-like character of old London Bridge, and indicated to its passengers that they were actually crossing a river. I know but of one engraving, Mr. Geoffrey Barbican, which gives us any view directly up the Bridge-street; and even that is so slight, that were it not that I am unwilling to lose any fragment relating to old London Bridge, I should omit mentioning it altogether. You will find it, however, in that half-sheet copper-plate, after Antonio Canaletti, published in *'Bowles's Perspectives,'* entitled *'The Monument of London in remembrance of the dreadfull Fire in 1666. Bowles delin. et sculp. Published according to Act of Parliament, 1752. Printed for John Bowles and Son, at the Black Horse in Cornhil.'* This prospect, then, being taken on Fish-Street-Hill, shews the Monument on the left hand, and the termination of the street in the first Northern gate of London Bridge, with some indication of the houses beyond it; though the whole view has certainly a far more spacious appearance, than this part of London ever possessed.

"Before I close my notices of the year 1757, I have to observe, from the printed document I have so frequently quoted, that from 1639 until this time, 'no addition of salary was paid to the Bridge-Masters, nor any other allowance; but when the houses were taken down on London Bridge, the sum of £10 per annum was ordered to be paid to each of the Bridge-Masters, in lieu of fees, &c. arising from the said houses. Order of the Committee made May 4, 1757. And also when certain warehouses were taken away, and laid into the Bridge-House, the annual sum of £6. 10s. was ordered to be paid in lieu of the said warehouses to the Senior Bridge-Master. And after the Bridge was finished, lighted, and watched, one of the Bridge-Masters was ordered to superintend the Watchman on the said Bridge, and in the Bridge-Yard, for which he received the sum of £12 by order of the Committee. The whole Income of the Senior Bridge-Master at the present time (1786) £100. 10s. Rental at Christmas 1785, £8280. 1s. 4d.

Present Income of the Junior Bridge-Master: Salary, &c. as before	72	0	0
In lieu of a stable	4	0	0
In lieu of fees for the houses lately standing on London-Bridge	10	0	0
In lieu of Warehouses	0	7	6
Total Income	£86	7	6'

"So terminates this very curious document, which has furnished so many authentic particulars of the Bridge accounts at different periods, shewing its increasing prosperity and revenues, between the times of Edward the Fourth, and those of George the Third.

"Whilst the alteration of London Bridge was being carried rapidly into effect, in the early part of the year 1758, an event occurred, which not only destroyed some portion of the building itself, but also nearly the whole of the works surrounding it. This was the fatal FIRE ON THE TEMPORARY BRIDGE,

which burst out about eleven o'clock, in the night of Tuesday, April 11th, as it is related in Entick's '*Continuation of Maitland*,' page 20; in the '*Gentleman's Magazine*,' volume xxviii., page 192; in John Noorthouck's '*History of London*,' 1773, quarto, page 390; and in Harrison's '*History of London*,' page 410, where there is an engraving of the fire, probably by Wale, after a drawing by Grignion. From these accounts, we learn that the conflagration brake out suddenly from the two ends of the Wooden Bridge, which, having been dried by several days of bright sunshine, appeared instantly to be in flames, entirely preventing any approach to suppress it. Though Sir Charles Asgill, the Lord Mayor, came very early to the spot, and remained there almost the whole time of the fire, exerting himself exceedingly to stop its progress, it continued raging until the next day, when the burning ruins fell into the river; and Entick observes, that he saw the drawbridge a-light at twelve o'clock at noon. All communication between the City and Southwark being thus suspended, excepting so far as it could be carried on by water, forty additional boats were licensed by the Lord Mayor to work as ferries on the three succeeding Sundays; though the inhabitants of Southwark suffered still greater privation from the destruction of the troughs which conveyed water to them over the Bridge whilst it was repairing, instead of the pipes which had been dug up from the water-works. The navigation was also equally interrupted by the vast timbers that fell across the arches, and the many large stones which almost blocked up the current of the tide; so that the locks at each end only remained entirely clear. As it was very generally suspected that this fire was not accidental, the Lord Mayor waited on Mr. Pitt by nine o'clock the next morning, by whom a Proclamation, dated Whitehall, April the 12th, was issued, containing the King's Pardon to any of the incendiaries, excepting the person who actually set the Bridge on Fire; with a reward of £200 for his discovery, from the Corporation of London. From the examinations of several persons, there appears to have been considerable grounds for this suspicion. The Watchmen and others in the vicinity, on both sides of the river, declared that about eleven o'clock they observed lights in several places under the Bridge; soon after which, the whole building burst into flames; and it was also reported, that about ten o'clock, on the night of the fire, several persons, apparently intoxicated, were seen coming over the Bridge, with a torch, which, in a struggle between themselves, was flung over the boarded fence, where the light disappeared, till all the timber beneath burst into flames. Another account, contained in the '*London Chronicle, or Universal Evening Post*,' for April the 11th to the 13th, 1758, page 350, states, that the Watchmen actually saw 'a person in a boat with a candle in a lanthorn, busy about the stone pier, which is to be taken down to lay two arches into one; and after a short time he was seen to extinguish the candle, and the boat went off, and in a few minutes after the Bridge burst out in flames, and continued so until there was no wood left above the water to burn.' The deposition, also, of Mary, wife of John Dennis, of George Alley, Thames Street, taken before the Lord Mayor on April 14th, stated, that about ten o'clock on the night of the fire, she was in the Watch House belonging to Dyers' Hall, near London Bridge, and, looking over the hatch of the door, she saw a lanthorn in the Chapel pier. Soon after, she observed another, and then, losing sight of both, there presently appeared three in the same place. At first, she supposed that some vessel was at the Bridge, but the appearance of the second light shewed her that they were between the wood-work at the great pier; and when the three lanthorns were visible together, she observed that one was held up and another down towards the timbers. These lights she imagined to proceed from workmen, but in a short time she saw a small flame burst out on the same spot, which was damped, and then brake out again, and, after having been damped a second time, blazed very fiercely; upon which the deponent went to the next wharf, and gave notice that London Bridge was on fire. This testimony of Mrs. Dennis was confirmed by that of several other persons, who declared that they also saw the lanthorns. The City was indeed filled with rumours and suspicions of every description; the lower orders accused the Watermen and Lightermen; another class attributed the fire to the supporters of the new Bridge at Blackfriars; whilst a third party intimated that the scheme lay still deeper, and believed the design to have been long concerted. We know, indeed, that the Temporary Bridge was the object of many an imprecation from the common people, who might be tempted to fire it from the inconveniences which they experienced upon it; as in the Winter it was so excessively dirty, that some supposed the Committee had contrived it so to increase the toll, by obliging all passengers to cross it in carriages: whilst in dry weather it was no less incommoded by dust. The real origin of the fire, however, was never discovered; and Noorthouck observes, that as there were enough of natural causes to have produced it, so it is not probable that persons interested in obstructing the works or creating new ones, would have exposed themselves to detection for such an attempt. 'In such a mixture of stone and wood,' says he, 'a heap of quicklime on the sterlings, accidentally wetted by the tide, might kindle any adjoining timbers: or, as it is usual for servants behind coaches, with flambeaux in their hands, to clear them by striking them on the hinder wheels, it is no forced supposition that some thoughtless fellow might have struck his flambeau on the pallisade of the Bridge for the same purpose; the flaming wax of which, dropping into some joint on the outside, would have been sufficient for such a disaster.' A curious letter on this subject, from which I have added many particulars to my information, will be found in the '*London Chronicle*' for April the 13th to the 15th, 1758, page 359. In consequence of this destruction, the Corporation of London addressed the Parliament for relief; and on Friday, April 21st, a resolution passed the House of Commons, that 'a sum not exceeding £15,000 be granted to his Majesty, to be applied towards the rebuilding of London Bridge.' This produced the Act to which I have already referred, which made any wilful attempt to destroy the Bridge or its works, to be death without benefit of clergy.

LONDON BRIDGE AFTER THE FIRE OF 1758

presented a truly ruinous prospect; for nearly all the centre houses being removed, there appeared a wide vacancy, with a broken chasm in the middle, down to the water's edge, where the new arch was being constructed. There are three engravings of this edifice taken immediately subsequent to the destruction, the rarest of which is an extremely slight and rude etching, on a small folio half-sheet, entitled *'The Melancholy Prospect of London Bridge South-East, April 12th, 1758. J. Jump Del. et Sculp. Published according to Act. To be had at the Acorn in the Strand.'* In this most barbarous prospect the buildings are represented in flames; and I have seen it marked so high as 4*s*. I cannot imagine why Gough, in his *'British Topography,'* volume i., page 735, calls the next of these engravings 'a miserable view,' since it is certainly as good as the generality of the prints of the period, and is very considerably better than the last. It consists of a large half-sheet, entitled *'An Exact View of London Bridge since the Conflagration of the Temporary Bridge,'* which is a copper-plate of 8 inches by 13¼; and beneath it, in letter-press, is *'A Chronological and Historical Account from the first building a Bridge across the River Thames from London to Southwark, till the late Conflagration of the Temporary Bridge, the 11th of April, 1758. Sold by William Herbert, under the Piazzas on the Remains of London Bridge. Price One Shilling, Plain. Colour'd, Eighteen Pence.'* The only additional information which we derive from this narrative, is, that 'as the wind providentially blew the whole time at East,—tho' all the day before it had blown strong from the Southward,—it did no damage to any of the houses at either end.' But by far the best representation of the effects of this fire, is a half-sheet copper-plate, entitled, in French and English, *'A View of London Bridge, with the Ruins of y*e* Temporary Bridge, Drawn the day after the Dreadfull Fire, April the 11th, 1758, by A. Walker.*

- 287 -

Published according to Act of Parliament, June 28, 1758. London: Printed for John Ryall, at Hogarth's Head in Fleet Street. A. Walker delin. et sculp.' All these prospects were taken on the West side of the Bridge, and represent the building horizontally across the picture: Herbert's extends from Fishmongers' Hall to the Southwark Gate; but Anthony Walker's takes in the whole Bridge, and part of the buildings on the Surrey shore.

"Yet, if this fire were sudden, and its destruction extensive, the exertions of the City Corporation were not less prompt and effectual in repairing of the damage. The Common Council, like Bunyan's Captains in *Mansoul*, being always true lovers of London, like so many Samsons, shook themselves and came together to consult upon and contrive a remedy. The Court of Common Council met by one o'clock on the day after the fire, and was attended by Mr. Dance, Mr. Taylor, and Mr. Phillips, the builder of the Bridge, whom the Lord Mayor had previously ordered to survey it; and their report was, that with a proper number of workmen, who should be allowed to labour on days, they would engage to make the old Bridge passable for carriages by the 1st of May. A new Temporary Bridge was ordered to be immediately erected, and upwards of 500 workmen were constantly employed upon it, by whose means, as it is stated in the '*Gentleman's Magazine*' for 1758, page 193, the Bridge was re-opened for foot-passengers, on Wednesday, the 19th of April; and the whole of the new wooden edifice was ready for carriages in less than a month after the fire. During the erection of this building, there seemed to be discovered an additional proof that the last conflagration was not accidental; for Daniel Capel, the Inspector of the Bridge, having been informed that Mary Dennis, before mentioned, and John Scott, one of the Bridge Watchmen, had seen lights about the new works at an unseasonable hour in the night of the 23rd of August, brought them to give their evidence before Mr. Alderman Francis Cokayne. The Inspector was then ordered to search if there were any appearance of fire, and make his report to the Lord Mayor; upon which he stated, that having carefully surveyed the Bridge with proper attendants, they found the appearance of an attempt in three places, where the new wood work was scorched quite black; and one of the Watchmen also produced the remains of a link found in the unfinished works of the Bridge. To prevent another conflagration, therefore, says Entick, in his '*Continuation of Maitland's History*,' page 21, it was ordered that two men, well armed, should be placed every night, from sun-set to sun-rise, in a gallery erected from end to end of the Temporary Bridge, just beneath the centre of the works, with lamps lighted, and a bell, to alarm the neighbourhood in case of an attack. This watch was continued under the direction of Mr. Capel, until the whole of the Temporary Bridge was taken down. Before this, however, as we are informed by '*Owen's Weekly Chronicle, or Universal Journal*,' for August 26th to September 2nd, 1758, page 173, five watermen, armed with blunderbusses and cutlasses, had watched for a fortnight, from ten at night until five in the morning, in a boat under the great Arch. The opening of the second wooden erection for carriages did not take place until Wednesday, the 18th of October, 1758, as we learn from 'Owen's Weekly Chronicle,' October 14th to 21st, No. 29, page 230: on page 206 of a former number of which, the watch is particularly mentioned; and we are also told that there was a convenient pathway for foot-passengers, railed in and elevated above the carriage-road. Pages 183 and 198 of the same authority, shew that the edifice was strewed over with gravel above the planks; that on each side there were uprights for covering it; and that a month intervened between the gravelling and the opening of the Bridge. In consequence, too, of the recent attempt to destroy the New Bridge, this paper likewise informs us, page 238, that orders were issued by the Lord Mayor, that no coaches nor foot-passengers should carry any lighted torches over the Temporary Bridge.

"It was not, however, until the middle of the year 1759, that the new Arch of London Bridge began to assume its intended form; though we can trace its progress only by slight occasional notices contained in the periodicals of the day. Thus we learn from a paragraph in the '*London Chronicle*,' of Saturday, July the 28th, 1759, page 88, that 'the grand Arch at London Bridge is now completed. It is finished in the Gothick taste, and the ballustrades upon it are fixing. The foot-paths will be rather wider than those at Westminster; and it is proposed to fix posts along them with chains from one post to the other, to secure foot-passengers from any damage which might otherwise happen from cattle.' The strength and complication of the timber used for forming this Arch, are particularly pointed out in an engraving and letter signed E. M., in '*The London Magazine*' for that year, volume xxviii., page 672; where it is stated, that about 17,000 feet of wood were contained within the arch, which, at some little distance, appeared to be entirely solid, the vacant spaces being exceedingly small in proportion to the beams themselves. Its actual contents were 13,872 cubic feet of timber, forming the centre; and 3570 feet more occupied in booms, guard-piles, struts, and trusses required for the preservation of the old and new works, and for keeping off the River craft, tide-water, and ice. This alteration was carried into effect by Sir Robert Taylor, Architect to the Bank of England, and Mr. Dance, Senior; and the Carpenter employed for the construction of this CENTRING OF THE GREAT ARCH OF LONDON BRIDGE, received 2*s.* per foot for the use of his timber, including labour, and took it back again at his own expense. It measured 70 feet span, by 48 feet wide, and the rise was 23 feet; it was formed of 16 ribs or frames, and was supported on three Sterlings; namely, the two side ones of about 6 feet each, and that from which the Chapel pier had been removed. The author of the letter which I have referred to, censuring the extraordinary quantity of wood used in the centre, observes that it employed nearly 10,500 feet more than were used at Westminster Bridge; notwithstanding the Arch at London Bridge is 4¾ feet narrower and 12 feet lower, though the Bridge itself is 4¾ feet wider. The author's own plan, which is also annexed to the letter, more resembles that adopted by the late Mr. Rennie, in his alteration of Rochester Bridge, in the year 1821. It consisted of five radii, supporting as many timbers placed pentagonally; occupied only 7000 feet of timber, and would have amounted to £1000 less than the plan actually adopted.

"Many months had not elapsed, however, when it was discovered, that, by the removal of the large centre pier, the excavations around and underneath its Sterlings were so considerable, as to place the adjoining piers, and even the new arch itself, in very imminent danger. The presentiments of many, and the apprehensions of almost all, were consequently so great, that but few persons would pass either over or under it; the Surveyors themselves were not prepared with any adequate remedy; and Mr. John Smeaton, the celebrated Engineer, was instantly summoned express from Yorkshire to relieve the difficulty. Having immediately proceeded to survey the Bridge, and to sound about the dangerous Sterlings, he advised the Corporation to buy back again the stones of the City Gates, and throw them into the water, to guard the Sterlings; preserve the bottom from farther corrosion; raise the floor under the Arch; and restore the head of the current required for the Water-works, to its original power. These City Gates, you will remember, had been previously sold and taken down, in 1760 and 61, as appears by the *'Gentleman's Magazine'* for those years; volume xxx., pages 390, 440, 591, and volume xxxi., page 187: where we are informed, that on Wednesday, July 30th, were sold to Mr. Blagden, a Carpenter in Coleman Street, before the Commissioners of City Lands, the edifice of Aldgate for £177: 10s.; Cripplegate for £91; and Ludgate for £148. Two months were allowed for the removal of each, the latter being begun on Monday, August 4th, and Aldgate on Monday, September 1st. Bishopsgate was sold on Wednesday, December 10th; and on Wednesday, April 22, 1761, Moorgate was also sold for £166, and Aldersgate for £91. It was probably the materials of the first of these, which lay in Moorfields, when Mr. Smeaton advised their being thrown into the Thames: and with so much promptitude was that advice followed, that the stones were bought the same day; horses, carts, and barges were instantly procured, and the work commenced immediately, although it was Sunday morning. These particulars are related in the Life of this Engineer, attached to his *'Reports made on various Occasions,'* volume i, London, 1812, quarto, page xix.

"Whilst we are speaking of this alteration of London Bridge, it seems to be a proper place to say something of the massive features of our ancient edifice, and the oldest contrivances used for the support of Bridges in general. First, then, the Piers are said to be raised, so far as their nature can at present be known, upon rough piles of oak and elm, shod with iron, and driven very close, but apparently not fastened. Upon the heads of these are frequently found pieces of plank, chiefly oak, 4 to 6 inches in thickness; and the insides of the Piers are filled up with rubble laid in mortar. This kind of building is supposed to have been anciently used when the bed of the river could not be laid dry; and the stilts or piles were then surrounded by a row of other piles and planks, like a wall, called a Sterling or Jettee, the vacant spaces of which were filled with loose stones, &c. to the top. The inconveniences attending such a method are, however, so great, that it is now entirely disused: as, on account of the very loose composition of the Piers, they must be made both large and broad, to prevent their entire destruction upon drawing the centre of the Arch. This great breadth, also, very materially contracts the water-way, and incommodes navigation; whilst the Sterling itself is in considerable danger of bursting."

"But, Mr. Postern," said I, as the Antiquary arrived at this part of his narrative, "although Maitland tells us, in his *'History,'* volume i., page 46, and volume ii., page 1349, that the use of Coffer-dams, or *Caissons*, for building of the Piers of Bridges, was first introduced into the Thames at the erection of Westminster Bridge, yet it has been supposed that even this of London was constructed somewhat after the same plan; and that those Sterlings are but the upper parts of the machines themselves, left in the water to guard the

Piers; though it is certain, that in most of the Reports, illustrative of the great repair of London Bridge, the Sterlings are mentioned as additions to the original structure for the support of the Piers. I have been obligingly furnished, however, with an interesting drawing, and extract from the MS. Journal of Mr. William Knight, of Mr. Rennie's office, by which we are enabled to understand the construction of these parts of the Bridge in a much clearer and more perfect manner. Mr. Knight observes, that having received several different statements as to the way in which the Piers of the old London Bridge had been erected, he determined upon convincing himself by an actual survey. This he effected on August 14th, 1821, when an excavation was made for ascertaining whether the original structure would support new Arches of a larger span; and he then found it to be built in the following manner. 'The foundation of the Piers on the North side,—between the Great Lock and what is called the Long Entry Lock,—and in the Sterling round it, appeared to be about 3 feet above low-water mark. The bottom of the masonry originally laid of the pier, is about 2 feet 3 inches above low-water mark; and the first course is laid upon a sill of oak, 16 inches wide, by 9 in thickness, and perfectly sound. Immediately beneath this is a mass of Kentish rubble, mixed with flint, chalk, &c., thrown in irregularly, but not mixed with any cement. The masonry above the sill seems well bonded together, with good mortar joints, but there are *no piles under the oak sill.* The external parts of the pier seem to have been new-fronted at some period,—probably at the time when the centre Arch was formed in 1759,—as the base of this new fronting projects about 1 foot before the original Pier. There are *no piles under the original part of the Pier;* but to the *new part there are some small ones driven into the rubble,*—which can be of little service,—with some planks laid upon their edges. The new masonry is well bonded into the old work.' Mr. Knight concludes, by observing that, in all the accounts which he has hitherto met with, the old Piers of this Bridge are described to *stand upon piles*; but that, as he found this to be erroneous in the present instance, he considers it to be a fair conclusion that all the other Piers were constructed upon the same principle. His drawing represents a SECTION OF THE NORTH PIER OF THE GREAT ARCH OF LONDON BRIDGE,

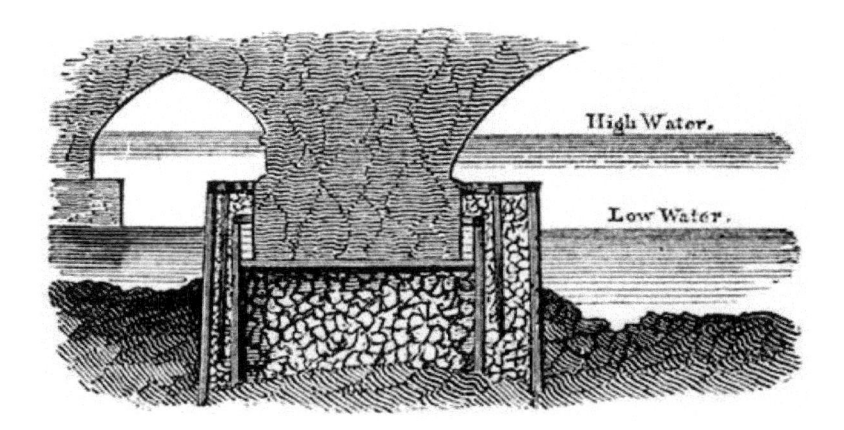

shewing the original manner of constructing it, and the Sterling, or ancient Coffer-dam, standing around it; which, it thus appears unquestionably evident that, not having the art to pump dry, was filled up with loose stones. The Arch on the right hand is denominated the Long Entry Lock, and that on the left is a part of the Great Arch in the centre. I should remark also, that Mr. Knight has examined several other parts of this edifice with no less care and industry, in order to ascertain the plans adopted at the famous alteration of London Bridge, of which we are now speaking; of all of which observations he has made interesting sketches and memoranda. He states that he has felt with his measuring rods the timber, &c., placed in the river to strengthen the piers of the Great Arch, and that his sounding leads have been broken by catching in it. In April, 1826, the opening of the roadway of London Bridge for throwing of two more Arches into one, to increase the water-way during the building of the New Bridge, also made a curious discovery of many of the more ancient parts of the original building. The crowns of the old Arches, observes Mr. Knight, were about 8 feet 6 inches from the present surface of the ground, which appeared to have been raised at different periods; and five several strata were evidently to be traced over the centre of the original Bridge, which was 20 feet in width. Immediately over the crowns of the Arches was a layer of fine gravel, about 20 inches in depth, perhaps the ancient roadway, as its upper surface had the appearance of being trodden down and dirty, when contrasted with that beneath it. The next stratum consisted of mixed chalk and gravel; the third of made ground of various materials; the fourth, a thick layer of burnt wood, ruins, and black earth; and the last another bed of different substances, over which was the granite paving. The filling-in between the Arches was composed of chalk and mortar, of so hard a nature that it was taken out with great difficulty. With respect to the building itself, he observes, that the stone of which the Arches were formed consists of two courses: that of the soffits or flying ribs, being Merstham Fire-stone, and the course above very similar to the stone of Caen, or Normandy. In the additions, or casings, on each side of the original structure, Portland stone has been used, as well for the facing, as for the Arches; whilst the backing and filling-in, between the spandrils of the Arches, was composed of chalk and mortar; which latter was evidently of a very bad quality and carelessly applied. Indeed, the ashler facing had been so little attended to in the bonding of the work together, that it is surprising, with the great weight behind, the careless manner of throwing in the backing, and the slight nature of the facing itself, that the whole work has not been thrown outwards some time since. Having thus, Mr. Barnaby, added these curious observations to your narrative, I must once more entreat you to proceed."

"After making you my acknowledgments," recommenced the Antiquary, "for the very curious illustration you have now furnished; and before quitting the Great Arch of London Bridge, let me observe, that it contains the Trinity Standard of High Water, which is placed there for the benefit of persons erecting buildings on the banks of the Thames, and originally inscribed upon a metal plate, affixed under the Great Arch upon the North East side, as it may be seen beneath the centre Arch of Blackfriars Bridge. It is at present engraven in the centre of each Pier of the Great Arch, in black Roman letters, about 7½ feet above the springing line of the Arch, or 8½ feet over the sterling; and consists of the inscription,—

```
Trinity.
H. W.
1800.

Λ
```

the character beneath being the average point of the ordinary rise of a Spring Tide at High Water, which, above Bridge, is 14½ feet or 15 feet, being 5 feet 3 inches above the Neap Tides. At high Spring Tides, however, it has risen 16 feet and upwards; and in that remarkable one combined with a land-flood on December 28th, 1821, it rose 2 feet, 10 inches, and five parts, above the mark below Bridge. From the official tidal observations of the Trinity Company, it has been ascertained, that, from Blackwall to London Bridge, the High Water ascends to the same level; and that from the upper side of London Bridge to that of Westminster the River is likewise generally level, excepting under the influence of winds or land-floods. During that of 1821, to which I have just referred, the banks of the River, and the marshes and gardens above Westminster, were overflowed and damaged to a very considerable extent; which has been attributed to the obstruction offered by the present London Bridge to the passage of the water towards the sea, as we learn from the '*Report of Ralph Walker, delivered into the House of Commons,*

11th of April, 1823,' octavo, page 9; where he states, that the tides below this edifice during the flood, rose only to the ordinary height, whilst at Low water the fall was increased by several feet. This celebrated fall is, of course, most evident at Low water, when it is about 4 feet 6 inches, or 6 feet in the Winter season; and the most hazardous time for passing through any of the Bridge Locks, is probably half an hour previous to, or, for barges, the last two hours before, Low water below Bridge. The safest time of the tide is at High water, or slack Low water: but boats may pass with safety for 2½ hours after flood, and the last half hour of the drain of the tide at ebb, above Bridge; the tide having then flowed nearly 4 feet below. Deeply laden barges also take the drain through at Low water. The Great Arch is doubtless one of the safest to pass under, and is always used by craft and barges; but before the erection of the New Bridge works, most of the other Locks were employed at the flood tide, when the fall is extremely trifling. When the tide is on the ebb, the Arches which are chiefly used for boats are, the Draw-Lock,—the 4th from the Great Arch,—on the South; and St. Mary's Lock,—adjoining the Great Arch,—on the North, which is always taken on the first part of the ebb. The Long-Narrow, once a favourite Lock, is now nearly abandoned; but the Draw-Lock is perhaps considered the safest, and is the most generally used since the erection of the New Bridge Coffer-dams. The approach, however, is dangerous, and requires a skilful waterman, who is obliged to pull his boat into the draft or eddy of the dam before he can make the Lock. Though the works of the New Bridge have at present closed several of the Arches of the ancient edifice, yet the 4th and 5th Locks from the Southwark end have been thrown into one, with a strong wooden vaulting, parapet, and roadway above, to increase the water-way beneath. Since the commencement of these works, the fall of the river has also become less dangerous for barges, from the returning tide sooner meeting with resistance; and instead of a direct fall of 6 feet in 50, it is now only about 6½ feet in 250. The draft of the tide, however, round the Coffer-dams, makes it very difficult for lightermen to enter the Locks fairly; and some of the outer rows of piles are driven inwards from their barges being carried against them. In 1820 and 1822, the average fall at High water was only from 8 to 13 inches; and in 1823, after the removal of the London Bridge Water-works, it decreased to between 3 and 4.

"Mr. Barnaby! Mr. Barnaby!" exclaimed I, fretted by this long digression in the Antiquary's narrative, "I protest you really put me out of all patience: there's no keeping you to one subject; for the last of your annals referred to that most wearisome alteration and repair of London Bridge which began in 1757, and now you are bewildered in a discourse on the navigation and tides of the Thames! Truly, it's intolerable!"

"I am aware," replied the placid Mr. Postern, whom there seemed to be actually no putting into a passion, "I am aware how much these observations serve to lengthen and interrupt our history; but still they are vastly important to its illustration. 'Our life,' says an interesting and romantic author, 'cannot be like an Arabian manuscript, all flowers and gold,' and neither can history be composed only of the facts which naturally belong to it. There must be various incidental notices, seemingly unconnected with it, which are at last found to combine with the story, and to render it much more intelligible; and if ever, Mr. Barbican, you publish these Chronicles of London Bridge, make my words both your defence and your apology. The fact is, I really am half unwilling to proceed to the close of the alterations of this edifice, because we have subsequently so few interesting particulars on record concerning it; and other events,—excepting the usual unhappy accidents beneath its Arches,—are almost entirely wanting. At the time of the formation of the Great Arch, it appears that the wooden Draw-Bridge was first taken away,—though it had then long ceased to be used,—and the present Stone Arch, entitled the Draw-Lock, about 30 feet in width, or 16 feet between the Sterlings, was erected instead of it. This we learn from the '*Public Ledger*,' of Monday, January 28th, 1760, which states 'that the centre of the new Draw-Lock Arch of London Bridge is struck; so that there is now a free passage for boats, &c.' In this very Lock, however, only a few months afterwards, an accident occurred which might have almost proved fatal to the Bridge itself; and it is thus related in the '*Public Advertiser*' of Monday, December 29th, 1760. 'On Tuesday, a large old French ship, that was coming through the Draw-Lock at London Bridge, to be broken up above Bridge, stuck in the Lock, and still continues there, having done considerable damage to the same; and it is thought that she cannot now be got out, but must be broken up where she now lies.' The same paper for Friday, January 9th, 1761, states, that 'yesterday the workmen, who have been employed, for this fortnight past, in breaking up the large French ship that stuck in the Draw-Lock at London Bridge, as she was going up the river, endeavoured, on the strong flow of the tide, to get her through the Bridge, but could not effect it. This ship, it appears, was but 18 inches wider than the Lock.' At length, however, in the same paper for Friday, January 30th, it was announced that 'Yesterday the watermen cleared the Draw-Lock at London Bridge, of the large French ship that stuck there some weeks ago.'

"The destruction of part of St. Magnus' Church, by most authors attributed to the year 1759, but which actually took place in 1760, was the cause of a further improvement of the North-East end of London Bridge; by the opening of that arched passage beneath the Church Steeple, which the wisdom of Sir Christopher Wren had foreseen, and provided for, fifty-five years before. This destruction then, took place by a fire, which brake out between 9 and 10 o'clock, in the morning of Friday, April 18th, at the house of Messrs. Barrow and Reynolds, Oilmen, in Thames street, adjoining to the Church. It consumed seven dwelling-houses, all the warehouses on Fresh

Wharf, with a considerable quantity of goods contained in them, and the roof of the Church itself; which, falling in, very much damaged the pews and altar-piece. The organ, the excellence of which we have already noticed, was taken away, but was considered to have received very serious injury in the removal. The whole of this destruction was estimated at £40,000; and it was occasioned, says Entick, in his *'Continuation of Maitland's History,'* page 29, by the neglect of a servant, who was appointed to watch the boiling of some inflammatory substances, and who left his charge on the fire, whilst he went to see the famous Earl Ferrers return from his trial and condemnation. Before he could get back, the whole shop was in flames. Some of these particulars you will also find recorded in the *'Public Advertiser'* for Saturday, April 19th, 1760; and in the *'Gentleman's Magazine'* for that year, volume xxx., page 199. Before this fire, the main body of St. Magnus' Church extended to the tower, which was originally about equal with the houses on London Bridge; but when they were taken away, the West end so greatly interfered with the foot-path, that it was proposed to take down so much of the building as enclosed the tower on each side, and to form a passage under the steeple by arches. This plan, however, does not appear to have been proposed, until after the Church had been repaired; because the first notice of it which we meet with, is in the *'Public Advertiser'* of Monday, September 29th, 1760, in the following terms. 'The workmen have paved a great part of the foot-path on the lower side of London Bridge; and the tower part of St. Magnus' Church has been lately surveyed, in order to make some alteration in the lower part thereof, conducive to the convenience of the passage of the Bridge.' The danger which was supposed to be attendant upon its alteration, was probably the cause of delay in its execution; but the surveyor who was employed, had the ingenuity to discover, that Sir Christopher, conceiving that such a convenience must be required at some future period, had contrived the arch on which the steeple stood, of such strength, that it was essential only to clear away the intermediate space to perfect the alteration. Still the work proceeded but slowly, since the next notice of it is contained in the *'Public Advertiser'* for Wednesday, August 4th, 1762. 'The North and West Porticoes adjoining to the tower of St. Magnus' Church at London Bridge, are taking down, in order to form a passage to and from that building, through the spacious arch upon which the steeple is built; the South Portico is also down, which fronts the Bridge, and makes a very agreeable appearance; and the taking down of the West Portico, to compleat that useful work, is in great forwardness.' It was yet, however, almost another twelvemonth before this improvement was perfected, as we learn by the following notice, from the last mentioned paper of Thursday, June 30th, 1763. 'On Saturday last,—25th,—the foot-passage under the arch of St. Magnus' steeple was opened; which, besides the convenience for foot-passengers, makes a very pretty appearance. A vestry, built of stone, is to be erected in the Church-yard, to front the new Toll-house, just erected at the corner of London Bridge.' Before we finally part with St. Magnus' Church, I must not forget to state, that Malcolm, in his *'Londinum Redivivum,'* volume iv., page 31, observes,—though without citing his authority,—that 'in October, 1713, the Rector received an anonymous letter, which discovered a design of setting fire to London Bridge, for the purpose of plundering the inhabitants. The greatest precautions were adopted in consequence, and nothing uncommon occurred.' I find, however, no notice of this letter in any of the periodical prints of the time.

"In the mean time, the alterations of the Bridge itself were in continual progression; though all the buildings were not even yet removed, and the Temporary Bridge was still standing. The *'Public Advertiser'* for Thursday, December 25th, 1760, states that 'notice has been given to the people on the West side of London Bridge, to quit their premises by the 25th of March next.' In the same paper, for Tuesday, February 3rd, 1761, an advertisement announces, that six houses on the West side of London Bridge, from the North end of the Temporary Bridge to the Toll House, were to be sold by auction at Guildhall, to be put up at £156: and in the paper for Wednesday, February 11th, we are informed that those houses were begun to be pulled down. In your notices, Mr. Barbican, of the tokens issued by the tradesmen of old London Bridge, you mentioned two who lived at the sign of the Bear, at the Bridge-foot, which, perhaps, was the building referred to in the following passage contained in the *'Public Advertiser'* of Saturday, December 26th, 1761. 'Thursday last, the workmen employed in pulling down the Bear Tavern at the foot of London Bridge, found several pieces of gold and silver coin of Queen Elizabeth, and other monies to a considerable value.'"

"By no means unlikely," replied I, "and I may also add, that at this period was probably removed the house of the original manufacturer of Walkden's Ink-powder, with which we are still familiar. We learn the situation of his dwelling by his Shop-bill, an impression of which is in the possession of Mr. Upcott of the London Institution, engraven on a copper plate, measuring 6¼ inches by 4⅛. Within a double line, and beneath an ornamented compartment containing a Bell, is inscribed:—*'Richard Walkden, Stationer, at y*^e *Bell on London Bridge, near S*^t *Magnus Church, Makes and Sells all Sorts of Accomptants and Shopkeepers Books, y*^e *greatest Variety of Paper-Hangings for Rooms, and all other Sorts of Stationary Wares, Wholesale or Retail at the Lowest Prices. Where may be had Bibles, Common Prayers, Testaments, Psalters, &c. N. B. He is also the Maker of the Fine British Ink-Powder, for making Black Writing Ink, w*^{ch} *is Universally Allowed to Excell all other whatsoever, yet made, and is of the greatest Convenience for Country Shopkeepers to make their own Ink, to Sell again, as Likewise for Merchants and Sea Captains who goe or Send Ventures to Sea, to whom great allowance will be given with printed Directions of its Excellence and Use. At the same place may be had y*^e *best*

Liquid Ink, in its Greatest Perfection. Customers may Depend on being Serv'd as well by Letter as if present.' I must also take this opportunity of mentioning another Shop-bill connected with this edifice, communicated to me by Henry Smedley, Esq.; and consisting of a copper-plate executed about the latter end of the 17th century, representing a circle surrounded by fruit and foliage, having two Cupids standing at the upper corners, and containing in the centre, two palm-branches, enclosing a Sceptre surmounted by a Heart. Round the whole are suspended lancets, trepans, saws, &c., and beneath the device is engraven, '*Samvell Grover, at the Sceptre and heart on London bridge, who maketh all sorts of Chirugeons Instruments, the best sort of Razors, pen-knives, Scissers, and Lancetts: there are also the best Hoans, and fine Fish Skin Cases.*' You may remember, Mr. Postern, that one of my former Shop Bills was that of James Brooke, Stationer, 'near the Square on London Bridge,' This Square was formed in the first opening on the Bridge, above the 8th Arch from the North end, called St. Mary's Lock. It was surrounded by massive iron rails, and Mr. J. T. Smith, in his '*Antiquities of London,*' page 26, states, that when the houses were taken down, the iron-work was bought by several inhabitants of the Parish of St. Botolph, Bishopsgate, and placed upon the dwarf wall on the Eastern side of the Church yard, where it is yet to be seen."

"I have again to offer you my thanks," answered the Antiquary, "for your very curious and *recherché* illustrations; and we will now close up the year 1761 by stating, that we are informed by the '*Continuation of Maitland's History,*' page 35, that on Monday, February 2nd, the tide flowed so short up the Thames, that at high-water there was not sufficient to cover the Sterlings; so that several persons waded over, both above, and a little below, the Bridge at low water. We may, I think, fairly consider the history of *Old* London Bridge terminated at this place; since the alterations we have recently described, made its features almost such as we now behold them. I should not forget, however, that one of the last pieces of poetry connected with it, was written by the famous Anne Killegrew, celebrated by Dryden, and entitled '*On my Aunt, Mrs. A. K. Drown'd under London Bridge in the Queen's Bardge: Anno 1641.*' You will find it printed in Southey's '*Specimens of the later English Poets,*' London, 1807, Octavo, volume i., page 15.

"As we are informed by the '*Public Advertiser*' of Monday, June 7th, 1762, that the workmen had then begun to lay down the iron pipes, for the conveyance of water from London Bridge into the Borough, we may conclude that the stone-work of the edifice was then perfect; although from those pipes leaking between the stones, there arose a report that the new Bridge was falling to pieces, which was, some years after, the origin of a particular inquiry.

"The destructive effects of some very high tides which happened early in 1763, are the principal events connected with London Bridge at that period; as the '*Continuation of Maitland's History,*' page 48, informs us that, on Tuesday,

February 15th, the tide rose to such a height in the River, that many parts of Westminster were overflowed; and, below London Bridge, the inhabitants of Tooley Street were obliged to keep to their upper rooms. In the *'Public Advertiser'* of the following Thursday, it is stated that the damage done to goods in warehouses adjoining the Thames, was estimated at upwards of £20,000; the great land-floods having occasioned the water to rise higher than it had ever been known. That the Bridge itself was in some danger, may be inferred from the same paper of Wednesday, February 23rd, where it is recorded that 'three engines are at work driving piles, for the security of the large Arch of London Bridge; some of the small ones, it is said, will be entirely stopt, to prevent the water from ebbing away too fast.' It was probably this circumstance that was alluded to by Mylne, the Architect, in his Report to the Corporation of London, concerning a new grant to the Water-works, made in June, 1767; and which you will find in the *'Public Advertiser'* for Friday, July 17th. He there states, that in the beginning of 1763, the first winter after taking up the Pier from under the Great Arch, when the other Arches were stopped up with ice, the whole force of the tide rushed so violently through it, as to tear up the bed of the river, and the Sterlings, being deprived of their support, gave way, and left the foundation-piles entirely exposed to the water. He adds, too, that only to repair this damage, the sum of £6800 was expended by the Bridge Committee. Mr. Smeaton's answers on the best manner of enlarging and improving London Bridge, delivered on March 18th, 1763, may also be seen in the paper last referred to, for Monday, July 20th, 1767, and subsequent numbers. In the same journal of Tuesday, April 15th, 1763, it had been related, that 'the water in the Thames rose so high on Sunday, that many houses on the Surrey shore were two or three feet deep in water; and at Lambeth, the long walk by the Bishop's Palace was overflowed, and boats were employed in the town to carry people from house to house.'

"Although the famous winter of 1766-67 continued with remarkable severity until January 16th, we find but few particulars of it connected with London Bridge; excepting that the *'Gazetteer and New Daily Advertiser'* for Monday, January 12th, states that several of its Arches were then stopped by the ice, and some accidents, which happened there, are recorded in the subsequent numbers of the same paper. In a notice of the proceedings of a Court of Common Council on Wednesday, July 30th, 1766, also contained in the *'Gazetteer'* of the following Friday, it is stated that the Committee for conducting the recent repairs of London Bridge, made the last report of their works; in which they set forth, that they had executed the several trusts reposed in them by the Acts of Parliament which I have recited to you, and at the same time rendered an account of the money then owing for the alterations. Of these it is observed by John Gwynn, in his *'London and Westminster Improved,'* London, 1766, quarto, page 120, *Note*, that they amounted to nearly £100,000, beside the materials of the houses, many of which were new. He adds, too, that the Bridge was rendered worse than it had been, by the exceeding rapidity of the stream under the Great Arch; and condemns both the appearance and effects of the Water-works. Of the remaining debt, then, the Court ordered that £3000 in the Chamberlain's hands should be immediately paid; and that bonds should be given for the remainder, not exceeding £12,000, redeemable by the City, and bearing interest at 4 per cent. The Committee was then dissolved, and the concerns of London Bridge were again restored to that belonging to the Bridge-House Estates.

"There seems, however, to have been but little satisfaction given by the extensive alterations and improvements of this edifice; for, at the very same Court, a petition for relief was presented from the Watermen's Company, stating that the navigation through the Great Arch of London Bridge was very dangerous, from the two adjoining Arches on the North side being stopped up; and vessels being caught in the eddy it occasioned, received considerable damage before they could escape, which had sometimes occasioned the loss of life. It was soon discovered, too, that the iron pipes belonging to the Water-works, laid across the Bridge, had greatly injured the stone-work and crowns of the Arches, by frequent leaking; whilst the piers of the Great Arch were weakened, and the current of the tide was altered, by a new Arch being granted to the Water-works. These particulars are noticed in the *'Gazetteer'* of Thursday, October 23rd, 1766; whilst in the *'Public Advertiser'* for Tuesday, November 4th, and the former paper for Saturday, November 22nd, a report is mentioned of entirely removing both the Bridge and Water-works, and greatly improving the whole of their vicinity. In the *'Gazetteer,'* too, for Friday and Monday, December 5th and 8th, the dirty and dusty state of the Bridge is mentioned as arising from total neglect of cleaning and watering it, though the usual advertisements for their performance were then publishing.

"For the consideration and removal of these defects, a very fair opportunity was now offered; a Committee of the Proprietors of the Water-works having presented a petition to the Corporation, for renting, and erecting a wheel in, the 5th Arch at the North end of London Bridge, which had been referred to a Committee, to examine, and report upon. This petition was read at the Court of Common Council on Thursday, November 28th, 1765, as we learn by the *'Public Advertiser'* of the following day; and you will find a copy of it in the same paper for Friday, July 3rd, 1767, forming part of a series of 13 official documents, on the subject, inserted in that journal down to Thursday, July 23rd, of the same year. I have already had occasion slightly to notice these proceedings, of which you may find several particulars in the *'Gentleman's Magazine'* for 1767, volume xxxvii., pages 337, 407; but I shall now give you some account of them from these more authentic sources, and close up my history of the Water-works with a short description of their mechanism, and final removal.

"The petition alluded to, contains a curious historical outline of the Water-works at London Bridge, tracing their gradual extension from one to four of its Arches; the leases of all which were to terminate in the year 2082, being 500 years from the time when the original grant was made, the remainder taking only the unexpired term. The 1st and 2nd Northern Arches were let for 500 years, from November 24th, 1582, at 10*s. per annum*; and the 4th Arch, from August 24th, 1701, for 381¼ years, also at 10*s. per annum*, and a fine of £300. The lease of the 3rd Arch, however,—formerly stopped up and let to a Wharfinger,—did not commence until Michaelmas day, 1761, when it was granted for the term of 321 years, at the old rent; though the Proprietors of the Water-works had made proposals for it in 1731 and 1743, when it was unoccupied, the last tenant having quitted it at Lady-day, 1718. These leases were the more readily granted, as it was supposed that the Water-works were a protection to the Bridge and the vessels below it; whilst it was asserted that the Arches they occupied were but very seldom used, and the lessees covenanted to secure their engines by piles, as well as to keep the Piers and Sterlings built upon, in proper repair. Their fire-plugs, too, were to be under the direction of the Committee of City-Lands; the Works were not to rise higher than the cellars of the buildings on London Bridge; and houses in general, in the City and its liberties, were to be supplied with water at 20*s. per annum*. In petitioning for a fifth Arch, it was represented, that, notwithstanding the great expense incurred for the Water-works, the engine was yet inadequate to the furnishing at all times a sufficient supply of water. The wheels under the other four Arches would never act with the same velocity as they did before the late alteration of the Bridge; but as the 5th Arch stood nearer the central current of the River, the continual flowing of the tide would give the works additional power, without being any obstacle to the navigation. On the other hand, however, several counter-petitions were presented from the Wharfingers and Lightermen, stating the dangerous eddy at the Great Arch, arising from the closing of those Arches called the Long Entry and Chapel Locks, to give force to the current at the Water-works; and praying that they might be opened, the middle of the River kept free, or that two Arches at the South end might be closed instead of them. We have already seen, that these suits made but slow progress; and accordingly we find that the petition from the Water-works was first referred to a Sub-committee by the Committee of City-Lands, on Wednesday, December 4th, 1765; to the Committee itself on Friday, November 28th, 1766: and on Tuesday, December 16th, their Report was delivered to the Court of Common Council. Before these Committees, the Proprietors of the Water-works appeared on Tuesday, October 21st, and Wednesday,

November 19th, 1766; when the complaints of their pipes leaking, and the navigation being endangered, were stated, and remedies ordered to be provided. They were also asked, whether they would undertake, on forfeiture of their lease, 'to keep their engine at work during the times of dead high and low-water, when their wheels lay still, provided they had leave to raise their tenants 1*s.* yearly for every house.' To this they ultimately agreed, the additional rent being made 2*s.*; and to remedy the leakage of such pipes as lay across the Bridge for the supply of Southwark, it was proposed that they should be entirely removed, the first Arch on the Surrey side of the Bridge being stopped up, and a wheel erected in the second, 10*s. per annum* being paid for each, whilst the Long Entry and Chapel Locks were to be re-opened. Such then were the measures recommended in the Committee's Report, as being without danger and of general benefit; but before they were acceded to, these particulars were ordered to be printed, and a copy sent to some of the most eminent Surveyors of the time, Messrs. Brindley, Smeaton, Yeoman, Mylne, and Wooler, whose answers were read to the Common Council, on Wednesday, February 25th, 1767. At the same time, too, as we are informed by the '*Gazetteer*' of the day following, the Proprietors of the Water-works were heard upon the subject of their alterations, though the decision was referred to the next Court. The Engineers generally agreed, that by opening the Long Entry and Chapel Locks, taking away the water-pipes upon the Bridge, erecting a wheel in the 5th Arch, and occupying the farthest two on the Surrey side, the edifice and navigation would be generally improved. Mr. Mylne, however, recommended that the 5th Arch should not be granted; but that so many Arches at the South end should be wholly stopped, as would be equal to compensate the Water-works for their loss by the Great Arch; adding, that the pipes were slowly, but certainly, ruining the Bridge; and that a Water-company, then established in Southwark, should be encouraged to supply the whole of the Borough. The Corporation, however, did not yet come to a decision, but on Friday, March 13th, 1767, the Town Clerk was again ordered to solicit the Engineers to re-consider the subject, and to point out the course most proper to be followed. The second series of answers, which was read at a Court of Common Council, on Tuesday, June 23rd, chiefly confirmed and referred to the former. Messrs. Wooler and Mylne were, however, decidedly against any new grants to the Water-works, of which they earnestly recommended the removal, as well as the opening of the closed-up Arches; proposing to substitute a horse, or fire, engine, on both sides of the river, or closing up three Arches on the Surrey shore. Mr. Yeoman also recommended the taking away of the Water-works; whilst Mr. Smeaton, considering that the bed of the Thames had become so unequal that it would require several centuries to restore its level, argued that the stoppage of London Bridge was useful both to the Water-works and navigation in general, and that it remained only to employ the force of water in the most beneficial manner. By his Report the Corporation seems to have been determined; since the *'Gazetteer'* of June 24th states, that Mr. Mylne was examined, and, after a long debate, the 5th Arch was granted to the Water-works, upon the conditions already mentioned: though there were, subsequently, several disputes on points of law, and particularly upon the power which the Corporation had to grant away the passage of a navigable river.

"The *'Gazetteer'* for Monday, Dec. 28th, 1767, informs us that the two Arches adjoining the South end of the Bridge were, at length, then stopped up, and wheels preparing to be erected in each of them; and on the 30th, most of the Locks at that part of the edifice were entirely closed by the ice. It was not, however, until the year 1770, as we are informed in Concannen's *'History of Southwark,'* page 233, that the Borough Water-works were perfected by the erection of a Steam-Engine; though a part of the machinery was originally erected on the River-banks for the supply of Mr. Thrale's Brewery, when it was worked by horses. These works were then known by the name of their proprietor, which was afterwards changed for that of the Company which bought them: and an engine erected, wherein the pressure of the atmosphere acted upon the Steam-piston.

"I proceed now, Mr. Barbican, to give you some account of the Water-works erected at the North end of London Bridge, which were considered to be far superior even to the celebrated hydraulics of Marli, in France. You are already aware, that the wheels beneath the Arches were turned by the common tide-water of the Thames; the axle-trees being 19 feet in length, and 3 in diameter, having 4 sets of arms, 8 in each place, on which were fixed 4 rings, or fellies, 20 feet in diameter, with 26 floats of 14 feet long, and 18 inches deep. The gudgeons, or centre-pins, of these wheels, rested upon brasses, fixed on 2 large levers 16 feet long, the tops of which were formed of arched timber, the levers being made circular on their lower sides to an arch, and kept in their places by 2 arching studs fixed in a stock, through 2 mortices in the lever. To the lower part of the arch on the lever, was fixed a strong triple chain, the links attached to circles of 1 foot in diameter, having notches or teeth, to take hold of the leaves of a cast-iron pinion, 10 inches in diameter, with 8 teeth in it, moving on an axis. The other end of this chain had a large weight hanging from it, to assist in counterpoising the wheel, and to preserve the chain from sliding on the pinion. On the same axis with the pinion, were 2 cog-wheels; one of 6 feet in diameter having 48 cogs, and another of 51 cogs, each working in a trundle of 6 rounds: on this axis there was also a winch, by which one man could raise or lower the wheels as occasion might require. Near the end of the great axle-tree, was another cog-wheel of 8 feet in diameter, and 44 cogs, working into a trundle of 20 rounds, 4½ feet in diameter; the axis of which was fixed in brasses at each end of the lever before mentioned, and communicated with iron cranks having 4 necks, each of which raised an iron spear attached to levers 24 feet in length. To the other ends were fastened iron rods and forcing-plugs, working in cast-iron cylinders 4¾ feet long, 7 inches in bore above, and 9 below, where the valves were. These cylinders were placed over a hollow trunk of cast-iron, with 4 valves in it, immediately beneath them; and as one end of the trunk was furnished with a sucking-pipe and grate going into the water, they were each filled alternately, and delivered their supplies through curved pipes into a second trunk, furnished with an iron pipe, through which the water was forced up to any height required. These were, however, only half the works; the whole of the mechanism being double to each wheel. The first wheel in the Arch next the City, worked 16 forcers; and in the third Arch were three wheels, one working 12, the second 8, and another 16 forcers. Their utmost power of raising water was estimated from four of the wheels, to be 2052 gallons per minute; 123,120 gallons—being equal to 1954 hogsheads—in an hour; or 46,896 hogsheads daily, to the height of 120 feet, including the waste, which might be considered as a fifth part of the whole. Every revolution of a wheel, made 2½ strokes in every minute in all the forcers, the wheels turning 6 times in a minute at high-water, and 4½ times at middle water; and it was stated before a Committee of the House of Commons, that in the year 1820, these Works supplied 26,322,705 hogsheads of water. It is usual to give Dr. Desaguliers as the authority for these particulars, but I have abstracted them from the '*Philosophical Transactions*,' already referred to; and they are also printed in Maitland's '*History*,' volume i., page 51, whence they have been copied into almost every subsequent account of London. After the grant of a fifth Arch to the Water-works, about July 1767, an improved wheel was designed by Mr. Smeaton, to be erected at that part; of which two engravings and several particulars, together with his remarks on the Water-engine, are inserted in the Second volume of his '*Reports*' already cited, Plates ii.-iii., pages 27-30.

"I have in my possession a large and curious old drawing, in colours, representing two elevations, and a ground-plan of these Works and the Water-Tower, executed before the grant of a fifth Arch, or the erection of wheels at the South end of the edifice, which is chiefly interesting, as shewing the courses of the main-pipes then attached to every wheel for conveying water to the various parts of London; which were connected and furnished in the following manner. Bishopsgate Main, supplied from the Wheels under the 3rd Arch, and Western end of the 4th, called 'the Upper, and Borough Wheels:' Cheapside Main, from those under the second and 3rd Arches, called the 'Three-Ringed, and Low Wheels:' Aldgate Main, from those under the 2nd Arch, and the Eastern end of the 4th, expressed by the same name: Fleet-street Main, from a small Wheel in the 1st Arch, and another at the Western end of the 4th, called 'the Two-Ringed, and Borough Wheels:'

Newgate-street Main, from those in the 2nd Arch, and the Western end of the 4th, or 'the Upper, and Three-Ringed Wheels:' Broad-street Main, principally from 'the Low-Wheel,' under the 2nd Arch; though it also derived some water from that at the Western end of the 4th: Grace Church-street Main, from those in the 1st and 2nd Arches, or 'the Two-Ringed, and Three-Ringed Wheels:' Cannon-street Main, from 'the Upper, and Borough Wheels,' or those beneath the 3rd and 4th Arches: Thames-street Main, from a 'Low Wheel' at the Eastern end of the 4th Arch; and the Borough Main, from the proper Wheel, which was situate at its Western extremity, forming ten sets of main-pipes in all. At each end of the Bridge, round the Western-sides of the Water-works, were wooden platforms or galleries, occasionally decorated with plants and flowers; and immediately over the Wheels at the City end, were the work-shops belonging to them. Their history is now, however, fast drawing to a close: in March, 1817, the managers gave notice that they were about to rebuild their largest Water-wheel; but on July 26th, 1822, the third Year of King George IV., an Act was passed for their entire removal, with a view of improving London Bridge, or erecting a new one. You will, of course, find this document in *'The Statutes of the Realm,'* by John Raithby, Esq., volume viii., London, 1822, quarto, pages 1049-1054; it being chapter cix. of the *'Local and Personal Acts declared public:'* and I shall now give you a slight idea of its contents. Having declared, that about 260 years of the original grants to the Water-works are yet unexpired, it is enacted that the Corporation of London shall raise £15,000 out of the Bridge-House Estates, for carrying the Act into effect; £10,000 of which should be paid to the Proprietors of the Water-works, for rendering void all their licences, and transferring all their machinery, buildings, &c. to the New-River Company, which Company was entitled to commence receiving rents and defraying expenses connected with the Water, from June 24th, 1822; and it was also licensed to procure leave from the Corporation, to cut the River-banks, &c. below low-water mark, not exceeding 100 feet from the East side of the present Bridge, for laying down pipes, &c., saving the City's rights in the Thames; paying the sum of 20*s.* as a fine for so doing, and 20*s.* annually afterwards. Full powers were likewise granted, that the Company might lay down pipes in the streets, and over the Bridges of London; and that it might resign the supply of a part of a district to another party, and receive a recompence in return; adding that it should neither be compelled to continue the supply, nor be considered to have an exclusive right to it. Upon conclusion of the agreement, the Company was to remove the whole machinery, &c. within the six months following, which was otherwise to be taken up and sold by the Corporation. The New-River Company was also charged with the payment of certain annuities to the former Proprietors of the Water-works, for the remainder of their lease, as well as with the pensions due to their servants, &c. to be defrayed out of the rents received. Such, then, was the end of the London Bridge Water-works; and the only other remarkable event which I find recorded in the year 1767, connected with our edifice is, that on Saturday, November 28th, about 5 o'clock in the morning, the tide ebbed and flowed at this place, and at Greenwich, twice within an hour and a half; as you will find recorded both in the *'Continuation of Maitland's History,'* page 71, and in the *'Gazetteer'* for Wednesday, December 22nd.

"The year 1768 commenced with so violent and general a frost, that its effects were felt equally upon the land and the water. 'It is said,' observes the *'Gazetteer'* of Friday, January 1st, 'that London Bridge is in great danger by this severe frost: the most essential of the piles which form the Sterlings have been lately observed to be quite loose, and playing in the water; and workmen have been ordered, notwithstanding the imminent danger, to throw Kentish rag-stone round the piers.' In addition to this, there were also several fatal accidents, arising from the River being frozen, which were likewise greatly detrimental to this edifice. The night of Tuesday, January 5th, was said to have been the most fatal ever known for damage done upon the Thames: one French vessel was thrown upon the Sterlings of the Bridge, with the loss of her bow-sprit, where it was obliged to be kept for several days secured by ropes; and two others were driven through the Centre Arch, losing their main-masts, and carrying away the lamps from the parapet. Some barges also got across the other Arches, and after the breaking up of the frost, which was about the middle of January, the *'Gazetteer'* of Thursday, 21st, states, that 'yesterday a great many tons of Kentish rag-stones were thrown under the Great Arch of London Bridge, as a supposed temporary remedy against the damage the foundation received during the late frost. An expedient productive of infinite ruin to the navigation, as they are soon scowered away again, and an accumulating expense to the City of an alarming nature.' It is also added in the same paper for Tuesday, February 2nd, that 'the damages done to London Bridge Water-works in the late severe weather, are not yet repaired, though the workmen have worked over hours, and on Sundays, ever since the weather broke. The last damaged wheel will be at work this week.' It had been frequently remarked in the papers of this period, that the amount of rents received from the Proprietors of the London Bridge Waterworks, was not, in any degree, proportionate to the expenses of their repairs, which were calculated at £2500 yearly; and in the *'Gazetteer'* for Friday, April 22nd, 1768, it is stated that they returned only £3000 clear of all expenses. It is also rather curiously observed, that ''tis computed that there are drowned at London Bridge, about 50 people upon an average every year; which, as they are the prime of watermen, bargemen, and seamen, amount, at £400 each, to £20,000 *per annum.*' The *'Continuation of Maitland's History,'* page 73, states, that on April 10th, in this year, the Thames was so remarkably low, that it was with difficulty even a wherry could cross it, the sand-banks on both sides of the Bridge being entirely dry. And now, as I have already mentioned to you several particulars concerning the foundation of Blackfriars' Bridge, let me conclude this year with a summary notice of its completion. The Architect, then, was Robert Mylne, Esq.; the first pile of it was driven in the middle of the Thames on Saturday, June 7th, 1760; and the first stone was laid by Sir Thomas Chitty, Lord Mayor, on Friday, October 31st. On Wednesday, November 19th, 1768, it was made passable as a bridle-way, exactly two years after its reception of foot passengers; and it was finally and generally opened on Sunday, November, 19th, 1769. The total expense of this building amounted to £152,840. 3*s.* 10*d.*; exclusive of £5830 for altering and filling-up the Fleet-ditch, and £2167, the cost of the Temporary Wooden Bridge. Until June 22nd, 1785, there was a toll of ½*d.* for every foot-passenger, and 1*d.* on Sundays; the yearly amount of which, from its commencement in 1766, with the purposes to which it was applied, may be seen in the '*Second Report of the Select Committee for Improving the Port of London,*' 1799, folio, *Appendix* B. 11, page 49. The Toll-house was burned down in the Riots of 1780, when all the account-books were destroyed.

"And now to return again to our memorials of London Bridge, I do not find, even after the most careful search, any particulars of this edifice, connected with the great Frost of 1785, notwithstanding its extent and severity for 115 days; and for that of 1789, though there are many descriptions of its appearance both up and down the River, there are but few notices of it at this identical spot. The '*Public Advertiser*' of Friday, January 9th, 1789, states, that the shipping below the Bridge was in considerable danger, from the tiers at Deptford, Greenwich, &c. being enclosed with ice; and that the Thames being frozen over on the day preceding, 'several purl-booths were erected, and many thousands of persons crossed upon the ice from Tower-wharf to the opposite shore.' The same paper for the day following, states, that the frost had then continued for about six weeks; whilst its severity down the River kept still increasing. Passages across the ice, strewed with ashes, were formed at Gun-Dock, Execution-Dock, &c.; and these parts seem to have constituted the principal scenes of attraction. 'No sooner,' says the '*London Chronicle*' from Saturday, January 10th, to Tuesday, January 13th, page 48, 'had the Thames acquired a sufficient consistency, than booths, turn-abouts, &c. &c. were erected; the puppet-shows, wild-beasts, &c. were transported from every adjacent village; whilst the watermen, that they might draw their usual resources from the water, broke in the ice close to the shore, and erected bridges, with toll-bars, to make every passenger pay a halfpenny for getting to the ice. One of the suttling booths has for its sign 'Beer, Wine, and Spirituous Liquors without a License.' A man who sells hot gingerbread, has a board on which is written 'no shop-tax nor window-duty.' All the adventurers contend in these short sentences for the preference of the company, and the Thames is in general crowded.' Another specimen of the humour exhibited at this place, was contained in the following inscription on a temporary building on the Thames, and printed in the *'Public Advertiser'* of Thursday, January 15th: 'This Booth to Let. The present possessor of the Premises is Mr. Frost. His affairs, however, not being on a permanent footing, a dissolution or bankruptcy may soon be expected, and the final settlement of the whole entrusted to Mr. Thaw.' On Wednesday, January 7th, a large pig was roasted on one of the principal roads; and on Monday the 12th, a young bear was hunted on the ice, near Rotherhithe. As usual, too, a printing-press was erected near the same spot, of which there is a curious memorial preserved in Mr. Crowle's *'Illustrated Pennant,'* volume viii., page 262, consisting of a bill, having a border of type flowers containing the following verses; afterwards altered and adopted in the Frost of 1814.

'The silver Thames was frozen o'er,
No diff'rence 'twixt the Stream and shore;
The like no Man hath seen before,
Except he liv'd in Days of Yore.

On the Ice, at the Thames Printing-Office opposite St. Catherine's Stairs in the severe Frost, January, 1789. Printed by me, William Bailey.' The same collection also contains a small stippled engraving, entitled *'A View of the Thames from Rotherhithe Stairs, during the Frost in 1789. Painted by G. Samuel, and Engraved by W. Birch, Enamel-painter.'* The severity of this frost, however, appears to have been felt considerably beyond these scenes of amusement. The East-India ships were hastily sent down to Gravesend, to which place, and even below it, large shoals of ice had already floated, extending almost through the whole Reach; the navigation of boats was entirely stopped, and it was supposed that the River would soon be completely impassable from London Bridge to Woolwich. Vast quantities of boiling water were poured every morning upon the Bridge Water-works, before the wheels could be set in motion, and 25 horses were daily employed in removing the ice which surrounded them: whilst at Blackfriars the masses of floating ice were said to be 18 feet in thickness, and were continually increasing from the many cart-loads of snow constantly thrown over the ballustrades. 'The various parts of the River,'— says the *'Public Advertiser'* of Friday, January 9th,—'present different appearances; in some, the surface is smooth for a mile or two, and then rough and mountainous, from the great quantities of snow driven by the wind, and frozen in large bodies.' Towards Putney Bridge and upwards, the scene on the ice again became really entertaining. 'Opposite to Windsor-street,' continues the same paper, 'booths have been erected since Friday last, and a fair is kept on the river. Multitudes of people are continually passing and repassing; puppet-shows, round-abouts, and all the various amusements of Bartholomew fair are exhibited. In short, Putney and Fulham, from the morning dawn till the dusk of returning evening, are a scene of festivity and gaiety.'

"At length, the expected thaw commenced with some rain, about two o'clock on Tuesday, January 13th; and before night the streets were almost overflowed. 'Perhaps,' says the '*London Chronicle*,' from that date to Thursday, January 15th, page 56, 'the breaking up of the Fair upon the Thames last Tuesday night below Bridge, exceeded every idea that could be formed of it, as it was not until after the dusk of the evening, that the busy crowd was persuaded of the approach of a thaw. This, however, with the cracking of some ice about 8 o'clock, made the whole a scene of the most perfect confusion; as men, beasts, booths, turn-abouts, puppet-shows, &c. &c. were all in motion, and pouring towards the shore on each side. The confluence here was so sudden and impetuous, that the watermen who had formed the toll-bars over the sides of the river, where they had broken the ice for that purpose, not being able to maintain their standard from the crowd, &c. pulled up the boards, by which a number of persons who could not leap, or were borne down by the press, were soused up to the middle. The difficulty of landing at the Tower stairs was extreme, until near 10 o'clock, occasioned by the crowding of people from the shore, who were attracted by the confusion on the water. The inconvenience to the shipping is now increased more than since the setting in of the Frost, as no persons will venture upon the ice to fetch or carry any thing for them, and it is not yet sufficiently disunited for a boat to live.' The succeeding number of this paper, page 60, mentions that on Thursday, January 15th, the ice was so powerful as to cut the cables of two vessels lying at the Old Rose Chain, and drive them through the Great Arch of London Bridge; when their masts becoming entangled with the ballustrades, both were broken, and many persons hurt. The Thames, however, continued to be considerably frozen for some time after this. I shall terminate the year 1789, by informing you, that it is stated in the '*Public Advertiser*' of Friday, January 16th, that the shares of the London Bridge Proprietors, which some years before had been worth £3000 per annum in Life Annuities, had then fallen below £2000.

"In the years 1793 and 1794, the Great Centre Arch again became a subject of consideration; for, in order to confine the rubble which had been deposited there to raise and preserve the form of its bed, nine strong beams of timber were sunk in it horizontally between the Sterlings, having upright pieces at each end fitting into grooves cut in the sides of the Sterlings, which forced them down and held them in their places. This contrivance, however, was only of temporary benefit, for, at the excellent survey of London Bridge, made by Mr. George Dance, in 1799, he supposed that only two of these timbers were remaining, the rest having been carried away by the ice. If we remember, indeed, the accidents that were continually happening to the

Bridge, by vessels driving through it at this very part, there can be no great reason to wonder at these defences being speedily destroyed. So early as January 19th, 1795, we find by *'Dodsley's Annual Register'* for that year, volume xxxvii., page 3 of the *'Chronicle'* part, that, about 12 o'clock, two vessels broke from their moorings a little below the Bridge, when the tide drove them violently against it. One of them being a large West-Indiaman, making the Centre Arch, had all its masts carried away close by the board, when it drove through with a violent crash, and continued up the river to Somerset House. In 1798, also, the same authority, volume xl., page 40 of the *'Chronicle'* part, mentions, that on May 23rd, a sprit-sail vessel, laden with hay, drove against the Bridge with great velocity, and the mast not being lowered in time, it struck the ballustrades over the Centre Arch and broke them away to the space of nearly ten feet; the two persons on board being killed by the stones. But if I were to record all the accidents of this nature, which are contained in the registers of every year, my narrative would be much longer, and more melancholy, than either of us would desire; and I shall add only, therefore, that even the timbers, sunk as an improvement to the passage of the Centre Arch, were found, in some degree, to injure the navigation of the Bridge. For in the examination of Mr. M. P.—now Alderman—Lucas, on June 26th, 1799, he stated, that the chalk, &c. thrown into the water to support the foundation of that part of the Bridge, had produced shoals both above and below it; and, that the timbers recently laid there having prevented the rubble being scattered, it was stopped up in the wake of the Great Arch, where it formed a bar. On this account, the last three hours of the ebb-tide, which were always attended with danger, became additionally hazardous; empty craft under 3 or 4 tons burthen, could not go through with safety, and loaded craft could not pass at all at that time. The stream being then sunk below the level of the Sterlings, the passage was reduced nearly one half; the fall commenced and increased until the ebb was over; a barge of 30 or 40 tons would consequently pass with her bows under water, of which it frequently shipped four or five tons; whilst it was impossible for any one to stand upon the deck, without holding on to some part of the vessel. Let me add, that you will find all these particulars, together with a *'Plan and description of the Timbers sunk in the Great Arch of London Bridge, in the years 1793 and 1794,'* in plate vii. of *'The several Plans and Drawings referred to in the Second Report from the Select Committee upon the Improvement of the Port of London,'* 1799, folio; and in the Appendix A 5, B 6, and pages 19 and 35 of the Report itself.

"As I do not find that the famous Frost of 1794 produced any very remarkable circumstance connected with London Bridge, I shall hasten to the year 1799, when it again became the subject of considerable inquiry and speculation, the particulars of which are so fully recorded in that Report to which I have now referred you: pages 5 and 6, section 2, and *'Appendix,'* B. 1,-B. 11, pages 21-49, plates v.-vii. The amount of these proceedings was, that after a minute survey of the Bridge and River, by Mr. George Dance, Clerk of the Works, and Mr. John Foulds, his assistant, and Engineer to the Water-works, executed between the months of May and July, it was ascertained, that, provided the Sterlings were kept in repair, the structure itself was likely to stand for ages. These defences, they added, had then been recently altered and improved in shape, size, and construction, so as to retain the chalk, &c. with which they were then filling; and though there were many fractures in the building, they had not increased in the last 30 years. The average cost of its repairs had exceeded £4200 annually, for the last six years, and the Wardens' receipts for the same period had varied from £9772: 2*s*. 1½*d*. to £24,848: 10*s*. 4½*d*. These financial particulars are recorded at length in the Report whence we derive our information; '*Appendix*,' B. 10, pages 38-49, in a document entitled '*An account of the produce of the Estates of the City of London, called the Bridge-House Estates, and the application thereof, from the year 1756 to Christmas 1798*;' which may properly be considered as a continuation of that paper which furnished us with the ancient revenues and expenditures. I should observe, however, that the Report still represents the dangers of the Bridge navigation; stating, that, although the stream was 10 feet deep under the Middle Arch at low-water, yet, at the distance of only a few yards below it, there were not more than 18 inches. These Reports contain also the following engravings.

"1. '*Ground-plan and Elevation of London Bridge in its present state, 2nd July, 1799, taken by Mr. Dance. R. Metcalf Sculp.*' A most curious and interesting print, measuring 8 feet 5 inches, by 2 feet; shewing the sizes of the several locks; the different heights of the tides; the singular forms of the Sterlings; a Section through one of the arches and roadway, and the measurement of every part set down in figures. See Plate v. in the large folio of Drawings, &c. belonging to the Second Report. If to these particulars we add the Water-works, the line of Soundings taken along the points of the Sterlings, a Section of the bed of the River beneath them, and Mr. Smeaton's new foundation of the Great Arch, we shall have the most accurate materials for constructing the GROUND-PLAN AND ELEVATION OF OLD LONDON BRIDGE.

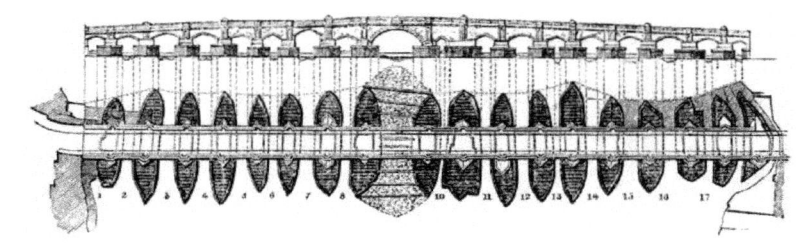

"2. Another print belonging to this Report, consists of the *'Soundings of the Great Arch of London Bridge, taken from the top of the Sterlings, 29th May, 1799, by J. Foulds and I. K.:*' to which are added the depths of the River, at, and between, London Bridge and Billingsgate, taken at low-water. Plate vi. in the same volume. The printed Report also contains three other engravings connected with this subject, from drawings made by Mr. Smeaton, to illustrate his observations on London Bridge, in March, 1763, and afterwards preserved by Sir Joseph Banks, with the original manuscript of his Report. They will be found at page 25, B. 5, of the *'Appendix,'* and they consist of—1. *'Section of the Water-way at London Bridge as it was before the opening of the Great Arch, and at the beginning of Feb. 1763:'*—2. *'Plan of the Sterlings of London Bridge, before the opening of the Great Arch;'*—3. *'Plan of the proposed Water-way under the Great Arch of London Bridge,'* shewing the bed of rubble, &c. laid down for lining the foundation, and the additions to the two centre Sterlings. All these engravings, however, you will find reduced upon one plate, by W. Lowry, and inserted in Smeaton's *'Reports'* already cited, volume ii., page 1.

"And now, Mr. Geoffrey Barbican, though I am rapidly advancing towards the end of my Chronicles, like the tired post-horse, which exerts all his remaining strength when he sees his resting-place is not far distant, though I may not delay my course to enlarge upon any part of our subject, yet I think it not only a fair opportunity, but a positive duty, to collect all the omissions that I can remember from the former part of my history; 'unconsidered trifles,' as *Autolycus* says, and add them to the end of the 18th Century, which is to us the great barrier between ancient and modern times.

"And firstly, I would observe, that so early as the year 1179-80, the inhabitants of the vicinity of London Bridge appear to have formed themselves into several of those fraternities anciently called Guilds; though, having done so without lawful authority, they were fined in various penalties. Whilst they all bore, however, the title of *Gilda de Ponte*, or Bridge-Guild, we can only suppose that the members of them lived in the Bridge-street, since the stone edifice had been at that time no more than three or four years begun. You will find these particulars recorded by Madox, in his *'History of the Exchequer,'* chapter xiv., section xv., pages 390, 391, note z, and cited from the Great Roll of the 26th year of Henry II.; the following being those articles which immediately refer to the present subject. 'The Bridge-Guild, whereof Thomas Cocus is Alderman, oweth 1 mark,'—13*s.* 4*d*.: 'the Bridge-Guild, whereof Ailwin Fink is Alderman, oweth 15 marks:'—'the Bridge-Guild, whereof Robert de Bosco is Alderman, oweth 10 marks:'—'the Bridge-Guild, whereof Peter Fitz Alan was Alderman, oweth 15 marks.'

"In speaking, too, of the reign of Queen Mary, I omitted to mention that short notice with which John Fox has furnished us, of certain 'vaine pageants,' exhibited to her upon London Bridge. You will find the passage in the second volume of that edition of his '*Acts and Monuments*' which I have already cited, page 1338, and it runs thus. 'And the next day, being Saturday, the xix. of August—1554,—the King and Queene's Majesties rode from Suffolk Place, accompanied with a great number as well of noblemen as of gentlemen, through the City of London to White Hall, and at London Bridge, as he entered at the Draw-Bridge, was a great vaine spectacle set vp, two images presenting two Giants, one named Corineus and the other Gogmagog, holding between them certain Latin verses, which, for the vain ostentation of flattery, I overpasse.' I can discover no other particulars of this exhibition, but the preceding paragraph was copied, by Holinshed, into his '*Chronicles*,' volume ii., page 1120.

"In mentioning the tradesmen who resided on London Bridge, I ought, also, to have pointed out to your notice that paragraph concerning them, first inserted in Strype's edition of *Stow's Survey*, edit. 1720, Book i.; chapter xxix., volume 1, page 242; where it is said that 'Men of trades, and sellers of wares in this City, have oftentimes,'—since the days of Fitz Stephen—'changed their places as they have found to their best advantage. For, whereas, Mercers and Haberdashers used then to keep their shops in West-Cheap, of later time they held them on London Bridge, where, partly, they do yet remain.'

"One would expect to find frequent references to London Bridge, in the works of our ancient Dramatists, yet my memory supplies me with but very few instances; though I may observe, that Shakspeare has an allusion to the heads of traitors erected over the gate of this edifice, in Act iii. Scene 2, of '*King Richard the Third*,' where *Catesby* says to *Hastings*:

'The Princes both make high account of you,—
For they account his head upon the Bridge.
[*Aside.*'

Another passage, referring to this custom, is also to be found in the second Act of George Wilkins's '*Miseries of Inforced Marriage*,' first printed in quarto, 1607, and inserted in Dodsley's '*Select Collection of Old Plays*,' London, 1780, duodecimo, volume v., page 27; where *Ilford* says to *Wentloe*, 'S'foot! you chittiface, that looks worse than a collier through a wooden window, an ape afraid of a whip, or a knave's head, shook seven years in the weather on London Bridge;—do you catechise me?' In Act v., Scene 1, of Shakerley Marmion's '*Antiquary*,' originally printed in 1641, quarto, and published in the preceding collection, volume x., page 97, is likewise the following passage, the idea of which appears to be taken from the noisy situation of the houses on the Old Bridge: 'That man that trusts a woman with a privacy, and hopes for silence, may as well expect it at the fall of a bridge.' But 'rare Ben Jonson,' in his '*Staple of News*,' Act ii., Scene 1, has a reference to those frequent, and almost useless, repairs of this edifice, of which we have recounted so many; since he makes *Shunfield* say of *Old Pennyboy*,

'He minds
A courtesy no more than London Bridge,
What Arch was mended last.'

"In William Gifford's '*Works of Ben Jonson,*' London, 1816, octavo, volume v., page 215, he has rather a violent note upon this passage, in which he says, 'Two hundred years have nearly elapsed since this was written, and the observation still holds. This pernicious structure has wasted more money in perpetual repairs, than would have sufficed to build a dozen safe and commodious Bridges; and cost the lives, perhaps, of as many thousand people. This may seem little to those whom it concerns, but there is blood on the City, and a heavy account is before them. Had an Alderman or a turtle been lost there, the nuisance would have been long since removed.' As I have already referred to the heads of the Regicides, &c. standing over the Bridge-gate at the time of the Great Fire, I may observe, that 'glorious John Dryden,' in his '*Annus Mirabilis,*' stanza 223, has this solemn mention of them, with a fine allusion to the infernal hymns chanted on a Witches' sabbath:

'The ghosts of traitors from the Bridge descend,
With bold fanatic spectres to rejoice;
About the fire into a dance they bend,
And sing their sabbath-notes with feeble voice.'

See '*The Works of John Dryden,*' edited by Walter Scott, Esq., London, 1808, octavo, volume ix., pages 144, 186, *Note* xlv.

"In recording these analecta of Old London Bridge, I may also take the opportunity of observing to you, that from about July to September, you may see almost every 'jutty, frieze, and coigne of 'vantage, made the pendent bed and procreant cradle' of the small yellow flowers and pointed leaves of the *Sisymbrium Irio,* or London Rocket. It probably made its first appearance on this edifice soon after the Great Fire of 1666, since the famous Botanist, Robert Morison, who lived at the period, has a singular dialogue upon it in his rare and curious '*Præludia Botanica,*' printed in 1669; where he states, that in 1667-68 it sprang up in such abundance from the City ruins, that in many places it might have been mown like corn, though London Bridge is not specially referred to. A coloured engraving of the plant, with the foregoing particulars, will be found in William Curtis's '*Flora Londinensis,*' London, 1767, folio. Fasciculus vi., plate 48, marked 311.

"I have but few other fragments to mention; and the first of them relates to the very extensive use which is made of London Bridge as a thoroughfare. What it must have been formerly, when it was the only passage across the Thames, we know not; but after the introduction of a toll, the rent at which I have told you it was farmed, affords some general idea of its importance. In July, 1811, however, when the Southwark Bridge was projected, the Directors of that Company attended one whole day, to ascertain the probable amount of passengers, &c. over London Bridge; when it was found that 89,640 persons on foot, 769 waggons, 2924 carts and drays, 1240 coaches, 485 gigs and taxed carts, and 764 horses, went across it.

"But, to descend from the roadway to the foundation, I shall next remark, that the natural soil of the Thames, where the present London Bridge is erected, consists chiefly of black gravel, for about 2 feet in depth, below which it is gravel with red sand: and this we learn from a table of *'Borings of the River betwixt London and Blackfriars' Bridges, performed betwixt the 19th of May and the 16th of June, 1800, by John Foulds and assistants;'* printed in the *'Third Report'* of the Port of London Committee, *'Appendix,'* A. 2, page 39.

"Another point, connected with this part of the edifice, concerning which I am very desirous of giving some little information, is the etymology of the word Sterling, or perhaps Starling, according to the general pronunciation; yet what can I presume to say upon it, when we find that, in the meaning of a defence to bridges, it is unnoticed in the learned glossaries of Somner, Minsheu, Stephen Skinner, Sir Henry Spelman, John Jacob Hoffman, Du Fresne, Edward Phillips, Francis Junius, Doctors Johnson and Jamieson, and Archdeacon Nares? In the last edition of *'Dr. Johnson's Dictionary,'* indeed, by the Rev. H. J. Todd, this signification is inserted, though the Editor candidly adds, 'I know not the etymology;' and, therefore, it seems alike futile to search after, and presumptuous to conjecture it; howbeit, take what hints I have met with upon the subject. And firstly, in a small tract entitled *'A short Review of the several Pamphlets and Schemes that have been offered to the Public, in relation to the building of a Bridge at Westminster,'* by John James, of Greenwich; London, 1736, octavo, at page 16, we find the following conjecture. 'It is very probable, that the *Stallings*,—as I choose to call them, our workmen after the Normans, having, perhaps, taken the name from the French word, *crèche*, which signifies a manger, or crib in a stall,—may have been much enlarged since the first building of the Bridge.' For my own part, however, I am greatly inclined to think that the term is of Northern origin, not very much corrupted, since the Danish word *Staer*, and the German, *Starr*, or *Starck*, a defence, evidently appear to be the root of it; and Christian Ludwig, in his *'Dictionary of English, German, and French,'* Leipsic, 1763, quarto, volume i., page 840, translates the word Starling by *Stahr*, explaining it to be 'a spur to the pillar of a stone bridge, for dividing the water.' It is common, in most

Dictionaries, to consider the word Sterling as referring only to that authorized coin, originally manufactured by the Flemings or Easterlings, whose name it has made immortal. Even in this sense, however, it is still connected with the history of London Bridge; since in Thomas Hearne's *'Collection of Curious Discourses,'* edit. London, 1771, octavo, volume ii., article xliii., page 316, is a paper on the derivation of the expression Sterling Money, written by that eminent Antiquary Arthur Agarde, containing a singular anecdote on this subject; which, however, I shall give from the original manuscript in the Cottonian collection, marked *'Faustina,'* E V., article 10, folio 52 a. 'I suppose,' says he, 'the name came by meanes the Easterlinges from vs, being Germaynes, brought vp in the mynes of syluer and copper there, were vsed here in Englaunde for the reducynge and refyninge the diuersyte of coynes into a perfecte Standarde. As in the beginning of the Quenes Mat^s raigne, they were brought hyther by Alderman Lodge, (wth whom I was famylyarlye acquaynted,) by her Mat^s order, for the refining of o^r base coignes: And this he toulde me, That the mooste of them in meltinge fell sycke to deathe wth the sauoure, so as they were advised to drynke in a dead man's skull for theyre recure. Whereupon he, wth others who had thoversyght of that worke, procured a warrant from the Counsaile to take of the heades vppon London Bridge, and make cuppes thereof, whereof they dranke and founde some reliefe, althoughe the mooste of them dyed.' This wild and romantic circumstance probably took place about the year 1560 or 1561, when Queen Elizabeth had all the base coin in the Realm brought to the Tower and melted there; when it is supposed that the fumes of the arsenic which it contained induced the illness of the foreigners: see Ruding's *'Annals of the Coinage,'* which I have already quoted, volume iii., page 38, *note*. When, to these particulars, I have added, that you will find a view of part of Old London Bridge with the houses, in the sixth plate of Hogarth's *'Marriage à la Mode,'* my reminiscences of this edifice are concluded to the end of the eighteenth century."

"Well, sir, well," said I, fetching a long breath, which sounded a good deal like a yawn, "I know what you would say,—another libation of Sack, to the memory of Old London Bridge; in the which I more readily join you, seeing that your history of it is rapidly closing, and that we are something like the Merchant Abudah, in Ridley's Tales of the Genii, when he first saw the distant light after his wanderings in the murky caverns of Tasgi: though, indeed, Master Barnaby, I should ask you, on your veracity, if we really are coming to a conclusion, or am I only deceiving myself in thinking so?"

"No, truly," answered the Antiquary, "I have but little more to speak, and you but little to hear; for, excepting the usual accidents of London Bridge, which I shall omit to notice, the great employment of the last quarter of a century has been coming to the resolution of building a new one, and considering the best means of doing it. Whilst, however, I give you my hearty thanks for your attention and assistance during upwards of eight hundred years of our Bridge-history, I would only remind you of the great mass of information which we have collected upon it, much of which was either never before brought together, or adapted to it."

"Why, really," said I, with that kind of half agreement with which men admit a truth not discovered by themselves, "there is something in your remark; and he who next writes the history of London Bridge will have some difficulty in finding new materials for it, at least in any ordinary authorities. But then, you know, others, who are not acquainted with the mass of matter relating to it, may accost us with the old Italian saying of, 'Where the Devil did you get all this rubbish from?'"

"Out upon them for unthankful knaves, then," replied Master Postern; "let us console ourselves with the thought that virtue rewards itself; and so, as I see that you are again set in a position either for listening or sleeping, I shall, for the last time, take up my tale." To this remark I nodded assent, and the old Gentleman thus went on.

"The present century, Mr. Barbican, commenced with some active exertions for the immediate erection of a new London Bridge, upon the most extensive and elaborate scale; of the numerous schemes for which, however, I can give you little more than a catalogue, referring you for full particulars to various parts of *The Third Report from the Select Committee upon the Improvement of the Port of London*,' 1800, Folio, and the large volume of engraved *'Plans and Drawings'* belonging to it. It is stated in sections i. ii. of the former authority, pages 4-6, that the great, continual, and ineffectual expenses of the old Bridge, its irremediable insecurity, and the dangers of its navigation, had induced the Committee to collect information and provide designs for the building of a new one. In this edifice it was proposed to construct a free passage for vessels not exceeding 200 tons' burthen, to that part of the River between London and Blackfriars' Bridges; where it was supposed, upon examination, that they would always have a depth of from 12 to 15 feet above low-water, formed and maintained at only a slight expense after the shoals had been cleared away. To ascertain the number of ships which might be expected to use this passage, the Committee procured an account of the Foreign and Coasting Trade of London for 1799, with the measurements of their masts, by which it appeared that an Arch of 65 feet above high-water mark, at medium Spring-Tides, would allow vessels of 200 tons to pass it with their top-masts struck; and that of Coasters under that burthen the number was 7248. Such, then, being the general design, the Artists, who proposed sending in drawings, were directed particularly to consider a convenient passage over the Bridge, with as little acclivity as possible, as well as its access to the principal avenues of London; to the attainment of these objects with the least interference with private property; to the embellishment of the Metropolis of London; and to the length of time, and expense of the whole work. The designs presented were of three different characters: being, firstly, for a Bridge with a lofty Centre Arch, and a descending causeway leading to some principal street on each side of the River; secondly, for a similar Bridge, having its approaches at right angles, and parallel to the shores, to be raised on Arches on a new embankment in front of the old wharfs, &c.; and, thirdly, for two Parallel Bridges, enclosing a space sufficient for so many vessels as would probably pass in one tide, their passage being through corresponding drawbridges, one of which should always remain lowered for the use of passengers. See the *'Third Report,'* already cited, page 7; and having mentioned these particulars, let us now take a glance at some of the plans themselves.

"1. Mr. Ralph Dodd, Engineer, proposed the erection of a stone Bridge of six Arches, 60 feet wide, and a centre one of iron 300 feet span, and about 100 high, to admit shipping up the River; calculating that the space between London and Blackfriars' Bridges contained 3,353,180 square feet, and would accommodate nearly 1000 vessels. As this Bridge was to be erected on the old foundations, and even to be built in such a manner over the original structure as not to interfere with the passage across it, it was to consist of two separate tiers, somewhat in the manner of an aqueduct, excepting at the Centre Arch; the lower range consisting of small elliptical Arches lying horizontally, and the upper,—which was to be about 100 feet high,—of segmental Arches. The whole was to be adorned with an entablature and ballustrade, statues, sculptures on the lower Piers, and Corinthian columns above them; and its declivity to extend from the upper corner of Monument Yard to St. Thomas's Street, Southwark, at an inclination of about 2½ inches in a yard. A pictorial elevation and ground-plan of this design, with its relative bearing to the old Bridge, are to be seen in Plates ii. and vii. of the Plans and Drawings belonging to the Third of the Port of London Reports. Vide also the *'Report'* itself, section 3, page 7, and *'Appendix,'* B. 1, page 49.

"This Plan, however, having led Mr. Dodd attentively to survey the foundations of old London Bridge, he became convinced of their insecurity and of its impracticability, and referring to it only as a specimen of its peculiar character, he sent the Committee another design (2) for a highly decorated Stone Bridge, which he proposed to be erected about 40 yards above the ancient one, on the East side of Fishmongers' Hall on the North, and near Pepper-Alley on the South Shore. It was to consist of five elliptical Arches, the centre being 160 feet span and 80 feet high, the succeeding two 140 feet span and 75 in height, and the outer two 120 feet span, and 70 in height; the structure was to be raised 90 feet from high-water, and occupy 210 feet of the river, leaving 840 for water-way. The whole was to be embellished with statues, columns, &c.; and the estimate for building it, including the avenues,

&c. &c. was £350,000 for a Centre Arch of 80 feet; £332,000 for one of 70 feet; and £314,000 for one of 60 feet; the erection to occupy five years. An Elevation and Ground-plan of Mr. Dodd's second design are in the volume of Plates already referred to, Plate iii.; and farther particulars will be found in the *'Report,'* page 7, *Appendix* B. 1, page 51. These plans are also farther illustrated by a pamphlet published in 1799, entitled *'Letters to a Merchant;'* for which see the *'Gentleman's Magazine,'* volume lxix., part ii., November, page 965.

"3. The next design, upon the principle of a large Centre Arch, was by Mr. Samuel Wyatt, constructed wholly of cast-iron, with granite piers, and the bulk of the superstructure filled up with chalk. This Architect, however, sent only a model, without drawings, plans, or estimates; see the *'Report,'* page 8.

"4. The design furnished by Mr. Robert Mylne, proposed that a Bridge of 5 Arches, the centre being 60 feet above high-water mark, and 150 feet wide, should be directed towards the Monument, which was to form the centre of a square, and terminate in a new road into Kent on the South. The particulars of this plan also propose a considerable improvement in all the streets connected with the Bridge, as may be seen in the *'Third Report,'* *Appendix* B. 2, pages 51-56; but it has neither estimates nor drawings.

"Mr. Thomas Wilson, Architect of the celebrated Bridge at Bishop's Wearmouth, near Sunderland, furnished a design (5) for one of cast-iron, with stone piers, consisting of three large segmental Arches, the centre one being 240 feet span, and 65 high, and the two sides of 220 feet: the breadth of the road above was to have been 45 feet; and his estimate for the iron-work alone amounted to £55,061. See the *'Third Report,'* pages 9 and 17, and *Appendix* C. page 76. A large engraving of the Elevation and Sections is also contained in the folio of Plans, &c. Plate viii. In section 4, article 9, page 14 of the *'Report,'* the Committee appears to have given a preference to this design, with the side-approaches and improvements of the shores by other Architects; it being supposed that an ascent of about 2½ inches in a yard would have been sufficient for such a Centre Arch.

"The next three designs (6, 7, and 8,) were also confined to Iron Bridges, and were furnished by Messrs. Thomas Telford, Surveyor, and James Douglass, Engineer, of which only one was published. Their first idea was to diminish the ascent by increasing the length of the Bridge on the Surrey side, and by placing the largest arch nearest the City shore; its dimensions being 160 feet span, and 65 rise. Their estimate, including some extensive improvements along the banks of the River, amounted to £988,154; but this design was particularly objectionable, both on account of its unsymmetrical appearance, and the inconvenience of its navigation; and in their subsequent plans, therefore, they placed the great arch in the centre, without any other material alteration. The estimate for this was £1,041,654; but their chief design (9) was constructed on the principle of inclined planes gradually descending at the sides on to the wharfs at each end of the Bridge, and rounded for the convenience of carriages. The edifice itself was to be of iron, having an ascent of 2¼ inches in a yard, and was to consist of five arches decorated with statues, trophies, &c., commemorative of the Naval Triumphs of England, which were to give it the name of 'Victory Bridge.' The principal Arch was to be 180 feet span, and 65 high; and the lateral approaches were to be formed upon wharfs gained out of the River by embankments, and supported also by iron Arches, having warehouses beneath them. As a protection to the Bridge and its adjoining buildings, it was proposed that all the Arches, but the centre, should be closed at night by a chain; that in the spandrils of the great Arch, watch-houses should be constructed; and that the communications with the wharfs should be cut off by gates. The site of this Bridge was proposed to be the very line which the New one is now taking, and the estimate for it was £1,054,804: see the *'Third Report,'* pages 8, 9, 17, *Appendix* B. 3, pages 57-73; and Plates ix.-xii. in the folio volume of Illustrations. The Report states that this plan would prove, in some degree, the most speedy and economical, and that it would interfere with existing buildings less than the former; though it is admitted that the turns to the ascent would be both inconvenient and dangerous.

"Mr. George Dance, Architect to the City, and Professor of Architecture in the Royal Academy, was the only person who at this time furnished the Port of London Committee with a design (10) for parallel Bridges with Drawbridges for the passage of vessels; and a single glance at the fac-similes of his drawings in Plates xiv-xix. of the folio of Plans, &c., will probably be quite convincing as to their inconvenience. The best idea of this peculiar design is, however, to be gained from a large coloured bird's-eye view of the perfect edifice, drawn by the Architect, and engraven in aqua-tinta by Thomas Daniell, dedicated to Lord Hawkesbury, and published November 10th, 1800; a copy of which is in volume xiii. of Mr. Crowle's Illustrated Pennant in the British Museum. It was intended to consist of two low level bridges, one on each side of the present; containing six elliptical Arches, having a drawbridge of two leaves in the centre of each, flanked by four round towers containing the mechanism for working them, and signal-staffs for flags, or reflecting lamps, to announce which of the passages was open. The space between the Bridges was to be 300 feet wide, furnished with mooring-chains, &c. &c., for securing the ships in tiers, so as not to interrupt the passage of smaller vessels. Each end of the edifice was to be formed into a grand semi-elliptical area, surrounding the Monument on the London side; and the estimate for executing the whole was £1,279,714; though Mr. Dance also sent in two more contracted plans, one amounting to £968,677, and the other to £807,537. In speaking of his Double Bridge, I should observe that he was led to the form of it by the great expense, steepness, deformity, and inconvenience attendant on an Arch high enough for the passage of vessels, which he explained in a Drawing marked Plate xiii. in the folio volume of Plans, &c. The inclination of Ludgate-Hill he found to be the steepest which he could adopt for an Arch of 60 feet, and that would have extended the approaches from East Cheap to beyond Union Street. The principal objections made to this plan were the great expense and delay connected with it; that the shipping moored in the basin would be exposed to a strong tide, with some danger; and that whenever their number was considerable, it would be difficult to provide for their uninterrupted passage, as well as for that of smaller vessels. For all these particulars, see the '*Third Report*,' pages 9, 10, 17; and the *Appendix* D. pages 77-81.

"Such, then, were the designs laid before the House of Commons; and the Committee concluded its labour for the year 1800, by recommending the rebuilding of London Bridge of iron, with a centre Arch of at least 65 feet above high-water. It was advised, also, that the old edifice should remain till the new one were completed; the place for erecting which was opposite the West end of St. Saviour's Church, as being the narrowest part of the River, and having buildings of the least value upon its banks, whilst the Northern end should form a street to the Royal Exchange. The removal of the Water-works was also recommended; and the funds for carrying these works into effect were proposed to be raised, firstly, by a Bridge-toll on horses and carriages, which, it was calculated, in 20 years would discharge a debt of £100,000; secondly, by a sum charged upon the Bridge-House Estates equal to their annual expenditure, which being taken at £4200, in 25 years would amount to £105,000; and, thirdly, £100,000 more were to be raised by an additional debt on the Orphans' Fund: this sum of £305,000 being considered as more than sufficient for erecting Mr. Wilson's Bridge, and making a proper compensation to the Water-works.

"Soon after the appearance of these resolutions, but too late for publication in the Committee's Report, two other designs were presented, an account of which was printed in a *Supplement* to it. The first of these, see *Appendix* H. pages 143-147, consisted of a design by Mr. James Black, Civil-Engineer, (11) for a Bridge of Granite, with three elliptical Arches; the centre being 230 feet span and 65 high, and the sides having a span of 220 feet each: the inclination was to be 2 inches in a yard, and the estimate, £294,089: 6*s*. Two folding engravings, consisting of a Profile and Sections, will be found in Plates xxii.-xxiii. of the Supplementary Illustrations of the folio volume of Drawings.

"The other design (12) was by Messrs. Telford and Douglass,—see *Appendix* I., pages 148, 149,—for a cast-iron Bridge of a single semi-circular Arch 65 feet high, and 600 feet in the clear; the roadway being 45 feet wide in the centre, and increasing to 90 feet at each granite abutment, to strengthen the foundation, afford a greater space, and communicate better with the inclined planes. The estimate was £262,289, and a very large engraving of it by Lowry, comprehending an Elevation and Sectional Ground-plan, with another outline of the ribs and framing, form Plates xxiv. and xxv. of the Supplemental folio Illustrations.

"In consequence of this last design, the attention of the Committee was directed to the consideration of a metal Bridge with one Arch; and on their meeting in 1801, a series of Questions was transmitted with this last plan to Dr. Nevil Maskelyne, Astronomer Royal; the Rev. A. Robertson, Savilian Professor of Geometry at Oxford; John Playfair, Professor of Mathematics at Edinburgh; John Robeson, Professor of Natural Philosophy at Edinburgh; Dr. Milner; Dr. Charles Hutton, of the Royal Military Academy, Woolwich; Mr. Atwood of Knightsbridge; Colonel Twiss, of Woolwich; Mr. William Jessop, of Newark; the late Messrs. John Rennie and James Watt; Messrs. John Southern, of Soho, Birmingham; William Reynolds, of Coalbrook-Dale; John Wilkinson, of Bradley in Staffordshire; Charles Bage, of Shrewsbury; and General Samuel Bentham, Inspector General of the Naval Works of the Admiralty; whose answers for an Appendix to the '*Report of the Select Committee*' for 1801: Nos. 1-16, pages 9-83. For the Questions themselves, see pages 4-7 of the *Report*; they were 21 in number, and inquired the nature of pressure and gravity in such a Bridge? whether it would be strengthened by increasing towards the abutments? how the weight should be distributed to make it uniformly strong? what weight it would bear? and what force would overturn it at any particular part? concerning the form of the Arch, and how to improve it? the importance of models and experiments? the means of keeping ships in the centre of the stream? the proportionate strength of the abutments? the possibility of constructing centering for it, without obstructing the ordinary navigation? the nature, power, dimensions, and method of casting the metal and cement to be employed? how the design might be improved and rendered more durable? and whether the estimates equalled or exceeded the execution of the works?

"It was probably the very great diversity of sentiment prevailing in the answers to these inquiries, which caused this design to be ultimately abandoned; for though its practicability, magnificence, and excellence, were universally admitted, yet there were so many doubts as to the actual strength and cohesion of cast-iron, the power of the crown of the Arch, the possibility of making the structure as one self-dependent frame, and of fortifying the haunches without overloading them, that few of the returns agreed with each other throughout. Drs. Maskelyne, Hutton, and Mr. Rennie, recommended an elliptical arch; Professors Robertson, Playfair, and Robeson, a circular one: some considered increasing the width of the roadway at each end of great importance; others proposed making it still wider; Professor Robeson thought it not very essential; and Professors Playfair and Robertson conceived that it took away from the strength of the whole. Dr. Hutton, Mr. Robeson, and Mr. Watt, supposed that the gravity of the Bridge would of itself be so great, that any additional weight would be trifling; and that the mast of a ship striking it, would break only that particular part, without damaging the rest, though repeated shocks might in time destroy it. For its construction, however, cast-iron of the soft-grey kind, or rather gun-metal, was generally preferred, as well as liquid iron for a cement; which some practical persons considered as not adapted for the purpose, and only advised the whole to be well fitted together. The papers of Col. Twiss and Mr. Watt recommended that the Bridge should consist of three arches; and with that of Mr. Southern was sent a drawing,—Plate xxvi. in the folio of Plans, &c.—of his method of more securely constructing the arch and frame-work.

"The return sent in by General, afterwards Sir Samuel, Bentham, see '*Appendix*,' No. 16, page 76-83, instead of considering the lofty Bridge of Messrs. Telford and Douglass, was occupied by detailing a new design, (13) engraven by Basire, on Plate xxvii., in the folio of Illustrations. Its principal characteristic was an enlargement in the centre, into a sexangular form of more than twice its ordinary breadth, having in the middle an octagonal basin, spacious enough for a ship to lie in, without touching a Drawbridge constructed in each side; which Drawbridges were to be 30 feet wide, and so contrived, that either should be sufficient for a temporary passage; and the vessel having passed through one, it was to be let down and fixed, before the other was opened. The edifice itself was to be of granite, on a rise of an inch in a yard, and to have eight segmental arches, with the Drawbridge-passage in the centre, guarded by four low round towers for the machinery: the estimate was £210,411.

"The '*Appendix*,' No. 17, pages 83-85, contains an additional paper from Mr. Wilson, giving a farther account of his design, and of a model which he had constructed of it; and concluding with an estimate of £163,496 for the whole work.

"An interval of several years now occurs before we meet with any farther proceedings concerning the erection of a New London Bridge; which I shall fill up with some notices of the engraved views of the present edifice, and a few memoranda of the other modern Bridges built over the Thames. The prospects of this part of London are extremely numerous; since it has not only frequently been delineated in separate prints, but is also to be found in almost every volume which treats of our metropolitan history. Perhaps some of the best representations are those drawn by Joseph Farrington, R. A., about the latter end of the last century, and engraven by F. C. Stadler to imitate the originals. One of these is a large folio, and the other will be found in Boydell's '*History of the River Thames*,' London, 1794, folio, volume ii., plate

16, page 226. A small neat print of London Bridge is also contained in Samuel Ireland's *'Picturesque Views of the River Thames,'* London, 1792, octavo, volume ii., plate 24, page 221: but etchings of an infinitely superior class, by William Bernard Cooke, are in his beautiful work of *'The Thames,'* London, 1811, octavo, volume ii., plates 16 and 18. Two of the most recent views of this edifice were published in Charles Heath's *'Views of London,'* 1825, octavo, both taken on the Eastern side, by W. Westall and P. Dewint. A perspective elevation of the Bridge, shewing the obliquity of its arches, and a curious section of the River bed, also on the Eastern side, surveyed by Mr. Ralph Dodd, is inserted in the folio volume of *'Plans, &c., belonging to the Third Report of the Port of London Committee,'* Plate vii.: and the same Engineer has likewise given a large and interesting print of the *'South Pier of the Great Arch of London Bridge,'* exhibiting the two chasms in it, the iron clamps which hold it together, and a section of the water-way. See Plate vi. of the same volume, and the *Report* itself, *'Appendix,'* B. 1, page 52.* A similar representation was furnished by Mr. Mylne, and is marked *'Drawing,* C.' on Plate i. of the same illustrations: it consists of a profile through the middle of the Great Arch, taken at still low-water in 1767, and shows the excavations above and below Bridge, made by the rushing of the current. The remainder of this Plate is occupied by Tables of Soundings, Measurements, &c. at various points of the River near this place; and *'A Section of the Locks and construction of the Piers of London Bridge as ascertained in taking up of the Pier under the Great Arch in 1762.'* See Drawing A. Of this I have already given several particulars, and in Mr. Mylne's paper belonging to it, printed in the *'Third Report,' 'Appendix,'* A. 1, page 26, he has a curious account of taking up the Piers, and its consequent effects. He was at that time occupied in erecting Blackfriars' Bridge, and a lighterman, named Parsons, employed under him, having contracted for removing the Pier, consulted him as to the best means of doing so. Having examined the building, he advised his procuring some powerful screws, used in raising the heavy wheels of the Water-works, which were fastened to the heads of the soundest and securest piles. They first drew out a few from the outer row, and then some of the original in the interior, when all the stone-work which was worth preserving being removed, and the remainder thrown into the River, the cross-ties of timber and iron were loosened, and the whole Pier soon fell into ruins. It was immediately carried away by the impetuosity of the fall; for the other piles being removed, the middle of the work was borne off so suddenly as scarcely to allow of its construction being examined and measured. The Arch being thus opened, the danger at first anticipated by Mr. Mylne soon followed; for the accumulated volume of water drawn from all the other arches acted so violently upon the River bed, as greatly to increase the depth and force of the tide; whilst the corrosion spreading to the old Piers of the new Arch, attacked the stability of the Sterlings beneath them: these defences being only 6 feet broad under the haunches of the Arch, and so close to the Piers, that there was neither room to make any substantial repairs, nor sufficient space for a pile-engine to act. It was in this difficulty that Mr. Smeaton advised the City-Gates to be thrown into the River, for transferring the deep water to the lower side of the Bridge; an idea which he seems to have taken from Henri Gautier's statement concerning the Bridge of St. Esprit. Mr. Mylne remarks, however, that the whole of this advice not being followed, a farther quantity of 2000 tons of rubble-stone was recommended for the construction of a new bed. And now, to come back to my starting-place, and conclude my notices of views of this edifice, let me remark that if you would see it in all its interest, with the water rushing through its Locks, and the building itself surmounted and bounded by the Monument and the Spire of St. Magnus' Church, then the very spot for such a prospect is the EASTERN SIDE OF LONDON BRIDGE.

"I come next to perform my promise of giving some account of the other modern Bridges of London, and shall begin by reminding you that the proposal for those at Westminster and Blackfriars was met by a steady and violent opposition. This objection to new Bridges appears, however, to have existed so early as the year 1671, when it was first designed to build one over the Thames at Putney; upon the argument of loss to the Thames watermen, to the tolls of London Bridge, and to the City of London, as natural consequences. You will find all the particulars of this subject contained in the Hon. Anchitell Grey's *Debates of the House of Commons, from the year 1667 to the year 1694,*' London 1763, octavo, volume i., pages 416-417: and it is singular, that in this discussion the very places at which Bridges are now erected, are mentioned as the most improper for such edifices. The kind of prophetic objection which runs through the whole debate has rendered it a very amusing article for modern reading; and an ingenious, but amplified, paraphrase of it was inserted in the '*European Magazine*,' for September, 1825, *New Series*, page 20-27. But even in the notes to the Debates themselves, it is stated that 'Experience has at length convinced us of the weakness and fallacy of the objections raised against another Bridge, though private interest, it may be presumed, was the principal motive: since, not to mention the many Bridges that have been raised higher up the River, this Metropolis now boasts,'—1763—'without any of the inconveniences, not only a Bridge at Putney, but one at Westminster, where use and magnificence go hand in hand; to which is adding a third at Blackfriars.' The first of these modern structures was the VAUXHALL BRIDGE, which was remarkable for having had, in consequence of disputes, four Architects, Mr. Ralph Dodd, Sir Samuel Bentham, Mr. Rennie, and lastly, Mr. James Walker, who carried the design into effect. It consists of nine arches of cast-iron, of 78 feet span, and 26 above high-water at spring-tides; the first stone was laid by Lord Dundas, as proxy for the Prince Regent, about 3 o'clock, on Thursday, May 9th, 1811; it was opened in July, 1816; and its cost amounted to upwards of £300,000. The Strand, or WATERLOO BRIDGE, was partly projected by Mr. George Dodd, but wholly brought to perfection by Mr. Rennie: it has 9 elliptical arches of 120 feet span, and 36 feet above high-water at spring-tides; the first stone was laid on the Surrey side of the River close to Cuper's Bridge, by the Chairman, Henry Swann, Esq., and the Directors of the Company, about 4 o'clock in the afternoon, of Friday, October 11th, 1811; the building amounted to about £400,000; and it was opened with great splendour by a procession of the Prince Regent, and the Dukes of York and Wellington, about 3 o'clock on Wednesday, June 18th, 1817, the anniversary of the Battle of Waterloo, when it received its name. The last was the SOUTHWARK BRIDGE, of which the first stone was laid by the late Admiral Lord Keith, at 12 o'clock on Tuesday, May 23rd, 1815, the Bill for erecting it having passed May 6th, 1811. It consists of three immense Arches of cast-iron, the centre being 240 feet in span, and those at the sides 210, and about 42 feet above the highest spring-tides: the whole work was estimated at £400,000; the Architect was the late Mr. Rennie; and the edifice was opened by lamp-light on Wednesday, March 24th, 1819, as the clock of St. Paul's Cathedral tolled midnight.

"I come now, Mr. Barbican, to speak of the last Fair held on the River Thames, by London Bridge, in the beginning of 1814. The Frost commenced with a thick fog, on the evening of the preceding December 27th, which lasted for several days; followed by heavier falls of snow than any within the memory of man, and continuing for almost two days, with very short intervals. During nearly four weeks' frost, the wind blew, with little intermission, from the North and North-East; and the cold was intense. The

River was covered with vast pieces of floating ice, bearing piles of snow, moving slowly with the tide, or collected into masses wherever their progress was obstructed. A thaw, which continued from January 26th to the 29th, floated so many of these down the River, that the space between London and Blackfriars' Bridges was almost impassable; and the severe Frost, which recommenced the day following, and lasted to February 5th, speedily united the whole into one immoveable sheet of ice. Even on Sunday, the 30th, some persons ventured to walk over it at different parts; and on Tuesday, February 1st, the usual entries were formed by the unemployed watermen; particularly between Blackfriars' Bridge and Three Cranes' Wharf, notices being written against the streets leading to them, announcing a safe footway over the River, by the toll on which, many of them received £6 per day. The standing amusements of an English Frost Fair now commenced, and many cheerfully paid to see and partake of that upon the frozen Thames, which at any other time they would not have deigned to look upon. Beside the roughly-formed paths paved with ashes, leading from shore to shore, there was a street of tents, called the 'City Road,' in which gay flags, inviting signs, music, and dancing, evinced what excellent entertainment was to be found there. That ancient wonder, peculiar to the place, the roasting of a small sheep over a fire, was exhibited to many a sixpenny audience, whilst the provision itself, under the name of 'Lapland Mutton,' sold for one shilling a slice! Several Printing-Presses were also erected, to furnish memorials of the Frost, in old verse, and new prose; and as I have already given specimens of the ancient Thames' printing, let us not pass over this last Great Frost without recording a few of its papers.

'You that walk here, and do design to tell
Your children's children what this year befell,
Come buy this print, and then it will be seen,
That such a year as this hath seldom been.'

'OMNIPOTENT PRESS! Tyrant Winter has enchained the noblest torrent that flows to the main; but Summer will return and set the captive free. So may tyranny for a time 'freeze the genial current of the soul;' but a Free Press, like the great source of light and heat, will, ere long, dissolve the tyranny of the mightiest. Greatest of Arts! what do we not owe to thee? The knowledge which directs industry; the liberty which encourages it; the security which protects it. And of Industry how precious are the fruits! Glowing and hardy temperaments which defy the vicissitudes of seasons, and comfortable homes which make you regret not the gloom that is abroad. But for Industry, but for Printing, you might now have been content, like the Russ and Laplander, to bury yourselves under that snow, over which you now tread with mirth and glee. Printed on the River Thames, and in commemoration of a Great Fair held upon it on the 31st of January, 1814, when it was completely frozen over, from shore to shore. The Frost commenced 27th December, 1813; was accompanied by a thick fog that lasted eight days; and after the fog came a heavy fall of snow, that prevented all communication with the Northern and Western parts of the country, for several days.'

"Another bill, on the same subject, ran thus:—

'Friends! now is your time to support the freedom of the Press! Can the Press have greater liberty? Here you find it working in the middle of the Thames; and if you encourage us by buying our impressions, we will keep it going in the true spirit of liberty, during the Frost.'

"One of the last papers printed on the River was as follows:—

'To Madam Tabitha Thaw.

'Dear Dissolving Dame,

'FATHER FROST and SISTER SNOW have *Bonyed* my borders, formed an *idol of ice* upon my bosom, and all the LADS of LONDON come to make merry: now, as you love mischief, treat the multitude with a few CRACKS by a sudden visit, and obtain the prayers of the poor upon both banks. *Given at my own Press*, the 5th Feb. 1814.

THOMAS THAMES.'

"During the obstruction of this Frost, the tide did not appear to rise above half its usual height; and about the Bridge the ice lay in enormous blocks, where their occasional splitting very much endangered the edifice, and caused several accidents; one of which forms the subject of a highly spirited etching in Mr. J. T. Smith's '*Antiquities of London*,' page 24, representing 'AN ARCH OF LONDON BRIDGE, *as it appeared during the Great Frost, Drawn February 5th, 1814.*' This is a North-East view of the Prince's Lock, or the 6th from the City-end; and is particularly curious for shewing at once the modern casing of the present Bridge, and the ancient edifice beneath it. In the evening of Saturday, the very day when this view was taken, Frost-Fair was visited by rain and a sudden thaw, when the ice cracked and floated in several places. On the following day, about 2 o'clock, the tide began to flow with great rapidity; the immense masses of ice were broken up in all directions, and the River was covered with wrecks; until returning industry and the rushing current removed every vestige of the last Frost-Fair. The features of this British Carnival are in the memories of the greater part of the present generation; though, if it were otherwise, the representations of it are few and scarce, and generally very inferior.

"It was, probably, the damage done to the Bridge by this Frost, which again called the public attention to its effectual improvement, by widening its water-way; and in November, 1814, Messrs. George Dance, William

Chapman, Daniel Alexander, and James Mountague, addressed a Report to a Committee of the Corporation, for substituting four large Arches for eight of the present. Their estimate amounted to £92,000, supposing the Piers to be strong enough to bear the increased weight; which were to be examined by Coffer-dams, each Coffer-dam amounting to about £20,000, additional; when, if the edifice should be found too weak, the expense would be considerably increased. By direction of the Corporation, one of the Piers was opened, when Messrs. Chapman, and Ralph and James Walker, were nearly satisfied as to the practicability of the alteration; though Mr. Rennie's confidence in the structure was rather decreased. These particulars are given at length in '*An Abstract of the Proceedings and Evidence relative to London Bridge, taken from the Reports of a select Committee of the House of Commons, the Journals of the Common-Council, and the Committee for letting the Bridge-House Estates,*' London, 1819, folio, pages 68-107: and also in a Report of a Committee of the House of Commons, printed in '*Reports and Evidences relative to London Bridge,*' 1820, 1821, folio, pages 49-52. This Report candidly states the uncertainty and expense of the whole plan, and earnestly recommends the erection of a new Bridge, with not more than five Arches, as near as possible to the site of the present: adding, from the evidence of numerous witnesses, the universal agreement on the decided advantages to be gained from a free current of water, and that the Water-works should certainly be removed, whether the Bridge were altered or rebuilt. The annual rental of the Bridge-House Estates, amounting to £25,800, and the property and stock of the Trustees, £112,000 more, were conceived to be sufficient for the proposed works; or that the remainder might be raised without levying a toll upon foot-passengers.

"This Report is dated May 25th, 1821, and its strenuous reccommendation of a new building was a natural result of the inquiries of the Select Committee of the House of Commons, specially appointed for that purpose; the Minutes of which are printed in the '*Reports and Evidences*' already cited, pages 7-47. This examination of witnesses took place in consequence of several Petitions from water-men, owners of barges, &c. relative to the dangerous navigation of London Bridge, Mr. Heathfield being agent for the Petitioners; and as the nature of their complaint is generally known, I shall be very brief in my account of it. They stated, then, that the craft, &c. on the River having increased one-third within the last 20 years, the water-way at London Bridge was no longer sufficient for them; since the larger loaded barges, in general, went through the Great Arch, which they could pass only for about 6 hours out of 24, or the first 3 after high-water. On this account, there was considerable danger at the flood-tide, because the loaded barges, then crowding to get through, were all equally impelled to the same point; and thus very frequently damaged, sunk, or locked together in the Arch. Another cause of great danger was the getting on a Sterling, when the water had covered it only enough to prevent its form being visible; for if a barge passed over it but a few feet, or even inches, and stopped upon not finding sufficient water, if it got on the edge, as the water sank, it fell over; or, if in the middle, was detained there until the next tide. This evil, too, was stated to be continually increasing, from the constant repairs of the Sterlings, which considerably extended their size; whilst much of the chalk, &c. being daily washed over, served only to fill up the Arches. For barges, however, not exceeding 25 tons' burthen, St. Mary's and the Draw-Locks were both occasionally used at high-water; but, besides their extreme narrowness,—neither of them being more than 16 feet between the Sterlings,—they are both subject to peculiar and contrary sets of tides; whilst the Sterling of the former has so great a projection, that a barge striking it would probably go stern foremost into the 4th Lock, where it would be detained the rest of the tide, and considerably damaged, or sunk. Omitting the numerous accidents at London Bridge recounted in these answers, I shall observe only, that some of the Lightermen, &c. estimated their losses by it at £100 yearly; and that Mr. Anthony Nicholl, a Wharfinger at Dowgate, stated, that, having, in April, 1820, lost goods there to the amount of £1000, he could not insure property passing through the Bridge, under a premium of 5 per cent.

"Whilst this evidence, however, seemed decisive as to the great importance of a new edifice, the Corporation of London appears to have been much more inclined to alter the old one; since, on February 22nd, 1821, the Committee for letting the Bridge-House Estates was ordered to attend the Select Committee of the House of Commons, during their deliberations respecting London Bridge: and on the 22nd of the ensuing March, the Select Bridge Committee was also directed to consider of the Report on altering the structure, as proposed by Mr. Dance, &c. The result of the latter inquiry was given in a Report dated April 11th, contained in the tract of Documents already cited, page 78; and it stated that, on March 30th, a conference having been held with the Earl of Liverpool and the Right Hon. Nicholas Vansittart, the Committee, &c. were informed that His Majesty's Ministers would not sanction the appropriation of the public revenue towards the erection of a new Bridge; though it was considered that tolls might be levied for that purpose. From this interview, the Committee was induced to recommend the alteration of the old London Bridge, as all the proposed funds for building a new one were either objectionable or wholly insufficient. The Corporation of London having agreed to this return, it was delivered to the Select Committee of the House of Commons, where evidence was being received on the part of the Corporation; as contained in the tract of Documents before referred to, *Appendix* No. 1., pages 53-129; the proceedings lasting from Wednesday, March 23rd, 1821, to Monday, May 14th, and the examinations on the part of the City being conducted by Mr. Randle Jackson. This evidence was divided into two principal parts; the first being intended to disprove the allegations of the petitioners respecting the inconveniences; and the second, that the proposed alteration of the Bridge would be both a practicable and sufficient improvement. To ascertain whether the centre had undergone any recent or continued settlement, since the great alteration of 1758, Mr. Francis Giles surveyed it on March 6th, 1821, and found, by a spirit-level on the cornice of the Great Arch, that the Western side inclined only 2½ inches below a right line of 83 feet, whilst the variation on the East was no more than 2⅜ inches; and even this depression was supposed to have taken place soon after the striking of the new Arch, as there appeared neither crevices in the joints, nor fractures in the stones, as indicating any later sinking. The Sterlings and Piles were stated to be in generally good repair, though the former had been increased from 4 to 5 feet each at the Great Arch, to make them of a more easy sweep, and form a smoother passage for the current. To guard against any increase of depth there, which might render the Piles insecure, it was stated, that monthly soundings were taken and registered, and large stones occasionally dropped in, which were found to remain; but it was not the custom to throw them in large quantities, though the Sterlings of St. Mary's and the 4th and 5th Locks had recently received about 153 tons of chalk.

"These particulars were chiefly communicated by James Mountague, Esq., Superintendant of the Works at London Bridge, and Mr. John Kitching, the Tide-Carpenter; but the most interesting and curious evidence, which was intended to shew the nature and amount of the Bridge-House funds, was given by Robert Finch Newman, Esq., Comptroller of the Bridge-House Estates; and embraced a great variety of information relating to the history, property, and officers belonging to this edifice. From his answers, it appeared, that the real and personal property of London Bridge produced an income of £30,503: 7s. 8d.; out of which the rental of the Bridge-House Estates amounted, in 1819, to £23,990: 5s., and in 1820 to £25,805: 13s. 2d. This rental consisted of 'Proper Rents,' or those arising from premises within the City; 'Foreign Rents,' derived from places without London; 'Quit Rents,' which have been already explained; and 'Lands Purchased,' or possessions formerly bought of the Crown. Before the Reformation, we have seen that some of these were subject to the expense of certain religious services; and the ancient estate at Stratford, producing a rent of £409: 4s., is still charged with the support of St. Michael's and Peg's Hole Bridges there, on which £2,467: 8s. 11d., have been laid out since 1724; and £50 per annum are paid as a composition for repairing the causeway. It was farther added, that the City was indebted to the Bridge-House the sums of £36,383: 4s. 6d. in cash, and £9,000 in 3 per cent. Consols; whilst its capital consisted of

4 per Cent. Consolidated Bank Annuities, vested in the names of the Chamberlain, Town-Clerk, and Comptroller of the Bridge-House Estates.	£54,000	0	0
3 per Cent. Consolidated Bank Annuities	17,257	1	6
3 per Cent. ditto, in the name of the Accountant General of the Court of Chancery, to be vested in Freehold property	3,860	12	6
Exchequer Bills, and Cash, for the same purpose.	850	17	1
Cash in the hands of the Chamberlain of London, as Banker to the Bridge-House Estates, and the Bridge Masters, about	4,200	0	0

"The next branch of the evidence was to shew the practicability and advantage of the proposed alterations, contrasted with the erection of a new Bridge; Mr. Rennie's estimate for which amounted to £450,000, including £20,000 for a temporary passage, as it was to be erected on the old site, with nearly the present approaches. The crown of the principal Arch of this structure was intended to be 29 feet 6 inches over high-water mark, being 14 feet 3 inches more than the present; and the quantity of stone for it was calculated at 70,000 tons. The principal argument for altering the old edifice was, that the Piers might be examined at low-water, at a trifling cost, without Coffer-dams, and in about a month's time; on account of the apparent strength of the fabric as discovered in an excavation made in May, 1821, on the City side of the North Pier of the Great Arch, about 14 feet from the Western front. There is a lithographic print of this opening, by Mr. James Walker; and particular descriptions of its construction are contained with it, in the tract of '*Reports and Evidences*,' as given by that Engineer, Mr. William Chapman, and Mr. Thomas Piper, Stone-Mason to the City, see pages 87, 102, 111, and 127; but with its formation, as examined in this very year by Mr. Knight, we are already perfectly well acquainted. As it was found, however, as he also stated, that, in all probability, none of the Piers rested solely on Piles, they were considered capable of bearing a much greater weight than the present Bridge, though that was proposed to be lightened in the alteration; and as the Piers of the Great Arch supported the superstructure when the depth under it was 24 feet at low-water, they were believed to be perfectly equal to carrying it with a depth of 10, to which the River-bed was proposed to be levelled. Mr. Chapman also stated, that though a new Bridge would admit of greater perfection, yet that the intended alteration might answer the purpose, and the whole work be rendered secure, if the Sterlings were kept in repair; though he thought they might be both lowered and contracted. And should this alteration prove even insufficient as to the water-way, he considered that two new Arches might be formed at the North end, giving an addition of 43 feet, for the expense of about £20,000 each. This alteration was expected to reduce the annual repairs of the Bridge, from one half to two-thirds of its former amount; and abate the quantity of the fall of water from 5 feet to 3 inches: though the velocity of the stream above Bridge would be thereby increased, since a greater quantity of water would have to run through in the same time; and as the tide would flow higher, and ebb lower, the inclination of the River's surface would likewise be increased. This inclination amounts at present to 6 inches in a mile, or 1 foot between Westminster and London Bridges, at low-water; and estimating it at double after the alterations, it was calculated by Messrs. James Walker, and Stephen Leach, Superintendant of Improvements in the Thames Navigation, that its effect would extend as far as Kew Bridge. They also supposed that the water would ebb sooner from the wharfs, and thus leave their barges less time afloat; from all which circumstances, it seemed important that the River should be artificially deepened, the shoals cleared, and the whole navigation gradually prepared to meet the effects of the enlargement of London Bridge.

"The last part of the evidence was intended to prove, that the increased water-way would be more than sufficient to satisfy the petitioners; but though the owners of the Coal-craft were contented with this, some of the Wharfingers still objected to the short time their vessels could work, from the rapid flow of the tide; and contended that the remaining six Arches on the North would collect ice enough to block up the River above the Bridge. From these examinations, the Bridge-Committee was convinced of the superior advantage of erecting a New Bridge, as expressed to the Corporation in a Report dated April 12th, 1821; though, from the difficulty of raising funds for it, unassisted by Parliament, on June 2nd, another Report was made, stating that a Select Committee having attended the House of Commons, it had adduced evidence to prove the stability of the Bridge; that the inconveniences complained of were exaggerated; and that the proposed alteration was both sufficient and practicable: notwithstanding which, however, the House of Commons' Committee, in its Report of May 25th, recommended a Bill for a new Bridge to be presented early in the next Session.

"These proceedings were followed by a survey of the Thames, from the present Bridge to Old Swan-Stairs, made by appointment of the City, about August, 1822, and taken at low-water mark, when the depth was found to vary from 9 feet to 33½; the greatest being at 84 feet from the Sterlings, and the least at 290. The measurements were taken by a line divided into spaces of 12 feet by pieces of red cloth, passing between two others; one being extended from the Old Swan entirely across the River, and the second from the Sterling-points at the Great Arch.

"To procure designs for a new Bridge, on June 15th, 1822, the Corporation advertised premiums of £250, £150, and £100, for the first, second, and third in merit, which produced about an hundred drawings; their inspection being referred, November 15th, by the Bridge-House Committee, to John Nash, John Soane, Robert Smirke, and William Mountague, Esqrs.: whose answers were given in three Reports in December, 1822, and the following January, and the premiums awarded to Messrs. Fowler, Borer, and Busby; though one of the designs of the late Mr. Rennie was that ultimately adopted. The rebuilding of London Bridge was then officially referred to Parliament by order of the Corporation, February 19th, 1823, when a Select Committee, formed from that for managing the Bridge-House Estates, provided a Bill; though the measure was still a matter of dispute, from the doubts existing of its effects on the navigation, the expense which it would incur, and on the designs already presented.

"On July 4th, however, 1823,—the 4th year of George IV. Chapter 50,—the Royal Assent was given to '*An Act for the Rebuilding of London Bridge, and for the improving and making suitable approaches thereto*;' which is printed in '*A Collection of the Public General Statutes*,' London, 1823, folio, pages 478-536. It commenced by noticing the title of the Corporation of London to be Conservator of the Thames, and its right to the Bridge-House Estates for the benefit of London Bridge; and after referring to the Acts for its improvement and removing the Water-works, the evils of the present building, and the expedience of a new one, it then proceeded to give the following powers, to remain in force for 10 years. To take down, and sell the old Bridge; either leaving it till the completion of the new one, or erecting a temporary structure before removing it: to build a new edifice of Granite, either on the present site, or within 180 feet Westward, with convenient approaches, according to the designs of John Rennie, Esq., with any alterations, being, with the Engineer and Contractor, previously approved by the Lords of the Treasury; the new building standing in the parishes where its abutments are placed, and marking the extent of any jurisdiction instead of the old one: to embank the River in a straight line, from the centre of the abutments of the present Bridge, to the distance of 180 feet West, and 110, East; to raise and lower, new pave, alter, or stop up, streets, &c. in the approaches; and close them during the execution of the Act, to the distance of 300 yards from the present edifice; to land materials free of duty, and to occupy places for storing them, also within 300 feet; to take down houses, &c. beside those entered in the schedule, upon recompense being previously made; to occupy the burial-ground of St. Magnus' Church, providing another; to set back houses on the Western side of Grace-Church Street, Fish-Street Hill, and High-Street, Southwark, between Lombard-Street and St. Margaret's-Hill; to sell, or grant leases of, ground not wanted, and apply the produce to the purposes of the Act; to receive from the Lords of the Treasury the sum of £150,000; additional funds being raised on credit of the Bridge-House Estates by mortgages, annuities, bonds, &c.; to set apart the yearly sum of £12,000 from the Bridge-House rents, for payment of existing charges, and expenses; and to form a sinking-fund for redeeming the monies borrowed; the residue of the rents being deposited with the Chamberlain, for paying of interest, &c.; the expenses of the Act, designs, &c. being discharged from other sums belonging to the Bridge-House Estates. It was also provided, that the Corporation should be answerable for the misuse of these funds, a yearly statement of accounts being laid before Parliament; though it is not to be liable for failure of the rents, &c. on which money is borrowed, for damage occasioned by removal of the Bridge, nor for the work being left unfinished, by the funds proving insufficient. The Act closed with powers for appointing Committees, with Clerks, &c., to execute it, saving interested persons; and with the usual clauses for lighting, watching, making compensation for tithes, &c. &c. The schedule of houses to be taken down contained the particulars of 43 buildings on the City side, and of 109 in Southwark.

"It being determined to retain the old edifice till the completion of its successor, the site of the new Bridge was fixed at about 100 feet Westward of the present, St. Saviour's Church standing above it; though the perfect plan of its approaches can scarcely yet be traced. The first Pile of the work was driven near the Southern end of the old Bridge, opposite the Arch called the Second Lock from the Surrey shore, at the East end of the Coffer-dam, of which it formed a part, on Monday, March 15th, 1824. About the same time, too, the whole of the open spaces between the ballustrades on the Western parapet of the present edifice, were closely boarded up; as well as those square recesses, open at the top, which would have allowed spectators to climb upon the cornice. The houses and other buildings abutting on London Bridge on the Western side of the Borough High-Street, were also rapidly sold, and some parts only of the lower fronts allowed to remain.

"It might have been expected that, in excavating the new foundations, several interesting antiquities would be discovered, illustrative of London history, and of the ancient Bridge in particular; though, if we consider the impetuous rush of the River at this place, it is not surprising that but few articles of value have been yet brought up. The most numerous have been, defaced brass and copper coins of Augustus, Vespasian, and later Roman Emperors; Venetian Tokens; Nuremburg Counters; and a few Tradesmen's Tokens, very perfect; though I have seen none of persons dwelling on the Bridge itself. There have also been found, an old red earthen pitcher, or bottle, nearly perfect; various rings and buckles of wrought and engraved brass, and silver; some very ancient iron keys, and silver spoons; the remains of a dagger which had once been engraven and gilt, and an iron spear-head, engraven on the shaft; most of which are in the possession of Robert Finch Newman, Esq., the Bridge-House Comptroller; whilst in the City Library, at Guildhall, are some ancient carved stones with dates, found in taking down the Arches of the old Bridge. There has also been discovered a particularly fine bronze lamp, representing a head of Bacchus, wreathed with ivy; standing upon the neck, which is made flat, and on its forehead a circular lid, raised by the two curling horns, whilst a handle is attached to the back of the head. This beautiful antique is in very excellent preservation. One of the most interesting reliques, however, which I have yet seen, is a small SILVER EFFIGY OF HARPOCRATES,

which was presented to the British Museum, by Messrs. Rundell, Bridge, and Rundell, of Ludgate-Hill, November 12th, 1825; and is preserved in the Hamilton Room, No. xii. of the Gallery of Antiquities, Case, No. 11, under the care of Mr. J. T. Smith. The figure is about 2½ inches in height, and one in breadth, and represents the son of Osiris as a winged boy, with his finger pointing to his mouth, as God of Silence; the horns, emblematical of his mother Isis, on his head; and at his feet his other attributes, of a dog, a tortoise, an owl, and a serpent twined round a staff; by the number of which we may guess the figure to have been made in Greece, after the time of Alexander the Great. The style of sculpture is firm and massive; and on the back is a strong rivet, through which pass a large ring and a very delicate chain of pure gold, crossing like four belts in front; it being probably of that class of figures which Winckelmann states to have been worn as amulets, or the attributes of Priests.

"To proceed, however, with New London Bridge, I should state, that, Mr. Rennie, senior, having died in 1821, the works have been principally superintended by his son, Mr. John Rennie; and that the builders, who have contracted to erect it, are Mr. William Jolliffe, and Sir Edward Banks; the original amount of whose contract was £426,000, and £30,000 for making alterations in the present structure; the whole to be completed in six years, from March 2nd, 1824: which contract is now increased to £506,000, by the addition of £8,000 for a new set of centering for the 4th Arch; and of £42,000 granted by the Treasury in 1825, for making the Bridge 6 feet wider; namely, 2 feet in each foot-path, and 2 feet in the carriage-way. The exterior of the edifice will be of three sorts of Granite; the Eastern side being of purple Aberdeen; the Western, of the light-grey Devonshire Haytor; and the Arch-stones of both, united with the red-brown of Peterhead: the heartings of the Piers being of hard Brambley-Fall, Derby, and Whitby stone. These materials are roughly shaped at the quarries; and after being carefully wrought at the Isle of Dogs, are finally dressed and fitted to their places, at the Bridge. The Pier-foundations are formed of piles, chiefly beech, pointed with iron, and driven about 20 feet into the blue clay of the River, about 4 feet apart; having two rows of sills, each averaging about a foot square, and filled in with large blocks of stone, upon which is laid a six-inch beech planking, bearing the first course of masonry. The proposed form of the Bridge is a very flat segment, the rise not being more than 7 feet; and it is to consist of 5 elliptical Arches, having plain rectangular buttresses, standing upon plinths, and cutwaters; with two straight flights of stairs, 22 feet wide, at each end. That on the Western side, at the City end, will, however, cut so deeply into Fishmongers' Hall, that it is to be taken down, the Corporation paying £20,000 to the Company. My narrative is now so near a termination, that I have to add only a few notices concerning the Bridge-Officers, and a more particular and exact account of the measurements of the new edifice than has yet been recorded. Which dimensions, from high-water line, are as follow:—

		Feet.		Feet.	Inches.
"Centre Arch of the New London Bridge,	*Span*	150	*Rise*	29	6
Piers to ditto, 24 Feet.					
Second and Fourth Arches	—	140	—	27	6
Piers to ditto, 22 Feet.					
Land Arches	—	130	—	24	6
Abutments at the base, 73 Feet.					

Total width of water-way, 690 feet; Length of the Bridge including the Abutments, 928 feet; Length within the Abutments, 782 feet; Width of the Bridge from outside to outside of the Parapet, 56 feet; Width of the Carriage-way, 36 feet, and of each Footpath, 9 feet; and the total height of the Bridge on the Eastern side, from low-water, 60 feet.

"All which particulars, however, are much better illustrated by A GROUND-PLAN AND ELEVATION OF THE NEW LONDON BRIDGE.

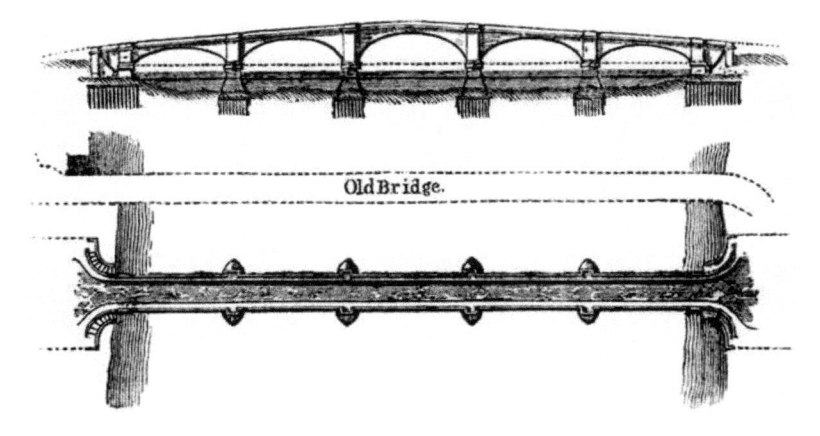

"The Officers of old London Bridge, and its estates, are, firstly, Two Masters, or Wardens, who receive and pay all accounts of the Bridge-House, oversee its concerns, watchmen, labourers, &c., summon and attend the Auditors, and Committees, and meet the Corporation on Midsummer and Michaelmas days. The yearly salary of the senior is £250, and a house; and that of the junior, £200, with £86 for house-rent and taxes: their incomes being further increased by some trifling official fees. The Comptroller of the Works and Revenues of London Bridge receives a salary of £300, with other emoluments; and attends all Committees, keeping their journals, and preparing their reports, leases, contracts, and all other documents; he has also the custody of the records, &c., and, being a solicitor, conducts all the Bridge-House law-proceedings. The Clerk of the Works is occupied as a general Architectural Surveyor, attending Committees, arbitrations, &c., and making surveys, valuations, designs, and estimates. He superintends all new buildings and alterations on the Bridge-House lands, inspects the covenants and dilapidations of the tenants; as well as the time and bills of the trades-men, and the Bridge-House stores, of all which he makes reports to the Committee: his yearly salary is £500. The Assistant Clerk at the Bridge-House resides in the upper part of that building, with a salary of £200; assisting the Bridge-Masters in keeping and copying their accounts. The Superintendent of the Works at London Bridge overlooks and directs the repairs, the measuring and examination of the articles, and certifies their quantities, &c., his yearly salary being £100. The Bridge-House Carpenter is foreman of those works, with a residence and £200 per annum; he keeps the workmen's accounts, and receives and portions out building stores; he also sets up marks on the Bridge-House estates, and repairs such water-stairs as they support. The Bridge-House Messenger is employed in summoning and attending the Auditors and Committees; in delivering notices to the tenants, and in various other duties at the Bridge-House, his salary being 36 shillings per week. To these officers is added a Collector of Rents of Tenants at Will in St. George's Fields, who resides in a house belonging to the estate, and is paid by a commission of 5 per cent. The manner of letting premises pertaining to the Bridge-House, is, on the expiration of a lease, to have them viewed by the Committee and Surveyor; when, if the Committee and tenant agree, it is so stated to the Common Council; and, if not, the premises are put up to auction. Finally, the Committee of Bridge-House Estates is composed of a certain number of Aldermen, and a Commoner from each Ward; but no payments exceeding £100 are made without the sanction of the Common Council, a brief statement of the accounts being annually laid before the Court, a copy of which is sent to every member. The accounts and vouchers are then examined by four Auditors, annually elected by the Livery, to whom a report is made; the documents being sworn to by the Bridge-Masters; and these statements, fairly transcribed on vellum, are deposited, one copy in the Chamber of London, and another in the Muniment-Room at the Bridge-House. And now, having observed, that these particulars were given in evidence before a Select Committee of the House of Commons, in April 1821, and are printed much more at large in the tract of '*Reports and Evidences*,' pages 72, 73, 135-138, here I conclude with a parting libation, and many thanks for your long-tried attention."

Such, then, were Mr. Barnaby Postern's historical notices of old London Bridge; in which the reader may perceive, that he evinced a fair proportion of antiquarian learning, and rather a large share of reading and memory. When he had arrived at this period, however, as I thought that my own information would enable me to add some curious modern particulars to his narrative, I addressed him with, "My best thanks are due to you, worthy Sir, for your interesting CHRONICLES OF LONDON BRIDGE; for, although you have sometimes been prosy enough to have wearied a dozen Dutchmen, yet, by my patience and your perseverance, the story is safely brought down to the present day. You have steered it, slowly enough, certainly, but surely, through all the intricate navigation of the Record Rolls, and have carefully avoided several of those rocks of error, upon which so many former historians have been wrecked. And since the narrative has now reached the building of a New London Bridge, pray allow me, so long your grateful hearer, to relate the ceremony of Laying the First Stone thereof, from my own observation, sketches, and memoranda."

"My very hearty thanks are your's for that most excellent proposal, Mr. Geoffrey," said the old Antiquary; "for I am now too far declined into the vale of years, to describe modern ceremonials and festivities with the spirit of a younger Citizen: whilst you are 'not clean past your youth;' having yet only 'some smack of age, some relish of the saltness of time in you;' therefore the story, good Mr. Barbican, the story."

"You shall have it, Sir," replied I; "you shall have it, and with all the skill I can; though, after your highly-finished ancient historical pictures, my modern delineations can appear only faint and imperfect.

"The Coffer-Dam, in which the ceremony of Laying the First Stone took place, was erected opposite to the Southern Arch called the Fourth Lock, and was constructed of three rows of piles, planks, and earth, substantially secured by timbers of great strength and thickness; and when the day for performing it was fixed, it was officially announced by the following notice:—

"'LONDON BRIDGE. MANSION HOUSE, 23rd May, 1825. The Committee for Rebuilding the New London Bridge having appointed Wednesday, the 15th day of June next, for Laying the First Stone of the New Bridge, Notice is hereby given, that the Foot and Carriage-way over the present Bridge will be stopped on that day, from Eleven o'clock in the Forenoon until Four o'clock in the Afternoon.

'By Order of the Right Honourable the LORD MAYOR.

'FRANCIS HOBLER.

'N.B. Southwark Bridge will be open free of Toll during the above hours.'

"As the intervening space passed away, the preparations for the ceremonial proceeded on a scale of equal celerity and magnitude. A Steam Engine, with a high funnel, was erected against the City side of the Coffer-Dam, for exhausting it of water, an entrance to which was made through a covered stone recess of the old Bridge, on the Northern side of the Dam. The rude and intricate walling of piles and other erections now began to assume a more regular appearance; a platform and flight of steps connected them with the parapet of the old edifice; a broad raised passage surrounded the area in the centre, and the whole was covered with an awning, above which rose numerous lofty flag-staves. These, then, were the earlier preparations for this splendid water-festival; and now let us proceed to recount the wonders of the day itself. A finer and more freshly-breathing air was certainly never abroad, than that which cooled the atmosphere and blew out the gaily-coloured flags around old London Bridge, on the morning of Wednesday, the 15th of June. At a very early hour, the workmen began erecting the barriers, which were double, and at a considerable distance apart. Across the whole space of Fish-Street Hill, from Upper and Lower Thames Street, and again at Tooley Street, there stretched wide wooden railings, having a moveable bar at each pavement, with an opening wide enough for one person only; whilst the centre of the Street was divided with posts and bars, allowing carriages to pass between them also, but in single lines. Within these, at each end of the Bridge, was erected a strong screen of rough planks, about fourteen feet high, having four gates, answering to the former foot-paths and carriage-ways. So long as the barriers continued open, the old Bridge was crowded with gazers; who were especially collected opposite that part of the parapet which was to form the grand entrance to the Coffer-Dam; while on the roofs of the houses, and other buildings in the vicinity, were platforms of seats, and awnings preparing, which were afterwards crowded with spectators; as well as the Monument, St. Magnus' Church, the towers of St. Mary Overies', and St. Olave, Fishmongers' Hall, and the Patent-Shot works. Many scaffolds were also erected for the purpose of letting, the prices varying from 2*s.* 6*d.* to 15*s.* each, according to their accommodations; and the following is a specimen of their announcements. 'Seats to be let for viewing the Procession, No. 2, Bridge Foot, for Laying the First Stone of the New Bridge. Tickets 7*s.* and 5*s.* each:' though more moderate exhibitions were set forth in the words, 'A full view of the whole works, Admission 6*d.*' Another bill of entertainment, also issued on that morning, stated, that 'This Evening, Wednesday, June 15th, the Monument will be superbly illuminated with Portable Gas, in commemoration of Laying the First Stone of the New

London Bridge, by the Right Honourable the Lord Mayor. Admittance Sixpence each, at Nine o'clock.' And in the evening a lamp was accordingly placed at each of the loop-holes of the column, to give the idea of its being wreathed with flame, whilst two other series were placed on the edges of the gallery; though the wind seldom permitted the whole of the gas to remain lighted at the same instant.

"Long before the time appointed for the closing of old London Bridge, the River and buildings around it were fully occupied with visitors; the vessels were decorated with flags; and crowded pleasure-boats, some carrying bands of music, floated round the Coffer-Dam. At eleven o'clock, the Bridge was begun to be cleared, and that of Southwark opened, for the first and only time, toll free. The various entries were guarded by constables, who ascertained that every person was provided with a ticket; and before noon, this famous passage across the Thames had so completely changed its character, that the very striking contrast to its usual appearance must have been seen to be appreciated. The building of the New London Bridge having been entrusted to the following Committee, the ceremonies of this day were also placed under the same direction; the Members being distinguished by painted wands, surmounted by the Arms of London and Southwark. These were,—

"THE LORD MAYOR, all the Aldermen, and Jonathan Crocker, Chairman of the Sub Bridge-House Committee; Robert Fisher, of the Ward of *Aldersgate within*; John Lorkin, of *Aldersgate without*; Samuel Favell, of *Aldgate*; Henry Hughes, of *Bassishaw*; William Austin, of *Billingsgate*; James Davies, and Sir William Rawlins, of *Bishopsgate*; William Mathie, of *Bread Street*; John Locke, of *Bridge*; Richard Webb Jupp, of *Broad Street*; Thomas Carr, of *Candlewick*; Robert Slade, of *Castle Baynard*; Charles Bleaden, of *Cheap*; Josiah Griffiths, of *Coleman Street*; Charles William Hick, of *Cordwainers*; Spencer Perry Adderley, of *Cornhill*; Hugh Herron, of *Cripplegate within*; Richard Lambert Jones, of *Cripplegate without*; James Ebenezer Saunders, of *Dowgate*; Josiah Daw, and Adam Oldham, of *Farringdon within*; William John Reeves, and James Webb Southgate, of *Farringdon without*; Joseph Carter, of *Langbourn*; Thomas Price, of *Lime Street*; Robert Carter, of *Portsoken*; William Routh, of *Queenhithe*; Peter Skipper, of *Tower*; Thomas Conway, of *Vintry*; and William Richardson, of *Walbrook*.

"The Tickets of admission to the Coffer-Dam were also issued by these gentlemen, and were, of course, in great request; but their number being limited, and the general arrangements peculiarly excellent, there was ample accommodation for even a more numerous company. The Tickets themselves—and how will they not be valued by the curious collectors of a future day?—were elegantly engraven, and printed on stout cards, measuring about five inches by eight: they consisted of an oblong elevation of the New

Bridge, looking down the River, '*Perkins, St. Mary Axe, Sculpsit,*' having beneath it the following words:

'ADMIT THE BEARER
TO WITNESS THE CEREMONY OF LAYING
THE FIRST STONE
OF THE
NEW LONDON BRIDGE,
ON WEDNESDAY, THE 15TH DAY OF JUNE, 1825.

        (*Signed*) HENRY
        WOODTHORPE, JUNR.
 Seal of the   *Clerk of the*
  City Arms.   *Committee.*

N.B.—*The Access is from the Present Bridge, and the time of Admission will be between the hours of Twelve and Two.*

No. 837.'

These, however, admitted only to the galleries of the Coffer-Dam, the lowest floor being reserved for the bearers of a second Ticket, printed in letter-press, on a pale pink card, of an ordinary size, and containing the following words.

'NEW LONDON BRIDGE.
ADMIT THE BEARER
TO THE
PLATFORM SEATS,
ON PRODUCING THE TICKET OF ADMISSION
WITH THIS CARD.'

"The general passage was along the outer gallery, but the latter admissions were conducted down a staircase, lined with crimson, opposite to the principal entrance. Both these Tickets, however, were required to be *shewn* only, being intended for preservation as memorials, and they were admitted at each end of the Bridge. Having passed the barriers, the visitors proceeded to the GRAND ENTRANCE TO THE COFFER-DAM,

which was formed by removing part of the stone parapet of the Bridge, adjoining the fourth recess from the Southwark end, on the Western side; the break being most expeditiously made just as the Bridge was cleared. It was then that the extreme elegance of this entrance became perfectly visible. Several steps, covered with crimson cloth, led up to a kind of tent formed of flags, gathered in festoons, with roses of the same, and surmounted by a white flag bearing a red cross, and having the Union in the first quarter, the Sword of St. Paul in the second, and the Saltire of Southwark in the fourth. The roof of this entrance was also formed of two immense red ensigns, charged with the Union in their quarters; the sides were elegantly divided into arches, richly festooned and entwined with flags; and, on the left-hand of the entrance, at the edge of the pavement, was erected a board, which stated, that 'All Carriages, not in the Procession, are, on setting down the company, to pass on into Southwark, and return from Southwark to take up.' Round the whole of the Dam itself was a broad stage; which formed a most delightful promenade, secured from the heat of the sun by the tent above, whilst the air, light, and prospect, might be enjoyed through the Arches. THE WESTERN END OF THE COFFER-DAM terminated in a circular form, and presented a peculiarly beautiful object from the water; whence a series of substantial ladders led to the platform: over which floated the Union Jack, and a St. George's Ensign. THE SOUTHERN EXTERIOR OF THE COFFER-DAM

formed, however, its most magnificent prospect; especially when seen from a point of sufficient elevation to comprise the whole extent of its splendid and capacious amphitheatre. The nearest objects were the thick and irregular walls of discoloured piles standing in the water, from which all boats were kept off by persons stationed for the purpose; and on the interior row was the outer gallery of the tent, with its decorated arches. The awning above was raised on a little forest of scaffold-poles, which would have appeared of unusual strength any where but by the side of the huge blocks of timber immediately beneath them: and, over the whole, the breeze unfolded to the sun the several banners. In the centre waved the Royal Standard of England; at the Western top of the tent was the flag of the Navy Board; at the opposite point that of the Admiralty; and above these a rope extended the whole length of the building, decorated with about five-and-twenty signal-colours, furnished, like all the others, from the Royal Dock-Yard at Woolwich.

"This erection was divided into four principal parts, consisting of a floor and three galleries, the whole being capable of containing 2000 persons; nearly which number was probably present. The floor was laid 45 feet below high-water mark, and measured 95 feet by 36, being formed of four-inch beechen planks, resting upon Piles headed with iron; upon which was a layer of timber two feet thick, and a course of brick-work and stone, each of 2½ feet deep. It was surrounded by three rows of seats, excepting at the entrance at the Eastern end; and on the North side was a chair of state, covered with crimson cloth, having behind it the seats appropriated to the Lord Mayor's family and private friends. The whole floor was capable of receiving 500 persons, and was entirely covered with red baize, excepting at a rectangular space in the centre, within which appeared a cavity, cut in stone, of 21 inches by 15, and 7 in depth, for the coins, &c., over which the First Stone was suspended by a strong fall and tackle, secured to the upright timbers of the Dam. Above the floor was a gallery, containing three rows of covered seats, sufficient to hold 400 spectators; and over it were two others; the lower one, of two rows for 400; and the upper tier for 300 more. Three other galleries also stretched along the cross beams above; whilst a still more lofty one, at the Western end, was appropriated to the Ward Schools of Bridge, Dowgate, and Candlewick. The general character of the Dam was strength and solidity; the tiers of seats being supported by massive cross-beams, wreathed and decorated with flags and rosettes; along the centre passed another very thick timber, bearing the uprights and their respective supporters; and from the roof several large flags hung heavily downwards. The taste and ingenuity which were exerted in the arrangements, had indeed left nothing to be wished for; whilst the general security was everywhere so palpably apparent, as to dispel the apprehensions even of the most timid. Such was the appearance of the INTERIOR OF THE COFFER-DAM, AND THE POSITION OF THE FIRST STONE, which was of the best hard Aberdeen Granite, weighing 4 tons. Its measurement was, 5 feet ⅝ of an inch long, 3 feet 6⅜ inches broad, and 2 feet 10 inches deep; containing 50 feet 7 inches in cubic measure; and its situation as nearly as possible the centre of the First, or South Pier, on the Southwark side. The Company continued rapidly to arrive until the barriers were closed at 2 o'clock, when most of the seats in the Coffer-Dam were occupied; and where, to lighten as much as possible the interval of waiting, the bands of the Horse-Guards, Red and Blue, and of the Artillery Company, which were stationed in a gallery at the entrance, were employed to furnish frequent entertainment: Refreshments of Tea, Coffee, Champagne, &c., being also liberally supplied by the Committee. About a quarter before three o'clock, the Lady Mayoress, and her family, came to the Dam in the private state-carriage; and at four, a signal-gun announced that the Procession had left the Court-yard of Guildhall, nearly in the following order; passing through Cheapside, Cornhill, and Grace-Church Street, to the Bridge, where it was received by the Committee, and other members of the Common Council; the principal persons being in their own carriages.

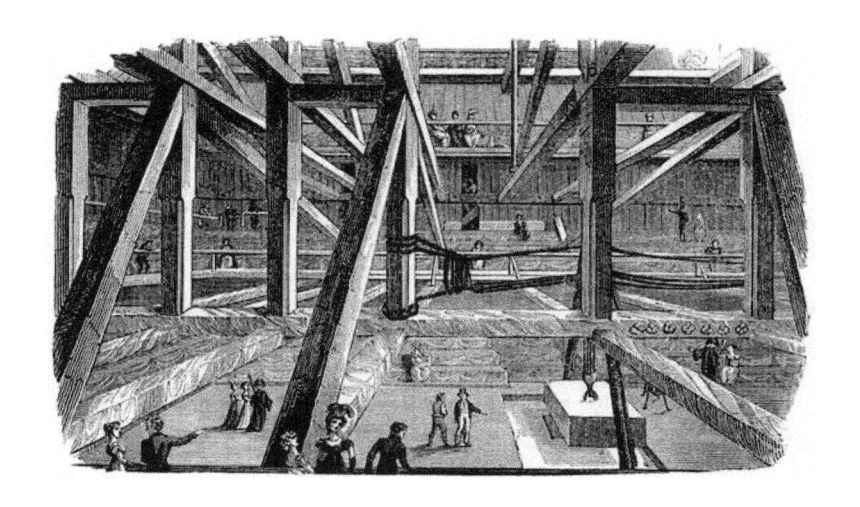

A Division of the Artillery Company, with their Field-pieces.
Constables.
Band of Music.
Marshalmen.
The Junior City Marshal, Mr. W. W. Cope, on horseback.
 Nathaniel Saunders, Junr., Esq., the Water-Bailiff, and Mr. Nelson, his Assistant.
Barge Masters.
City Watermen, bearing Colours.
Remainder of the City Watermen.

Bridgemasters and Clerk of the Bridge-House.
Contractors, William Jolliffe, Esq., and Sir Edward Banks.
Model of the Bridge, borne by Labourers.
Architect and Engineer, John Rennie, Esq., F.R.S.
Members of the New Bridge Committee.
Comptroller of the Bridge-House, Robert F. Newman, Esq.
Visitors and Members of the Committee of the Royal Society.
High Bailiff of the Borough of Southwark, John Holmes, Esq.
Under Sheriffs, George Martin, and John S. Tilson, Esqrs.
Clerk of the Peace of the City of London, Thomas Shelton, Esq.
City Solicitor, William Lewis Newman, Esq.
Remembrancer, Timothy Tyrrell, Esq.
Secondaries of Giltspur Street and the Poultry Compters.
Comptroller of the Chamber, Lewis Bushnan, Esq.
Common Pleaders, Wm. Bolland, Esq., George Bernard, Esq.
Hon. C. E. Law, and John Mirehouse, Esq.
Judges of the Sheriff's Court.
Town Clerk, Henry Woodthorpe, Esq.
Common Serjeant, Thomas Denman, Esq., M. P.
Deputy Recorder, Mr. Serjeant Arabin.
Chamberlain, Richard Clark, Esq.
Members of Parliament and other Gentlemen, Visitors.
Sir Humphrey Davy, President of the Royal Society.
The Sheriffs, Anthony Brown, and John Key, Esqrs., Aldermen.
Aldermen below the Chair.
The Recorder, Newman Knowlys, Esq.
Aldermen past the Chair.
Visitors, Privy Councillors.
Visitors, Peers.
Officers of State.
Music and Colours, with the Court of the Lord Mayor's Company, the Goldsmiths.
Marshalmen.
The Senior City Marshal, Mr. Neville Brown, on horseback.
The Lord Mayor's Household.
The Lord Mayor's Servants in their State Liveries.
The Lord Mayor in his State Carriage, accompanied by His Royal Highness the Duke of York.
Carriage of His Royal Highness the Duke of York.
The remainder of the Artillery Company, as a guard of honour to the Lord Mayor.

"The streets through which the Procession passed, were all thronged; every window was filled with spectators; and, on arriving at its destination, the

River, the Wharfs, the most distant buildings, and even Southwark Bridge, were equally crowded with thousands of impatient gazers. It was not, however, until a quarter before five, that the field-pieces of the Artillery Company, at the old Swan Stairs' Wharf, announced the cavalcade's actual approach, when the bands played the famous Yäger Chor of Weber's '*Freyschutz*.' The City-Watermen, bearing their richly emblazoned standards, soon afterwards entered the Coffer-Dam, when, after the colours had been very ingeniously passed between the timbers, and grouped around the Stone, it being found that they would materially obstruct the view, they were, with similar difficulty, conveyed back again. The narrow and winding passages of the Dam destroyed much of the stately order of the Procession; but nearly the whole Court of Aldermen, and a large party of the Common-Council, in their scarlet and purple gowns, having appeared on the floor beneath, they were followed by the City Officers; the Lord Mayor, in his robes of state; and His Royal Highness the Duke of York, in a plain blue coat, wearing the Garter round his knee, and the star of the order upon his breast. In the same part of the Procession also came the Earl of Darnley; Lord James Stuart; the Right Hon. C. W. W. Wynn, President of the Board of Controul; Admiral Sir George Cockburn, M. P.; Admiral Sir Isaac Coffin, Bart, M. P.; Sir George Warrender, Bart, M. P.; Sir Peter Laurie; Sir Robert Wilson, M. P.; Thomas Wilson, Esq., M. P.; William Williams, Esq., M. P.; George Holme Sumner, Esq., M. P.; and several other personages of distinction.

"The Lord Mayor and His Royal Highness having arrived at the state chair, amidst the waving of handkerchiefs, and the loudest cheers, and having both of them declined that seat of honour, they remained standing during the whole of the ceremony; which then commenced by the Ward Schools and the visitors singing '*God save the King*,' verse and chorus, in which the Duke also joined with great enthusiasm. The Lord Mayor then removed towards the Eastern end of the Platform, in the centre of the Coffer-Dam floor, where there was a small stage covered with crimson cloth, attended by four members of the Bridge Committee, bearing the bottle for the coins, an inscription incrustated in glass, the level, and the splendid SILVER-GILT TROWEL FOR LAYING THE FIRST STONE.

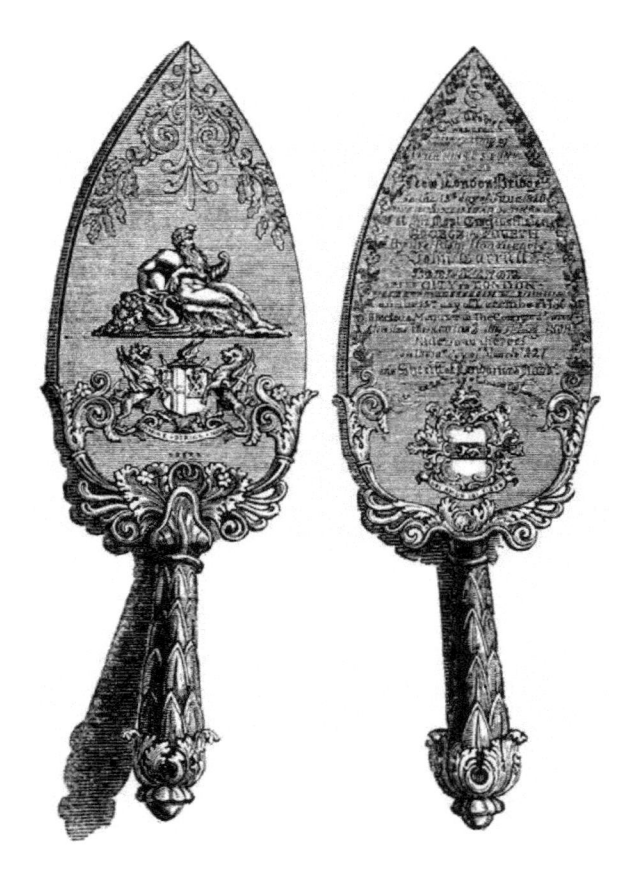

This elegant instrument, which was designed and executed by Messrs. Green, Ward, and Green, of Ludgate Hill, measured 15 inches in its extreme length, and 5 inches at the widest part of the blade; the handle being 5½ inches long, composed of wrought laurel, terminating in very rich acanthus foliage at the end; and its depository, a green Morocco case lined with white satin. The upper side was embossed with a reclining figure of the Thames, with a vase, swan, and cornucopia; beneath which was a shield, charged with the impaled arms of London and Southwark, and surrounded by the supporters, crest, motto, and badges of the City. The other side was perfectly flat, and was decorated with a border of flowers; the armorial ensigns, crest, and motto, of the Lord Mayor; and the following Inscription, engraven in ornamental characters:—

'THIS TROWEL
WAS USED
IN THE LAYING OF
THE FIRST STONE
OF THE

NEW LONDON BRIDGE,
ON THE 15th DAY OF JUNE, 1825,
IN THE SIXTH YEAR OF THE REIGN
OF HIS MOST GRACIOUS MAJESTY
GEORGE THE FOURTH,
BY THE RIGHT HONOURABLE
JOHN GARRATT,
LORD MAYOR
OF THE CITY OF LONDON:
WHO WAS BORN IN THE WARD IN WHICH THE BRIDGE IS SITUATED,
ON THE 15th DAY OF DECEMBER, 1786;
ELECTED A MEMBER OF THE COMMON COUNCIL
FOR THAT WARD, ON THE 3rd DAY OF AUGUST, 1809
ALDERMAN THEREOF,
ON THE 10th DAY OF MARCH, 1821;
AND SHERIFF OF LONDON AND MIDDLESEX,
ON THE 24th DAY OF JUNE FOLLOWING.'

"Mr. John Rennie having exhibited to the Lord Mayor and the Duke of York a large and excellent drawing of the elevation of the New Bridge, Richard Clark, Esq., the venerable Chamberlain of London, next produced a white satin purse, containing a series of new coins of the reign, each separately enveloped, which being uncovered, and deposited by the Lord Mayor in an elegant square bottle of cut-glass, were placed in the cavity; four glass cylinders, 7 inches long and 3 in diameter, intended to support the engraved Inscription-plate, being fixed at the corners in plaster-of-Paris. Another member of the Committee then handed to the Lord Mayor a block of solid glass, 7¼ inches broad, 3½ in height, and 1½ in thickness, enclosing these words, in Messrs. Pellats' and Green's Ceramic Incrustation:—

'THE FIRST STONE OF THIS BRIDGE
WAS LAID BY THE RIGHT HON[BLE] JOHN GARRATT,
LORD MAYOR OF LONDON, IN JUNE, 1825:
AND IN THE 6TH YEAR OF THE REIGN
OF KING GEORGE THE 4TH.'

'PELLATS & GREEN.'

"The Town-clerk, Henry Woodthorpe, Esq., who had recently received the Degree of LL.D., then came forward with the brass Depositum-plate, and read aloud this very fine Inscription, composed, at the request of the Bridge Committee, by the Rev. Edward Coplestone, D.D., Master of Oriel College, Oxford, and late Professor of Poetry in that University; whose *'Prælectiones*

Academicæ' have so excellently illustrated the beauties of the ancient Classic Poets.

'PONTIS VETVSTI
QVVM PROPTER CREBRAS NIMIS INTERIECTAS MOLES
IMPEDITO CVRSV FLVMINIS
NAVICVLAE ET RATES
NON LEVI SAEPE IACTVRA ET VITAE PERICVLO
PER ANGVSTAS FAVCES
PRAECIPITI AQVARVM IMPETV FERRI SOLERENT
CIVITAS LONDINENSIS
HIS INCOMMODIS REMEDIVM ADHIBERE VOLENS
ET CELEBERRIMI SIMVL IN TERRIS EMPORII
VTILITATIBVS CONSVLENS
REGNI INSVPER SENATVS AVCTORITATE
AC MVNIFICENTIA ADIVTA
PONTEM
SITV PRORSVS NOVO
AMPLIORIBVS SPATIIS CONSTRVENDVM DECREVIT
EA SCILICET FORMA AC MAGNITVDINE
QVAE REGIAE VRBIS MAIESTATI
TANDEM RESPONDERET
NEQVE ALIO MAGIS TEMPORE
TANTVM OPVS INCHOANDVM DVXIT
QVAM CVM PACATO FERME TOTO TERRARVM ORBE
IMPERIVM BRITTANICVM
FAMA OPIBVS MVLTITVDINE CIVIVM ET CONCORDIA
POLLENS
PRINCIPE
ITEM GAVDERET
ARTIVM FAVTORE AC PATRONO
CVIVS SVB AVSPICIIS
NOVVS INDIES AEDIFICIORVM SPLENDOR VRBI ACCEDERET.

PRIMVM OPERIS LAPIDEM
POSVIT
IOANNES GARRATT ARMIGER
PRAETOR
XV DIE IVNII
ANNO REGIS GEORGII QVARTI SEXTO
A. S. M.D.CCC.XXV.

JOANNE RENNIE S. R. S. ARCHITECTO.'

"The following English translation of this truly elegant composition was also engraven on the reverse of the plate; though not then read.

'THE FREE COURSE OF THE RIVER
BEING OBSTRUCTED BY THE NUMEROUS PIERS
OF THE ANCIENT BRIDGE,
AND THE PASSAGE OF BOATS AND VESSELS
THROUGH ITS NARROW CHANNELS
BEING OFTEN ATTENDED WITH DANGER AND LOSS OF LIFE
BY REASON OF THE FORCE AND RAPIDITY OF THE CURRENT,
THE CITY OF LONDON,
DESIROUS OF PROVIDING A REMEDY FOR THIS EVIL,
AND AT THE SAME TIME CONSULTING
THE CONVENIENCE OF COMMERCE
IN THIS VAST EMPORIUM OF ALL NATIONS,
UNDER THE SANCTION AND WITH THE LIBERAL AID OF
PARLIAMENT,
RESOLVED TO ERECT A BRIDGE
UPON A FOUNDATION ALTOGETHER NEW,
WITH ARCHES OF A WIDER SPAN,
AND OF A CHARACTER CORRESPONDING
TO THE DIGNITY AND IMPORTANCE
OF THIS ROYAL CITY:
NOR DOES ANY OTHER TIME SEEM TO BE MORE SUITABLE
FOR SUCH AN UNDERTAKING
THAN WHEN, IN A PERIOD OF UNIVERSAL PEACE
THE BRITISH EMPIRE
FLOURISHING IN GLORY, WEALTH, POPULATION, AND
DOMESTIC UNION,
IS GOVERNED BY A PRINCE,
THE PATRON AND ENCOURAGER OF THE ARTS,
UNDER WHOSE AUSPICES
THE METROPOLIS HAS BEEN DAILY ADVANCING IN
ELEGANCE AND
SPLENDOUR.

THE FIRST STONE OF THIS WORK
WAS LAID
BY JOHN GARRATT, ESQUIRE,
LORD MAYOR,
ON THE 15th DAY OF JUNE,

IN THE SIXTH YEAR OF KING GEORGE THE FOURTH,
AND IN THE YEAR OF OUR LORD, 1825.

JOHN RENNIE, F.R.S. ARCHITECT.'

"Printed copies of these Inscriptions, with an embossed border, were presented to each person on entering the Dam; as was also another edition of the Latin, engraven on copper, of the same size as the admission-ticket, and having the same view of the New Bridge above it. The brass plate was then placed upon the glass pillars, when Mr. Richard Lambert Jones, Sub-Chairman of the Committee for erecting the edifice, presented the splendid Trowel to the Lord Mayor, with this address: 'My Lord, I have the honour to inform your Lordship, that the Committee of Management has appointed you, in your character of Lord Mayor of London, to lay the First Stone of the New London Bridge; and that I am directed to present your Lordship with this Trowel, as a means of assistance to your Lordship in accomplishing that object.' Upon which the Lord Mayor turned towards the Duke of York, and thus addressed His Royal Highness, and the other witnesses of the ceremony.

"'Though it is not essential for me to speak at any length upon the purpose for which we are this day assembled, since its importance to this great commercial City must be clearly evident; yet I cannot refrain from offering a few observations, feeling, as I do, more than an ordinary interest in the accomplishment of the undertaking, of which the present ceremony is only the primary step. I cannot consider the present a favourable moment for entering into any chronological history of the present venerable Bridge, which is now, from the increased commerce of the country, and the rapid strides made by the Sciences in this Kingdom, found inadequate to its purposes; but would rather advert to the many advantages which must naturally result from the completion of this great national enterprise. Whether there be taken into consideration the rapid, and consequently dangerous, currents arising from the obstruction incidental to the defects of this ancient edifice, which have proved so destructive to human life and property, or its difficult and incommodious approaches and acclivity, it must be matter of sincere congratulation, that we are living in times when the resources of this highly-favoured country are competent to a work of such great public utility. If ever there were a period more suitable than another, for engaging in national improvements, it must be the present; governed as we are by a Sovereign, the munificent and accomplished Patron of the Arts, beneath whose mild and paternal sway, by the blessing of Divine Providence, we now enjoy profound peace; living under a government, by the enlightened policy of which, our trade and manufactures so extensively flourish; and represented by a Parliament, ever ready to foster, by the most liberal grants, any plans for the improvement of the Empire; to which the present undertaking is so deeply indebted for its munificent support. Thus happily situated, it is impossible to hail such advantages with other feelings than those of gratitude and delight; and it is to me a source of unqualified pride and pleasure, that this great undertaking should have occurred in the year when I have been honoured by the office of Chief Magistrate of this great, this greatest, City, not of England only, but of the world; and that this important ceremony should take place in the Ward which I have the honour to represent in the Civic Councils. I cannot conclude without acknowledging how highly complimentary I feel it to the honourable office which I now fill, to meet such an auditory as now surrounds me; in which I see the illustrious Prince, Heir-presumptive to the Throne of this Kingdom; many of His Majesty's Ministers, and the distinguished Nobles of the land; my active brother-magistrates; my kind fellow-citizens; and, above all, so brilliant an assemblage of that sex, whose radiant smiles, this day, shed a lustre on our meeting. Under such auspices, I rejoice to lay the Foundation-Stone of a structure, which, I trust, will, through all future time, prove an ornament to the Metropolis; reflect credit on the Architect; and redound to the honour of this Corporation: and I offer up a sincere and fervent prayer, that, in executing this great work, there may occur no calamity; that, in completing what is most particularly intended as a preventive of future danger, no mischief may overcloud the universal rejoicings on the undertaking.'

"The very warm applauses which followed this most appropriate address subsided only upon the commencement of the Masonic ceremonies, by a portion of fine mortar being placed around the cavity of the Stone, by several of the Assistants, and spread by the Lord Mayor with his splendid Trowel; after which, precisely at 5 o'clock, the First Stone was gradually lowered into its bed by a brazen block of four sheaves, and the power of a machine called a crab. When it was settled, it was finally secured by several Masons, who cut four sockets close to it on the stone beneath, into which were fitted strong iron clamps, cured with plaster of Paris. The Lord Mayor then struck it with a mallet, and ascertained its accuracy by applying the level to its East, North, West, and South surfaces. The work being thus perfected, the City Sword and Mace were disposed in Saltire upon the stone; successive shouts burst from the numerous spectators; the bands again played the National Anthem of England; and a flag being lowered as a signal on the top of the Dam, the guns of the Artillery Company, and the carronades on Calvert's Brewery Wharf, fired a concluding salute. The declining Sun, also, contributed to shed a golden glory upon the closing ceremony; for, as the day advanced, its radiance streamed through an opening in the tent-covering above, and, gradually approaching the Stone, shone upon it with a dazzling brilliancy, at the very moment of its being deposited. The whole ceremonial terminated with an universal repetition of *'God save the King,'* and three series of huzzas, for the Duke of York, Old England, and Mr. Rennie; after which, when the Procession had left the Dam, amidst similar acclamations to those which first greeted it, many of the visitors went down to the floor, to view the Stone more closely, and to boast to posterity that they had stood upon it, or walked over it.

"To conclude the festivities of the day with appropriate Civic hospitality, the Lord Mayor, at his own private expense, gave a most sumptuous banquet to the Corporation, and his noble visitors, at the Mansion House. The dinner and wines included Turtle, Venison, Champagne, Claret, and every other luxury; to which the following card of Invitation, thus commemorated the event:—

'THE LORD MAYOR REQUESTS THE HONOUR OF

COMPANY TO DINNER AT THE MANSION HOUSE,
ON WEDNESDAY THE 15th OF JUNE, AT SIX O'CLOCK PRECISELY,
ON THE OCCASION OF LAYING THE FIRST STONE OF THE NEW LONDON BRIDGE.

The favour of an answer is particularly requested by the 6th of June.

Mansion House, May 25th, 1825.'

"A Royal dinner at Carlton Palace, on the same day, deprived him of the presence of the Duke of York, who quitted the Bridge through Southwark, immediately after the ceremony. His Lordship's guests, however, amounted to a greater number than had ever before dined within the Mansion House, since, in addition to upwards of 360 in the Egyptian Hall, nearly 200 of the Artillery Company dined in the Saloon; the whole edifice being brilliantly illuminated with gas, both within and without, and the entertainment superintended by a Committee of his Lordship's private friends.

"To mark the very deep public sense of the Lord Mayor's munificent conduct upon this memorable occasion, at a Court of Common Council held on the following day, Thursday, June 16th, Adam Oldham, Esq., Deputy of the Ward of Farringdon Within, called the attention of the Court to the very splendid manner in which his Lordship had conducted himself towards the Members of the Corporation, at the recent ceremony of Laying the First Stone of the New London Bridge; and suggested that the Court should make some early and suitable acknowledgment of his Lordship's distinguished liberality. In consequence of which, at a subsequent Court held on July 28th, a motion was made by R. L. Jones, Esq., 'That a Gold Medal be prepared, with a suitable Inscription, commemorative of the circumstance of Laying the First Stone of a New London Bridge, and presented to the Right Honourable the Lord Mayor in the name of this Court:' which was unanimously agreed to, and its provision referred to the said Committee.

"This Medal, however, has not yet been presented; and of two others which were prepared, as memorials of this work, one had the die break in the hardening, and the other was struck for private distribution only: as their extreme rarity is, therefore, not to be questioned, I shall give a short account of each of them; at the same time, expressing my surprise, that so important an event has not called forth an host of these classical memorials. The first private Medal was executed by Peter Rouw, and William Wyon, Esquires, Modeller, and Die-sinker, to his Majesty; the obverse containing a MEDALLION OF THE LORD MAYOR AND LADY MAYORESS;

and the reverse being occupied by the following Inscription:—

'TO COMMEMORATE THE
LAYING OF THE
FIRST STONE OF LONDON BRIDGE
BY
THE RIGHT HON. JOHN GARRATT, LORD MAYOR,
ON THE 15th OF JUNE 1825, IN THE PRESENCE OF
H.R.H. THE DUKE OF YORK, VARIOUS BRANCHES
OF THE NOBILITY, AND THE CORPORATION OF THE CITY,
AND IN TESTIMONY OF HIS LORDSHIP'S

PUBLIC WORTH AND PRIVATE VIRTUES,
THIS MEDAL WAS DESIGNED
AT THE REQUEST
OF HIS FELLOW CITIZENS,
BY JOSEPH YORK HATTON.'

"The other Medal had about twenty impressions struck in silver, which were distributed to the Engineers, assistants, &c., on the day of the foundation. These were 2½ inches in diameter, and nearly ⅛ of an inch in thickness. The obverse consisted of a fine head of the elder Mr. Rennie, from a former Medal; and the reverse contained a design, by Mr. William Knight, of the New London Bridge Works, consisting of an elevation of the edifice, with representations of the First Stone, Mallet, and Trowel: the Inscription being as follows:—

'. LONDON . BRIDGE .
. THE . FIRST . STONE . OF . THIS .
. WORK . WAS . LAID . BY . THE .
. RIGHT . HON. . JOHN . GARRATT, .
. LORD . MAYOR . OF . LONDON. .
. ON . THE . XV . DAY . OF . JUNE, .
. MDCCCXXV . AND . IN . THE . SIXTH .
. YEAR . OF . THE . REIGN .
. OF . GEORGE . IV. .
. JOHN . RENNIE . ESQ. . F.R.S. . ENGINEER .
. JOLIFFE . & . BANKS . CONTRACTORS.'

"Such are the few remaining reliques of this Ceremony, which have been provided for posterity; for, with the exception of a slight etching of the Western end of the Coffer-Dam, in a Memorandum Book, and an Indian Ink Drawing, by Dighton, of some of the principal persons standing about the First Stone, there is no other representation to record it. There are, indeed, several prospects of the finished Edifice; though of its exact features, it is probable we can form no very correct idea, until we are a few years older; so then let us here take our last VIEW OF THE NEW LONDON BRIDGE;

for such are all the particulars and memorials which I can give you concerning this interesting Civic ceremony; and if the Italian of old could give his famous 'ESTO PERPETUA!' to his water-seated Venice, how much rather shall every true-hearted citizen bestow it upon this rising edifice, beneath whose expansive arches,

'The time shall come, when, free as seas or wind,
Unbounded Thames shall flow for all mankind;
Earth's distant ends our glories shall behold,
And the new world launch forth to seek the old!'"

I concluded these lines of Pope's "*Windsor Forest*" with so much enthusiasm, that I did not immediately remark the silence which followed; but upon looking up to wish my auditor a good night, how greatly was I astonished to find myself alone! with only a few dim lights in the empty coffee-room, and the waiter sleeping in a distant box. Hastily starting from my seat, I inquired what had become of Mr. Postern, when, to my great surprise, he absolutely denied that he had seen him either come in or go out. Since that time, too, I have everywhere, but in vain, sought "the learned Pundit" who had so long conferred with me. I certainly cannot discredit the evidence of my own senses, but, upon reconsidering all the circumstances, it appears to me that I must have seen and conversed with the shade of Peter of Colechurch, the original Architect of London Bridge! Our narrative, however, rests upon more solid foundations; for, as I have verified every authority referred to, these CHRONICLES are presented to posterity as the collected memorials of that once-famous edifice, which within a few years will exist no longer."

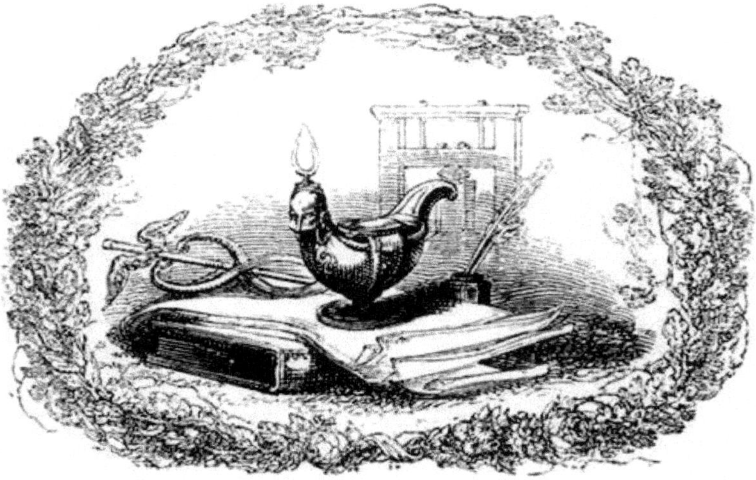